Upper Intermediate Teacher's Book

with Resource and Assessment Disc

Jane Comyns Carr and Louis Rogers
with Nick Witherick

contents

TEACHER'S BOOK

Introduction

Teacher's notes

Resource bank

TEACHER'S RESOURCE AND ASSESSMENT DISC

Extra resources

- Class audio scripts
- Class video scripts
- BBC interviews
- Worksheets for BBC interviews

Tests

- Unit tests
- Achievement tests
- Mid-course test
- End of course test
- Test audio
- Test audio scripts
- Test answer key

STUDENTS' BOOK CONTENTS

DVD-ROM: BBC DVD CLIPS AND SCRIPTS — BBC INTERVIEWS AND SCRIPTS — CLASS AUDIO AND SCRIPTS

LISTENING/DVD	SPEAKING	WRITING
understand informal conversations	have interesting conversations	write an advice forum message; edit for accuracy
	talk about new experiences	
handle phone enquiries	make phone enquiries	
BBC **50 Things To Do Before You Die**: watch a BBC documentary about adventures	recommend an experience	write a forum entry
	talk about different issues	
listen to opinions about surveillance	discuss surveillance	write a letter of complaint; use formal written language
listen to people discuss issues	give and respond to opinions; support your viewpoint	
BBC **A quiet revolution**: watch a BBC programme about changes in working patterns	give a presentation about traditional gender roles	write notes for a presentation
	tell anecdotes	write a narrative; use adverbs
listen to a BBC radio programme about very short stories	talk about life stories	
listen to people recommending books	talk about your reading; summarise a plot	
BBC **Tess of the D'Urbervilles**: watch a BBC drama	describe a TV/film scene	describe a TV/film scene
	discuss how you use your time	write an opinion essay; use linkers
listen to people talk about holidays	plan an alternative holiday	
listen to people describing TV game shows	describe procedures; use mirror questions	
BBC **The Happiness Formula**: watch a BBC programme about happiness	do a class survey	write your top tips for how to be happy
	talk about inventions	
listen to a programme about advertising	describe adverts	write a report; make writtten comparisons
listen to a brainstorming session	take part in a brainstorming session	
BBC **Genius**: watch a BBC programme about presenting ideas	present a novel idea	write a product review

LISTENING/DVD	SPEAKING	WRITING
	discuss different ages and generations	
listen to a BBC programme about letters to your future self	talk about your future	write an informal email; focus on informal style
listen to a phone-in about life's milestones	discuss the right age for different things	
BBC **Horizon: How to Live to 101**: watch a BBC programme about living longer	hold a debate	write a forum comment
	talk about TV programmes	
listen to an expert talking about hoax photographs	talk about celebrity and media	write a discursive essay; use linkers of contrast
listen to people talking about recent news stories	express strong reactions	
BBC **The Funny Side of the News**: watch a BBC programme about live news	retell a news story	write a short news article
	talk about a difficult decision you've made	
listen to an experiment about fairness	talk about values and behaviour	write an informal article; use linkers of purpose
	deal with awkward situations	
BBC **The Human Animal**: watch a BBC documentary about body language	give advice on how to behave in your culture	write about behaviour in your culture
	discuss how good a witness you are	
listen to people talk about getting tricked	speculate about scams	write a 'how to' leaflet; learn to avoid repetition
listen to someone report an incident	talk about emergency situations	
BBC **Horizon: How to Survive a Sea Disaster**: watch a BBC programme about a sea rescue	agree priorities	write a story about a lucky escape
listen to people talk about films	talk about a film you never get bored with	write a film review
	talk about popular culture and arts experiences	
listen to tours of two very different places	show a visitor around part of your town	
BBC **The Culture Show: The People's Palace**: watch a BBC programme about an innovative building	discuss an artistic project for your town	write a competetion entry

COMMUNICATION BANK page 158 AUDIO SCRIPTS page 164

Frances Eales • Steve Oakes
speakout
Upper Intermediate
Students' Book
with DVD-ROM
2ND
EDITION
GLOBAL SCALE
of English
BBC
ALWAYS LEARNING
PEARSON
Frances Eales • Steve Oakes • Louis Harrison
speakout
Upper Intermediate
Workbook
with key
2ND
EDITION
GLOBAL SCALE
of English
BBC
ALWAYS LEARNING
Jane Comyns Carr and Louis Rogers
with Nick Witherick
speakout
Upper Intermediate
Teacher's Book
with Resource and Assessment Disc
2ND
EDITION
GLOBAL SCALE
of English
BBC
ALWAYS LEARNING
PEARSON

speakout
Upper Intermediate
Class Audio CDs
Frances Eales • Steve Oakes
2ND
EDITION
BBC
PEARSON
speakout
Upper Intermediate
DVD-ROM
2ND
EDITION
BBC
PEARSON
speakout
Upper Intermediate
Resource & Assessment Disc
2ND
EDITION
BBC
PEARSON

Our first priority in writing *Speakout Second Edition* was to find out what people liked about the first edition and what could be improved. To that end, we asked teachers and learners around the world for feedback on every level of the course. What did they like? What worked well in class? What changes would they like to see?

We then took a fresh look at every single exercise in the series and improved or updated it based on the feedback we'd received. We revised the grammar, vocabulary and skills syllabuses in line with the *Global Scale of English*, we ensured that there was more recycling and practice of key language, and we included a wealth of up-to-date new material:

- **New BBC video clips** – The BBC video clips which accompany each unit are one of the most original features of the course. We've retained the most popular clips and included some wonderful new material from the BBC archive to engage and motivate learners.
- **New reading/listening texts** – Teachers really appreciated the range of authentic texts in the first edition. We've broadened the range of genres in the second edition to reflect the types of texts learners read outside the classroom. Listening texts are also more authentic and we've included a wider variety of international accents.
- **New pronunciation sections** – We've developed a stronger pronunciation syllabus. Teachers wanted more support in this area, so we now have a wider range of pronunciation features in the three input lessons in each unit. Further pronunciation practice can also be found in *Speakout Extra*.
- **New images and clearer design** – The overall design is lighter, less cluttered and easier to navigate. We've refreshed the photos and illustrations completely, and selected dramatic images to introduce each new unit. Great images motivate learners, and provide excellent prompts for language activities.
- **New supplementary material** – One thing teachers always ask for is 'more'. More grammar, more vocabulary, more pronunciation. There's only so much we can fit into the Students' Books but, for those who want more practice in specific areas, *Speakout Extra* provides a bank of additional exercises that can be accessed via the *Speakout* website. *Speakout Extra* includes grammar, vocabulary, pronunciation and skills practice as well as ideas and activities for exploiting the BBC clips and interviews. *Speakout Extra* will be updated regularly so don't forget to check it out.

We really appreciate the feedback you've given us and hope you find *Speakout Second Edition* even more stimulating and user-friendly than the first edition.

From left to right: Steve Oakes, Antonia Clare, JJ Wilson and Frances Eales

OVERVIEW OF THE COMPONENTS

STUDENTS' BOOK WITH DVD-ROM

- Ten units with 90 to 120 hours of teaching material
- Comprehensive *Language bank* with detailed explanations and extra practice
- *Vocabulary bank* to expand vocabulary
- Audio material for use in class
- DVD content (BBC clips and interviews)
- Audio and video scripts

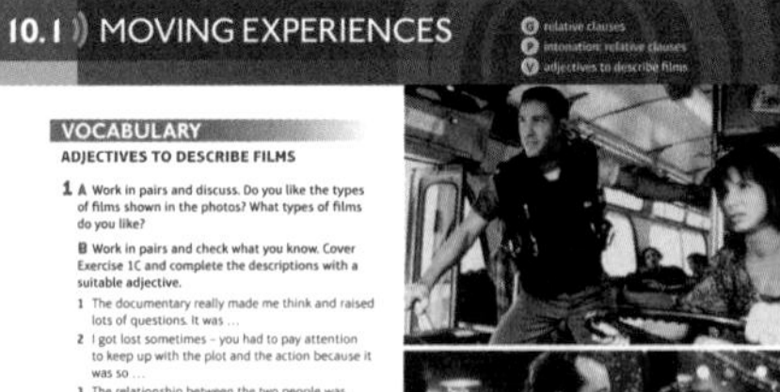

CLASS AUDIO CDs

- Audio material for use in class

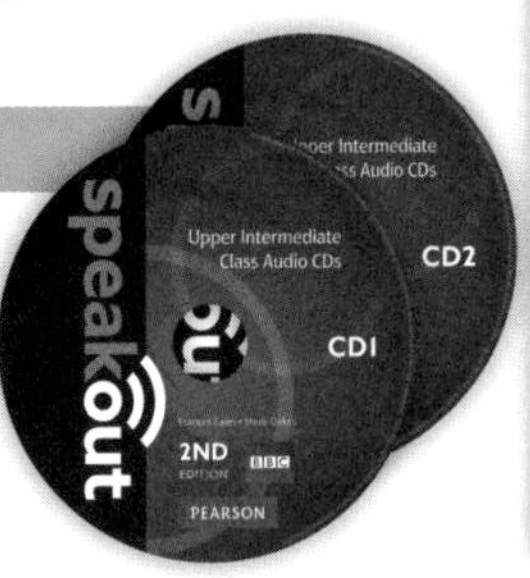

WORKBOOK

- Additional grammar, vocabulary and pronunciation exercises to complement material in the Students' Book
- Additional functional language practice exercises
- Additional reading, listening and writing practice
- Regular review sections
- With- and without-key versions

WORKBOOK AUDIO

- Audio material to practice listening, pronunciation and functional language
- Visit www.english.com/speakout to download the audio

MYENGLISHLAB

Learning Management System that provides:

- Interactive Workbook with instant feedback
- Extra practice in grammar, vocabulary and skills
- Unit and achievement tests
- Mid- and end of course tests
- BBC interviews and interactive exercises

MyEnglishLab speakout 2ND EDITION Upper Intermediate

8.1 Behaviour Switch to Student view

Exercise 1A Grammar – conditionals

Read the article. Find the mistake in each picture.

EURO-MILLION DILEMMA

One morning in 2006, Jim Farley was outside a Dublin bank when five bundles of cash fell from a security van which was driving away. He took them home and kept them for two days before phoning the bank. He rang from a payphone in a terrible state of anxiety as he didn't know what to do. The security director persuaded him to hand in the money. It came to almost €1,000,000.

PARIS MÉTRO RESCUE

Jean LeBois was waiting for his métro train with his son, Roger, aged four. Suddenly, a man collapsed on the platform and then fell onto the tracks. A train was approaching and LeBois had to make a split-second decision whether to help. He leapt off the platform and pressed the man into the space between the tracks. Five carriages went overhead before the train stopped. Both men emerged safe to the applause of the onlookers.

1 Euro-Million Dilemma
- In the picture, the man is phoning from a payphone; in the article, he phones from home.
- In the picture, the man is phoning from home; in the article, he phones from a payphone.
- In the picture, the man is phoning from a payphone; in the article, he phones from a mobile phone.

2 Paris Metro Rescue
- In the picture, the man is saving a boy; in the article, he saves another man.
- In the picture, the man is saving a girl; in the article, he saves another man.
- In the picture, the man is saving a boy; in the article, he saves a woman.

Close

ALWAYS LEARNING PEARSON

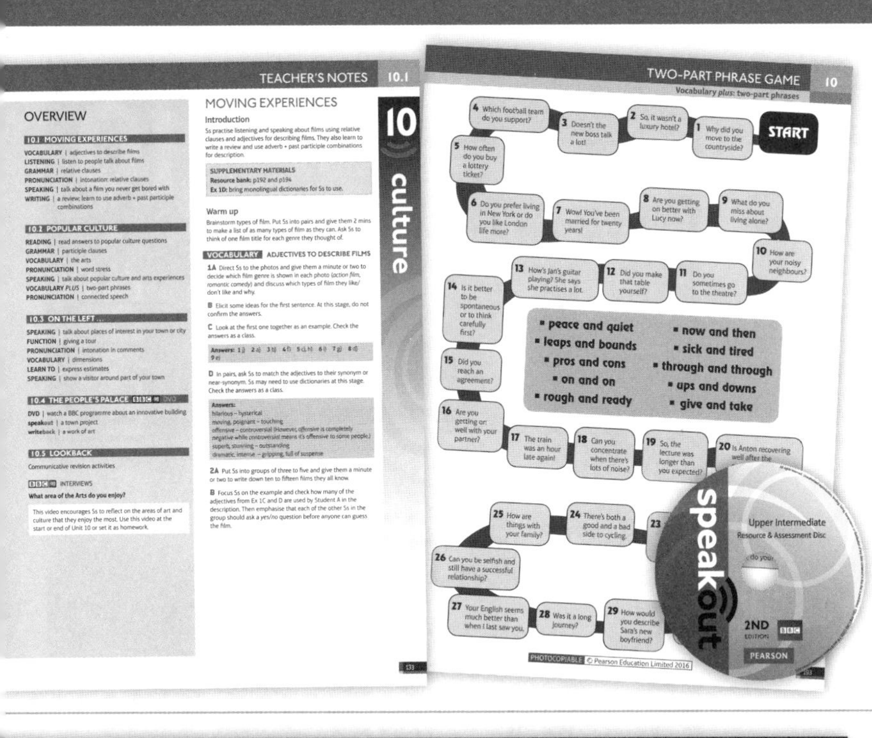

TEACHER'S BOOK WITH RESOURCE AND ASSESSMENT DISC

- Teacher's notes for every unit with warmers, fillers, alternative suggestions, culture notes and answer keys
- Generic teaching tips on useful areas such as grammar, lexis, pronunciation, using video, etc.
- Photocopiable grammar, vocabulary, and functional language worksheets for every unit
- Class audio and video scripts
- BBC interviews, worksheets and scripts
- Unit and achievement tests
- Mid- and end of course tests
- Test audio, audio scripts and answer keys

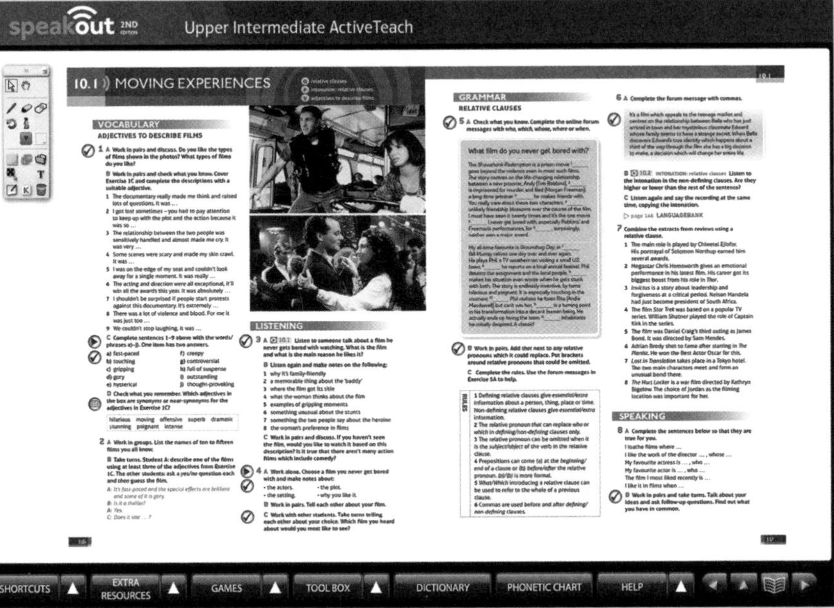

ACTIVETEACH

Software for classroom use to help teachers get the most out of the course:

- Integrated audio and video content
- Answer-reveal feature
- Large extra resources section
- Grammar and vocabulary review games
- BBC interviews and worksheets
- Assessment package containing all the course tests
- A host of useful classroom tools

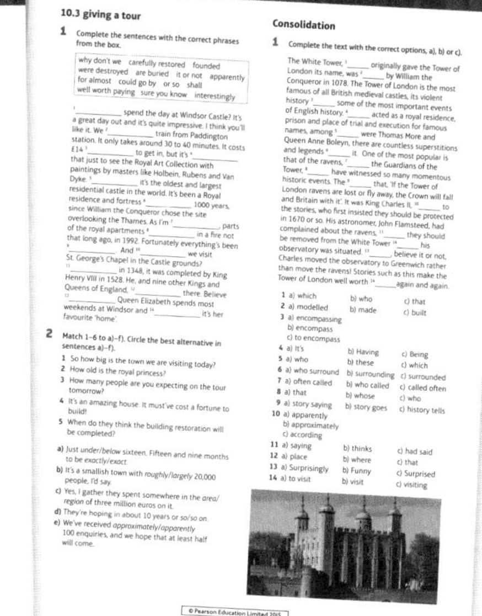

WEBSITE AND *SPEAKOUT EXTRA*

- Information about the course
- Sample materials
- Placement test
- Teaching tips and ideas
- Free downloadable worksheets provide additional grammar, vocabulary, pronunciation and skills practice (*Speakout Extra*)
- Extra video-exploitation activities to help learners get the most out of the course (*Speakout Extra*)

Speakout Extra and other teacher's resources available at:

www.pearsonelt.com/speakout

A UNIT OF THE STUDENTS' BOOK

Speakout Second Edition Students' Book is clearly designed and easy to use. Each unit follows the same pattern with an introductory page, two main input lessons covering grammar, vocabulary, pronunciation and skills work, a functional lesson and a skills-consolidation lesson based on a clip from a BBC programme. The unit culminates with a page of *Lookback* exercises and there is a detailed *Language bank*, *Vocabulary bank* and *Communication bank* at the back of the book.

1. Striking images provoke interest in the topic
2. Language focus and outcomes clearly stated at the start of each lesson
3. BBC interviews provide 'models' of authentic language
4. Grammar presented in context with clear explanations and plenty of practice
5. Learners referred to Language bank at the back of the book for further practice
6. Key vocabulary introduced and practised in context
7. Vocabulary *Plus* sections focus on word-building skills and other useful areas such as collocation, affixation, multi-word verbs, etc.
8. Special pronunciation sections in each lesson
9. Focus on reading and/or listening in every spread
10. Writing sections focus on different genres and sub-skills
11. Useful learning tips included in each unit
12. Speaking activities encourage learners to personalise language

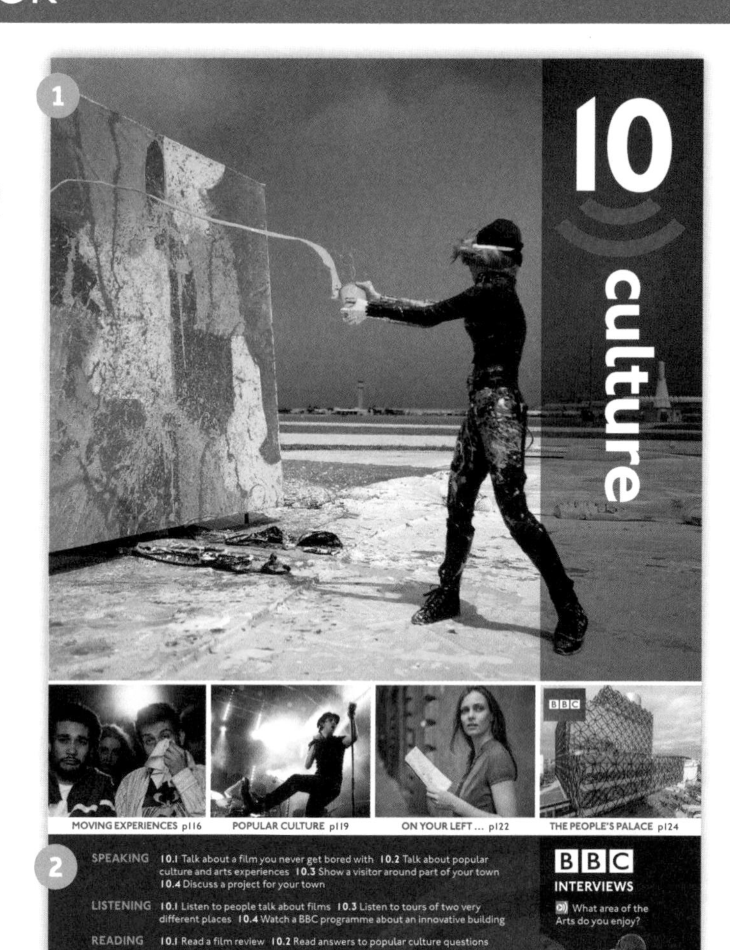

10

culture

MOVING EXPERIENCES p116 | POPULAR CULTURE p119 | ON YOUR LEFT ... p122 | THE PEOPLE'S PALACE p124

SPEAKING **10.1** Talk about a film you never get bored with **10.2** Talk about popular culture and arts experiences **10.3** Show a visitor around part of your town **10.4** Discuss a project for your town

LISTENING **10.1** Listen to people talk about films **10.3** Listen to tours of two very different places **10.4** Watch a BBC programme about an innovative building

READING **10.1** Read a film review **10.2** Read answers to popular culture questions

WRITING **10.1** Write a film review **10.4** Write a competition entry

BBC INTERVIEWS

What area of the Arts do you enjoy?

115

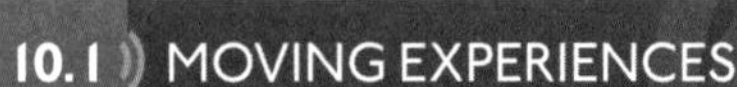

G relative clauses
P intonation: relative clauses
V adjectives to describe films

VOCABULARY

ADJECTIVES TO DESCRIBE FILMS

1 A Work in pairs and discuss. Do you like the types of films shown in the photos? What types of films do you like?

B Work in pairs and check what you know. Cover Exercise 1C and complete the descriptions with a suitable adjective.

1 The documentary really made me think and raised lots of questions. It was …
2 I got lost sometimes – you had to pay attention to keep up with the plot and the action because it was so …
3 The relationship between the two people was sensitively handled and almost made me cry. It was very …
4 Some scenes were scary and made my skin crawl. It was …
5 I was on the edge of my seat and couldn't look away for a single moment. It was really …
6 The acting and direction were all exceptional, it'll win all the awards this year. It was absolutely …
7 I shouldn't be surprised if people start protests against this documentary. It's extremely …
8 There was a lot of violence and blood. For me it was just too …
9 We couldn't stop laughing, it was …

C Complete sentences 1–9 above with the words/phrases a)–j). One item has two answers.

a) fast-paced
b) touching
c) gripping
d) gory
e) hysterical
f) creepy
g) controversial
h) full of suspense
i) outstanding
j) thought-provoking

D Check what you remember. Which adjectives in the box are synonyms or near-synonyms for the adjectives in Exercise 1C?

hilarious moving offensive superb dramatic stunning poignant intense

2 A Work in groups. List the names of ten to fifteen films you all know.

B Take turns. Student A: describe one of the films using at least three of the adjectives from Exercise 1C. The other students: ask a *yes/no* question each and *then* guess the film.

A: *It's fast-paced and the special effects are brilliant and some of it is gory.*
B: *Is it a thriller?*
A: *Yes.*
C: *Does it star … ?*

116

LISTENING

3 A 10.1 Listen to someone talk about a film he never gets bored with watching. What is the film and what is the main reason he likes it?

B Listen again and make notes on the following:

1 why it's family-friendly
2 a memorable thing about the 'baddy'
3 where the film got its title
4 what the woman thinks about the film
5 examples of gripping moments
6 something unusual about the stunts
7 something the two people say about the heroine
8 the woman's preference in films

C Work in pairs and discuss. If you haven't seen the film, would you like to watch it based on this description? Is it true that there aren't many action films which include comedy?

4 A Work alone. Choose a film you never get bored with and make notes about:

- the actors.
- the plot.
- the setting.
- why you like it.

B Work in pairs. Tell each other about your film.

C Work with other students. Take turns telling each other about your choice. Which film you heard about would you most like to see?

10.1

GRAMMAR

RELATIVE CLAUSES

5 A Check what you know. Complete the online forum messages with *who, which, whose, where* or *when*.

What film do you never get bored with?

The Shawshank Redemption is a prison movie [1]_____ goes beyond the violence seen in most such films. The story centres on the life-changing relationship between a new prisoner, Andy (Tim Robbins), [2]_____ is imprisoned for murder, and Red (Morgan Freeman), a long-time prisoner [3]_____ he makes friends with. You really care about these two characters, [4]_____ unlikely friendship blossoms over the course of the film. I must have seen it twenty times and it's the one movie [5]_____ I never get bored with, especially Robbins' and Freeman's performances, for [6]_____, surprisingly, neither won a major award.

My all-time favourite is *Groundhog Day*, in [7]_____ Bill Murray relives one day over and over again. He plays Phil, a TV weatherman visiting a small U.S. town, [8]_____ he reports on a local annual festival. Phil detests the assignment and the local people, [9]_____ makes his situation even worse when he gets stuck with both. The story is endlessly inventive, by turns hilarious and poignant. It is especially touching in the moment [10]_____ Phil realises he loves Rita (Andie Macdowell) but can't win her, [11]_____ is a turning point in his transformation into a decent human being. He actually ends up loving the town [12]_____ inhabitants he initially despised. A classic!

B Work in pairs. Add *that* next to any relative pronouns which it could replace. Put brackets around relative pronouns that could be omitted.

C Complete the rules. Use the forum messages in Exercise 5A to help.

RULES

1 Defining relative clauses give *essential/extra* information about a person, thing, place or time. Non-defining relative clauses give *essential/extra* information.
2 The relative pronoun *that* can replace *who* or *which* in *defining/non-defining* clauses only.
3 The relative pronoun can be omitted when it is the *subject/object* of the verb in the relative clause.
4 Prepositions can come (a) at the *beginning/end* of a clause or (b) *before/after* the relative pronoun. *(a)/(b)* is more formal.
5 *What/Which* introducing a relative clause can be used to refer to the whole of a previous clause.
6 Commas are used before and after *defining/non-defining* clauses.

6 A Complete the forum message with commas.

It's a film which appeals to the teenage market and centres on the relationship between Bella who has just arrived in town and her mysterious classmate Edward whose family seems to have a strange secret. When Bella discovers Edward's true identity which happens about a third of the way through the film she has a big decision to make, a decision which will change her entire life.

B 10.2 INTONATION: relative clauses Listen to the intonation in the non-defining clauses. Are they higher or lower than the rest of the sentence?

C Listen again and say the recording at the same time, copying the intonation.

▷ page 146 **LANGUAGEBANK**

7 Combine the extracts from reviews using a relative clause.

1 The main role is played by Chiwetel Ejiofor. His portrayal of Solomon Northup earned him several awards.
2 Megastar Chris Hemsworth gives an emotional performance in his latest film. His career got its biggest boost from his role in *Thor*.
3 *Invictus* is a story about leadership and forgiveness at a critical period. Nelson Mandela had just become president of South Africa.
4 The film *Star Trek* was based on a popular TV series. William Shatner played the role of Captain Kirk in the series.
5 The film was Daniel Craig's third outing as James Bond. It was directed by Sam Mendes.
6 Adrian Brody shot to fame after starring in *The Pianist*. He won the Best Actor Oscar for this.
7 *Lost in Translation* takes place in a Tokyo hotel. The two main characters meet and form an unusual bond there.
8 *The Hurt Locker* is a war film directed by Kathryn Bigelow. The choice of Jordan as the filming location was important for her.

SPEAKING

8 A Complete the sentences below so that they are true for you.

I loathe films where …
I like the work of the director … , whose …
My favourite actress is … , who …
My favourite actor is … , who …
The film I most liked recently is …
I like it in films when …

B Work in pairs and take turns. Talk about your ideas and ask follow-up questions. Find out what you have in common.

117

MIDNIGHT IN PARIS

Midnight in Paris is set in Paris in the present and in different periods in the past. It stars Owen Wilson as Gil, a Hollywood screenwriter, and Rachel McAdams as Inez, his beautiful fiancée.

As the film opens, Gil is on holiday in Paris with Inez and her wealthy parents. He is supposed to be in love with his girlfriend but his love affair really seems to be with Paris in the springtime. One evening while wandering around the city, he gets lost and as the clock strikes midnight an old Peugeot car pulls up. Inside the car are a group of party-goers who are dressed in 1920s clothes and who invite him to join them. They go to a party where Gil realises he has been transported to the 1920s, a period which he loves. We see him meeting some of his intellectual and artistic heroes from that time and falling in love with Adriana, Picasso's mistress. Meanwhile, in the present, Gil's bride-to-be and her parents become more and more annoyed and suspicious about his nightly disappearances. Eventually Gil realises Inez is not right for him and breaks up with her. He decides to stay and live in his beloved Paris.

Skilfully directed by Woody Allen, the film cuts between the glitter of Paris in the twenties and the present-day city. The script is alternately gripping, shocking and hilarious and the camerawork is stunning. As Gil, Owen Wilson is appealing in his enthusiasm and love of Paris in the past. However, for me, it is the character of Adriana, convincingly acted by Marion Cotillard, who is the most fascinating of all.

With its charm, sparkling wit and engaging leaps forwards and backwards in time, *Midnight in Paris* is a light, delightful film which I'd thoroughly recommend.

10 WRITING

A REVIEW; LEARN TO USE ADVERB + PAST PARTICIPLE COMBINATIONS

9 A Work in pairs and discuss the questions.

1 Where do you usually read film reviews (e.g. on the internet, in magazines)?
2 What is the main purpose of a film review?
 • to make people want to see the film
 • to help people decide if they want to see a film
 • to give factual information about the film
3 Which of the topics in the box do you usually find in a film review?

plot summary description of the film's ending actors' names recommendation ticket prices setting of the film reviewer's opinion of different elements

B Read the film review above. Would you like to see the film? Why/Why not?

C Read the review again and write the topic of each paragraph. Use the topics in the box to help.

10 A Underline two adverb + past participle combinations in paragraph 3 of the review.

B Write three adverbs from the box next to each participle to complete the phrases. Some can be used more than once.

convincingly harshly skilfully widely sensitively overwhelmingly highly poignantly heavily

1 ______ / ______ / ______ directed by …
2 ______ / ______ / ______ acted by …
3 ______ / ______ / ______ praised by …
4 ______ / ______ / ______ criticised by …

11 A Make notes about a film you have seen recently or a film you never get bored with. Use the topic areas from Exercise 9C.

B Write a first draft of your review (120–180 words). Use adjectives and at least two adverb + past participle combinations.

C Exchange with another student and read each other's review. Is it interesting and clear? Suggest two or three improvements.

D Write a final version of the review.

POPULAR CULTURE

G participle clauses
P word stress; connected speech
V the Arts; two-part phrases

9 READING

1 A Work in pairs and look at the photos. What do you think is the most difficult part of each performer's job?

B Work in pairs and discuss these questions from a magazine article. Make notes on your answers.

1 How do actors cry on demand?
2 Do big stars have to audition for film roles?
3 How do singers keep their voices steady when they're dancing?
4 Why is rock music played so loud at concerts?
5 Who decides whether something is 'art' or not?
6 Why do works of art get stolen if they can't be sold without attracting attention?
7 What's the secret to making an audience laugh?
8 How does a comedian deal with hecklers?

C Work in pairs. Student A: turn to page 163. Student B: quickly read the text on this page. Which four questions above does it answer?

D Read the text again. Write a maximum of five key words for each answer to help you remember the information.

E Work in pairs. Cover the text and look at your notes from Exercise 1D. Tell your partner about the answers.

POPULAR CULTURE Q&A

Want to know the best-kept secrets of popular culture? Read our Top Questions & Answers to find out.

Q:

A: Rock music is characterised by a strong bass line and hard, driving rhythm and percussion parts, which are greatly enhanced by amplification. At some point in the evolution of rock, audiences became almost addicted to the sensations of the music they loved 'vibrating' inside them at concerts. The listeners go beyond hearing the music and feel it through their whole body, feel its vibrations, provided it is loud enough. Heavy metal music played softly sounds stupid and can only be played as it was intended to be: very, very loudly.

Q:

A: A big star auditioning for a part is almost unheard of. Actors such as Tom Hanks go straight from film to film, so directors and producers have access to a whole portfolio of their work. The closest such actors ever get to anything resembling an audition is when they're invited to chat about the project informally, which gives the director and producer a chance to evaluate the actor without it feeling like a test. The stars don't usually even have to read part of the script. More often, it's actually a matter of the actor choosing whether to work with the director!

Q:

A: Every stand-up comedian knows that making people laugh with prepared material, on stage, is very different from making your friends or colleagues laugh in an informal setting. You need to focus on technique, such as which words to stress, when to pause, how to use facial expressions and body movements, as well as sensing how to work each individual audience. Interestingly, shows with paying audiences are better than freebies. Having paid to be entertained, people are often more ready and willing to laugh.

Q:

A: Criminals steal paintings only when they already have a buyer. Sometimes, a wealthy private collector actually requests a particular piece to be stolen – essentially orders it – for part of their private collection. The collector knows that it can never be shown publicly but that's not why they want the piece in the first place. Valuable works of art are a favourite commodity for criminal organisations, who will use them in place of cash for making deals with each other. They are also useful for money launderers, as works of art are easier to transport and harder to trace than cash, as well as easily traded on the black market.

4 GRAMMAR

PARTICIPLE CLAUSES

2 A Read the article below. In what situations do celebrities use fake names? What is the joke in each chosen name?

Do stars use their real names when travelling?

In short, no. In fact, stars [1]**registered at hotels under their real name** are a rarity – their day can be ruined by paparazzi [2]**trying to take their pictures** and members of the public [3]**taking selfies**. So if you're going to change your name, why not have fun doing it? Names [4]**involving wordplay** are common: Britney Spears uses Ms Alotta Warmheart among other names, and Brad Pitt and Jennifer Aniston, [5]**married in 2000 but divorced five years later**, used to call themselves Mr and Mrs Ross Vegas. And the fun doesn't end there – the name [6]**used by George Clooney** when he was travelling caused him great amusement: Arnold Schwarzenegger. 'It was funny, the hotel staff had to call me Mr Schwarzenegger, when they knew of course, I wasn't him,' said Clooney.

B Work in pairs and look at the participle clauses in bold in the article. Then answer the questions.

1 Which participle clauses in bold replace relative clauses?
2 What is the full relative clause in each case?
3 Which two verb forms can a participle clause begin with?

C Compare the sentences below and underline the participle clauses. Then complete the rule.

1 a) Names which involve wordplay are common.
 b) Names involving wordplay are common.
2 a) The people who worked in the hotel thought the name was funny.
 b) The people working in the hotel thought the name was funny.
3 a) The hotel, which was built in the 1980s and which is often used by film stars, is famous.
 b) The hotel, built in the 1980s and regularly used by film stars, is famous.

RULES
1 When a relative clause has an active verb in the present simple or past simple, the participle clause uses a ______ participle.
2 When a relative clause has a passive verb in the present simple or past simple, the participle clause uses a ______ participle.

3 A Rewrite the sentences using a participle clause.

1 People who take photos should ask their subjects' permission first.
2 Films that are based on books are disappointing.
3 It's great to see rock stars in their sixties who still play concerts.
4 Architecture which was designed in the 1960s is generally quite ugly and ought to be pulled down.
5 Photos of people who are posing for the camera don't work as well as spontaneous pictures.
6 Film and TV stars who appear at the theatre attract huge audiences.
7 Jokes which involve racial stereotypes are not funny.
8 Photographers who used software to enhance their photos were justifiably banned from entering a national competition last month.

B Work in pairs and discuss. Do you agree with the statements in Exercise 3A? Give examples.

11

Using participle clauses can improve the level of your writing and speaking. Try to improve this sentence by using a participle clause: *I couldn't concentrate on the concert because there were so many people who took photos.*

▷ page 146 LANGUAGEBANK

VOCABULARY

THE ARTS

4 A Which of the forum comments are generally positive (✓), negative (✗) or mixed (–)?

"I'd read a lot about this new singer in the music press. She's certainly **creating a stir** with her **ground-breaking** mix of rap and folk. Ever since she got those **rave reviews** in the press, each performance has been a **sell-out** and it's impossible to get tickets. Everyone says it's the **must-see** performance of the year. Is she really that good?"

"Well, after all the **hype** surrounding her concerts, I went to see her on Friday, expecting something really sensational … but the concert was a real **letdown**! It was a complete **flop** because we couldn't hear her properly."

"Yeah, I was at that gig and the technical side was pretty bad but her album is amazing, really innovative. I've never heard anything quite like it before. I just hope she doesn't go **mainstream** and boring like all the other **alternative** artists."

B Work in pairs. What do you think the words and phrases in bold above mean? Use the context, grammar and your knowledge of similar words to help. Then check in a dictionary.

C ▶ 10.3 WORD STRESS Work in pairs and say the words and phrases in bold. Which syllable(s) is/are stressed? Listen to the words in context and check.

D Think of a performance you have seen or heard. Write a forum entry about it using at least four of the words which are new to you.

E Read other students' forum entries. Find a performance you would like to see or hear.

▷ page 157 VOCABULARYBANK

7 SPEAKING

5 A Choose three of the questions below to answer. Write the name of the thing/person and two or three words to explain why you liked it/him/her.

1 What's the best gig/concert or dance performance you've ever been to?
2 What's the best music album ever made?
3 Who's the funniest comedian you know?
4 What's the most moving, scary or exciting film you've ever seen?
5 What's the most memorable exhibition you've ever been to?
6 What's the best photo you've ever taken?
7 Who's the painter or other type of artist you most like? What's your favourite work of his/hers?
8 What's the most unforgettable show or play you've ever seen?

B Work in pairs and take turns. Talk about your experiences and feelings.

C Work in groups and take turns. Recommend something you've recently been to/seen/heard.

VOCABULARY *PLUS*

TWO-PART PHRASES

6 A Work in pairs and look at the two-part phrases in sentences 1 and 2. What do you think they mean?

1 There are some basic **dos and don'ts** when taking a good photo.
2 I've worked in the film business **off and on** for most of my life.

B Check your ideas with the dictionary entries.

D **dos and don'ts** things that you should and should not do: *the dos and don'ts of having a pet*

O **off and on/on and off** for short periods of time but not regularly: *I worked as a secretary off and on for three years.*

From Longman Active Study Dictionary

7 A Match a word from A with one from B to make a two-part phrase.

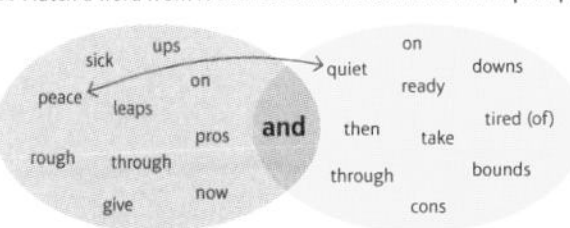

8 B ▶ 10.4 CONNECTED SPEECH Listen and check. Then listen and repeat, paying attention to the linking, the weak form of *and* /ən/ and the dropping of /d/ in connected speech.

ups_and downs

8 A Work in pairs. Student A: turn to page 163. Student B: turn to page 161. Read the definitions and then complete five of the sentences below.

1 I hate having music on in the background. I prefer some ______ and ______.
2 I used to go to rock concerts a lot but nowadays I only go ______ and ______.
3 I'm a reggae fan ______ and ______.
4 I'm ______ and ______ of having to listen to people's favourite music on the train. I wish they'd turn their MP3 players down.
5 Any skill such as playing the piano improves in ______ and ______ if you practise enough.
6 Every relationship has its ______ and ______ so it's not surprising that most bands break up after a few years.
7 I don't like jazz. Some of the pieces go ______ and ______ for far too long.
8 It's OK for my neighbours to play music I don't like. You have to have a bit of ______ and ______. I'm sure they don't like my music!
9 There are ______ and ______ to listening to a live recording as opposed to a studio album.
10 Some of the music videos made by ordinary people on *YouTube* are a bit ______ and ______ but that's OK.

B Work in pairs and take turns. Help your partner to complete the sentences and understand the two-part phrases.

C Change five of the sentences so that they are true for you. Then compare with a partner. How many do you agree on?

▷ page 157 VOCABULARYBANK

10.3 ON YOUR LEFT ...

G giving a tour
P intonation in comments
V dimensions

A

B

C

Greenwich Village, New York, USA

D

E

F

Oxford, England

SPEAKING

1 Work in pairs and discuss the questions.

1 Have you ever shown anyone around your town/city?
2 What places of interest in your town/city would you take a visitor to? Why?

FUNCTION

GIVING A TOUR

2 A Work in pairs. Look at the photos of Greenwich Village and Oxford and discuss. What do you know about each place? Which would you most like to visit?

B 10.5 Listen to two people showing visitors around Greenwich Village and Oxford. Number the photos in the order you hear them.

C Listen again and write one fact you hear about each place.

1 The Blue Note Jazz Club
2 The Café Reggio
3 Greenwich Village in general
4 Washington Square Park
5 The Bodleian Library
6 The Oxford colleges
7 The Bridge of Sighs
8 New College
9 The 'Schools'
10 Christ Church College

3 A Work in pairs and complete the phrases. Sometimes there is more than one possible answer.

Leading the way

Let's [1]______ over to Washington Square Park and then [2]______ back.
Why don't we [3]______ our steps and go back to the Café Reggio?

Giving facts

It was [4]______ on the Arc de Triomphe.
It was built to [5]______ the hundredth anniversary of the inauguration of George Washington as president.
In front of us is the Bodleian, [6]______ after the [7]______ – Thomas Bodley.

Commenting on facts

[8]______ I'm sure you [9]______, Greenwich Village has always been a centre of artistic life – very bohemian.
[10]______, the oldest college was actually only founded a hundred or so years earlier!
[11]______, the biggest room can seat somewhere in the region of 500 students although I haven't seen it myself.
We can actually go inside if we're quick. It's well [12]______ a visit.

B Compare your answers with the audio script on page 175.

C 10.6 **INTONATION IN COMMENTS** Listen to the intonation in the phrases. Then listen again and repeat.

Interestingly, the statue disappeared at the time of his death.

The story goes, he threw it in the lake.

Apparently, it was made of gold.

Surprisingly, no one has ever tried to find it.

▷ page 146 **LANGUAGEBANK**

4 A Complete A's part in the extracts from a tour of Paris.

A: [1]Let's / head / over / the cathedral, Notre Dame.
B: On the island? Do we have time to go inside?
A: [2]Yes, / well worth / visit it.

B: ... So that's the Arc de Triomphe?
A: [3]Yes, / model / a famous Roman arch.
B: And why was it built?
A: [4]celebrate / one / Napoleon's great victories.

A: [5]... So here we are / the Eiffel Tower / named / its designer, Gustave Eiffel.
B: Wow! It's impressive.
A: [6]Yeah / apparently / can sway six to seven centimetres in the wind!

B Work in pairs and take turns. Practise the conversations using the prompts above.

VOCABULARY

DIMENSIONS

5 Complete the tourist's questions with the noun or verb form of the adjectives in brackets.

1 What is the ______ of the tower? (high)
2 So the road goes the ______ of the town? (long)
3 When did they ______ the entrance? (wide)
4 What is the ______ of the wall here? (thick)
5 The road ______ here. Why's that? (narrow)
6 What's the ______ of the river and ______ of the water here? (broad, deep)
7 Why don't they ______ the map? It's so small. (large)
8 It's nine o'clock and it's still light. When do the days ______ here? (short)

LEARN TO

EXPRESS ESTIMATES

6 A Look at the extracts and underline five phrases for expressing estimates (when we don't know the exact number).

1 A: How many colleges are there?
B: Just under forty. Well, thirty-eight to be exact.
2 A: How 'new' is new?
B: Roughly 1370.
A: You're kidding!
B: No, really! Interestingly, the oldest college was actually only founded a hundred or so years earlier!
3 Apparently, the biggest room can seat somewhere in the region of five hundred students.
4 A: How many students are there at the university in total?
B: To be honest, it depends. In term time, you'd probably get upwards of twenty thousand.

B Which phrases in Exercise 6A could be replaced by 1) *fewer than,* 2) *more than* or 3) *about/around/approximately?*

C 10.7 Listen and tick the exact number.

1 a) 1,400 b) 1,518
2 a) 30 b) 38
3 a) 1,180 b) 1,220
4 a) 712 b) 746
5 a) 2.13 b) 1.10
6 a) 318 b) 371

D Work in pairs and take turns to estimate:

- the number of students in your school/employees in your workplace.
- the age of the building you're in.
- the population of your town/city.
- the distance from your home to where you are now.
- the cost of dinner in a good restaurant in your town/city.
- the number of contacts on your mobile phone.
- the number of English words you know.

SPEAKING

7 A Work in pairs. Design a one-hour walking or cycling tour of a town/city you know for a visitor. Make notes on:

- four or five places to see.
- a fact or personal opinion about each place.
- some approximate numbers associated with the place (how many people visit it; how much it costs; how old/long/high, etc. it is).

B Work with a new partner and take turns. Role-play the tour. Student A: lead the way. Student B: ask questions.

10.4 THE PEOPLE'S PALACE

DVD PREVIEW

1 A Look at the photos of a new library and discuss the questions in pairs.

1 Which words/phrases in the box would you use to describe the building?

crazy makes a bold statement unique fresh pleasing on the eye modern too busy delicate too elaborate beautiful amazing unsightly

2 How is it different from what you expect a library to look like?
3 What facilities would you expect to be included in a 21st-century library?

B Read the programme information and look at the photos. Which of the following do you think you will see in the DVD?

1 The reporter interviews local people, the designer of the building and celebrities.
2 The designer explains why she used rings as part of the design.
3 The local people feel mostly positive about the new library.

The Culture Show: The People's Palace

BBC

At a time when many libraries across Britain face budget cuts and closure, Birmingham is opening the biggest public library in Europe. Is this a new breed of super library for the future?
This programme explores the cutting-edge building to discover what a 21st-century library looks like, what goes into its design, and how local people – the taxpayers – feel about it. Perhaps most importantly, we find out what role the library has in the internet age.

DVD VIEW

2 A Watch the DVD and check your answers to Exercise 1B.

B Work in pairs and answer the questions. Then watch the DVD again and check.

1 Why and how is Birmingham regenerating its city centre?
2 How does the designer describe the city of Birmingham? What characteristics did she try to reflect in the library's design?
3 Why did she call it a 'People's Palace'?
4 What is there inside the library besides shelves of books?
5 What is the 'façade bench' and what can you do there?
6 What do people say they like once they're inside the library?

C Watch the DVD again and underline the correct alternative.

1 We started with this idea, that's the *tradition/heritage* of the proud industrial city, with the steel industry.
2 I think any *funding/investment* of money put into libraries at the moment is fantastic.
3 And in a time of economic *austerity/strictness*, what a bold step to take. Wonderful stuff!
4 There's a lot of people, students, they want to be *independent/individual* but be part of a bigger collective.
5 It's brilliant, yeah, I really like it, it's very *user-friendly/easy-to-use*.
6 I love this in *particular/especially*. I love this outside *bit/section* with the balcony.

3 Work in pairs and discuss whether you agree/disagree with the statements.

1 Local governments shouldn't spend taxpayer's money on expensive architecture.
2 Libraries still have an important role in the internet age.
3 For a society to be healthy, it needs public spaces like libraries, parks and theatres.

speakout a town project

4 A 10.8 Listen to three people discussing a new public space or artistic project for their town. Which project does each person, Tim, Nigel and Sarah, like from the list below? Why?

- an outdoor sculpture (modern or traditional)
- a concert space
- a theatre workshop space for young people
- a state-of-the-art multiplex cinema
- a botanical garden
- a skateboarding park

B Listen again and tick the key phrases you hear.

KEY PHRASES

I'm really in favour of the ...
I think that it would be [beneficial for the community/popular/ ...].
The only thing that would concern me though is that ...
I'd rather have something that would [appeal to all ages/make a statement/...]
We have to consider [costs/maintenance/ ...]
Can you see the [older/younger] generation [using/liking] it?

5 A Work in pairs. You are responsible for choosing an artistic project for your town/city. Choose two items from the list in Exercise 4A. The items must:

- have artistic and/or architectural merit.
- represent the town/city in some way.
- convey a positive image.

B Work with other students. Discuss your ideas and decide on one project.

C Present your decision to the class.

writeback a work of art

6 A Work in pairs. Read about the competition and tell your partner what you would choose and why.

> We want you to write about a favourite work of art or building. It could be a statue or sculpture, a fountain or bridge, a painting or even a favourite room. Send us your description in 150–250 words, and we'll put the five best entries on our website.

B Read the description and tick (✓) the topics in the box that the writer mentions.

setting when it was made material colour size who made it why he/she likes it

> My favourite building is in fact a bridge, the Millau Viaduct in southern France. It's an awe-inspiring structure, as much a work of art as it is a bridge. It towers over the valley that it crosses, but is so graceful that it seems to me more an integral part of the natural environment than the architectural and engineering achievement that it is.
> It was designed by a French engineer and a British architect who conceived it as a series of towers, which look like the masts of a ship, from which cables are suspended, the cables that support the road surface that runs 2500 metres across the valley. The highest tower is the tallest structure in France, taller than the Eiffel Tower, and I think the tallest bridge in the world.
> This 21st-century masterpiece is breathtaking to behold, and it gives me a sense of calm every time I look at it. No one should miss it if they are visiting this part of France.

C Write your competition entry. Use the box in Exercise 6B for ideas of what to include.

D Read your classmates' competition entries. Which one makes you most want to visit the place they write about?

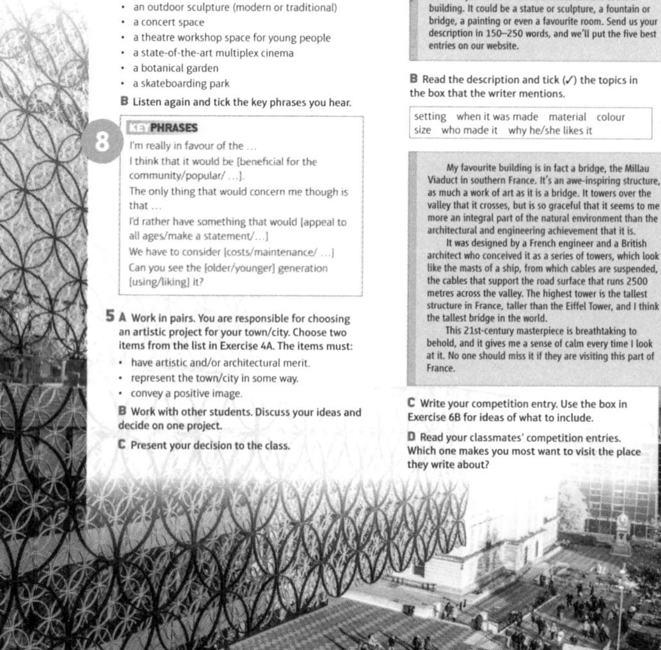

Speakout Second Edition Students' Book places particular emphasis on listening and speaking skills. Each unit has a functional lesson which develops useful communication skills as well as a motivating BBC DVD spread which is designed to revise key language and act as a springboard for further speaking and writing tasks.

Each unit culminates with a *Lookback* page that provides a review of key language covered in the unit. There is a detailed *Language bank*, *Vocabulary bank* and *Communication bank* at the back of the book for further practice and consolidation.

1. Speaking and discussion exercises are a motivating lead-in to the lesson
2. Focus on useful functional areas such as giving a tour, commenting on facts and figures, etc.
3. *Learn to* sections develop listening and speaking skills
4. Learners read about the DVD clip in preparation for viewing
5. Different viewing tasks help learners understand and appreciate the DVD clip
6. *Speakout* tasks consolidate language and build learners' confidence
7. 'Models' are provided to help learners perform the task
8. Key phrases give learners the language they need to perform the task
9. *Writeback* tasks provide further communicative practice
10. *Lookback* exercises are an enjoyable 'test' of language covered in unit
11. *Language bank* provides detailed explanations and further practice
12. *Vocabulary bank* focuses on word-building and useful areas such as collocation, affixation and multi-word verbs.

10.5 LOOKBACK

10

ADJECTIVES

1 A Work in pairs. Make a list of as many adjectives for describing films as you can remember.

B Complete comments 1–4 with a suitable adjective.

1 The ending was sensitively handled and made me cry! Very ________!
2 The script was basically one joke after another. Absolutely ________!
3 It kept my attention for two hours. Utterly ________!
4 My friends and I are still arguing about it. Quite ________!

C Work in pairs. Write four review comments similar to the ones above. Use a suitable adjective for describing films in each review.

RELATIVE CLAUSES

2 A Underline the correct alternative.

I'd like to find …
1 a person *who/for whom/whose* main interests include **doing sports**.
2 a place *that/which/where* I can **speak English with native speakers**.
3 someone *that/whose/whom* knows **a famous person**.
4 a shop *where/which/that* I can buy **reasonably priced clothes**.
5 a person for *whose/that/whom* **money** is not important.
6 three **interesting places** in **this town/city** *which/to which/where* I've never been to.

B Change the words in bold in four of the sentences above so that they are about things/people you'd like to find.

C Ask other students questions about your sentences in Exercise 2B.

A: Do you know anyone whose main interests include going to the cinema?
B: Yes – me.
A: Right. Who's your favourite actor?
B: At the moment, Christian Bale.

PARTICIPLE CLAUSES

3 A Complete the quiz with the present or past participles of the verbs in brackets.

Trivia quiz

1 It's an arts building ______ (stand) in Sydney Harbour and ______ (make) of white tiles to look like sails.
2 It's a company ______ (start) by Steve Jobs, Steve Wozniak and Ronald Wayne, best ______ (know) for its iPod and iPhone products.
3 It's a game ______ (play) by two players, ______ (involve) a small rubber ball and racquets and ______ (take) place in a four-walled court indoors.
4 He was a great leader, born in Corsica, ______ (crown) Emperor of France in 1804 and ______ (defeat) at Waterloo in 1815.
5 It's a statuette ______ (award) to people in the film world every year by the American Academy of Motion Picture Arts and Sciences.
6 They're a group of people ______ (live) in cold, snowy parts of the USA and Canada, and ______ (use) blocks of ice to build their houses, ______ (call) igloos.
7 It's a Japanese dish ______ (consist) of raw fish and rice ______ (roll) up in seaweed.
8 It's a play ______ (write) by Shakespeare and ______ (feature) a Danish prince.

B Work in pairs and do the quiz.

C Check your answers on page 163.

THE ARTS

4 The words in bold in the wrong sentences. Put them in the correct sentences.

1 The musical was a complete **sell-out** and had to close early.
2 Does the Picasso exhibition deserve all those **hype** reviews?
3 The new sculpture is **alternative**. Everyone's arguing about it.
4 He's famous for his **mainstream** work in photography, never done before.
5 You can't get tickets for the show. It's a complete **rave**.
6 I thought the new album was a real **must-see**, very poor.
7 That new comedian is certainly creating a lot of **flop**. Everyone's talking about him.
8 This Virtual Worlds Exhibition is a **letdown** event. Don't miss it!
9 I don't listen to **ground-breaking** pop music much. It all sounds the same.
10 During **creating a stir** Fashion Week you can see some shockingly original clothes.

GIVING A TOUR

5 A Complete descriptions 1–3 below with the words in the box. Where are the places?

was story worth it you honour named rebuilt

1 It was built in the 17th century by Shah Jahan in of his wife. As may know, it's made of white marble and is well a visit.
2 It was after its designer and was built in 1889. The goes that many Parisians hated it because it was too modern.
3 Parts of it were many times. Believe or not, millions of Chinese died in its construction.

B Write two sentences about a tourist site you know.

C Read out your sentences. The other students guess the place.

126

10 LANGUAGE BANK

11

GRAMMAR

10.1 relative clauses

defining relative clauses

- give essential information about a noun.
  *That guy is the actor **who is going to play the president**.*
  Don't use commas before or after the clause.
- can use *that* instead of *who* or *which*.
  *Ken's just seen a woman ~~who~~ **that** he went to university with.*
- can omit the relative pronoun/adverb when it is the object of the relative clause.
  Ken's just seen a woman (who) he went to university with.
  He is the subject of the relative clause, *who* is the object, so we can omit *who*.

pronouns and adverbs in relative clauses

Use the relative pronouns *who/that* (people), *which/that* (things), *whose* (possession) and the relative adverbs *when* (time) and *where* (place).
*I remember the time **when** you were just a little girl.*
Whose can be used to refer to cities, countries and other nouns which suggest a group of people. It is rarely used with things.
*It's a city **whose** inhabitants always seem to be upbeat.*
Omit words which have been replaced by the relative pronoun.
NOT *She's someone **who** I know ~~her~~ well.*

non-defining relative clauses

- give additional, non-essential information.
  *That's Sam, **who is going to play the president**.*
- use commas to separate this clause from the rest of the sentence.
- cannot use *that* instead of *who* or *which*.
  *The film, **which** won the Oscar last year, was made in India.*
  NOT *~~The film, that won the Oscar last year, was made in India.~~*
- cannot omit the relative pronouns/adverbs.
  *Gwen, **who** I'm going to see later, is my fiancé.*
  NOT *~~Gwen, I'm going to see later, is my fiancé.~~*
- can use *which* to refer to the whole of a previous clause.
  *The plane was delayed, **which** meant we were late.*

prepositions in relative clauses

In informal spoken and written English prepositions usually come at the end of the relative clause.
*This is the book **which** she's famous **for**.*
In formal and in written English prepositions often come before the relative pronoun. Use *whom* for people.
*He is someone **with whom** I can work.*
Where can be replaced by *which … in, on,* or, in more formal English *in which*.
*The room **where** she slept/**which** she slept in/**in which** she slept is over there.*

10.2 participle clauses

- Use participle clauses (clauses that start with a present participle or a past participle) to vary your style or to include more information in a sentence.
- Use them as a shorter alternative to relative clauses. In this use they are also known as 'reduced relative clauses'. Form the participle clause by omitting the relative pronoun and any auxiliary verbs.
- Clauses beginning with a past participle have a passive meaning.
  *The children **caught in the rainstorm** came home soaked.*
  = The children who were caught …
  *The film, **directed by Miyakazi**, won an award for animation.*
  = which was directed by Miyakazi …
- Clauses beginning with a present participle have an active meaning.
  *The team **playing in red** is Chile.*
  = The team that is playing in red …
  *Do you know the man **standing in the corner**?*
  = the man who is standing …
- Clauses beginning with a present participle replace continuous and simple verbs in different tenses.
  *Give me a number **beginning** with three.*
  = Give me a number which begins with three.
  *Anyone **cheating** in the exam failed.*
  = Anyone who cheated in the exam failed.
  *The bus **leaving** tomorrow will stop at Lima.*
  = The bus which is leaving/leaves tomorrow …

10.3 giving a tour

commenting on facts
As you may know,/As I'm sure you know, …
The story goes that …
Apparently,/Supposedly,/Interestingly, …
Surprisingly,/Strangely,/Believe it or not, …
It's well worth (going/seeing/a visit)

leading the way		
Let's/We could	head over to	the park.
Shall we	head back to	the café?
Why don't we	retrace our steps to	

giving facts		
It was	built	to celebrate … / to commemorate … / in honour of …
	founded by/ named after	(Thomas Bodley).
	modelled on/ modelled after	(the Arc de Triomphe).
	burnt down / destroyed / rebuilt / restored	in the 15th century. / in the 1990s.

146

VOCABULARY BANK

12

Lesson 9.1 DEPENDENT PREPOSITIONS

1 Complete the headlines with a dependent preposition.

1 Innocent man mistaken ______ gang leader
2 Woman jailed for hiding robbers ______ police
3 Couple punished ______ balloon hoax
4 Mugger caught after boasting ______ crimes in local bar
5 Jailed criminal prohibited ______ selling his story
6 Politician condemned ______ involvement in banking scandal
7 Murderess given strong sentence for joking ______ crime
8 Local teacher fired for participating ______ protest march
9 College president conceals financial woes ______ board of trustees
10 Mother fined ______ leaving baby unattended in car

Lesson 9.3 CARS AND ACCIDENTS

2 Match the car parts 1–12 to A–L in the picture.

1 boot J
2 bonnet
3 number plate
4 indicator
5 wing
6 wing mirror
7 tail light
8 windscreen
9 tyre
10 windscreen wiper
11 sun roof
12 steering wheel

3 Complete the sentences with the verbs and verb phrases in the box in the past simple.

skid collide with pull out overtake drive the wrong way swerve exceed the speed limit scratch

1 The car ______ on the ice.
2 She ______ to avoid hitting the dog.
3 She increased her speed and ______ the blue car.
4 He ______. He was going at 100 kph.
5 She ______ the side of the car by parking too near a wall.
6 He was driving too fast in a narrow street and ______ another car.
7 A car ______ in front of him and he almost crashed into it.
8 He ______ down the motorway.

156

WORKBOOK

Speakout Second Edition Workbook contains a wide variety of review and practice exercises and covers all of the language areas in the corresponding Students' Book unit. It also contains regular review sections to help learners consolidate what they have learned.

1. Extensive practice of vocabulary and grammar covered in the Students' Book
2. Additional practice of pronunciation points covered in the Students' Book
3. Reading and listening texts develop learners' skills
4. Writing exercises focus on useful sub-skills

Speakout Second Edition Workbook Audio is available online. Visit www.english.com/speakout to download audio material to accompany the pronunciation, listening and functional practice exercises.

10.1

10 CULTURE

3 READING

1 A Look at the photo and read the question on the forum. How would you answer it? Can you give an example?

B Read the forum and match comments 1–7 with categories a)–d).

a) sound *1*
b) image
c) situation
d) other

C Seven sentences have been removed from the article. Complete the article with sentences a)–g).

a) I guess I identify with the character from the start and so it feels like it's me who's trapped.
b) Maybe it reminds me of my early childhood, that feeling of being lost, of hearing my own voice crying out for help.
c) And then there's that fast bit in *Friday the 13th*, they have the whole orchestra playing …
d) Darkness and shadow can have the same effect – the effect of hiding the evil character but letting you see just enough to imagine its shape and form.
e) You know that partly because they're not a main character and they're not needed to play the story out.
f) It's similar, I guess, when there's a sinister little boy or girl, or twins in old-fashioned clothes …
g) Some are also made from made-up compound nouns, like *Cloverfield, Skinwalkers, Wickerhouse.*

D Find words in the forum that mean:

1 make a high-pitched sound (paragraph 1) ______
2 strange and frightening (paragraph 3) ______
3 damaged or made immoral (paragraph 4) ______
4 talking quickly (paragraph 6) ______
5 quick moment (paragraph 7) ______

FILM FAN FORUM

This week we asked:
What makes a horror film scary for you?

1 I'm a big fan of horror film music and I think that's the thing that really carries the fear factor for me. You get slow creepy music like in *Jaws*, you know buh-dup-buh-dup-buh-dup-buh-dup, … [1] ______, or the screaming shock music like in *Psycho*, where suddenly when the shower curtain opens, the violins shriek incredibly loudly. Every time I see that scene I jump out of my seat and it's the music that does it.

2 Vulnerability is what gets me. A character is put into a position where they can't really protect themselves against something terrible, whether they're alone, trapped in a closed space, or walking down a dark stairway or narrow hallway, or in a forest that's overgrown and hard to walk through, and basically not knowing what's going on, but knowing it's not good. [2] ______

3 I think the title of a film has quite an impact. If it's good, it somehow captures the whole experience of the film, so even years after seeing *The Omen*, if I heard that title, I'd relive the feeling. The really good titles seem to follow a pattern, for example, 'the' followed by a word ending with *-ing*, for example, *The Haunting, The Shining, The Vanishing*. [3] ______ Or you get odd, eerie words after 'the': *The Ring, The Uninvited* and, of course, *The Omen*. Very scary, I don't know why.

4 A kid's bicycle upside-down with one of its wheels turning. A broken doll. A child's shoe. I see a shot of one of those and I hide under my seat. [4] ______ I think it has to do with the innocence of childhood being corrupted by evil.

5 There's a kind of scene in a lot of horror films that always gets me. I call it the 'innocent victim' scene. You'll have a character who's often a very likeable old guy or old lady who does a simple job like running a shop or working in a restaurant. What happens is something like they close up the shop, get into their car, drive home in darkness, pull into their driveway … and so on, and you know that at any moment something very bad is going to happen to them, but you don't know exactly when. [5] ______

6 When the sound track has sound effects that sound a bit like human voices, that really scares me. So like religious chants or women's voices chattering. You almost hear words but not quite. Or a child's voice, that gives me the shivers. [6] ______

7 When you get just a glimpse of the villain or evil being. So he or she walks by a window or is spotted by a character just for a flash and then is out of sight. [7] ______ It really makes the evil come alive in your mind because your imagination starts racing, generating images.

65

10.1

1 VOCABULARY
ADJECTIVES TO DESCRIBE FILMS

2 Add vowels to make words.

1 f_st-p_c_d
2 g_ry
3 hyst_r_c_l
4 c_ntr_v_rs_ _l
5 f_ll_f_s_sp_ns_
6 gr_pp_ng
7 t_ _ch_ng
8 cr_ _py
9 _ _tst_nd_ng
10 th_ _ght-pr_v_k_ng

GRAMMAR
RELATIVE CLAUSES

3 A Underline the correct alternatives.

THE PROBLEM WITH CINEMAS

[1]What/When/Whose I was younger, one thing I used to do was to go and see new films as soon as they came out but I've stopped because of the way [2]who/what/that people behave there. The cinema should be a place [3]which/where/when you are transported to another world but this is impossible because:

- a mobile phone rings, [4]when/which/what completely kills the moment. People [5]who/whose/what leave their mobile phones on are thoughtless; people [6]who/whose/when phones ring should be sent out.
- people act like they're at home, by [7]whom/where/which I mean they have conversations, sometimes [8]where/when/which there's something really moving happening on screen. You hear about times in the day [9]what/when/which something went wrong instead of the dialogue.
- children, [10]which/who's/whose parents should control them better, kick your seat every time they laugh.

B In which examples above is it possible to leave out the relative pronoun?

4 Make sentences containing relative clauses with the prompts. The word in bold immediately follows the relative pronoun.

1 A biopic / be / a film / **tells** / the life story / famous person.
A biopic is a film which tells the life story of a famous person.
2 The biopic / I want to review today / be / *Raging Bull*, / **be** / the story of a famous boxer.
3 Robert de Niro, / **play** / the part of Jake La Motta, / be / absolutely extraordinary.
4 The film / be / made at a time / **most** biopics / be of heroic figures.
5 The film, / **be** / directed by Martin Scorsese, / be / now recognised as a masterpiece.
6 De Niro / become / interested when he read the book / on / **story** / be / based.

4 WRITING
A REVIEW; LEARN TO USE ADVERB + PAST PARTICIPLE COMBINATIONS

5 A Rearrange the letters to make adverbs that collocate with the past participles.

1 ghlhyi ______ / ylediw ______ praised
2 hyhlars ______ / oyghlwelrminve ______ / eahvliy ______ criticised
3 klulfysil ______ / iisetvsynle ______ directed
4 ptlnnoagyi ______ / nlngvnoiicyc ______ acted

B Complete the sentences with one of the collocations above.

1 a) Audiences all over the world have applauded the film.
The film has been ______.
b) Critics have given it very positive reviews.
It has been ______.
2 a) There wasn't a critic who said a positive thing about his last movie.
His last movie was ______.
b) The reviews weren't just negative, they were very negative.
The film was ______.
3 a) It wasn't an easy script, but Spielberg showed his talent in the way he directed it.
The script was ______.
b) The topic is a delicate one, but Bigelow showed she could handle this in her direction of the film.
The film was ______.
4 a) The acting in that scene made me cry.
That scene was ______.
b) Morgan Freeman's acting was so good, I actually believed he was the real Nelson Mandela.
The role of Nelson Mandela was ______.

66

10.3

FUNCTION
GIVING A TOUR

1 A Put the words in the correct order.

1 visit / worth / it's / a / well
2 the / over / let's / to / head
3 to / they / interrupt / had / supposedly,
4 not, / or / it / believe / took / it
5 was / as / originally / it / built
6 were / well, / founded / they / in
7 he / that / goes / story / the / used

2

B 10.4 Listen and draw any links between the words in the phrases. Then listen and repeat.
It's well worth a visit

C Complete the conversation with phrases from Exercise 1A. Write the number of the phrase in the correct place.

A: Here we are at the famous Leaning Tower of Pisa. [a] ______ a bell-tower for the cathedral.
B: It looks like it's going to fall over!
A: It won't. Not today. [b] ______ 177 years to build.
B: Why did it take so long?
A: [c] ______ its construction because Pisa was constantly at war.
B: Didn't Galileo live in Pisa?
A: Yes. [d] ______ the leaning tower to demonstrate the rules of gravity, by dropping things off the top.
B: Is that true?
A: Who knows, really. [e] ______ Piazza dei Cavalieri.
B: Oh yes, that's such a beautiful square.
A: Well, my favourite restaurant, Ristorante alle Bandierine, is on the way. [f] ______.
B: Sounds good to me.

VOCABULARY
DIMENSIONS

2 A Write the noun and verb forms of each adjective.

	noun	verb
1 long	*length*	*lengthen*
2 short		
3 narrow		
4 wide		
5 broad		
6 thick		
7 deep		
8 high		
9 large		

B Complete the sentences with the correct form of words from Exercise 2A.

1 The jury needs to ______ down its choices before choosing the finalists.
2 He doesn't have much experience in other companies. He's a good candidate, but I think he needs to ______ his work experience.
3 The mystery of strange lights appearing in the sky in Russia ______ today as scientists said they couldn't explain them.
4 The ______ of the mixture is important – it shouldn't be too thin, so when you mix together the flour and water, wait for it to ______ before pouring it into the pan.
5 The ______ of the road isn't enough to add another lane – they'll have to ______ it.
6 We need to check the ______ of the sofa to make sure it's not too long.
7 Lessons should be shorter and they should ______ the breaks in between.
8 This video tutorial will show you how to ______ a small photo.
9 The bridge was ______ enough for normal trucks to go underneath, but the ______ of those particular lorries was above the legal limit.
10 This exercise is too long – it needs to be ______.

LEARN TO
EXPRESS ESTIMATES

3 Correct the mistakes in the sentences.

1 There were under just 200 people at the party.
2 The homework should take you rough an hour to do.
3 We'll be arriving at 4 o'clock or so what?
4 The renovations cost downwards of one million euros.
5 We're expecting somewhere on a region of a thousand people for the conference.

69

MYENGLISHLAB

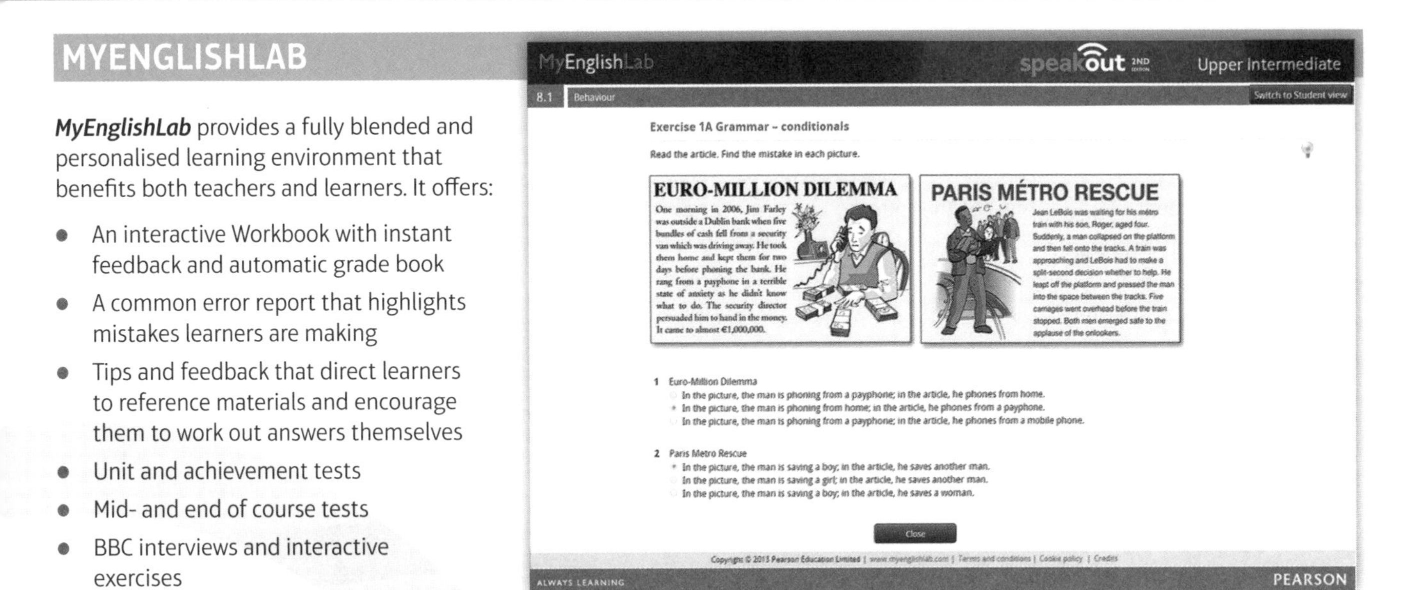

MyEnglishLab provides a fully blended and personalised learning environment that benefits both teachers and learners. It offers:

- An interactive Workbook with instant feedback and automatic grade book
- A common error report that highlights mistakes learners are making
- Tips and feedback that direct learners to reference materials and encourage them to work out answers themselves
- Unit and achievement tests
- Mid- and end of course tests
- BBC interviews and interactive exercises

ACTIVETEACH

Speakout Second Edition ActiveTeach contains everything you need to make the course come alive. It includes integrated whiteboard software that allows you to add notes, embed files, save your work and reduce preparation time.

- Answers to exercises are revealed at the touch of a button
- Audio and video content fully integrated with time-coded scripting
- Shortcuts to the relevant pages of the *Language bank* and *Vocabulary bank* make navigation easy
- Extra resources section includes editable scripts, photocopiable worksheets, tests and BBC interviews for every unit with accompanying worksheets
- Grammar and vocabulary review games
- Assessment package containing all the course tests
- Useful tools include a regular keyboard, a phonetic keyboard, a stopwatch and scoreboard.

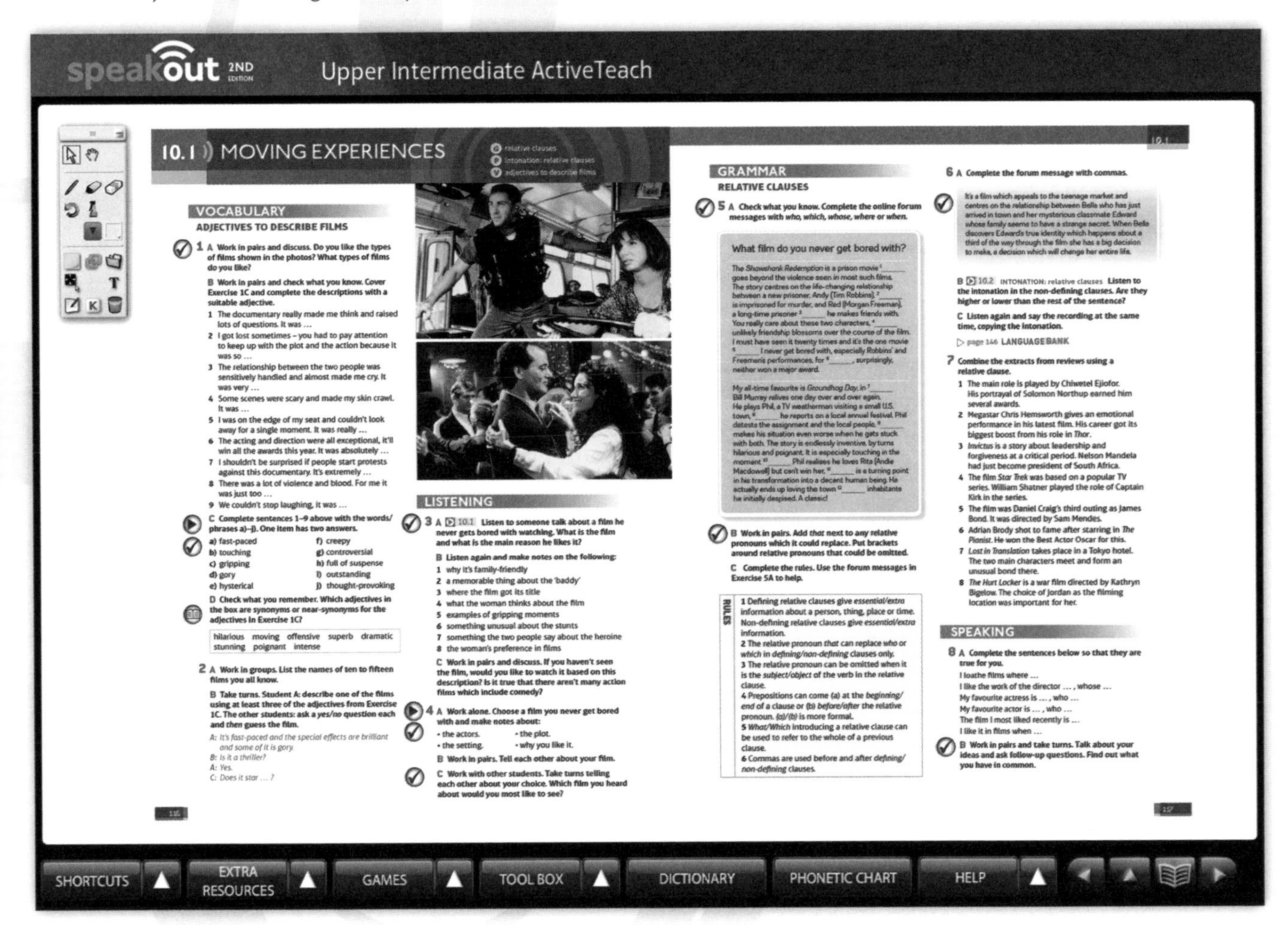

WEBSITE

Speakout Second Edition's website provides a wealth of information to support the course including:

- Information about the course, components and authors
- Introductory videos by the authors of the course
- Sample materials and free downloadable worksheets
- Teaching tips
- Placement test
- Editable audio and video scripts
- Global Scale of English mapping documents

Visit www.pearsonelt.com/speakout to check out the range of material available.

SPEAKOUT EXTRA

Speakout Extra provides a bank of additional downloadable exercises that can be accessed via the companion website:

- Downloadable grammar, vocabulary, pronunciation and skills worksheets
- BBC interviews and accompanying worksheets
- Additional worksheets to accompany DVD clips in the Students' Books
- Updated regularly with new material

Visit www.pearsonelt.com/speakout to check out the range of material available.

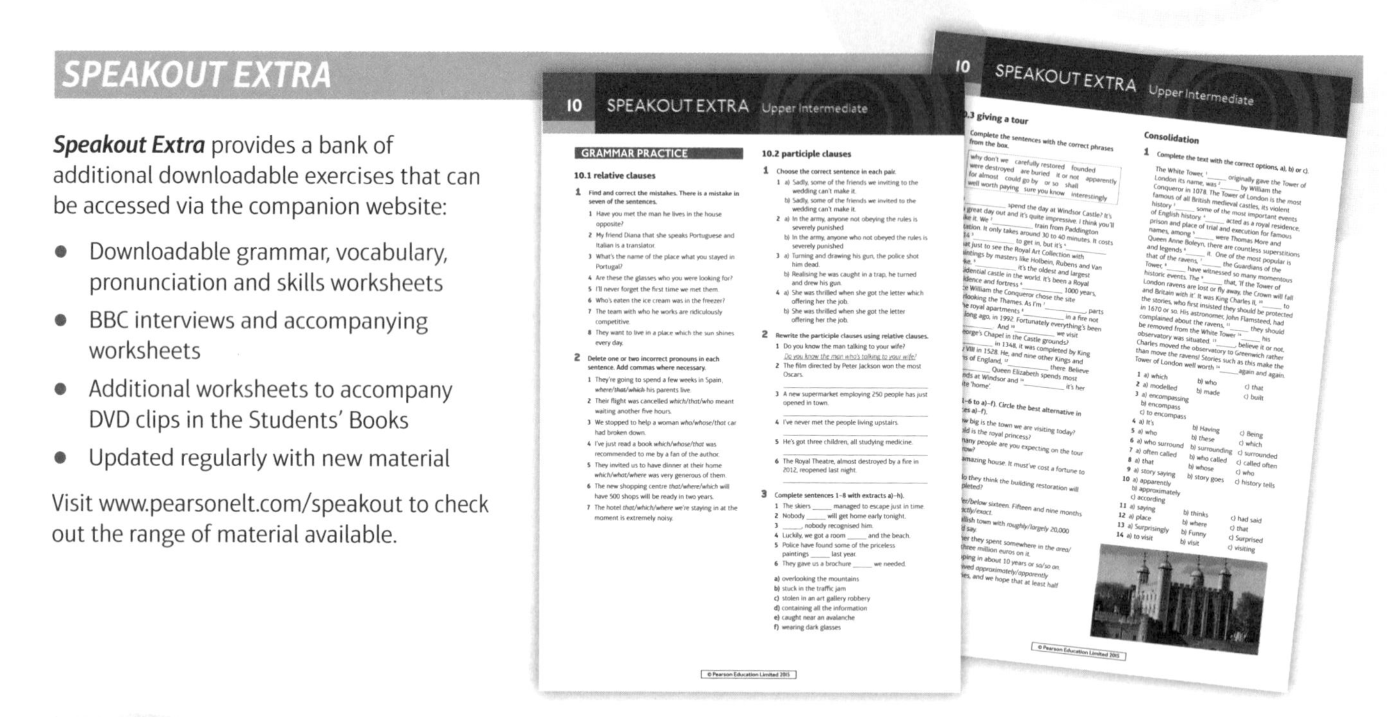
10 SPEAKOUT EXTRA Upper Intermediate

GRAMMAR PRACTICE

10.1 relative clauses

10.2 participle clauses

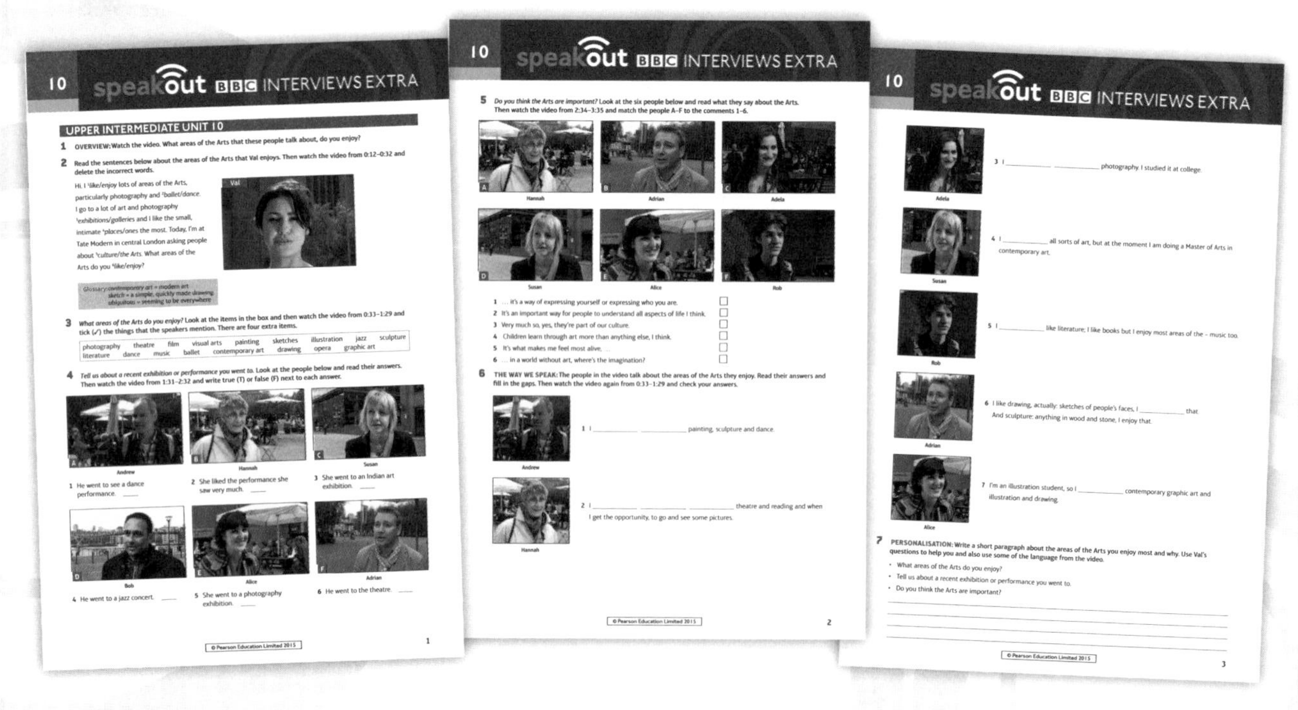
10 speakout BBC INTERVIEWS EXTRA

UPPER INTERMEDIATE UNIT 10

The thinking behind *Speakout Second Edition*

Speakout Second Edition has been significantly updated and refreshed following feedback from students and teachers from around the world. It offers engaging topics with authentic BBC material to really bring them to life. At the same time it offers a robust and comprehensive focus on grammar, vocabulary, functions and pronunciation. As the name of the course might suggest, speaking activities are prominent, but that is not at the expense of the other core skills of reading, writing and listening, which are developed systematically throughout.

With this balanced approach to topics, language development and skills work, our aim has been to create a course book full of 'lessons that really work' in practice. Below we will briefly explain our approach in each of these areas.

TOPICS AND CONTENT

In *Speakout Second Edition* we have chosen topics that are relevant to students' lives and are global in nature. Where a topic area is covered in other ELT courses we have endeavoured to find a fresh angle on it. It is clear to us that authenticity is important to learners, and many texts come from the BBC's rich resources (audio, visual and print) as well as other real-world sources. At lower levels, we have sometimes adapted materials by adjusting the language to make it more manageable for students while trying to keep the tone as authentic as possible. We have also attempted to match the authentic feel of a text with an authentic interaction. Every unit contains a variety of rich and authentic input material including BBC interviews (filmed on location in London, England) and DVD material, featuring some of the best drama, documentary and light entertainment programmes that the BBC has to offer.

GRAMMAR

Knowing how to recognise and use grammatical structures is central to our ability to communicate with each other. Although at first students can often get by with words and phrases, they increasingly need grammar to make themselves understood. Students also need to understand sentence formation when reading and listening, and to be able to produce accurate grammar in professional and exam situations. We share students' belief that learning grammar is a core feature of learning a language and believe that a guided discovery approach, where students are challenged to notice new forms, works best. At the same time, learning is scaffolded so that students are supported at all times in a systematic way. Clear grammar presentations are followed by written and oral practice.

In *Speakout Second Edition* you will find:

- **Grammar in context** – We want to be sure that the grammar focus is clear and memorable for students. Grammar is almost always taken from the listening or reading texts, so that learners can see the language in action, and understand how and when it is used.
- **Focus on noticing** – We involve students in the discovery of language patterns by asking them to identify aspects of meaning and form, and complete rules or tables.
- **Cross-references to *Language bank*** – As well as a summary of rules within the unit, there are also cross-references to the *Language bank* at the back of the book which provides further explanation of the grammar point in focus as well as additional practice.
- **Plentiful and varied practice** – We ensure that there is plenty of practice, both form- and meaning-based, in the *Language bank* to give students confidence in manipulating the new language. Additional form-based grammar practice is also provided in the Workbook and in *Speakout Extra*. On the main input page we include personalised practice, which is designed to be genuinely communicative, and to offer students the opportunity to say something about themselves or the topic. There is also regular recycling of new language in the *Lookback* pages. Again, the focus here is on moving learners towards communicative use of the language.

VOCABULARY

Developing a wide range of vocabulary is key to increasing communicative effectiveness; developing a knowledge of high-frequency collocations and fixed and semi-fixed phrases is key to increasing spoken fluency. An extensive understanding of words and phrases helps learners become more confident when reading and listening, and developing a range of vocabulary is important for effective writing. Equally vital is learner-training, equipping students with the skills to record, memorise and recall vocabulary for use.

There is a prominent focus on vocabulary in *Speakout Second Edition*. We include vocabulary in almost all lessons, whether in a lexical set linked to a particular topic, as preparation for a speaking activity, or to aid comprehension of a DVD clip or a listening or reading text. Where we want students to use the language actively, we encourage them to use the vocabulary to talk about their own lives or opinions. At lower levels, the *Photo bank* also extends the vocabulary taught in the lessons, using memorable photographs and graphics to support students' understanding. Vocabulary items have been selected according to their usefulness with a strong focus on the following:

- **Vocabulary 'chunks'** – As well as lexical sets, we also regularly focus on how words fit together with other words, often getting students to notice how words are used in a text and to focus on high-frequency 'chunks' such as verb-noun collocations or whole phrases.
- **Vocabulary systems** – We give regular attention to word-building skills, a valuable tool in expanding vocabulary. At higher levels, the *Vocabulary plus* sections deal with systems such as affixation, multi-word verbs and compound words in greater depth.
- **Recycling** – Practice exercises ensure that vocabulary is encountered on a number of occasions: within the lessons, on the *Lookback* page, in subsequent lessons and in the *Photo bank/Vocabulary bank* at the back of the book. Additional vocabulary practice is also provided in the Workbook and in *Speakout Extra*.
- **Learner training** – One of the main focuses of the *Speakout* tips – which look at all areas of language learning – is to highlight vocabulary-learning strategies, aiming to build good study skills that will enable students to gain and retain new language.

FUNCTIONAL LANGUAGE

One thing that both teachers and learners appreciate is the need to manage communication in a wide variety of encounters, and to know what's appropriate to say in given situations. These can be transactional exchanges, where the main focus is on getting something done (buying something in a shop or phoning to make an enquiry), or interactional exchanges, where the main focus is on socialising with others (talking about the weekend, or responding appropriately to good news). As one learner commented to us, 'Grammar rules aren't enough – I need to know what to say.' Although it is possible to categorise 'functions' under 'lexical phrases', we believe it is useful for learners to focus on functional phrases separately from vocabulary or grammar.

The third lesson in every unit of *Speakout Second Edition* looks at one such situation, and focuses on the functional language needed. Learners hear or see the language used in context and then practise it in mini-situations, in both a written and a spoken context. Each of these lessons also includes a *Learn to* section, which highlights and practises a useful strategy for dealing with both transactional and interactional exchanges, for example, asking for clarification, showing interest, etc. Learners will find themselves not just more confident users of the language, but also more active listeners.

SPEAKING

The dynamism of most lessons depends on the success of the speaking tasks, whether the task is a short oral practice of new language, a discussion comparing information or opinions, a personal response to a reading text, or a presentation where a student might speak uninterrupted for a minute or more. Students develop fluency when they are motivated to speak. For this to happen, engaging topics and tasks are essential, as is the sequencing of stages and task design. For longer tasks, students often need to prepare their ideas and language in a structured way. This all-important rehearsal time leads to more motivation and confidence as well as greater accuracy, fluency and complexity. Also, where appropriate, students need to hear a model before they speak, in order to have a realistic goal.

In *Speakout Second Edition* there is a strong focus on:

- **Communicative practice** – After introducing any new language (vocabulary, grammar or function) there are many opportunities for students to use it in a variety of activities which focus on communication as well as accuracy. These include personalised exchanges, dialogues, flow-charts and role-plays.
- **Fluency development** – Opportunities are included in every unit for students to respond spontaneously. They might be asked to respond to a series of questions, to comment on a BBC DVD clip, interview or text, or to take part in conversations, discussions and role-plays. These activities involve a variety of interaction patterns such as pairs and groups.
- **Speaking strategies and sub-skills** – In the third lesson of each unit, students are encouraged to notice in a systematic way features which will help them improve their speaking. These include, for example, ways to manage a phone conversation, the use of mirror questions to ask for clarification, sentence starters to introduce an opinion and intonation to correct mistakes.
- **Extended speaking tasks** – In the *Speakout Second Edition* BBC DVD lesson, as well as in other speaking tasks throughout the course, students are encouraged to attempt more adventurous and extended use of language in tasks such as problem solving, developing a project or telling a story. These tasks go beyond discussion; they include rehearsal time, useful language and a concrete outcome.

LISTENING

For most users of English, listening is the most frequently used skill. A learner who can speak well but not understand at least as well is unlikely to be a competent communicator or user of the language. We feel that listening can be developed effectively through well-structured materials. As with speaking, the choice of interesting topics and texts works hand in hand with carefully considered sequencing and task design. At the same time, listening texts can act as a springboard to stimulate discussion in class.

The listening strands in *Speakout Second Edition* focus on:

- **Authentic material** – In *Speakout Second Edition*, we believe that it is motivating for all levels of learner to try to access and cope with authentic material. Each unit includes a DVD extract from a BBC documentary, drama or light entertainment programme as well as a BBC Interview filmed on location with real people giving their opinions. At the higher levels you will also find unscripted audio texts and BBC radio extracts. All are invaluable in the way they expose learners to real language in use as well as different varieties of English. Where recordings, particularly at lower levels, are scripted, they aim to reflect the patterns of natural speech.
- **Sub-skills and strategies** – Tasks across the recordings in each unit are designed with a number of sub-skills and strategies in mind. These include: listening for global meaning and more detail; scanning for specific information; becoming sensitised to possible misunderstandings; and noticing nuances of intonation and expression. We also help learners to listen actively by using strategies such as asking for repetition and paraphrasing.
- **Texts as a context for new language** – We see listening as a key mode of input and *Speakout Second Edition* includes many listening texts which contain target grammar, vocabulary or functions in their natural contexts. Learners are encouraged to notice this new language and how and where it occurs, often by using the audio scripts as a resource.
- **Texts as a model for speaking** – In the third and fourth lessons of each unit the recordings serve as models for speaking tasks. These models reveal the ways in which speakers use specific language to structure their discourse, for example, with regard to turn-taking, hesitating and checking for understanding. These recordings also serve as a goal for the learners' speaking.

READING

Reading is a priority for many students, whether it's for study, work or pleasure, and can be practised alone, anywhere and at any time. Learners who read regularly tend to have a richer, more varied vocabulary, and are often better writers, which in turn supports their oral communication skills. Nowadays, the internet has given students access to an extraordinary range of English language reading material, and the availability of English language newspapers, books and magazines is greater than ever before. The language learner who develops skill and confidence in reading in the classroom will be more motivated to read outside the classroom. Within the classroom, reading texts can also introduce stimulating topics and act as springboards for class discussion.

The reading strands in *Speakout Second Edition* focus on:

- **Authentic texts** – As with *Speakout Second Edition* listening materials, there is an emphasis on authenticity, and this is reflected in a number of ways. Many of the reading texts in *Speakout Second Edition* are sourced from the BBC. Where texts have been adapted or graded, there is an attempt to maintain authenticity by remaining faithful to the text type in terms of content and style. We have chosen up-to-date, relevant texts to stimulate interest and motivate learners to read. The texts represent a variety of genres that correspond to the text types that learners will probably encounter in their everyday lives.
- **Sub-skills and strategies** – In *Speakout Second Edition* we strive to maintain authenticity in the way the readers interact with a text. We always give students a reason to read, and provide tasks which bring about or simulate authentic reading, including real-life tasks such as summarising, extracting specific information, reacting to an opinion or following an anecdote. We also focus on strategies for decoding texts, such as guessing the meaning of unknown vocabulary, understanding pronoun referencing and following discourse markers.
- **Noticing new language** – Noticing language in use is a key step towards the development of a rich vocabulary and greater all-round proficiency in a language, and this is most easily achieved through reading. In *Speakout Second Edition*, reading texts often serve as valuable contexts for introducing grammar and vocabulary as well as discourse features.
- **Texts as a model for writing** – In the writing sections, as well as the *Writeback* sections of the DVD spreads, the readings serve as models for students to refer to when they are writing, in terms of overall organisation as well as style and language content.

WRITING

In recent years the growth of email and the internet has led to a shift in the nature of the writing our students need to do. Email has also led to an increased informality in written English. However, many students need to develop their formal writing for professional and exam-taking purposes. It is therefore important to focus on a range of genres, from formal text types such as essays, letters and reports to informal genres such as blog entries and personal messages.

There are four strands to writing in *Speakout Second Edition* which focus on:

- **Genres** – In every unit at the four higher levels there is a section that focuses on a genre of writing, emails, for example. We provide a model to show the conventions of the genre and, where appropriate, we highlight fixed phrases associated with it. We usually then ask the students to produce their own piece of writing. While there is always a written product, we also focus on the process of writing, including the relevant stages such as brainstorming, planning, and checking. At Starter and Elementary, we focus on more basic writing skills, including basic written sentence patterns, linking, punctuation and text organisation, in some cases linking this focus to a specific genre.
- **Sub-skills and strategies** – While dealing with the genres, we include a section which focuses on a sub-skill or strategy that is generally applicable to all writing. Sub-skills include paragraphing, organising content and using linking words and pronouns, while strategies include activities like writing a first draft quickly, keeping your reader in mind and self-editing. We present the sub-skill by asking the students to notice the feature. We then provide an opportunity for the students to practise it.
- **Development of fluency** – At the end of every unit, following the DVD and final speaking task, we include a *Writeback* task. The idea behind these tasks is to develop fluency in their writing. While we always provide a model, the task is not tied to any particular grammatical structure. Instead the emphasis is on using writing to generate ideas and personal responses.
- **Writing as a classroom activity** – We believe that writing can be very usefully employed as an aid to speaking and as a reflective technique for responding to texts – akin to the practice of writing notes in the margins of books. It also provides a change of pace and focus in lessons. Activities such as short dictations, note-taking, brainstorming on paper and group story writing are all included in *Speakout Second Edition* and additional writing practice is provided in *Speakout Extra*.

PRONUNCIATION

In recent years, attitudes towards pronunciation in many English language classrooms have moved towards a focus on intelligibility: if students' spoken language is understandable, then the pronunciation is good enough. We are aware, however, that many learners and teachers place great importance on developing pronunciation that is more than 'good enough', and that systematic attention to pronunciation in a lesson, however brief, can have a significant impact on developing learners' speech.

In *Speakout Second Edition*, we have taken a practical, integrated approach to developing students' pronunciation, highlighting features that often cause problems in conjunction with a given area of grammar, particular vocabulary items and functional language. Where relevant to the level, a grammatical or functional language focus is followed by a focus on a feature of pronunciation, for example, the weak forms of auxiliary verbs or connected speech in certain functional exponents. Students are given the opportunity to listen to models of the pronunciation, notice the key feature and then practise it.

Each input lesson looks at a specific feature of pronunciation and the following strands are covered:

- **Sentence stress** – We help learners to identify which words are stressed in a sentence. This is particularly important for helping learners to understand rapid spoken English where the important information is highlighted by the speaker.
- **Word stress** – When dealing with new vocabulary, we emphasise the importance of using the correct word stress patterns. This helps listeners to identify the word being used and helps the speaker to use the correct vowel sounds.

- **Intonation** – We look at how intonation and the way we deliver a sentence can influence its meaning, or how the sentence is received.
- **Connected speech** – We help learners to understand rapid spoken English by looking at how the sounds change in fast speech. To encourage fluency we also help learners to produce rapid speech.
- **Individual sounds** – Sometimes specific individual sounds can cause problems for learners. We help learners to identify and produce specific sounds where they are important.

Additional pronunciation practice is provided in the Workbook and in *Speakout Extra.*

TEACHING UPPER INTERMEDIATE LEARNERS

An upper intermediate learner represents a great achievement in having moved from being a total beginner to a competent user of the language. Students at this level probably have extensive experience learning in classroom contexts, are familiar with different procedures and activities, and often know what they like and don't like. They may have a very strong opinion about what's worth doing and how. That can work to the teacher's advantage, if the teacher is open to students' comments, suggestions and requests.

By the upper intermediate level, learners normally can communicate comfortably on a wide range of everyday topics, with relatively little of the sort of hesitation that is common at lower levels, and which can cause some listener irritation. Many students at this level can come across as impressive if they are on a topic that they have conversed about a lot, and this can be deceptive; a relaxed, smooth conversation can come to a screeching halt, or at least a significant slow-down, if the topic shifts to a specialised area or any topic that the student hasn't 'worked with' in English. A teacher needs to be aware of this, taking into account the need to challenge students and push them out of their comfort zone – and keeping in mind that their strategies for avoiding difficulty will be more sophisticated than at lower levels.

Students at this level have a great capacity and need to use the language to express themselves, to create their own meanings rather than only generate sentences that demonstrate or practise their knowledge. Lessons should be conducted with this in mind, giving space to individual expression and reducing the amount of sustained restricted practice.

Upper intermediate students also need to become more sophisticated in their use of functional language, focussing on its appropriacy in different situations. They will also be refining their use of speaking and listening strategies to increase competency in a range of contexts.

Learners at this level have made the rounds of the grammar syllabus at least once if not several times, and yet are likely still to have significant confusion with regard to certain areas; future and perfect forms and the article system are often an issue and remain so into the advanced level. As well as consolidating previous learning, upper intermediate learners will be exploring these areas in greater depth and also encountering more complex, clause and discourse level grammar, particularly in writing and reading.

As in other levels, there may be widely-ranging strengths and weaknesses across the skills and this may cause tensions in a class. Also motivations may differ, with some students needing to focus more on exam-style accuracy and on writing, and others more interested in developing fluency in speaking.

Here are our top tips for teaching at this level:

- Find out about your learners' experience studying English. What have they enjoyed most and found most useful? What sort of activities do they dislike? What do they find most challenging? Maintain a channel of communication with students over the course, and they will help you be most effective in your teaching.
- Challenge students. Don't let them cruise through a course using language they're already comfortable with, but rather push them to express themselves in greater depth and detail, and on topics that are not a comfortable part of their repertoire.
- In dealing with language errors, don't just correct, but upgrade and enrich the learners' language. Show them how more sophisticated structures and vocabulary, including lexical phrases, can help them make the 'quality step' they need to be truly above intermediate.
- Devote more time than you have at lower levels to freer activities so that students have the opportunity to both articulate more complex ideas and to build greater fluency expressing themselves.
- Be as systematic and rigorous in focusing on grammar and vocabulary as you are with lower levels. Don't be fooled by the impression an upper-intermediate group can give, particularly those one or two strong students, of knowing it all already. Post-systematic errors – where the student knows the rule but makes the error – need to be handled mindfully, as it may well be that the learner doesn't know, or has forgotten, the relevant rule.
- Encourage personalised learning out of class so that learners can focus on areas they need to strengthen.
- Encourage extensive, out-of-class reading and listening by identifying sources of texts and videos that are easy for them to access and of course likely to interest them. Along with vocabulary that is overtly taught on a course, students at this level have the capacity to make great gains in building their passive vocabulary as well as knowledge of syntax through reading and listening.
- As always, don't forget to praise your students. Praise can be a powerful motivator, and motivation is essential to making real progress in learning a language.

Antonia Clare, Frances Eales, Steve Oakes and JJ Wilson

The Global Scale of English

The Global Scale of English (GSE) is a standardised, granular scale that measures English language proficiency. The scale is part of a wider GSE ecosystem that includes Learning Objectives or 'can do' statements that describe exactly what a learner can do at each point on the scale, teaching and learning materials in a variety of media, and low- and high-stakes tests – all aligned to the Global Scale of English. Using the Global Scale of English students and teachers can now answer three questions accurately: Exactly how good is my English? What progress have I made towards my learning goal? What do I need to do next if I want to improve?

Unlike some other frameworks that measure English proficiency in broad bands, the Global Scale of English identifies what a learner can do at each point on a scale from 10–90, across each of the four skills: listening, reading, speaking and writing. This allows learners and teachers to understand a learner's exact level of proficiency, what progress they've made and what they need to learn next.

The Global Scale of English is designed to motivate learners by making it easier to demonstrate granular progress in their language ability. Teachers can use their knowledge of their students' Global Scale of English levels to choose course materials that are precisely matched to ability and learning goals. The Global Scale of English serves as a standard against which English language courses and assessments worldwide can be benchmarked, offering a truly global and shared understanding of language proficiency levels.

Visit English.com/gse for more information about the Global Scale of English.

SPEAKOUT SECOND EDITION AND THE GSE

The authors and editorial team were informed by the GSE Learning Objectives for Adult Learners during the writing and development of *Speakout Second Edition*. Revisions to the grammar, vocabulary and skills syllabuses were influenced by these GSE Learning Objectives, and they helped to ensure that the outcomes of each lesson are clear, meaningful and relevant to learners. The spread below shows how the GSE Learning Obectives for Adult Learners are reflected in the skills content of a typical lesson in *Speakout Upper Intermediate Second Edition*:

1. Can find specific information in simple letters, brochures and short articles. (Reading GSE 38)
2. Can understand TV documentaries, interviews, plays and most films in standard speech. (Listening GSE 64)
3. Can follow the main points of recorded material on familiar topics if relatively slow and clear. (Listening GSE 54)
4. Can exchange information on a wide variety of topics within their field with some confidence. (Speaking GSE 59)
5. Can justify a viewpoint on a topical issue by discussing pros and cons of various options. (Speaking GSE 60)
6. Can write clear, detailed descriptions on a variety of subjects related to their field of interest. (Writing GSE 64)

Visit www.pearsonelt.com/speakout for the full list of GSE Learning Objectives for Adult Learners covered in each level of *Speakout Second Edition*.

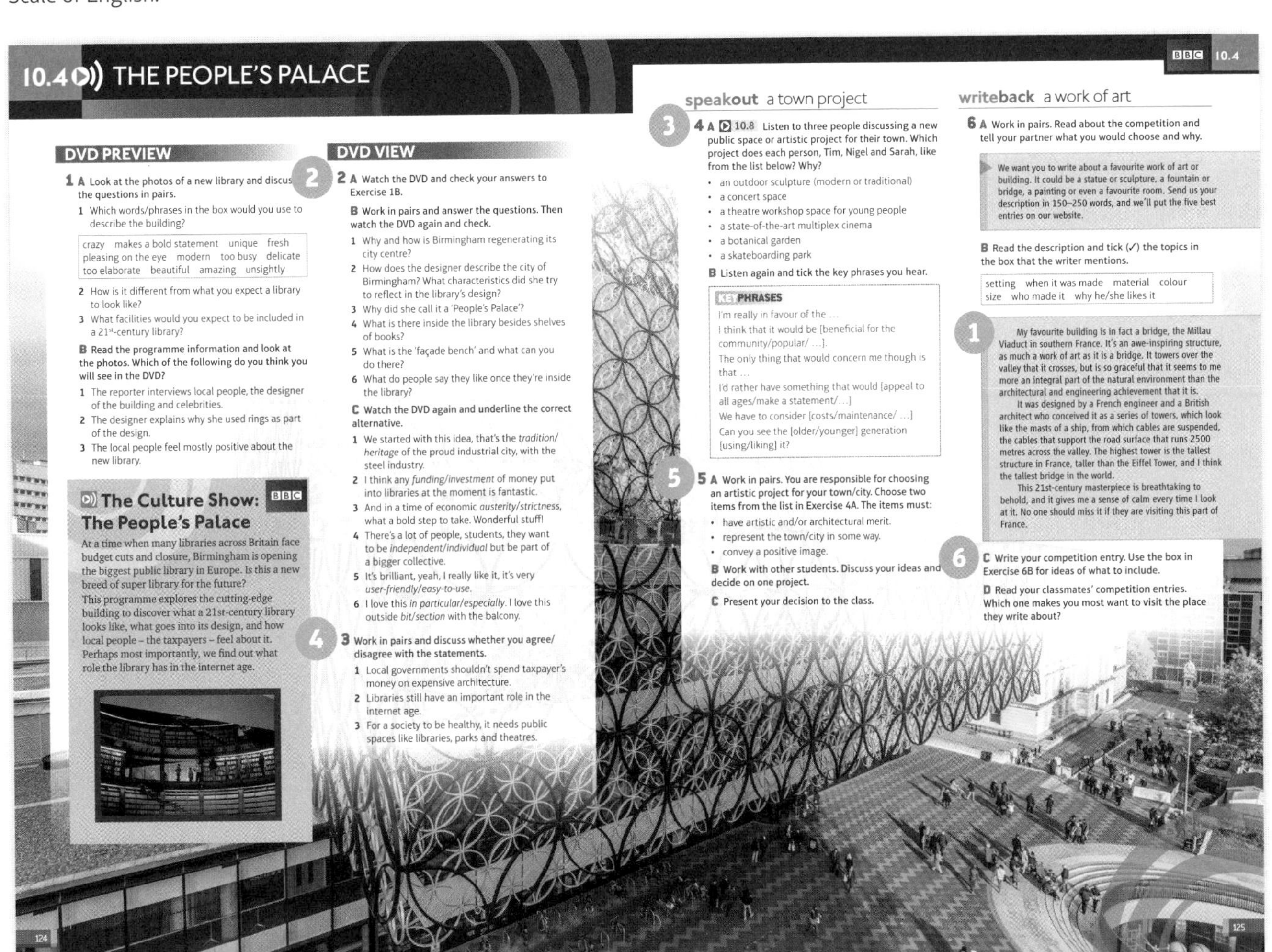

10.4 THE PEOPLE'S PALACE

DVD PREVIEW

1 A Look at the photos of a new library and discuss the questions in pairs.
1 Which words/phrases in the box would you use to describe the building?

crazy makes a bold statement unique fresh pleasing on the eye modern too busy delicate too elaborate beautiful amazing unsightly

2 How is it different from what you expect a library to look like?
3 What facilities would you expect to be included in a 21st-century library?

B Read the programme information and look at the photos. Which of the following do you think you will see in the DVD?
1 The reporter interviews local people, the designer of the building and celebrities.
2 The designer explains why she used rings as part of the design.
3 The local people feel mostly positive about the new library.

The Culture Show: The People's Palace

At a time when many libraries across Britain face budget cuts and closure, Birmingham is opening the biggest public library in Europe. Is this a new breed of super library for the future?
This programme explores the cutting-edge building to discover what a 21st-century library looks like, what goes into its design, and how local people – the taxpayers – feel about it. Perhaps most importantly, we find out what role the library has in the internet age.

DVD VIEW

2 A Watch the DVD and check your answers to Exercise 1B.

B Work in pairs and answer the questions. Then watch the DVD again and check.
1 Why and how is Birmingham regenerating its city centre?
2 How does the designer describe the city of Birmingham? What characteristics did she try to reflect in the library's design?
3 Why did she call it a 'People's Palace'?
4 What is there inside the library besides shelves of books?
5 What is the 'façade bench' and what can you do there?
6 What do people say they like once they're inside the library?

C Watch the DVD again and underline the correct alternative.
1 We started with this idea, that's the *tradition/heritage* of the proud industrial city, with the steel industry.
2 I think any *funding/investment* of money put into libraries at the moment is fantastic.
3 And in a time of economic *austerity/strictness*, what a bold step to take. Wonderful stuff!
4 There's a lot of people, students, they want to be *independent/individual* but be part of a bigger collective.
5 It's brilliant, yeah, I really like it, it's very *user-friendly/easy-to-use*.
6 I love this *in particular/especially*. I love this outside *bit/section* with the balcony.

3 Work in pairs and discuss whether you agree/disagree with the statements.
1 Local governments shouldn't spend taxpayer's money on expensive architecture.
2 Libraries still have an important role in the internet age.
3 For a society to be healthy, it needs public spaces like libraries, parks and theatres.

speakout a town project

4 A 10.8 Listen to three people discussing a new public space or artistic project for their town. Which project does each person, Tim, Nigel and Sarah, like from the list below? Why?
- an outdoor sculpture (modern or traditional)
- a concert space
- a theatre workshop space for young people
- a state-of-the-art multiplex cinema
- a botanical garden
- a skateboarding park

B Listen again and tick the key phrases you hear.

KEY PHRASES
I'm really in favour of the …
I think that it would be [beneficial for the community/popular/ …].
The only thing that would concern me though is that …
I'd rather have something that would [appeal to all ages/make a statement/…]
We have to consider [costs/maintenance/ …]
Can you see the [older/younger] generation [using/liking] it?

5 A Work in pairs. You are responsible for choosing an artistic project for your town/city. Choose two items from the list in Exercise 4A. The items must:
- have artistic and/or architectural merit.
- represent the town/city in some way.
- convey a positive image.

B Work with other students. Discuss your ideas and decide on one project.

C Present your decision to the class.

writeback a work of art

6 A Work in pairs. Read about the competition and tell your partner what you would choose and why.

We want you to write about a favourite work of art or building. It could be a statue or sculpture, a fountain or bridge, a painting or even a favourite room. Send us your description in 150–250 words, and we'll put the five best entries on our website.

B Read the description and tick (✓) the topics in the box that the writer mentions.

setting when it was made material colour size who made it why he/she likes it

My favourite building is in fact a bridge, the Millau Viaduct in southern France. It's an awe-inspiring structure, as much a work of art as it is a bridge. It towers over the valley that it crosses, but is so graceful that it seems to me more an integral part of the natural environment than the architectural and engineering achievement that it is.
It was designed by a French engineer and a British architect who conceived it as a series of towers, which look like the masts of a ship, from which cables are suspended, the cables that support the road surface that runs 2500 metres across the valley. The highest tower is the tallest structure in France, taller than the Eiffel Tower, and I think the tallest bridge in the world.
This 21st-century masterpiece is breathtaking to behold, and it gives me a sense of calm every time I look at it. No one should miss it if they are visiting this part of France.

C Write your competition entry. Use the box in Exercise 6B for ideas of what to include.

D Read your classmates' competition entries. Which one makes you most want to visit the place they write about?

124 125

INDEX

LEAD-IN

The activities on the Lead-in page are designed to provide revision and communicative practice in lexical sets and functional language that upper intermediate Ss should be familiar with. Use the Lead-in page to assess your Ss' existing knowledge and revise/teach the target language in each activity.

PARTS OF SPEECH

1A Before Ss look at the questionnaire, ask them to discuss with a partner how they learn languages. Refer Ss to the questionnaire and ask them to answer the questions with a partner. In class feedback, elicit the reasons for Ss' choices.

B Look at the example together and then set the task as individual work. Check the answers as a class.

Answers: a) 8 **b)** 14 **c)** 7 **d)** 10 **e)** 12 **f)** 2 **g)** 3 **h)** 11 **i)** 1 **j)** 9 **k)** 6 **l)** 5 **m)** 13 **n)** 4

VERB PATTERNS

2A This could be done as an individual exercise or as a competitive pair race. Check the answers as a class.

Answers:
1 I can't stand *working* with music on.
2 I learnt *to drive* last year.
3 I *want the teacher to correct* everything I say.
4 I'd rather ~~to~~ eat out than at home.
5 I'd like *to travel* abroad this year.
6 I enjoy *being* alone.
7 I like it when the teacher tells *me/us* to repeat words.
8 I'd better ~~to~~ spend more time studying or I'll never make progress in English.

B Look at the example together and then set the task as individual work. Check the answers as a class.

Answers: 1 verb + gerund 1 and 6 **2** verb + infinitive 4 and 8 **3** verb + infinitive with *to* 2 and 5 **4** verb + object + infinitive with *to* 3 and 7

C Ask Ss to discuss which statements are true for them and to change any that are not true. Elicit an example of a change to each one from the class.

PRONUNCIATION

3A Draw Ss' attention to the table and ask them to read the pairs of words in the table out loud. In pairs, ask Ss to complete the table with words from the box.

B Play the recording and check the answers with Ss. Play the recording again and ask Ss to repeat.

Answers: 1 minutes, system **2** extremely, reach **3** completely, future **4** guarantee, absolutely **5** public, thorough **6** push, took

C Ask Ss to discuss the question in pairs and then elicit some suggestions.

Suggested answer: If Ss know phonemic symbols and use a dictionary, they'll know how to pronounce a word without having to hear it.

COLLOCATIONS

4A Do the first one as an example with the class. You could do this by asking Ss to vote on the one they think does not collocate with the verb. Set the rest of the task as individual work. Check the answers as a class.

Answers: do ~~a problem~~; make ~~the housework~~; take ~~a noise~~; have ~~care~~; give ~~fun~~

B Put Ss into pairs. They take it in turns to say a noun or noun phrase and respond with the verb that collocates with it.

OVERVIEW

1.1 TIME FOR A CHAT

SPEAKING | have interesting conversations
LISTENING | understand informal conversations
VOCABULARY | personality
GRAMMAR | direct and indirect questions
PRONUNCIATION | sentence stress
WRITING | write an advice forum message; learn to edit for accuracy

1.2 TRY SOMETHING NEW

VOCABULARY | feelings
PRONUNCIATION | word stress
READING | read a web article about trying something new
GRAMMAR | present perfect
PRONUNCIATION | connected speech
SPEAKING | talk about new experiences
VOCABULARY *PLUS* | word building: nouns

1.3 I'D LIKE TO ENQUIRE

VOCABULARY | adverts
FUNCTION | polite enquiries
PRONUNCIATION | polite intonation
LEARN TO | manage enquiries
SPEAKING | make phone enquiries

1.4 GREAT EXPERIENCES BBC DVD

DVD | watch a BBC documentary about adventures
speakout | a recommendation
writeback | a forum entry

1.5 LOOKBACK

Communicative revision activities

BBC INTERVIEWS

What makes a good flatmate?

This video looks at the topic of house or flatsharing and examines the question of what makes a good flatmate. Use this video at the start or end of Unit 1 or set it as homework.

TIME FOR A CHAT

Introduction

Ss practise finding out about people using direct and indirect questions and personality vocabulary. They also practise listening to people socialising and role-play socialising.

SUPPLEMENTARY MATERIALS
Resource bank: p147 and p149

Warm up

This activity leads into the topic and gives Ss a chance (especially if this is a new class) to get to know each other. It also gives you an opportunity to assess Ss' language skills, especially the use of the present perfect, which is covered in Lesson 1.2. Write *New Things* on the board and elicit examples of times that people start something new in their lives, e.g. a school, a job, a course, a hobby, a relationship, life in a new town, etc. Write these on the board and put Ss into small groups to discuss which of these they have done, giving specific examples. Their aim is to find out how many of the 'New Things' all the people in their group have experienced. One person from each group feeds back to the class.

Teaching tip

It is often a good idea, when asking Ss to speak about personal experience, to give an example of your own first, e.g. for the above activity talk about something new you have started. This should encourage Ss to speak about themselves and demonstrate how much detail you expect them to give when they are speaking.

SPEAKING

1A Ask Ss when they last met someone new. Choose one or two Ss and elicit examples of who they met and the things they discussed. Ask Ss to work in pairs and to write down three things they often talk about when meeting new people. In feedback, choose two or three Ss to tell the class about the things they discussed.

B Give Ss a minute or two to read the text and then ask them to answer the first question before going on to discuss the other two questions with a partner.

Answer:
1 The conversations are about unusual topics, you speak to a number of different partners and you can eat mixed mezé at the same time.

LISTENING

2A Play the first conversation and ask Ss to identify the topic discussed from the opening text. Check the answer and then repeat the same process with the second conversation. Check the answer again, before asking Ss to discuss in pairs the things they remember from each conversation.

Answers:
Conversation 1:
What three questions would you ask a potential flatmate?
Conversation 2:
Which three adjectives might people use to describe you?

1 new things

Unit 1 Recording 1

Conversation 1

M = Man W = Woman

M: What would you say?
W: Erm, for me, an important question is 'Do you keep yourself to yourself, or do you tend to be around a lot?'
M: Hmm. What are you trying to find out?
W: I suppose I'm looking for a balance, because the last thing you want is a person who comes in and goes straight up to their room and you never see them again till the morning. You know, antisocial. I'm quite sociable, you know, I like having friends around. I suppose I'm a people person.
M: Yeah.
W: ... but on the other hand, you don't want a flatmate who's always there, so you never get any privacy. And especially in the morning. I'm not a morning person – I can't stand people who are all bright and cheerful first thing. You know, when I haven't woken up yet. So yeah, I'd like someone who is quite sociable but not too sociable.
M: Mm, yeah, I agree. I suppose another question is about housework and cleaning.
W: Yes, something like 'Who cleans the place where you live now?'
M: How would you answer that question?
W: Who cleans my flat now? I do.
M: Yeah, me too.
W: And I'd also ask: 'Are you tidy?'
M: What answer do you want the person to give?
W: I'd want the answer to be 'Oh yes, extremely.' I don't know. I'd hate to live with someone who was really untidy all the time, that never did the washing up, someone that left their stuff just lying all over the place. Someone who doesn't do their fair share of the housework. No, that would just drive me crazy. I suppose I'm quite tidy myself.
M: Yeah, yeah. Um and what about money?
W: Yeah it can be a big problem. I had a flatmate once and she used to say 'I know I have to pay the electricity bill but can I pay it next week?' She promised to pay and then never did. Really unreliable.
M: Oh yeah. It doesn't matter how nice people are if they've got money problems. You need to know they can afford the rent.
W: But I wouldn't ask 'Could you tell me how much you earn?' I think I'd say the rent and the bills have to be paid in advance, so I'd ask 'Can you pay three months in advance?' and see what they say.

Conversation 2

M = Man W = Woman

M: Ooh that's really difficult to answer ... I would like to think: 'handsome', 'witty', 'cool.'
W: Well at least you're witty. You're quick and you make me laugh, and you're good with words.
M: No, but I don't think they'd describe me like that. I dunno. Let me think. Erm. I suppose they'd say I'm good at coming up with new ideas ... yes ... So I think people would describe me as quite creative.
W: And the second one?
M: Erm ... well, people know I like doing new things, things that are out of the ordinary.
W: Such as?
M: Oh well, like last week I was by the sea with some friends and it was a lovely warm evening. And we decided to go for a midnight swim. I mean, we hadn't planned to, it just seemed like a great idea at the time. I like doing new things, different things. So I suppose that means I'm adventurous ... or maybe a better word is spontaneous. Yeah, that's more like it. I get an idea and I do it, no hesitation, so I'm spontaneous. That's useful in my job, too.
W: Can I ask what you do?
M: I work for a web design company. We design websites for new businesses.
W: Mmm, sounds interesting.
M: Most of the time!
W: So that's two very positive words so far. What's your third one?
M: Well, I think people that know me would say that I'm quite messy and disorganised. You should see my desk – papers everywhere – and my bedroom! And I'm always losing things. So yes, my friends would say 'creative, spontaneous and disorganised'.
W: I'd be interested to know if you agree with them. What words do you think describe you best?
M: Now that's an interesting question. Actually, I'd like to think that I'm fair, you know, non-judgemental.
W: What do you mean by non-judgemental?
M: Well, I try not to make up my mind about people until I get to know them, so yes, non-judgemental. But I'd stick with 'spontaneous' and 'disorganised'. I think they describe me quite well. What about you?
W: Erm. Well, people say I'm fun to be with, a good laugh, if you know what I mean. Erm, I'm very practical and down-to-earth.
M: What do you do?
W: I train people in advanced computer software. But don't worry, I'm not a computer geek. I don't sit in front of my computer for hours.

B Before you play the recording again, focus Ss on the sentences and check the following vocabulary: *sociable* (someone who enjoys being with other people), *salary* (a monthly or weekly income from work) and *outdoor adventure school* (a place to learn activities such as rock climbing, sailing and canoeing).

Teaching tip

After Ss have listened to the recording, put them into pairs to compare/discuss what they understood. This helps to build their confidence before giving their answers to the class. It also helps you, if they are struggling with the answers, to decide whether you need to play the recording again.

Answers:
1 F She would like someone who's quite sociable (not antisocial) but not too sociable (gives you privacy). A balance.
2 F She's not a morning person.
3 T
4 F She wouldn't ask a flatmate about their salary.
5 T
6 F He likes doing unplanned things.
7 F He works for a web design company.
8 T He agrees with the adjectives although he prefers 'non-judgemental' to 'creative'.

C Check the following vocabulary: *antisocial* (not good with other people) and *non-judgemental* (open-minded and not quick to judge). Ask Ss to discuss just the first question. Elicit answers from the class before moving on to the second question. Give Ss a few minutes to discuss the second question in pairs.

Answers:
Conversation 1:
antisocial: She gives the example of someone who goes straight up to their room when they come home and stays there.
tidy: She gives the example of someone who isn't tidy: they never do the washing-up, leave their stuff lying around and don't do their fair share of the housework.
reliable with money: She gives the example of someone who never pays the electricity bill on time – keeps promising to pay it but never does.
Conversation 2
creative: People say he's good at coming up with new ideas.
adventurous: He gives the example of going for a midnight swim with friends without planning it in advance.
non-judgemental: He says he tries not to make up his mind about people until he gets to know them.

Teaching tip

Weaker Ss might not be able to give you many ideas when you try to elicit examples from them. If this is the case, play the audio again or refer Ss to the audio script on p164 to build their confidence.

VOCABULARY PERSONALITY

3A Ask Ss some questions to check their understanding of the words and phrases in the box. For example, ask Ss: *Which two describe funny people?* (*witty* and *a good laugh*) *Which one is the opposite of 'a people person'?* (*keep yourself to yourself*) Give Ss a few minutes to complete the gaps and check the answers together.

Answers: **1** keep yourself to yourself **2** a people person **3** a morning person **4** witty **5** spontaneous **6** a good laugh **7** down-to-earth **8** a computer geek

B Ss may want to work alone on this for a few minutes before discussing their answers in pairs. In feedback, elicit an example person for each word or phrase in the box.

▷ VOCABULARYBANK p148 Personality adjectives

Let Ss check the personality adjectives in their dictionaries if they have difficulty in matching the words in Ex 1A. In feedback, elicit the main stress in each adjective. Elicit from the group which adjectives they think the photos in Ex 1B represent.

Answers:
A **1** sympathetic **2** cautious **3** naive **4** genuine **5** outgoing **6** mean **7** flexible **8** eccentric **9** trustworthy **10** moody
B **A** eccentric/outgoing **B** sympathetic **C** moody

GRAMMAR DIRECT AND INDIRECT QUESTIONS

4A Before completing the questions Ss could read the extracts quickly and see which conversation from Ex 2A they come from. They then complete the questions and check with the recording.

Answers: **1** Who cleans **2** how much you **3** as **4** what you do **5** if you **6** do you mean

B Ss work on the exercise alone, then discuss their answers in pairs. At this level you may have Ss in the class who are fluent but not very accurate and weaker at analysing language. If so, pair them with ***stronger Ss*** who can help them. In feedback, ask Ss how they know if a question is indirect (there is an 'introductory phrase' before the actual question). Before moving on to Ex 4C, you could elicit more information from the class about why we use indirect questions and how they are different from the direct form.

Answers: **a)** 6 **b)** 2, 4, 5 **c)** 1 **d)** 3

C As they work through this exercise, Ss should find an example from Ex 4A to support each rule. In feedback you could have the following indirect questions on the board to help you check the answers:

Do you mind me asking if you're in a relationship? (The question is personal – rule 1; it is also a *yes/no* question – rule 4.)

Could you tell me where you are staying? (The word order is not *Where* are you *staying?* – rule 2.)

Have you any idea how long you want to stay? (The auxiliary *do* is not used – rule 3.)

Answers: **1** personal, polite **2** the same as **3** don't use **4** isn't

5A Ss should write out the full sentences in their notebooks, as they will need them for marking the stress in Ex 6A. Monitor and check if Ss are forming the direct and indirect questions correctly but don't check answers at this point.

B Play the recording for Ss to check their answers. Ask Ss to look at the questions again and decide which one is the most personal.

Answers:
1 why you are studying English
2 how long you plan to study
3 what you do in the evenings
4 if/whether you have a full-time job
5 which countries you've visited
6 where you got that watch
7 if/whether there's a good café anywhere near here
8 if/whether you'd like to come for a coffee
Do you mind me asking … ? is best for asking a very personal question.

6A Do the first sentence as an example on the board with the class, underlining the main stressed syllables. Play the rest of the sentences, stopping after each one if necessary to give Ss time to mark the stress.

Teaching tip

Point out to Ss that the main stressed words are always the ones that carry the message, i.e. if the other words weren't there, the message could still be understood. If Ss have difficulty hearing the stressed words and syllables, you could model the questions yourself, emphasising the stresses a little more and/or clicking your fingers or tapping your foot on the stresses.

Answers:
1 Can you tell me why you're studying English?
2 Do you have any idea how long you plan to study?
3 Can I ask what you do in the evenings?
4 Do you mind me asking if you have a full-time job?
5 I'd be interested to know which countries you've visited.
6 Could you tell me where you got that watch?
7 Do you know if there's a good café anywhere near here?
8 I was wondering if you'd like to come for a coffee.

B Play the sentences again for Ss to focus on the stress. You could also drill the sentences, either after the recording or from your own model. Even at this level, Ss still need help with word order and natural stress in oral work.

7A Ss choose three questions and write two of their own. You might need to provide some prompts to help Ss generate their own questions. Topics could include: hobbies, interests, personal life, studies, work, etc.

B Ss can work on this in pairs and practise saying the questions with the appropriate stress before they work with other Ss.

C Before doing this stage you could elicit a range of the new questions from Ss and add them to the board. Check the grammar and drill for pronunciation. If Ss wish, they could substitute one or two of their questions for the ones you have added to the board. Give Ss time to ask and answer the questions in pairs or small groups.

Teaching tip

While Ss are asking each other their questions, monitor and make notes of examples of good language use and problem areas (particularly with the word order and intonation in indirect questions). You can then write the examples on the board for Ss to look at and correct or make a handout for Ss to work on in the next lesson.

D Tell Ss to work with someone different and to exchange information about the things they learnt. After Ss have exchanged information elicit some answers from the class.

▷ LANGUAGEBANK 1.1 p128–129

Depending on how well Ss have coped with the language so far, either give them time to read the notes in class and ask you any questions, or tell them to study the notes at home. Ss can do the exercises in class if you feel they need more practice in word order. Ask ***stronger Ss*** to make their own conversations using the questions in Ex A. They could also act out their dialogues for the class.

Answers:
A 1 Where have you been?
2 Who were you with?
3 What was the meeting like?
4 Do you know what time it is now?
5 Can I ask why you didn't phone?
6 Do you have any idea how worried I was/I've been?
B 1 Do you know if they accept credit cards here?
2 Do you mind me asking how you became a model?
3 Do you have any idea where I can get a coffee at this time?
4 Would you mind telling me when the computer becomes available?
5 Can I ask if you're planning to get married?
6 I was wondering where you bought that briefcase.
C 1 come 2 to 3 with 4 much 5 time 6 not

SPEAKING

8A Give Ss a few minutes to look at the questions in the text on p8 again. Tell them to choose one each to discuss with a partner.

B Ss change partners and talk about new conversation topics. Elicit which conversations people discussed and a range of answers.

Alternative approach

You could tell Ss to discuss as many of the questions from the text as possible. Tell Ss they can only ask each question to one person and they only have 30 seconds to discuss each question.

C If you have time, you could make this slightly competitive by asking Ss to briefly present their idea for a conversation evening. Each pair has to attract as many people to their night as possible. Ss then vote on the night they would most like to attend.

WRITING AN ADVICE FORUM MESSAGE; LEARN TO EDIT FOR ACCURACY

9A Set this task as pairwork discussion and then elicit answers. During feedback discuss question 1 by writing a scale of 1 to 10 on the board and asking Ss to rank the importance of English for them. Then discuss the other questions as a class.

B Ask Ss if they have ever given or asked for advice on an online forum. Ask Ss to read the messages and to discuss the questions with a partner. Elicit reactions to the suggestion. Elicit genres of videos and ask for a show of hands for the most popular genre.

C To help Ss do this task, you could write some alternative expressions showing these features on the board, e.g. *I understand how you feel …; Something that I found useful …; Hope this is useful.; Best of luck.* Check the answers as a class and check Ss know which features they correspond to.

Answers:
1 *I know exactly how you feel …*
2 *I know a really great idea which has really helped me …* and the whole of the second paragraph
3 No examples in the messages
4 *Hope that helps. Good luck!*

10A Point out to Ss that the advice contains errors (indicated by the blue teacher's correction code) but that they do not need to worry about these yet. Ask Ss to read the advice and to identify the features from Ex 9C used here.

Answers: 2, 4

B Before Ss read the advice again, direct them to the correction code and elicit an example of a mistake for each category, e.g. *oportunities* [sp], *We was* [v], *cant'* [p], *I exactly know* [wo], etc. Ss correct the mistakes in the advice. Also, ask Ss about the advantages of using a correction code (it forces them to think about the mistake).

Answers: 1 do some research 2 on the internet 3 you can find 4 aren't 5 practice (Br E spelling) 6 meeting new people very much 7 good luck (for the future)

11A Ask Ss to read Miki's forum question and to identify the context. Give Ss 10–15 mins to write a reply to either Miki or Rafael's post.

B Ask Ss to swap their replies and to first identify the features their partner has used from Ex 9C. They then identify and mark three mistakes in their partner's post. They should also tell their partner things they like about the advice when handing it back.

Watch out!

When asking Ss to mark mistakes in a ***monolingual class***, many will often not spot mistakes, as they are common ones to speakers of the same language. If you know typical mistakes your Ss might make with this task, elicit five very typical mistakes and tell Ss to see if their partner has made any of them.

C After Ss have checked their own posts again, ask Ss to exchange their posts with other Ss and to choose their favourites.

D Put the posts on the wall: one wall for advice for Miki and one for advice for Rafael. Tell Ss to read the posts to the person they didn't give advice to and decide which is most useful.

Optional extra activity

Take in Ss' posts. Choose one mistake from each post and create a worksheet using the correction code. In the following lesson, use this as a correction activity or play it as a competitive game.

speakout TIP

Ss check their posts using the techniques described. Many of the speakout tips throughout the course would also make ideal homework tasks.

Homework ideas

- Ss research opportunities for socialising in English online and in their hometown and report their findings to the class in the next lesson.
- **Ex 11:** write to the person you didn't choose.
- **Language bank:** 1.1 Ex A–C, p129
- **Vocabulary bank:** p148
- **Workbook:** Ex 1–5, p4–5

TRY SOMETHING NEW

Introduction

Ss practise speaking about how different activities make them feel, using adjectives and modifiers. They practise reading a text giving advice for lifestyle changes and they revise and practise the present perfect in the context of discussing experiences, unspecified time and incomplete states or actions. Finally, Ss work on noun building to further be able to describe feelings.

SUPPLEMENTARY MATERIALS

Resource bank: p148 and p150

Warm up: prepare pieces of paper with names of activities and criteria, as described below.

Ex 1D and **Ex 10B:** bring monolingual dictionaries for Ss to use.

Warm up

Lead into the topic via a discussion of a range of activities. Before class, write twelve to fifteen activities on pieces of A4 paper, e.g. *baking a cake, riding a horse, giving a speech, changing a tyre, singing karaoke, ballroom dancing, painting a portrait, sailing, redecorating a room, putting up shelves, planting a garden, going up in a balloon*, etc. On small slips of paper, write different criteria, e.g. *indoor/outdoor, interesting/boring, expensive/cheap, easy/difficult*, etc. Stick the activities on the board, divide Ss into groups of three or four and give each group a 'criteria' slip. Ss discuss how to divide the activities on the board according to their criteria. In feedback, one person from each group comes up to the board and puts the activities into two groups, without saying what their group's criteria were. The rest of the class has to guess.

VOCABULARY FEELINGS

1A This follows on naturally from the Warm up. However, if you haven't done the Warm up, you might want to spend a few minutes brainstorming new things Ss have done recently. To start Ss off, you could give them an example yourself. Ask Ss to tick the statements individually and then compare in pairs.

B Ask Ss to look at the photos and elicit a description of what they can see in each picture. Then ask Ss to read the comments and match them to the photos.

Answers: 1 B 2 C 3 A 4 D

C Ss work in pairs circling the words and phrases. With ***weaker Ss*** you might want to work through the first comment together as a class. With ***stronger Ss*** you could elicit their own adjectives for how they would feel before doing this task. Check the answers as a class.

Answers:
Comment 1: scared out of my wits; relieved
Comment 2: made my stomach turn; awkward; impressed
Comment 3: fascinated; over the moon
Comment 4: shaking like a leaf; frustrated; wished the earth would swallow me up
Positive: relieved, impressed, fascinated, over the moon

D For this task you might want to allow Ss time to use a monolingual dictionary. Ask Ss to work individually on these and then to compare their answers with a partner. Check the answers as a class.

Answers: **1** frustrated **2** wished the earth would swallow me up **3** over the moon **4** made my stomach turn **5** relieved **6** fascinated **7** shaking like a leaf **8** scared out of my wits **9** impressed **10** awkward

Optional extra activity

If you have time, put Ss into groups and ask them to mime the adjectives and phrases to the other people in their group. The other Ss should try to guess the word being mimed.

E Using *frustrated* as an example, ask Ss where the stress is and show them how to mark it by underlining the 'tra', i.e. *frustrated*. Ss work in pairs identifying and marking the stress, then check with the recording. Use the recording as a model for Ss to repeat, or model the words in short phrases yourself, e.g. *I was over the moon. I felt really relieved.*

Answers: **1** frustrated **2** wished the earth would swallow me up **3** over the moon **4** made my stomach turn **5** relieved **6** fascinated **7** shaking like a leaf **8** scared out of my wits **9** impressed **10** awkward

2A This will be revision for most Ss at this level, so they should be able to identify the incorrect alternatives and explain the reasons in pairs. However, for ***weaker Ss*** when checking answers, make sure Ss are familiar with the concept of an ungradable/extreme adjective, i.e. an adjective which already means *very* whatever the state the adjective represents may be and therefore cannot be made stronger or weaker in meaning, e.g. *fascinating* means *very interesting*, so you can't say *It was very fascinating.*

Answers:
1 **A** ~~frustrating~~ **B** ~~embarrassed~~ – adjectives ending *-ed* refer to how a person feels; adjectives ending *-ing* refer to the thing/person that causes the feeling.
2 **A** ~~totally~~ **B** ~~very~~ – *interested* is a gradable adjective and can be used with the modifier *very* but cannot be used with *totally*; *fascinating* is an ungradable/extreme adjective and cannot be used with *very*. It needs a stronger modifier such as *totally* or *absolutely*. *Really* can be used with both gradable and ungradable adjectives.
3 **A** ~~absolutely~~ **B** ~~very~~ – *relieved* is gradable and *over the moon* is ungradable/extreme, so the same rules apply here as in the previous item.

B If Ss are struggling to think of different modifiers, you could play hangman quickly with the two words.

Answers: completely, utterly

3A Ask Ss to work individually and make notes. You might want to model this first with an example for yourself.

B Ask Ss to discuss their experiences in pairs. Elicit some examples afterwards.

READING

4A Tell Ss they are going to read an article about lifestyles. Lead into the text by writing the title on the board and asking Ss to speculate about the contents of the article.

Teaching tip

Making predictions and analysing the title of an article before doing other tasks can help to raise schemata on a topic before moving on to look at it in more detail.

B Give Ss a couple of minutes to read the first two paragraphs and check their predictions. Briefly elicit thoughts from Ss about the effectiveness of this advice.

C Ask Ss to discuss whether they agree with the classification of the suggested activities or not. Ask Ss to regroup any of the ideas that they think are in the wrong place. Elicit the rationale behind Ss' new lists.

5A Ss work in pairs to discuss the comments. In feedback ask them to tell the class which of the challenges from the comments they would most like to do.

B Find the first phrase together as a class and then set this task for individual work. In feedback elicit some examples of when Ss were last outside their comfort zone, or what they did the last time they had some time on their hands.

Answers:
1 outside your comfort zone
2 how you get on
3 had more time on (my) hands
4 digging into
5 made much more of an effort to
6 carry on

C Give Ss a few minutes to discuss the question in pairs. Elicit the activities Ss would want to do and add them to the board. Ask Ss to vote on the best activity from those suggested by the class.

GRAMMAR PRESENT PERFECT

6A Ask Ss to complete the sentences using the given words. Then ask Ss to check their answers against the text.

Answers: **1** 've never done **2** 've just finished **3** 've learnt **4** 've done

B Elicit the basic structure for the present perfect and write it on the board. Then ask Ss to match the sentences to the rules.

Answers:
Rule 1 = sentences 1, 3
Rule 2 = sentence 2
Rule 3 = sentence 4

7A Draw three columns on the board and write *present perfect, past simple* and *both* at the top of each. Tell Ss to copy the table into their notebooks. Do an example, then put Ss into pairs to help each other put the time phrases in the box into the correct columns. As you check the answers in feedback complete the table on the board.

Answers:
up to now PP
so far PP
this time last week PS
recently PP
this morning B (PP if it is still the morning when you are speaking or PS if it is now the afternoon and you are looking back at a finished period, i.e. the morning)
over the last fortnight PP
not + yet PP
still + not PP
for several years B

B Here Ss are focusing on connected speech. The first time you play the recording Ss just need to write down the sentences they hear. With ***weaker Ss*** you might want to pause after each pair of sentences.

Answers: See Ex 7C.

C Play the example sentence again and show clearly how it has been marked for the different features of stressed, weak and linked words. Either drill the class or play the recording again and ask Ss to repeat the phrases as they listen.

Answers:
1 Have you tried it before?
2 I've thought about it a lot.
3 Has he seen my last email?
4 She's changed her address.
5 My kids have gone out.
6 Has she phoned anyone yet?

▷ LANGUAGEBANK 1.2 p128–129

Ss can read the notes in class or at home, depending on how confident they are about the rules. If you feel Ss need more basic practice of the present perfect and past simple before moving on to Ex 8A, they can do Ex A. Otherwise, set both exercises for homework.

Answers:
A **1** haven't written **2** was **3** haven't seen **4** has been **5** took **6** arrived **7** checked **8** saw **9** 've stayed **10** was **11** decided **12** forgot **13** got **14** called **15** 've been/gone **16** has handed
B **1** before **2** this morning **3** Until I took this course **4** for **5** So far **6** until **7** since **8** this month **9** yet **10** this time last week

8A Give Ss a few minutes to work alone on this, then check answers with the class. Vocabulary to check: *paranoid* (having an extreme and unreasonable worry about something), *hiking* (going for long energetic walks) and *loads (of)* (a large amount of).

Answers: **1** 've always been **2** learnt **3** 've just got **4** gave **5** 've played **6** haven't tried **7** 've never bought **8** 've lived **9** has been/gone **10** still haven't done

B Ss discuss the activities for a few minutes. In feedback, encourage them to use *both* and *neither*, e.g. *We'd both like to learn to play the guitar. Neither of us would like to edit a film. Sylvia has bought something online, but I haven't.*

SPEAKING

9A Help Ss with ideas by giving an example for each category for yourself. Give Ss a few minutes to write down their ideas for each one.

B Put Ss into groups to discuss their experiences. Elicit one or two examples for each from the class. Check the use of the present perfect as you elicit sentences and write any good examples on the board.

VOCABULARY PLUS WORD BUILDING: NOUNS

10A Explain to Ss how you would feel in each of the two situations and explain why. Ask Ss to choose adjectives from the box, or use their own ideas, to describe to a partner how each activity would make them feel and why.

B Write the endings on the board and tell Ss to match the words in the box to the correct endings. If monolingual dictionaries are available, encourage Ss to use them to check the noun forms if they are unsure.

Answers:
1 -ion: frustration, fascination
2 -ment: embarrassment, disappointment, amusement
3 -ity/-ety: creativity, anxiety, spontaneity
4 -ness: awkwardness, nervousness
5 other: anger, worry

C Using *frustration* as an example, show Ss how the main stress is indicated in a dictionary: *fru'stration*. They can then work in pairs to identify the stress in the other nouns. When you play the recording for Ss to check, stop after each noun for Ss to repeat.

Answers:
1 frustration, fascination
2 embarrassment, disappointment, amusement
3 creativity, anxiety, spontaneity
4 awkwardness, nervousness
5 anger, worry

D Use *frustration* and *embarrassment* as examples, then give Ss a few minutes in pairs to work out the rules.

Answers:
1 *-ion, -ity/-ety* – the stress is on the syllable before the suffix.
2 *-ment, -ness* – the stress is on the same syllable as in the adjective.

11A Focus Ss on the quiz and elicit the first answer as an example. Point out that they need to be careful with form, as one of the nouns is plural. Vocabulary to check: *intense* (very strong).

Answers: **1** spontaneity **2** frustrations **3** awkward **4** amusement **5** disappointed **6** anger **7** nervousness **8** anxiety

B Ask Ss to use nouns and adjectives from Ex 10A and 10B to write two more sentences. With ***weaker Ss*** you might want them to complete this task in pairs. Monitor and check Ss' use of the nouns and adjectives.

C Ss work individually to complete the quiz. Tell them to think about why they agree or disagree as they work through the questions.

D Ss work in pairs to compare and give reasons for their answers.

▷ **VOCABULARYBANK** p148 Word building

Give Ss time to work through Ex 2A and B before comparing their answers in pairs. Check the answers and then give Ss time to complete Ex 2C before they take it in turns to ask and answer the questions.

Answers:
A identify, appreciate; argue, develop; exist, defend; sign, please
B -tion/-ation: contribution, preparation, donation, reaction, prevention
-ment: involvement, treatment
-ence: interference, preference, reference
-ure: failure, mixture
C **1** signature **2** appreciation **3** defence **4** pleasure **5** contributions **6** preference **7** identification **8** arguments **9** reference **10** development

Homework ideas

- Ss try out a new activity in English for a number of days, for example, they choose a 'phrasal verb of the day' to learn, or watch a TV programme in English each evening. In class they feed back on how they felt doing this task using the nouns and adjectives taught in the lesson.
- **Language bank:** 1.2 Ex A–B, p129
- **Vocabulary bank:** p148
- **Workbook:** Ex 1–5, p6–7

I'D LIKE TO ENQUIRE

Introduction

Ss listen to and practise making polite enquiries on the phone. They also learn to recognise vocabulary commonly used in adverts.

SUPPLEMENTARY MATERIALS
Resource bank: p151

Warm up

Lead into the topic via a brief discussion about making phone calls in English. If you have had problems understanding or being understood on the phone in another country, tell Ss about your experience then invite them to tell the class about any problems they've had. Alternatively, ask Ss why speaking on the phone in English can be difficult (you can't see the other person's gestures or expressions, you don't know how to deal with a misunderstanding, there are certain phrases commonly used which you don't know, etc.) and what they can do to make phoning in English easier.

VOCABULARY ADVERTS

1A Give Ss a few minutes to discuss these questions in pairs. If you did the Warm up then you can just discuss the first question as a class and focus directly on the adverts. If you know of any examples, e.g. newspapers, websites, etc., you could show these in class.

B Give Ss a couple of minutes to scan the adverts quickly and decide which ones interest them the most. They compare their answers with a partner, explaining why they are interested.

C Ss should find the words/phrases in bold and try to guess their meaning before looking at the definitions.

Answers: **1** two-for-one deal **2** free trial **3** non-refundable deposit **4** negotiable **5** sign up for **6** limited enrolment **7** fill in your details

D Ss discuss this in pairs. Point out that many of the phrases can be used in different contexts. You could do *a restaurant* as an example with the class first.

Suggested answers:
restaurant: two-for-one deal
cookery course: two-for-one deal, free trial, non-refundable deposit, sign up for, limited enrolment, fill in your details
buying a used car: negotiable, non-refundable deposit
hotel booking: two-for-one deal, non-refundable deposit, fill in your details

FUNCTION POLITE ENQUIRIES

2A Give Ss time to read the questions before you play the recording. Ss discuss their answers in pairs then check with the class.

Answers:
1 The English Language College
2 She wants to change from a general English course (which she booked online) to a business English course.
3 Yes, the receptionist agrees to hold a place open for her until the caller can come in to the school to do the level test.
4 Yes, she does.

Unit 1 Recording 6

M = Man W = Woman

M: Hello, English Language College. Can I help you?
W: Yes, I'd like to enquire about a course.
M: OK. Have you seen the information on our website?
W: Well, actually the situation is that I booked myself onto a course through your website yesterday, and now I'd like to change.
M: Uh-huh. Could you tell me your name?
W: Maria Hidalgo.
M: And which course was it?
W: A general English course, pre-advanced.
M: Bear with me a minute. Yes, I've got it. What would you like to change to?
W: I've just noticed this morning that you have an advanced course in business English starting next week.
M: That's right.
W: I was wondering if it would be possible for me to change to that group.
M: OK, let me just check. There are still a few places in that group, but you'll have to do a level test.
W: But I've already done an online test for the other course.
M: Mmm. I appreciate that, but for this course you need to do a level test in person.
W: Erm … Can you tell me why I have to do it in person?
M: It's because it's a specialised course and there's an oral component to the level test.
W: I see. Would there be any chance of doing the level test on the phone?
M: Hold on, let me check … Sorry to keep you. No, I'm afraid it has to be in person.
W: I see. Do you mind me asking what it involves?
M: There's a written task that you have to do under timed conditions, and preparation materials for the oral interview.
W: I see. Sorry to be difficult, it's just that I'm really busy this week and can't make it up to the school for the level test.
M: That's going to be a bit of a problem. I'm not sure what we can do about that.
W: I'd really appreciate your help.
M: Hmm … You couldn't come in on Thursday evening, could you?
W: No, I'm afraid not. But I tell you what. I could come in on Saturday to do the level test.
M: The problem is, that's leaving it very late and we might have other applicants.
W: I'd be really grateful if you could hold a place for me till Saturday morning.
M: Can you hold on a minute? I'll just see … OK, we can do that. We'll provisionally transfer the course fee over as a deposit.
W: That's great. Oh, I've got one more question, if I'm not keeping you.
M: No, go ahead.
W: If I don't get into this group, do I lose my course fee?
M: I'm afraid we can't refund the deposit, but you could transfer it to another course.
W: Oh, that's a relief. Would you mind putting that in an email for me?
M: Certainly.
W: Thanks. Could you tell me when the school opens?
M: We're open from nine on Saturday. I won't be here myself, but I'll tell my colleague to expect you.
W: Thank you very much for your help.
M: You're welcome. Thank you for calling.

B Ss can work in pairs to help each other complete the sentences. If they find the more complex ones too challenging, you could put a 'key' word from each of these sentences on the board, to prompt them (e.g. *possible*, *chance*, *asking*, *could*). Play the recording, pausing after each sentence for Ss to check their answers.

Answers: 1 'd, enquire 2 was, if, would, possible, me 3 you, me 4 there, chance 5 mind, asking 6 grateful, could 7 putting 8 Could, when

C Play the examples, telling Ss to listen for what happens to the intonation at the end of each enquiry. You may then prefer to play the rest of the sentences one at a time, checking the intonation pattern before asking Ss to shadow the enquiries. The tendency is for the intonation to go down and then up at the end of questions (as in 3, 4, 5, 7 and 8) and to go down on other types of sentences (as in 1, 2 and 6).

D Ask Ss to discuss this in pairs. Ss can refer to any language they know well and not only their own. Elicit examples, e.g. in many languages there are formal and informal versions of 'you', etc.

▷ LANGUAGEBANK 1.3 p128–129

Give Ss a few minutes to study the tables showing the forms that the polite enquiries have in common. Check by asking, e.g. *Which phrases use an* -ing *form? Which use an infinitive? Which use* if *or a* wh- *question word?* Ss practise these forms in the next exercise (Ex 3A) in the lesson, so they could do Ex A from the Language bank for homework.

Answers:
A: Yourpick.net. My name's Dave. How can I *help* you?
B: Hi, I'm phoning to find *out* about a DVD I ordered. The reference number is 3714.
A: OK. Is *there* a problem?
B: Yes, it hasn't arrived yet and I ordered it a month *ago*. Could you tell me when I can expect it?
A: Bear *with* me a moment. I'm afraid we have no information about the arrival date.
B: And you don't know when it *will* be in?
A: It's coming from the USA so I'm *afraid* not. Do you want to cancel?
B: No, but I'd *be* grateful if you could look into it.
A: No problem *at* all.
B: And would there be any *chance* of phoning me when it arrives?
A: Sure … let me just *check* if we have your phone number …

3A Do the first one as an example, then give Ss 3–4 mins to write out the enquiries, then compare answers in pairs. As you check the answers with the class, you could drill the enquiries, paying attention to Ss' intonation.

Answers:
1 Could you tell me where you're located?
2 I was wondering if/whether I can use your two-for-one deal more than once.
3 I'd like to know if/whether my dog can come with me.
4 Would you mind telling me about the other people living there?
5 Do you mind me asking how many other people have inquired?
6 I'd be grateful if you could explain how the free trial works.

B Elicit examples of situations for the first enquiry then put Ss into pairs to discuss the rest.

Suggested answers:
Situation A: 1, 3, 4, 5
Situation B: 1, 5
Situation C: 1, 6
Situation D: 2, 3, 6

LEARN TO MANAGE ENQUIRIES

4A Elicit from/Remind Ss that in the original phone conversation they listened to, the caller asked the receptionist a few 'difficult' questions, which he couldn't answer straightaway. Direct them to the phrases and give them time to decide if the speaker is the receptionist or the caller and mark them R or C.

B Ask Ss to check their answers against the audio script.

Answers: 1 R 2 R 3 C 4 C 5 R 6 C

C Once Ss have found the phrases they could practise saying them as preparation for the next stage.

Answers:
1 Sorry to be difficult, it's just that …; I've got one more question, if I'm not keeping you.
2 Bear with me a minute.

5 Tell Ss not to write out the conversation, but to use the flow chart to help them speak. Encourage Ss to try to look at the prompts, then look up to speak, rather than 'reading' from the page, which will make them sound unnatural. For a ***weaker class*** you could go through the flow chart with the whole class first, eliciting examples at each step. When they have finished, tell Ss to reverse roles and practise the conversation again. Monitor the pairwork and note down examples of good language use and problems for feedback and correction.

SPEAKING

6A Make sure you give Ss enough time to read their instructions carefully and prepare notes to help them in the conversation. Circulate while Ss are preparing and provide help if required. While Ss are talking, monitor and make notes for feedback. You could invite one or two pairs to act out their conversations for the class.

B Repeat the same process in this task you did in Ex 6A. If you don't have time for Ss to do both situations in class, you could use the second one for homework (see below).

speakout TIP

Before directing Ss to the tip, ask them what advice they would give someone who is nervous about making phone enquiries in English.

7 Put Ss into new pairs and ask them to prepare to role-play the two situations in Ex 1B which they haven't worked on in this lesson, i.e. 'Flatmate wanted' and 'Walk & Talk English', or to think of situations they themselves have been in. Give Ss a few minutes to prepare for the situations before role-playing them.

Homework ideas

- Ss arrange to phone each other after class and practise the conversation for the situation in Ex 6B.
- If you are in an English-speaking environment, Ss find adverts in the local newspaper and underline examples of the vocabulary from Ex 1C. They could also choose one advert to phone and make an enquiry about, then report back to the class in the next lesson.
- **Language bank:** 1.3 Ex A, p129
- **Workbook:** Ex 1–4, p8

GREAT EXPERIENCES

Introduction

Ss watch an extract from the BBC programme *50 Things To Do Before You Die*, where various people talk about activities they've done. Ss learn and practise how to recommend something they've tried and write about an experience.

SUPPLEMENTARY MATERIALS

Warm up: Bring in some photos of activities on 'Bucket Lists', (this is another term for things to do before you die and there are many examples on the internet).

Warm up

If you have prepared photos of activities people often want to do before they die then display these around the room. Ask Ss to look at the photos and choose their top three. In pairs, Ss could discuss which activities they would want to do and why. If you have not prepared photos, lead into the topic by brainstorming the title *50 Things To Do Before You Die*. Write the title on the board (Ss' books are closed) and put Ss into small groups to write as many things that could be on the list as they can in 3 mins. Conduct feedback, eliciting examples from each group and writing a list on the board for Ss to refer back to later.

DVD PREVIEW

1 Set this task up by answering the questions yourself first. Ask Ss to work in pairs and to discuss the questions. Elicit activities and places from Ss and reasons why they haven't done them or visited them. Alternatively, you could find out what activities Ss wanted to do or places Ss wanted to visit in the past and elicit when they did/visited them and how they felt.

2A If you did the Warm up, Ss could quickly scan the article first, to see which of the activities on their list are mentioned and find out who decided the top fifty things for the programme.

Answer: BBC viewers

B Ss match the activities mentioned in the text with the photos. Tell Ss that one activity matches two photos.

Answers:
A observing rare and exotic animals in their natural habitat
B husky dog sledding
C travelling a historic route by train, car or jet plane
D wing-walking
E bungee jumping
F observing rare and exotic animals in their natural habitat

Culture notes

Route 66 is a road many Americans want to drive as it is considered historically important. Many people drove this road to escape from the Great Depression and it is seen as a road to prosperity.

DVD VIEW

3A Give Ss a few minutes to think of words that could be used to describe each activity. Elicit some example words for each activity.

B Play the DVD and ask Ss to check their ideas.

Answers: The speakers in the video use the following adjectives:
husky sledding – beautiful, fantastic, silent, incredible, exhilarating
wing-walking – wonderful, amazing
Route 66 – legendary, incredible, famous, wonderful
bungee jumping – awesome, fun
swimming with dolphins – magical, incredible, amazing, fantastic, wonderful
Photo A is not in the DVD.

DVD 1 Great experiences

P = Presenter HC = Helen Child AT = Andy Thomas W = Woman
RO = Rebecca Over KE = Kyle Emert DF = Dave Farris
NB = Nick Bryant NBr = Nick Brans LR = Lucia Rushton
AW = Alan Woods KS = Katie Siddals

P: At number 38 it's husky sledding.
I've come to Saariselkä in Finland for a test drive.
Absolutely beautiful here, the snow is just like … it's got little bits of crystal all over it and you can really take it in because the dogs are doing all the hard work.
HC: Just the sound of the snow and the dogs panting with all the silence around, I think that would be fantastic.
AT: Totally silent apart from the sound of the sled and the dogs' paws. Incredible.
W: Are you ready?
P: As I'll ever be.
This is much, much more exhilarating than just sitting in the sled, actually having the dogs work for you and feeling like you're in (or out of) control is definitely where it's at.
Meet Rebecca Over, an estate buyer from Surrey, who like hundreds of you crazy people, wanted nothing more than to be strapped to the outside of a plane and take part in your very own wing-walking display.
The craze started when World War One pilots would strap their poor girlfriends to the outside of their planes to entertain the crowds at air shows. We sent Rebecca off to Rendcomb in Gloucestershire.
RO: I'm feeling excited, a little bit nervous, can't wait, raring to go.
P: So buckled and braced our daredevil is ready to go.
RO: The wind is really, really strong and it's really hard to do the waving. It's been wonderful, an amazing day.
P: Still in America now and time to go west on the legendary Route 66: 2,400 miles, eight states, three time zones, one incredible journey.
KE: Once upon a time it was, the kind of the thing to do.
P: The famous route from Chicago to Los Angeles was used by thousands of Americans attempting to flee the hard times of the Great Depression, and for many it's remembered as the road to opportunity.
DF: I'd love to experience what they did travelling over two and a half thousand miles, and experience that wonderful feeling of getting somewhere which is better.
P: Next up something you've let get as high as 17 on this list. You're crazy, it's bungee jumping.
NB: The feeling you get when you jump off, fall off, dive off, or whatever, is just awesome.
NBr: Just to fly like that and just sort of end up being stretched and bounced back up, great fun.
P: Throughout history they've intrigued mankind with tales of their mystical powers and super intelligence; their legendary curiosity and playfulness have enchanted us for generations. Thousands and thousands of you have bombarded us with emails and calls to say the number one thing to do before you die is to go swimming with dolphins.
LR: They're absolutely amazing animals. They're so gentle they're so, um, sensitive.
AW: Once you swim with them, you don't want to … you don't want to leave them.
KS: A one-off, magical experience.
P: And it was incredible.
It's … It's amazing because, they're so responsive and they have, they feel fantastic. Don't you? You feel wonderful, you feel so lovely. And they're so huge and so powerful and yet so playful and, I'm really, really lucky to be here with them.

C Give Ss a few minutes to read through the sentences. Explain some of the difficult vocabulary to Ss: *scenery* (the natural views around us), *strap* (to tie to something), *stretched* (made longer by pulling) and *bounced* (to move quickly up and down). Play the DVD again and then check the answers as a class.

Answers:
1 F People say they love the silence, the sound of the snow and the dogs.
2 T '... having the dogs work for you and feeling in (or out of) control is definitely where it's at.'
3 F '... pilots would strap their poor girlfriends to the outside of their planes ...'
4 F '... it's really hard to do the waving.'
5 F It runs to Los Angeles.
6 T '... great fun.'
7 T '... their legendary curiosity and playfulness have enchanted us for generations.'
8 F 'They're so gentle ...', '... so responsive ...', '... so huge and so powerful and yet so playful ...'

D Ss should spend a few minutes reading through the sentences and trying to predict some of the missing words before you play the DVD again. You may need to play the DVD a fourth time for Ss to confirm their answers.

Answers: **1** take **2** where **3** take **4** thing **5** whatever **6** yet

E After Ss have ranked the activities, elicit the most popular order. As an extension you could ask Ss to create their own top five list.

speakout a recommendation

4A Check that Ss understand the instructions, pointing out that these don't need to be particularly unusual activities, just two that they would recommend, e.g. going camping or backpacking, riding a horse/donkey/camel, visiting a wildlife park, working on a farm, skateboarding, water skiing, scuba diving, windsurfing. You could demonstrate how Ss should answer the three questions, e.g.

1 *activity: windsurfing*
2 *before: nervous, not very confident*
  while: very frustrated but determined to pull the sail up
  after: exhausted but pleased that I'd managed to stay up for longer than a few seconds!
3 *worth trying because: really test your strength and balance as you try to stand up and pull the sail up; get a great feeling of freedom when surfing along the water and a feeling of achievement.*

Give Ss time to make notes on their own. Circulate and help with vocabulary, etc.

B After you have played the recording, Ss can compare their answers to the questions.

Answers:
1 skydiving
2 before: scared (it was scary); while: he felt sick because he was spinning so fast – but also he was laughing because it was so much fun; after: he doesn't say.

Unit 1 Recording 8

I'm not the kind of person who likes to be a daredevil or do anything too exciting. But the most incredible thing I think I've ever done was when I went skydiving. So, we went up in a tiny plane. I mean it's so small, so it was quite scary. And the build-up was just epic.

I was attached to another guy, an expert, by a harness. And I was sitting in front of him in this sort of, it was like a, a tiny tube little plane. And we went higher and higher and higher. And um, the suspense was building up. And then suddenly they just open this door and you're flying through the sky, and you can just see for miles. And it's freezing cold and the thing I'll remember most is the cold air hitting my teeth, 'cos it was just absolutely freezing. And er, we sort of scuttled out to the edge and our legs were dangling through the door of the plane. And erm, he just said, I remember him shouting, he just said 'Smile!' 'Cos there was a camera guy as well, so you can film it.

And we just, we sort of fell forward and we were just spinning, until he sort of levels you out. It was like I was completely weightless. And it didn't feel like you were falling at all, you were just sort of hovering. And it was still freezing cold on my teeth as well like that. And then the parachute, I remember lifting out. And it just sort of pulled me all up – I was like oh! Ugh! like that. And we started spinning round, you know he was doing all these kind of tricks and stuff. And that's when I started feeling sick, 'cos it was spinning so fast. But it was just so much fun, it was hilarious, I was laughing, you know even though I felt sick it was just the experience of it all and the adrenaline rush. It was one of the best experiences I've ever had in my life. And it's an activity I'd like to recommend to all my friends because I know they'd absolutely love it, it's hilarious.

C Give Ss a minute to read the key phrases. Point out that where there are options in the phrases (e.g. *It's one of the [best/most challenging] experiences I've ever had.*), they need to underline the option(s) they hear. Play the DVD again and ask Ss to tick the phrases they hear.

Answers: I'm (not) the kind of person who likes ...; It's one of the [best/most challenging] experiences I've ever had.; The thing I'll remember most is [the feeling of .../the moment when ...].; It's an activity I'd like to recommend to all my friends.

D Give Ss time to prepare their recommendation before you put them into groups. Monitor the group work and make notes of good language use and areas for improvement to discuss in feedback.

writeback a forum entry

5A Tell Ss they are going to read a web forum entry and response. Give them a few minutes to read the text and identify the activity the person is doing.

Answer: observing rare and exotic animals (probably orang-utans) in their natural habitat (Photo A on p16 in the Students' Book)

B Before Ss write their entry, ask them what other kinds of things Stacey wrote about in her entry, e.g. before the extract on the page (what made her decide to go and look at the orang-utans, which country she went to, who she went with, where she stayed, etc.) and after it (how she felt when their eyes met, whether she saw any more orang-utans on the trip, what her travelling companions thought of it, etc.). Ss can write their entry in class or for homework.

C Remind Ss about the correction code they used on p10. While they are checking each other's work, be available to deal with any queries about grammar, etc. However, tell Ss that the focus should be on improving the texts by finding any ways to make the experiences sound more exciting.

D You could either collect in all the entries and pass them round for other Ss to read, or put them on the walls of the classroom. Ask Ss to make a note of the most interesting entries as they read them, then put them into pairs to discuss the experience they'd most like to have, giving at least two reasons for their choice. In feedback you could have a show of hands to find out which was the most popular experience.

Homework ideas

Ss research the top fifty things to do before you die on the internet (there are a number of websites devoted to the topic) and choose three they would like to do. They write a short paragraph about why they've chosen each one.

LOOKBACK

Introduction

The aim of these activities is to provide revision and further practice of the language from the unit. You can also use them to assess Ss' ability to use the language, in which case you need to monitor but avoid helping them. You may feel that you don't need or have time to do all the activities. If so, you could allocate the activities that would be most beneficial for your Ss, or get individual Ss to decide which activities they'd like to do.

PERSONALITY

1A Ss work alone completing the sentences, then compare answers in pairs. They could also discuss people they know who match the descriptions.

Answers: **1** witty **2** keeps himself to himself **3** spontaneous **4** people person **5** down-to-earth **6** good laugh **7** morning person **8** geek

B After Ss have discussed this in pairs, they can compare and justify their ideas in feedback and try to agree as a class on the qualities for each type of person.

DIRECT AND INDIRECT QUESTIONS

2A For ***weaker classes***, you could choose one of the topics in the box and elicit a set of example questions, e.g. for 'transport' – *Do you like driving? What's going up in a hot-air balloon like? How often do you travel by plane? Have you ever driven a really powerful sports car? Would you like to travel in space? Why do you not like public transport?*

Write these up on the board and then give Ss some time to generate their own set of questions, either individually or in pairs.

B Tell Ss to imagine that they are going to interview a famous or important person (e.g. a politician, musician, actor, sportsperson) and ask this person their questions. This gives them a reason for making the questions polite and indirect.

C If Ss have written questions for a famous person, they need to tell their partner who it is and what topic they've chosen, so the partner can think about how that person would respond. After asking and answering the questions, Ss can tell the class about their partner's answers.

FEELINGS

3A Ss work alone then compare answers.

Answers: **1** over the moon **2** relieved **3** shaking like a leaf **4** awkward **5** wished the earth would swallow me up **6** impressed

B Give Ss a few minutes to discuss which adverbs belong in front of each adjective, then check with the class. Encourage Ss to add more lines to the conversations while they are practising, e.g. with follow-up questions. The extra lines can be added anywhere in the conversation, not just at the end. Ss act out their conversations for the class and are awarded points for the most convincing additions and best performance.

Answers: **1** really/absolutely/totally/completely **2** very/really **3** no modifier (it's a verb phrase) **4** very/really **5** no modifier (it's a verb phrase) **6** very/really

PRESENT PERFECT

4A With a ***weaker class***, you could elicit/check the rules of use for the present perfect and past simple before giving Ss a few minutes to work on the exercise. With a ***stronger class***, you could set up the exercise as a race. Ss work in pairs on the sentences and put up their hands (or make a pre-arranged 'buzzer' sound) when they have finished. If their sentences are not all correct, the next pair to finish have the chance to win, etc.

Answers: **1** started, 've improved **2** 've been, haven't been **3** 've never met, thought **4** played, 've started **5** didn't eat, haven't had

B Ss work in pairs and find out how many of the sentences are true for each of them. Then tell them to change the rest of the sentences to make them true. Ss report back to the class on their partner's new sentences.

POLITE ENQUIRIES

5A You could set this up as a team competition. Tell Ss to close their books and divide the class into teams of four or five. Write/Display the first sentence on the board and give the teams a chance to confer on the answer (remind them about the need for polite intonation). When a team is ready, they put up their hands and nominate one student to give the answer. You award points for accuracy and good pronunciation.

Answers:
1 I'd like to enquire about train times to Vienna.
2 Can you tell me which train I need to take to get to Vienna by 3p.m.?
3 Can I ask how far it is from the western to the southern train station?
4 Do you mind me asking where I can get information on local transport in Vienna?
5 I was wondering if/whether I need to book a seat on the train.
6 Could you tell me if/whether I can book on the phone?
7 I was wondering if you could book it for me.
8 I'd be grateful if you could send me an email confirmation.

B Give pairs a few minutes to prepare the role-play. The travel agent needs to think of answers to the questions and the customer can rehearse the questions, saying them to themselves and working on the correct intonation. After the first conversation, Ss could reverse roles and enquire about a flight, changing the questions as necessary.

BBC interviews and worksheet

What makes a good flatmate?

This video looks at the topic of house or flatsharing and examines the question of what makes a good flatmate.

OVERVIEW

2.1 MAKING A DIFFERENCE

VOCABULARY | issues
PRONUNCIATION | word stress
READING | read an article about small actions with big results
GRAMMAR | present perfect simple and continuous
PRONUNCIATION | weak forms: auxiliaries
SPEAKING | talk about different issues
VOCABULARY *PLUS* | verbs/nouns with the same form

2.2 YOU'RE BEING WATCHED

VOCABULARY | surveillance
LISTENING | listen to opinions about surveillance
GRAMMAR | the passive
PRONUNCIATION | sentence stress: passives
SPEAKING | discuss surveillance
WRITING | a letter of complaint; learn to use formal written language

2.3 GOOD POINT!

SPEAKING | give and respond to opinions
FUNCTION | opinions
PRONUNCIATION | intonation for partially agreeing
LEARN TO | support your viewpoint
VOCABULARY | opinion adjectives
SPEAKING | agree and disagree with statements

2.4 A QUIET REVOLUTION BBC DVD

DVD | watch a BBC programme about changes in working patterns
speakout | a joint presentation
writeback | notes for a presentation

2.5 LOOKBACK

Communicative revision activities

BBC INTERVIEWS

Does money make you happy?

This video encourages students to reflect on and discuss how much money contributes to our happiness. Use this video at the start or end of Unit 2 or set it as homework.

MAKING A DIFFERENCE

Introduction

Ss practise reading and speaking about social issues, using the present perfect simple and continuous and related vocabulary. They also learn about verbs and nouns with the same form.

SUPPLEMENTARY MATERIALS

Resource bank: p152 and p154

Ex 1A: bring some headlines from online newspapers or cut some out from physical papers.

Ex 2A: bring monolingual dictionaries for students to use.

Warm up

Lead into the topic via a discussion of charities. Elicit some names of charities (e.g. Oxfam, Amnesty International, the World Wide Fund for Nature, the Red Cross) and examples of what they do. Then elicit on the board examples of things people can do for charity, e.g. *do a sponsored walk or run, give money to people collecting in the street, give used clothes to a charity shop, organise an event to raise funds, work as a volunteer*. Then write *Have you ever… ?* in front of the list above and put Ss into small groups to discuss what they've done/would like to do. This will also allow you to assess how well Ss are using the present perfect.

VOCABULARY ISSUES

1A If you have brought in some headlines then put Ss into small groups and ask them to pass them from group to group, discussing each briefly. If you don't have any headlines, brainstorm news stories as a class and write the topics on the board.

B Tell Ss that they are going to listen to a number of news headlines. Check Ss understand the words in the task by playing a quick word association game, e.g. you say the word *food* and they have to associate this with one of the words. If you say a word such as *health*, Ss might link it to more than one, but as long as they can explain the link it will demonstrate their understanding. Play the recording and ask Ss to match each headline to a topic.

Answers: **1** hunger **2** disease **3** street crime **4** poverty **5** unemployment **6** pollution

Unit 2 Recording 1

1 A report out today says that over 800 million people in the world don't have enough to eat. The report, which was published …
2 Twenty people have died in an outbreak of the deadly Ebola virus. The virus, which has resulted in over …
3 If you're travelling to the city centre today, be careful of pickpockets, especially around the central square. Our reporter Will Nakama is there in …
4 The government has promised that their changes to income tax will help the poorest people in the country. A spokesperson said …
5 The number of people out of work has risen in the last quarter to seven percent and is now reaching three million. The situation is worst …
6 After four days of smog, only cars with even number plates can enter the city today. It is hoped that this move will improve the air quality after the levels of …

2A Give Ss a couple of minutes to read through the sentence halves and match them. Allow Ss to use a monolingual dictionary if necessary. Check the answers as a class.

Answers: 1 c) 2 h) 3 b) 4 f) 5 a) 6 e) 7 d) 8 g)

B Read the first sentence out loud to Ss. Restate the word *domestic*, and ask Ss to match it to a pronunciation pattern. Ask Ss to match the other words and then play the recording to check the answers.

Answers: **1** rural, urban, global **2** ethical **3** domestic
4 political, industrial **5** economic

C Ss do this activity quickly in pairs. Check the answers as a class. You could briefly extend this by asking Ss to think of other common collocations with these words, e.g. *environmental, international, regional*, etc.

Answers: issue, question, problem

D Ask Ss to think back to either the headlines you showed them or the ideas they generated in Ex 1A and to use the adjectives to describe these headlines. Many will probably have multiple collocations, e.g. one thing can be *economic, political* and *environmental* all at the same time.

▷ **VOCABULARYBANK** p149 Issues

Give Ss plenty of time to match the photos with the natural disasters in Ex 1A before feeding back with the answers as a class (make sure you check the pronunciation and word stress). Ss match the other words to the new items in Ex 1B and in Ex 1C decide what type of problem each is.

Answers:
A **A** flood **B** landslide **C** drought **D** volcanic eruption
B **1** obesity **2** debt **3** homelessness **4** drug abuse
5 domestic violence **6** earthquake
C ND – flood, volcanic eruption, earthquake, drought, landslide
S – homelessness, drug abuse, domestic violence, debt, obesity
H – drug abuse, obesity

READING

3A Choose one of the pictures and explain to Ss how the picture might be related to one of the problems in Ex 1B. Then ask Ss to work in pairs to describe the other pictures and the problems they might show.

B Ask Ss to read the article and check their answers. Elicit the words that helped Ss decide.

4A Ask Ss to choose one option for each statement before reading the text again. After Ss have checked their answers against the text, ask which person they find most inspiring and why.

Answers: 1 c) 2 b) 3 c) 4 a) 5 b) 6 a)

B With ***weaker Ss*** you might want to give more clues, e.g. a line range or the grammatical function of the word/phrase. Point out to Ss that the introductory paragraph is not paragraph number 1 and is not included in this task. Set this task for individual work and then check as a class.

Answers: **1** vet **2** a one-off (deal) **3** donates **4** eye-opening
5 pledge **6** keep up with

C Put Ss into pairs to answer the question. You could then extend the task by discussing the following questions as a class: *Have you ever done any charity work? Which charities would/do you raise money for? Have you ever watched TV programmes raising money for charities?*

GRAMMAR PRESENT PERFECT SIMPLE AND CONTINUOUS

5A Ask Ss to cover the article while they choose the correct alternatives. For ***stronger classes***, you could tell the pairs to think about why the simple or continuous is used in each case and if there are any examples where both are possible.

Answers:
1 've been doing (used in the text, although *'ve done* is also possible)
2 has cleaned **3** has always loved **4** has turned
5 've already raised **6** 've been dancing

B Many Ss will know that the present perfect can be used to link the past with the present, but often they do not consider the details of how. Look at sentences 1 and 4 in Ex 5A as a class and explain to Ss how they are different. Set the task individually and then check the answers as a class.

Answers:
Sentences 1, 2 and 3 – The perfect is used here to describe activities or states which started in the past and continue up to now.
Sentences 4 and 5 – The perfect is used to describe an event/action in the past which is completed although we don't know when. The link is that we are interested now in the result this has had.
Sentence 6 – The perfect is used because the activity has only just finished and we can see the result now.

C Ss discuss the rules in pairs. Monitor their discussions closely: if they are struggling, you may want to direct them to the examples in the Language bank during feedback.

To summarise, you could ask Ss: *Which form focuses on the completion of the activity? Which form focuses on the duration or repetition of the activity?*

Answers:
Rule 1: continuous, e.g. Sentences 1 and 6
Rule 2: simple, e.g. Sentences 2, 4 and 5
Rule 3: simple, e.g. Sentences 2 and 5
Rule 4: simple, continuous, e.g. Sentence 1
Rule 5: simple, e.g. Sentence 3

6A Point out that Ss are going to hear three pairs of questions and answers. If necessary, stop the recording after each question or answer, to give Ss time to write.

Answers:
1 **A:** How long have you been working here?
B: I've been here for over ten months now.
2 **A:** How many chocolates have you eaten?
B: I've only had three!
3 **A:** What have you been doing? You're filthy!
B: I've been running.

B Put Ss into pairs and encourage them to read out the questions and answers to each other, so they can work out the stresses and weak forms.

Teaching tip

Weak forms are the 'unstressed' vowel sounds. Demonstrate for Ss that the auxiliary verbs in the examples are 'squashed' between the main stressed words and the resulting vowel sound is extremely short. You could use circles on the board, e.g. for *How long have you been working here?* draw oOoooOoO. (The big circles represent *long, work* and *here*.)

To help Ss to produce the examples with a natural rhythm, drill only the stressed words first, then 'fill in' the unstressed words: *long – work – here?*
How long have you been working here?

▷ LANGUAGEBANK 2.1 p130–131

Read through these rules and examples before going on to Ex 7A. You may also want Ss to do Ex A and/or B to give them more basic practice in choosing between the present perfect simple and continuous.

Answers:
A 1 've been looking, 've just bought
2 've run, 've been running
3 've been trying, 've decided
4 's hurt, 's been fighting
5 've eaten, 've been eating
B 1 have you been teaching
2 **a)** have you been collecting **b)** have you collected
3 have you been studying
4 **a)** have you been saving **b)** have you saved
5 have you had
6 have you known

7A Find out what Ss know about Fairtrade. Tell them that the text is about someone who works with Fairtrade organisations. Ask Ss to read and find out who Kufuo is.

Answer: Kufuo is a friend of the writer's. He's a cocoa grower in Ghana and does work for Fairtrade.

Culture notes

Fairtrade is a charitable organisation that aims to help producers in developing markets to get a fair price for their goods.

B Ask Ss to complete the gaps individually and then check the answers as a class. Ask Ss to explain why both forms are possible in some cases. Vocabulary to check: *recruit* (to find new people to work in a company).

Answers:
1 've worked/'ve been working (*'ve been working* emphasises the length of time)
2 've visited
3 've lived/'ve been living (*'ve been living* here slightly emphasises the idea that it's temporary)
4 've met
5 've known
6 's grown/'s been growing (*'s been growing* emphasises the length of time)
7 has followed/has been following (*has been following* emphasises the length of time)
8 's recruited
9 've doubled
10 has become

C Ss discuss the question in pairs. You could extend this to discuss as a class organisations that make a difference at a local level where Ss live.

SPEAKING

8A Ask Ss to work in pairs and to quickly brainstorm some of the biggest problems facing the world. Elicit ideas and then ask Ss to compare their ideas with the ones in the text and decide which one they think should win.

B Ss discuss their views and ideas for solving the problems in their groups. Monitor the discussions and make notes of good language use and any problems, for praise and correction later. In feedback, Ss report to the class on their discussions and decide on the best suggestions for solving each problem.

9A If you brainstormed issues at the start of this section, you could ask Ss to work in pairs and add two of those to the list. If not, ask Ss to think of other issues to add to the list. Tell Ss to prepare to justify their choices to the group.

B Depending on your class size, these presentations could be done informally to the whole class and a class vote held. If your class is too large, break your group down into two or three sub-groups. The winner of each sub-group should go on to the class vote.

C Ask Ss to find out the winner and elicit their reaction – do they think the right cause won?

VOCABULARY PLUS VERBS/NOUNS WITH THE SAME FORM

10A Look at the example with the class, then give Ss a few minutes to complete the sentences. Check the answers as a class.

Answers: 1 Project, projected 2 decreased, decrease 3 appealed, appeal 4 recorded, record 5 permits, permitted

B Ss work in pairs to complete the sentences. Elicit a prediction for each sentence and then play the recording to check Ss' answers.

Unit 2 Recording 4

1 The environmental group Ocean Project has projected that sea levels will rise one metre in the next fifty years.
2 Fortunately, malaria has decreased in recent years, and the decrease is due to the use of nets and pesticides.
3 When a major charity appealed for donations to help the deaf, their appeal was broadcast mainly via radio.
4 Bonnie Tyler recorded her song *Total Eclipse of the Heart* in 1983, and in 2008 it set a record for the most popular karaoke track ever.
5 Tourists in a well-known site were given permits to take photos, but they were not permitted to take in their cameras.

C Ss can work in pairs to label the words (N) or (V). Check the answers as a class.

Answers: 1 Project N, projected V 2 decreased V, decrease N 3 appealed V, appeal N 4 recorded V, record N 5 permits N, permitted V

D Remind Ss to mark the stress by underlining the stressed syllable. Check the answers and then drill the sentences as a class.

Answers: For word stress see the underlining in the answers in Ex 10C above.
Appeal has the same syllable stress in the noun and verb form. The others have different stress.

11A Emphasise that Ss should not show their quiz questions to each other. Give them a few minutes to mark the stress on the words and practise saying their questions to themselves.

Answers:
Student A: imports, present, suspect, desert, Research
Student B: recorded, exports, produce, suspects, record

B Ss work in pairs asking and answering the quiz questions. Remind them to make a note of their partner's answers.

C Give Ss a few minutes to check the quiz answers on p162 and feed back to their partners. Conduct a brief feedback on which answers Ss found most interesting/surprising.

▷ **VOCABULARYBANK** p149
Verbs/Nouns with the same form

Encourage Ss to work through Ex 2A the first time without using their dictionaries. They should check their answers in pairs before using a dictionary. They can work with a different partner in Ex 2B to take it in turns to ask and answer the questions.

Answers:
A **1** delay **2** test **3** shout **4** queue **5** guess **6** cure **7** fine **8** tip **9** lie **10** hurry

Homework ideas

- Ss write about a charity that they feel is worthwhile. They could give a short talk about it in the next lesson.
- Ss write five quiz questions for a partner using the vocabulary and ideas from the unit so far.
- **Language bank:** 2.1 Ex A–B, p131
- **Vocabulary bank:** p149
- **Workbook:** Ex 1–5, p9–10

YOU'RE BEING WATCHED

Introduction

Ss practise listening and speaking about surveillance, using the passive and related vocabulary. They also learn to use formal written language and write a letter of complaint.

SUPPLEMENTARY MATERIALS
Resource bank: p153 and p155
Ex 7A: be prepared to talk about an official complaint that you or someone you know made.

Warm up

Ask Ss to close their books and write the title *You're being watched* on the board. Put Ss into pairs and give them a minute or two to discuss what they think the title means. In feedback, you may want to pre-teach *surveillance* and *CCTV (closed circuit television) camera.*

VOCABULARY SURVEILLANCE

1A Direct Ss to the photo and ask them which type of technology they can see. Ss discuss the questions in pairs. Elicit some ideas for each question.

B Draw Ss' attention to the small text boxes on the photo and the phrases in bold within them. Put Ss into pairs and tell them to match the phrases in bold with the meanings.

Answers: **1** the authorities **2** to monitor, keep track of **3** store the information **4** an invasion of privacy **5** identify **6** crime prevention, deterrent to crime **7** accesses data **8** surveillance

C Work through one of the techniques as a class, for example, *mobile phone tracking: + police could follow a suspect's route; – a jealous boy/girlfriend could track their partner*. Ask Ss to work with a partner and to think of at least one positive and one negative aspect of each surveillance technique. Discuss the question at the bottom of the photo as a class.

LISTENING

2A Suggest that Ss copy the table into their notebooks. Play the recording, telling them to listen only for whether the people like it or not.

Answers: See answers to Ex 2C.

Unit 2 Recording 5

W = Woman **M** = Man

W: Have you read this article?
M: Which one?
W: This is really shocking. This, look, look at this about surveillance techniques, on page three.
M: Oh yeah, yeah I did have a look.
W: There's gonna be absolutely no privacy for anyone.
M: What you mean like C, the CCTV camera bit?
W: Yeah, yeah, yeah, yeah, exactly that.
M: Well I'm glad they're there actually.
W: Why?
M: Well, not long ago a friend of mine he was, um, he was robbed at a bus stop, and, and they got the guy because of CCTV, they captured his image and um all the people who did it were arrested.
W: OK …
M: So I think it's, I think it's a good thing.
W: Well it's good if it's used for that, but don't you feel nervous about the fact that whatever you do, wherever you go, whatever you're doing, someone is watching you and recording what you're doing.
M: But I haven't got anything to hide so it's not really a problem.

W: Anyway, that's not the point though is it, it's an invasion of privacy.
M: Look, I think statistically more crimes are solved because of CCTV than not.
W: Right, what about that, that look – this one on page two – CCTV facial recognition did you see that bit there at the bottom?
M: Yeah, I didn't really get that bit.
W: Right, so basically, just imagine you're walking down the road and a camera, a CCTV camera takes your picture, yeah. And then a computer programme can then find your name, all your personal information, based on recognising your face. So where you shop, where you live, what you, what you like, what you buy, who your friends are. And there's nothing you can do about it.
M: That can only be a good thing, 'cos its gonna catch criminals, isn't it? And if you've got nothing to worry about then you know it's never really gonna be an issue for you.
W: If it's for that, yeah I get your point. But …
M: If you haven't done anything wrong.
W: No, no, absolutely, but …
M: The thing that really bothers me though is, is the way that marketing, marketing companies can target you, um, because of microchips in, in food packaging and stuff, so people get an idea of, of your shopping habits. I don't want to be sent adverts from companies that I don't know.
W: But we're being sent stuff all the time anyway, from companies, that we don't know. I wouldn't mind being sent adverts from, you know uh companies that I don't know if it's something that I want to buy.
M: Yeah. It's a little confusing really the way I, I feel about the whole thing, because you know on the one hand I'm, I'm, I'm pro, uh, using the technology to you know catch criminals or whatever. I mean serious criminals. But then on the other hand I occasionally drive a little bit over the, the speed limit.
W: Right OK.
M: Occasionally. And you know I, I've been given quite a few fines over the years because my number plate gets recognised and I, you know I think more money should be spent elsewhere to be honest.
W: I take your point, but I do actually think, although I'm really anti the amount of kind of you know filming and, and information they have – when it comes to speeding, I do actually think that's quite sensible that they, that they can clock what people are doing.

B Divide Ss into As and Bs. Tell the As that they are only listening for the woman's opinion. Tell the Bs that they are only listening for the man's opinion. Play the recording again but do not check answers at this stage.

C Ask Ss to work in A and B pairs to complete both columns in the table. Check the answers as a class.

Answers:

	technology	woman	man
1	CCTV	✗ Makes her feel nervous. Feels like an invasion of privacy.	✓ People who commit a crime are arrested. Helps prevent crimes.
2	facial recognition technology	✗ You can't stop them from finding everything out about you.	✓ Can only be a good thing, can catch criminals. Not a problem if you haven't done anything wrong yourself.
3	microchips in products	✓ She doesn't mind getting adverts for things she might want.	✗ Doesn't want adverts.
4	number plate recognition	✓ It's sensible (but she doesn't give details).	✗ Drives a lot and speeds, so he has had a lot of fines. Thinks the money spent on this technology should be spent on something else.

D Ask Ss to work in pairs to compare their opinions from Ex 1C with those of the speakers. They then discuss the questions as a class and say whether either of the speakers has made them change their mind or not.

GRAMMAR THE PASSIVE

3A Do the first sentence as an example, underlining *was* and *robbed*. Ss can work on the rest of the sentences in pairs. For a ***stronger class***, tell them to think about why the passive is being used in each case. In feedback, check the form of the passive: *be* + past participle. Point out that *be* can be used in different tenses, with modal verbs and in the *-ing* and infinitive forms. If your Ss would benefit from seeing more examples at this stage, direct them to the table in the Language bank on p130.

Answers:
1 Not long ago a friend of mine was robbed at a bus stop.
2 I think statistically more crimes are solved because of CCTV than not.
3 I don't want to be sent adverts from companies that I don't know.
4 But we're being sent stuff all the time anyway.
5 I've been given quite a few fines over the years.
6 Money should be spent somewhere else to be honest.

B Encourage Ss to look back at the sentences in Ex 3A as they complete the rules.

Answers:
1 affected by the action
2 **a)** is **b)** is unknown **c)** isn't **d)** isn't
3 the beginning
4 impersonal, formal

4 Remind Ss that the words carrying the important information in the sentence are usually stressed and do the first phrase with the class as an example.

Answers:
1 A friend of mine was robbed.
2 More crimes are solved.
3 I don't want to be sent adverts.
4 We're being sent stuff all the time.
5 I've been given quite a few fines.
6 Money should be spent somewhere else.

▷ LANGUAGEBANK 2.2 p130–131

Depending on how confident Ss seem with the passive, they can look at this in class or at home. If you feel they need more basic practice before moving on to Ex 5A, they could do Ex A and/or Ex B. Ex B is a short text about the use of Google Street View in finding a missing child, so might be more appropriate to use in the lesson. You could set Ex A for homework, asking Ss to expand each sentence into a two- or three-line dialogue.

Answers:
A 1 My cat's being operated on this afternoon.
2 He'll be caught sooner or later.
3 Kim was burnt badly/badly burnt in the fire.
4 They don't mind being woken up in the middle of the night.
5 It is said that the early bird catches the worm.
6 I've been asked to give a speech to the whole school.
7 She's expected to be at her desk by 9a.m. every day.
8 Employees' emails are sometimes monitored by their supervisor.
9 Someone could get hurt if you don't take care.
10 It is believed that nobody has survived the crash.
B 1 has been used 2 was found 3 was discovered 4 put 5 has been arrested 6 's believed 7 being separated 8 might be given

5A Ask Ss to read the text quickly and to underline the uses of the microchip. Check how many chips there are and what they do.

Answers: Four: (in fridge) to remind you when it's time to buy something; (babies) to monitor a person all their lives; (criminals) to keep track of them; (attached to any object) to help you find it when you lose it

B Do the first one as a class and elicit the reason for the form used. Give Ss time to finish the task individually. When checking, ask for the reason from Ss each time.

Answers:
1 they can be placed (this keeps microchips as the main focus)
2 you can be reminded (now the focus shifts to 'you' and what 'you' do, i.e. it's not focusing primarily on the microchips anymore)
3 you to buy something (keep the focus on 'you')
4 microchips could be implanted (keep the focus on microchips, the main topic of the whole text)
5 Microchips could also be implanted (keep the focus on microchips)
6 keep ('police' is the subject or agent of the verb, so it needs an active verb)
7 a crime is committed (we don't know who commits the crime)
8 you can buy a set of clip-on microchips (the new focus is on 'you', established at the beginning of this sentence)
9 both answers are possible, but 'can be attached' sounds better since the focus has just shifted to 'a set of clip-on microchips'
10 both answers are possible; the first ('you can use your phone') sounds slightly less formal

C Ask Ss to discuss this in pairs. As an extension you could talk about other ways people are tracked. Examples include: Google Glasses revealing data about people around the wearer; Facebook tracking everyone that uses it; toys listening to children; phone GPS tracking your location; apps that read your messages, emails and calendar.

SPEAKING

6A Focus Ss on the headline and the first sentence of the article, explaining that a *surge* is a sudden increase. Direct them to the questions and point out that in question 3 they need to think of a reaction for each of the three groups. Conduct a brief class feedback.

B Put Ss into pairs or small groups by type (e.g. all the parents together) to prepare the points they want to make. Circulate and help as required. Tell Ss to think about what the other groups might say and to plan how they could argue against these opinions.

C You could set up this role-play in different ways:
1 All Ss together as a class, with people of the same 'type' (police, teenagers, etc.) sitting together. In this case you need to ensure that all Ss have a chance to get involved, so you may need to moderate the discussion or appoint a student to do so. To avoid interrupting the discussion by calling out names, you can throw a small ball to the person you want to speak next.
2 Ss work in small groups, each with one representative from each 'type' (police, teenager, etc.). In this case, after the role-play ask each group what the outcome of their meeting was. Monitor the role-play(s) and make a note of good language use and problem areas for feedback.

D Hold a class vote by showing hands. Elicit reasons for the winning team.

WRITING A LETTER OF COMPLAINT; LEARN TO USE FORMAL WRITTEN LANGUAGE

7A Start by eliciting some examples of things people might make an official complaint about, e.g. the food/service in a restaurant; the room/cleanliness/service in a hotel; an item they bought; the maintenance of a road/park/service by the local council. You could give an example of your own and encourage Ss to ask you questions about it. If Ss have no experience of complaining themselves, they can think about people they know, e.g. friends/family members/neighbours.

B Focus Ss on the questions and tell them to be prepared to explain their answers to someone who hasn't read the letter. This will stop them reading out sections of the letter verbatim and encourage them to summarise simply.

Answers:
1 LaGrande Travel Agency
2 A personal photo of her and her friends was used without her permission.
3 She wants the company to remove the picture and to issue a public statement of their policy in relation to the use of photos.

C Ss look at the parts of a complaint a)–f) and order them individually. Ss then check their answers in pairs and against the letter in Ex 7B.

Answers: a) 3 b) 5 c) 1 d) 6 e) 4 f) 2

8A Before Ss match the phrases, they could look through the letter and put a tick in the margin next to any phrases they think would be useful for formal letter writing. They compare their ideas with a partner, then work together to match phrases 1–6.

Answers:
1 Please contact me within one week of the date of this letter to confirm that these steps have been taken.
2 To resolve this matter, I request that you …
3 I am writing with regard to …
4 Yours faithfully,
5 Thank you for your prompt attention to this matter.
6 I have taken up this matter …

B Find the first example of the passive with the class, then put Ss into pairs.

Answers:
Passive: *might be taken, have been taken* – in both cases the passive is used to sound very formal and even legalistic. The tone is more distant and impersonal than using the active (*we might take, you have taken these steps*).
Active: *has advised, has (also) indicated* – in both cases keeping the focus on the lawyer and what she has done. The message is 'I've got a lawyer behind me!'; *should you fail, you remove, you issue, contact me, you need* – the tone is more immediate, less distant and therefore more threatening and personal, keeping the emphasis on you. The recipient of the letter will understand clearly that these actions are to be taken by them, the recipient.

speakout TIP

You may need to check that Ss understand *concise* (short, with no unnecessary words), *constructive* (intended to be helpful) and *considerate* (thinking about other people and avoiding upsetting them) before asking them to look at the letter again. Ss may disagree as to whether the letter is *considerate*, but it is polite and one could argue that this is all that is necessary to get the response they hope for.

9A Once Ss have chosen the situation and planned their letter, they can show their plan to a partner and give each other advice on what to add/change. Alternatively, you could give Ss the option of working in pairs, choosing the same situation so that they can discuss and plan it together.

B Before Ss start writing, remind them about the formal language phrases they looked at and the use of the passive. While Ss are writing, be available to answer queries, but avoid correcting at this stage.

C Circulate and help as required while Ss are checking their work, prompting them to correct their mistakes for themselves as much as possible, e.g. by saying things like: *Check the tense here. Look at the word order in this sentence. Is this formal enough?*

D So that Ss see more than one other letter, you could put them up on the walls for Ss to walk round and read.

Homework ideas

- Ss look at the letters page of a UK newspaper (these can be found online, e.g. at thepaperboy.com (correct at the time of going to press)), and check whether the letters follow the four Cs. They can bring a letter they found interesting to show each other in the next lesson.
- **Ex 6C:** Ss write a newspaper article about the 'meeting' they had about surveillance, describing what happened and what the outcome was.
- **Language bank:** 2.2 Ex A–B, p131
- **Workbook:** Ex 1–5, p11–12

GOOD POINT!

Introduction

Ss practise listening to and giving opinions. They also learn to support their viewpoint and to incorporate opinion adjectives.

SUPPLEMENTARY MATERIALS
Resource bank: p156

Warm up

Lead into the idea of giving opinions via the following activity: *Don't say yes or no!* Demonstrate by putting a topic, e.g. *homework*, on the board and telling Ss to avoid saying *yes* or *no* when they answer your questions. Ask one or two Ss a question, e.g. *Do you think it's a good idea to do homework? Do you think you get enough homework?* If they answer *yes* or *no*, award yourself a point. If they answer *It depends/I'm not sure/I suppose so*, etc., award the class a point. Once Ss have got the idea, put them into pairs and put another topic on the board, e.g. *exams* or *learning English*.

SPEAKING

1 Focus Ss on the photos and discuss briefly with the class what they can see in each one. Give Ss a few minutes to read the extracts and match them to the pictures before putting them into pairs to discuss the questions. Make sure that Ss make a note of their reasons in question 2 so they can compare them with the speakers in the listening in Ex 2C.

Answers: **1** B (against) **2** C (for) **3** A (against)

FUNCTION OPINIONS

2A Tell Ss they are going to hear three conversations about the topics they've just discussed. Play the recording and tell Ss to take notes as they listen.

Answers:
1 The woman agrees that violence in gaming is a problem.
2 The man agrees that illegal downloading is a problem.
3 The man agrees that cosmetic surgery is a good thing.

Unit 2 Recording 7

Conversation 1

M = Man W = Woman

M: Have you seen this? There's a new law about computer games. They want to limit the kind of violent things that can happen in the games so kids don't see so much.
W: Really? Well, that makes sense. I do think that the violence in those games can make kids more aggressive.
M: Well, according to one article I read, kids are *less* aggressive if they play these games.
W: How could that be true?
M: Apparently the games give them a chance to use up some of their energy. So they're calmer in real life.
W: That's hard to believe. In my experience, playing those games makes kids *more* aggressive. So I'm in favour of some kind of control.
M: Hmm. I don't know … I agree to a certain extent but I think kids can separate real life from computer games. I mean, I don't like computer games and I hate violence, but actually I think it's more of a problem to put these limits on.
W: I think we'll have to agree to disagree.
M: I suppose so.

Conversation 2

W = Woman **M** = Man

W: Do you ever download music for free?
M: You mean illegally? No, I'm probably one of the few people that doesn't do it. I've always paid for downloads.
W: Why? I mean nobody I know pays.
M: Exactly! And it's just theft, isn't it? I mean, …
W: Oh, I totally disagree.
M: I mean, artists have copyright on their songs, so you're stealing from them. It's as simple as that.
W: But as far as I know musicians these days get very little money from CD sales or downloads anyway. So they don't lose out. I mean, they want people to hear their music.
M: Hmm. I'm not so sure about that. If people share the music without paying, how can musicians make any money?
W: Well, the famous ones, they don't need more money and for newer groups, file-sharing is the way they get known, so they don't have to spend a fortune, you know, on things like record companies and managers and …
M: Yeah, but …
W: … anyway, nowadays singers and groups make most of their money from concerts.
M: Hmm. I'm still not convinced. Aren't you worried about being found out? For instance, what about that man in the USA? Did you hear about that? Apparently, he got fined about one and a half million dollars for downloading and sharing films.
W: One and a half million dollars? Ouch!
M: Yeah, so maybe you'd better think again.
W: Hmm. Good point.

Conversation 3

M = Man **W** = Woman

M: Do you think you would ever have cosmetic surgery?
W: Me? No, I don't think so. I'm really against it actually. I think it's …
M: Really, why?
W: Well, basically I think it can be quite dangerous – some of the implants you can have, um –
M: Yeah, I see what you mean.
W: Like, like Mike's girlfriend – she actually had some Botox injections in her forehead.
M: Did she?
W: Yeah, and she couldn't, you know, she couldn't –
M: Couldn't move her face?
W: Yeah, she couldn't smile or frown – her face was just frozen solid.
M: Fair enough, but if someone's very depressed because of the way they look maybe then they should have some kind of surgery, you know, to help their self-esteem.
W: I think there are other ways to help.
M: And what about if they have a serious health problem? Such as maybe they're extremely overweight.
W: For health reasons maybe, yes, I mean, I see your point, but I still don't like the sound of it. Personally, I think it's too much of a risk. I wouldn't do it myself.
M: I might, if it was to do with my health.

B Tell Ss to make short notes about the speakers' opinions and reasons for these opinions. Play the recording again, stopping after each conversation to give Ss time to process what they've heard.

Answers:
Conversation 1:
Man's opinion: it makes kids less aggressive because they use up their energy; kids can separate real life from computer game fantasy
Woman's opinion: it makes kids more aggressive
Conversation 2
Man's opinion: it's the same as stealing
Woman's opinion: musicians don't make much money from CDs; famous musicians don't need the money; newer musicians can get their music heard
Conversation 2
Man's opinion: dangerous and damaging
Woman's opinion: helps people's confidence; may be good for health reasons

C Ss discuss their answers in pairs, commenting on which opinions match their own from Ex 1.

D Ask Ss to complete each gap with one word. With ***weaker Ss*** you could give them the first letter of each word.

E Ask Ss to check their answers against the audio script on p165.

Answers: **1** against **2** favour **3** makes **4** see **5** point **6** certain **7** think **8** convinced

3A Do the first one as an example, then put Ss into pairs to work on the rest. Check the answers as a class.

Answers:
Giving opinions: Personally, I think …; Basically, I think …; I do think …
Agreeing: Exactly!; Good point.
Partially agreeing: I suppose so.; Fair enough, but …
Disagreeing: I totally disagree.; I'm not so sure.

B Explain that partial agreement is generally expressed via a high pitch on the main stress (see the underlined words in the audio script), and a fall-rise at the end. Play the recording and ask Ss to repeat the sentences.

Unit 2 Recording 8

1. I see your point, but …
2. I agree to some extent, but …
3. I suppose so.
4. Fair enough, but …

▷ LANGUAGEBANK 2.3 p130–131

Point out that the phrases Ss have been working on are summarised in the Language bank for their reference. If you feel that Ss need some accuracy practice with the phrases before moving on to Ex 4A, you could do Ex A in class. Otherwise, Ss could do it for homework.

Answers:
A: I'm *in* favour of the idea of compulsory school uniforms.
B: Are you? I'm really against *it*.
A: Well, personally I *think* with uniforms everyone's the same, rich or poor.
B: I see your *point*, but they can be very expensive – especially as children get bigger.
A: I'm not so *sure*. Kids' clothes are expensive anyway.
B: Fair *enough*, but having uniforms stops children expressing their personality.
A: I agree *to* a certain extent, but I do think uniforms provide a sense of belonging.
B: I suppose *so*. But actually I don't think kids really feel any less lonely just because they have a uniform on.
A: Maybe not, but I'm *still* not convinced.

4A You could start by putting the two topics on the board (*banning smoking in public places* and *banning cars in the city centre*) and eliciting some examples from the class of reasons for and against them. Ss use the prompts to practise the conversations in pairs. Monitor the practice and invite one or two pairs who did well to act out their conversations for the class.

Answers:
Conversation 1:
A: I'm in favour of banning smoking in all public places.
B: Actually, I think people should be free to choose.
A: Fair enough, but what about the rights of other people?
B: Personally, I think the freedom to choose is more important.
A: I see your point, but passive smoking can be very bad for you.
B: I suppose so, but banning smoking in all places is too much!
Conversation 2
A: What do you think about banning cars in the city centre?
B: I'm against it. Basically, I think it's bad for business. And you?
A: I'm not sure. I agree to a certain extent, but I do think that it's better for the environment.
B: Good point. And people could use public transport more. It makes sense.
A: Exactly!

B Ask Ss to discuss in pairs who they agree with most and why. Take feedback as a class.

LEARN TO SUPPORT YOUR VIEWPOINT

5 Tell Ss they are going to look at some examples from the conversations in Ex 2 that will help them to make their opinions stronger and more convincing. You could do an example each for a) and b), then give Ss a minute or two (alone or in pairs) to look at the rest. In feedback, drill the phrases in bold, making sure that Ss sound natural.

Answers: a) 4, 5, 6 **b)** 1, 2, 3

6A Remind Ss to cover Ex 5 before they start and point out that they need to add a capital letter if the phrase starts a new sentence. After feedback Ss could practise the conversation in pairs.

Answers:
1 According to this article
2 for instance for memorising content/for memorising content for instance
3 such as spending time
4 apparently homework is essential
5 in magazines like that
6 As far as I know

B Ask Ss to look at the points about homework in Ex 6A and to discuss whether they agree or disagree with them and why. With ***stronger Ss*** you could ask them to rewrite the dialogue so that it includes their opinions and also uses the underlined phrases.

Optional extra activity

To give Ss more practice in using the phrases, you could give them other stereotypes to discuss, e.g. teenagers, politicians. Give them time to prepare their arguments, using at least three of the phrases. Alternatively, Ss could do some research for homework, then discuss the topic in the next lesson.

VOCABULARY OPINION ADJECTIVES

7A Do the first one as an example and then give Ss time to match the rest of the adjectives.

Answers: a) reasonable **b)** illegal **c)** unethical **d)** outrageous **e)** disturbing **f)** irresponsible

speakout TIP

After Ss have read the tip, write the following on the board: *That politician was really bad.* Ask Ss *What do you think he/she did?* Then change *bad* for *unethical* and ask again *What do you think he/she did?* Ss will then see how this is more specific (e.g. something which it was not acceptable to do in a position of power). Change *unethical* for *irresponsible* and ask again (e.g. something that might have put the population in danger).

B You could demonstrate this by doing a couple of examples with Ss in open pairs, across the class. Then put Ss into closed pairs and suggest they swap roles after four exchanges.

Teaching tip

Open versus closed pairs

An open pair is when Ss ask/answer from opposite sides of the classroom. This means that the rest of the class can hear them, so it's useful for demonstrating and setting up pairwork activities, especially if you choose two ***stronger Ss***.

A closed pair is two Ss sitting next to each other. This interaction maximises student speaking time because all the pairs are speaking simultaneously.

SPEAKING

8A Once Ss have chosen their three topics, give them time to prepare their arguments in their pairs. Remind them to look back at the phrases in Ex 5, as well as the adjectives in Ex 7A. Circulate and help as required.

B Ss can work in groups of three to five for this discussion. Split up the pairs so that Ss have to defend their opinions on their own without their partner's support. Alternatively, you can let Ss stay in their pairs and work in groups of four or six, the pairs presenting their case together. Monitor and make notes of good language use and problems, for praise and correction in feedback.

Optional extra activity

Instead of putting Ss into groups, you could set up a 'discussion ladder': Ss sit in two lines facing each other and start discussing a topic with the person opposite them, then on a signal from you, one line moves up one 'step' so that Ss have new partners. This will mean that Ss will sometimes be discussing a topic they haven't prepared, but this will give them practice in more spontaneous production of language. This also provides more challenge for ***stronger classes***.

Homework ideas

- Ss watch a TV programme in English (e.g. on the internet) which features a panel discussion and listen out for the phrases they've learnt for giving and supporting opinions.
- **Language bank:** 2.3 Ex A, p131
- **Workbook:** Ex 1–3, p13

A QUIET REVOLUTION

Introduction

Ss watch an extract from the BBC News called *A quiet revolution*. Ss then learn and practise how to give a joint presentation and write notes for a presentation.

SUPPLEMENTARY MATERIALS

Ex 1A: Write some stereotypical/traditional gender roles onto individual pieces of paper. Prepare enough for one set per group.

Warm up

Write *men's roles* on one half of the board and *women's roles* on the other half of the board. Give Ss a couple of ideas, e.g. *housework* and *childcare*, and ask which role they would associate these with. Put Ss into pairs to brainstorm what they see as men's roles or women's roles. Conduct a brief feedback, so Ss can see how many ideas the class have generated.

DVD PREVIEW

1A In pairs, Ss discuss traditional gender roles in their country. If you did the Warm up, ask Ss to discuss which of these roles are changing or have changed in recent years. Elicit ideas from the class. Draw Ss' attention to the pictures on the page. Ask Ss how many men they think behave like this in their country.

B Give Ss a minute or two to read the statements and tick the ones they agree with. After Ss have compared their answers in pairs, hold a vote on how many agree and how many disagree with each statement.

Optional extra activity

Extend the topic by asking Ss to work individually and write one or two sentences on the topics of the sentences in Ex 1B, i.e. men's and women's roles; their values regarding roles; who should take care of children. In pairs, Ss compare their views.

2 Ask Ss to look at the title and elicit what they think the programme might be about. Ask Ss to read the programme information and check their predictions. Finally, Ss list possible reasons for the change and then compare them in pairs. Elicit ideas as a class.

Answers:
1 The quiet revolution is that some British men are reducing their work hours, with some going part-time.
2 Suggested answers: to reduce stress; to spend more time with the family; to pursue a hobby or another interest; to help their partner (i.e. the man helping the woman) in her work/career

DVD VIEW

3A Write the ideas from Ex 2 and any additional ideas from Ss on the board before playing the DVD. Play the DVD for Ss to check how many were mentioned.

Answers: Answers will depend on what Ss listed in Ex 2. The ideas mentioned in the clip are: to spend more time with the family, to help his wife's career, to pursue an interest (writing), to slow the pace of life, to recharge, to have more time for himself, to make money, to keep from getting bored.

DVD 2 A quiet revolution

ES = Emma Simpson RSi = Rob Sinclair RSt = Richard Steele
BB = Bernard Brody

ES: Meet three men, with three different personal stories on why they pushed to work part-time.
Rob Sinclair is an accountant from Sutton Coldfield. With two young boys he and his wife realised something had to give.
RSi: Just proving to be a big challenge for us to keep both our careers progressing as they had been, whilst also making sure we didn't disrupt the home life, and make sure we actually spend time with the boys.
ES: Sound familiar? But it was *Rob* who cut his hours.
RSi: It seemed to make sense for me to take the lead in moving down to working part-time, to give me time, more time with the boys, let my wife concentrate on her corporate career, and let me do some more time with my writing as well.
ES: He has to make do with less money, but for Rob life's now on a more even keel. That's what Richard Steele had in mind when he went part-time.
RSt: I'd been working very hard for ten years. There was never a time to stop. The emails, with Blackberries, and then tablets and mobile phones meant that there was no sort of barrier to when work finished.
ES: But his pace of life has changed. Richard now works for a food business in Kent, with Fridays off.
RSt: It's a sort of transition really, from a very busy week to recharging and having time for me, and to build up again so that I can spend quality time with the family at the weekend.
ES: Rob and Richard are part of what feels like a quiet revolution. It's women of course who do the vast majority of part-time work. But more and more men are now choosing to do less than a full week.
There are nearly a million of them, a figure that's almost trebled in the last twenty years. But most of this growth is down to older men, like Bernard Brody. He could have retired two years ago and put his feet up, instead he's choosing to stay busy. Why are you working part-time at the age of 67?
BB: A: Money. Well not 'A: money' but that helps a heck of a lot.
B: Boredom. I can't sit around doing nothing.
ES: And he doesn't intend stopping any time soon. How to find the right work–life balance in today's demanding world. It's never easy but these men are breaking the mould. Emma Simpson, BBC News.

B Elicit a description of Rob, Richard and Bernard so that Ss are clear who is who before attempting this task. Ss could mark names next to any they remember before watching the DVD again. Check the answers as a class.

Answers:
to make money 3
to get back lost energy 2
to help his partner's career 1
to have more time for himself 2
to avoid getting bored 3
to spend more time with his family 1, 2

C Give Ss time to read the sentences and to choose an option before playing the DVD again. When checking their answers, elicit what Ss understand by each expression.

Answers: 1 give 2 lead 3 do, keel 4 up 5 mould

D Give Ss a few minutes to match the phrases to the meanings. As an extension you could ask Ss to discuss some additional questions, e.g. *When was the last time you felt like something had to give? When was the last time you had to take the lead? Have you ever made a decision that meant you had to make do with less money?*

Answers: a) on a more even keel **b)** make do with less (money) **c)** break the mould **d)** put your feet up **e)** something has to give **f)** take the lead (in doing something)

E Once Ss have discussed the questions, elicit some ideas. Find out from Ss whether they think these changes are positive or negative.

speakout a joint presentation

4A Give Ss a few minutes to discuss the pros and cons of traditional gender roles and tell them to think of reasons for their ideas.

B Tell Ss they are going to listen to two people giving a presentation on the pros and cons of traditional gender roles. They can tick the topics that the speaker mentions from their list.

Answers: Answers will depend on what Ss listed in Ex 4A. The ideas the two people mention are:
pros – roles clearly defined, no confusion about who does what; woman can manage family life because she has time to do so; more contact between mother and children; men are better at tasks considered traditionally 'male', and women at tasks traditionally considered 'female'
cons – too little contact between father and child; woman might in fact be better at traditionally 'male' tasks, and vice-versa; woman may want a career for herself, and traditional roles restrict this

Unit 2 Recording 9

D = Denise J = James

D: Our presentation is about the pros and cons of traditional roles in a family. I'll talk about the pros, and James will talk about the cons. Then you can decide.

J: First, to make it clear what we mean by traditional roles, we're thinking of the man as breadwinner, as the one who earns the money to support the family, while the woman stays at home and takes care of the children. At home, generally speaking the woman does the housework – the cooking, cleaning, etc. – while the man might do home repairs and take care of the car. Denise?

D: So, on the positive side, the roles are very clearly defined – both the man and woman know who does what, so there's less confusion and fewer conflicts about that. If there are children, there's less pressure on family life, in that if the woman doesn't work, she has time to manage things such as birthdays, paying bills, taking children to and from the various activities that children do. Also, there's more contact between the mother and children, and that's bound to be good for the health of the whole family. And in reality, a lot of men *are* better at doing heavier or more mechanical work, such as car repairs. And let's face it, many women *do* notice more than men things like how clean or tidy a room is, so they're the best person to take care of this. Over to you, James.

J: Thanks Denise. So, on the negative side, if the man is always the one who works, there can be too little contact between father and child, and that can't be good for the family. Also, in some couples the woman *will* be good at tasks traditionally done by the man, and vice-versa. For instance, if the man is a better cook than the woman, or is happier staying at home with the children, while the woman is better at fixing the car and mowing the lawn, then it would be silly for the one who is less good at the task to be the one to do it. Finally, and perhaps most importantly, a lot of women will of course want to work and develop a career, both for their own satisfaction and independence, and also to be a role model for their children.

D: Those are just some of the pros and cons. Over to you now to decide which are stronger, the pros or the cons.

C Focus Ss on the key phrases and give them time to read them through. Set the task for the listening and point out that where there are options in the phrases (e.g. *On the [positive/negative] side* ...), they need to underline the option(s) they hear.

Answers: Our presentation is about ...; First, to make it clear what we mean by [traditional roles] ...; Generally speaking [the woman does the housework]; On the [positive/negative] side ...; That's bound to be [good/bad] for ...; Finally, and perhaps most importantly ...

5A Allow Ss time to choose a topic. Where necessary, help Ss with ideas for their talk.

Alternative approach
An option here is to first do the writeback section on how to make notes for a presentation. This will allow Ss to make more effective notes for their presentation in this part of the speakout section.

B Before Ss prepare their talk in detail, spend some time brainstorming good features of a presentation, e.g. maintain eye contact, move around but only a little, organise your presentation into sections, make use of pauses, stress and intonation to engage your audience, clear voice projection, etc. Circulate and help as Ss practise their presentations. You could suggest that Ss aim to include at least five of the key phrases.

C After each presentation, encourage the class to ask the presenters one or two questions. Finally, hold a vote on the stronger argument in each case.

writeback notes for a presentation

6A Tell Ss to read the three possible presentation topics and to discuss with a partner which one sounds most interesting. Ask Ss to read the notes and to match them to one of the topics. Finally, hold a vote on which side of the argument is stronger.

Answers: The topic is gender-blind hiring. Ss can decide for themselves which argument is stronger.

B Tell Ss to write the first item in the pro column out as a full sentence. Elicit which words they had to add in order to make it a full sentence. Ask Ss to look at the other sentences in pairs and to identify which types of words are left out.

Answers:
The writer makes the notes short by:
- omitting subjects and *there is/are* (~~*There are*~~ *no problems* ..., ~~*It*~~ *may change* ..., ~~*There would be*~~ *resistance* ...)
- using abbreviations (*re* = *about/concerning*; *e.g.* = *for example*)
- using slashes instead of linkers (*men/women, people/cultures*)
- omitting articles (~~*the*~~ *best person chosen for* ~~*the*~~ *job*; *casting* ~~*a*~~ *female role in* ~~*a*~~ *film*)
- omitting the verb *be* (*best person* ~~*is*~~ *chosen for job*)

C Ss work alone to write their notes on one of the topics. Circulate and help as required, prompting Ss to keep their notes as brief as possible.

D Ss exchange their notes with a partner and first look at which argument is stronger. Next Ss cross out words they do not think are necessary. Elicit why making notes is generally a good technique as opposed to writing ideas out in full. (Generally, presentations written out in full tend to be read out loud. This can have a negative impact on intonation, stress, eye contact, voice projection and speed.)

Homework ideas
Ex 6C: Ss prepare a presentation using the notes they made.

LOOKBACK

Introduction

The aim of these activities is to provide revision and further practice of the language from the unit. You can also use them to assess Ss' ability to use the language, in which case you need to monitor but avoid helping them. You may feel that you don't need or have time to do all the activities. If so, you could allocate the activities that would be most beneficial for your Ss, or get individual Ss to decide which activities they'd like to do.

ISSUES

1A Ss can work on this in pairs, or work alone and compare answers with a partner. You could give Ss a time limit, e.g. 2 mins, to introduce an element of competition.

Answers: 1 urban, rural 2 domestic, global 3 ethical 4 economic 5 pollution, industrial

B Ss discuss the questions in pairs. Choose one or two questions which you notice Ss have had lots to say about to discuss as a class.

PRESENT PERFECT SIMPLE AND CONTINUOUS

2A For ***weaker classes***, you may need to let Ss refer to the rules and examples in the Language bank on p130–131. Ss work alone, while you circulate and help as necessary. For ***stronger classes***, you could either put Ss into pairs and conduct this as a race, or you could run it as a team game, with teams of four or five Ss. Tell Ss to close their books, then display the prompts on the board, one at a time. Teams confer on each question and put up their hands when they're ready to answer. They are awarded points for correct grammar and bonus points for good pronunciation.

Answers:
1 How long have you been learning English?
2 Your English has improved a lot recently. What have you been doing?
3 How many teachers have you had?
4 How far have you travelled on public transport today?
5 Have you done your homework for today?
6 How long did it take you to do it?
7 Have you studied/been studying a lot this week?
8 Have you ever forgotten to bring anything to class?

B This could be done in closed pairs, or in open pairs, to give some variety of interaction. Ss take turns to choose a question and nominate someone from the other side of the class to answer it.

SURVEILLANCE

3A This could be done as an individual exercise or as a competitive pair race. Check the answers as a class.

Answers: 1 crime prevention, deterrent 2 identify 3 access, invasion of privacy 4 authorities, monitoring 5 keep track 6 store information

B If you have time, Ss could choose one or two of these issues to hold a class debate on. To set up the debate, tell half the class they have to agree with the chosen statement and half that they have to disagree. Hold the debate. The winning group is the one with the most convincing standpoint and accurate use of structures and language taught in the unit. After finishing the debate, allow Ss to express their own opinions briefly.

THE PASSIVE

4A Look at the example with the class, pointing out that the agent *people* has disappeared in the passive sentence, because it's not necessary and drawing Ss' attention to the use of the *-ing* form *being* after the verb *like*. Ss work alone or in pairs to change the rest of the sentences.

Answers:
1 I don't like being called by my nickname.
2 I was brought up in a house full of pets.
3 I've never been robbed.
4 I hate being given clothes as a present.
5 I'm often told I look like my father.
6 I've always wanted to be admired for my intelligence.

B You could start by doing an example about yourself, e.g. *I don't mind being called by my nickname.* (changing one word) or *I don't like being called by my nickname at work.* (adding two words). Then give Ss a few minutes to work on their sentences alone.

C Encourage Ss to extend their sentences into conversations, e.g. *A: I've been robbed three times. B: Really? Did you lose anything valuable?* etc. Ss can report back to the class about what they found out.

5A Ss should write the questions in their notebooks rather than in the Students' Book, so that they can use the prompts for oral practice in the next stage.

Answers:
1 Have you ever been bitten by an animal?
2 Would you like to be invited to dinner by a celebrity?
3 Do you enjoy being photographed?
4 Do you always want to be told the truth even if it hurts?
5 What will you be remembered for after you die?

B Encourage Ss to extend this practice beyond the question and answer, giving reasons for their answers and asking follow-up questions. Ss could also stand up and walk round the class, asking different people the questions. Conduct feedback, asking Ss what surprising/interesting things they heard.

OPINIONS

6A Ss work alone or in pairs to correct the mistakes. As you go through the answers, write/display the corrected phrases on the board, e.g.
A: *I'm in favour of …*
B: *I'm really against it …*
A: *I see your point, but …*, etc.
Ss can then use these prompts for their own conversations in the next stage.

Answers: 1 I'm in favour of 2 I'm really against it. 3 I see your point, but 4 Actually, I think 5 I agree to a certain extent, but 6 I'm still not convinced. 7 I see what you mean.

B Ss should spend a minute or two thinking about what to say before starting the conversation. If you have time, Ss could talk about all three topics, then choose their 'best' one to perform for the class.

Homework ideas

Workbook: Review 1, p14–17

BBC interviews and worksheet

Does money make you happy?

This video encourages students to reflect on and discuss how much money contributes to our happiness.

OVERVIEW

3.1 AND THE MORAL IS …

READING | read stories with a moral
GRAMMAR | narrative tenses
PRONUNCIATION | weak forms: auxiliaries
VOCABULARY | sayings
SPEAKING | tell anecdotes
WRITING | a story

3.2 A LIFE IN SIX WORDS

VOCABULARY | adjectives for stories
LISTENING | listen to a BBC radio programme about very short stories
GRAMMAR | *I wish, if only*
PRONUNCIATION | sentence stress
SPEAKING | tell a six-word story
VOCABULARY *PLUS* | multi-word verbs
SPEAKING | talk about life stories

3.3 IT'S A GREAT READ

VOCABULARY | reading genres
FUNCTION | expressing likes and dislikes
PRONUNCIATION | sentence stress
LEARN TO | summarise a plot
SPEAKING | talk about your reading

3.4 TESS BBC DVD

DVD | watch a BBC drama
speakout | a favourite scene
writeback | a description of a scene

3.5 LOOKBACK

Communicative revision activities

BBC INTERVIEWS

What was the last book you read?

This video looks at the topic of what people like reading. Use this video at the start or end of Unit 3 or set it as homework.

AND THE MORAL IS …

Introduction

Ss practise reading, speaking and writing about stories, using narrative tenses. They also learn some common English sayings and how to use adverbs in a story.

SUPPLEMENTARY MATERIALS

Resource bank: p157 and p159

Warm up: be prepared to tell Ss about an important possession of yours and the story behind it. Take the possession into the lesson to show Ss if possible.

Ex 7A: be prepared to tell a personal story that illustrates one of the sayings in Ex 6A and prepare a list of eight to ten key words to help you tell the story.

Warm up

Diagnose Ss' use of narrative tenses via a storytelling activity.

Either: Ss tell a 'chain story' round the class. Start by eliciting some key words that are to be included in the story, e.g. a day, a time, a city, a country, the names of two people, the names of two/three objects and one method of transport, and write these on the board. Invite a student on one side of the classroom to start the story and to include one of the key words from the board. Once they've said a couple of sentences, they 'pass' the story on to the next student and so on. The idea is that once the story reaches the last student on the other side of the classroom, all the key words have been used and that student finishes the story.

Or: Tell Ss about an important possession of yours and the story behind how you got it, e.g. who gave it to you, when, why, etc. or where, why and when you bought it. Then put Ss into pairs to tell each other the story behind an important possession of theirs.

READING

1A Draw two columns on the board and write the story titles at the top of each column, then make sure that Ss cover the texts before directing them to the pictures and the titles. Elicit one or two ideas from the class about what they can see, then put Ss into pairs to predict what might happen in the stories. Conduct feedback, writing some of the Ss' ideas in the columns on the board for them to compare with the actual stories.

B Give Ss about 5 mins to read the stories, then they can compare what they've read with the ideas on the board. You could elicit a few ideas for the endings from the whole class, then put Ss into pairs to write them, using about three sentences for each ending. Invite two or three pairs to read out their endings to the class.

C Give Ss a minute or two to read the endings and discuss briefly with the class who came closest to either of the endings in their predictions.

2A Tell Ss to cover Ex 2B while they do this exercise. You could look at the first bold word with the class, as an example, reminding them to use the part of speech, the context and the 'look' of the words to help them. Put Ss into pairs to look at the rest of the words and make a note of possible meanings.

B Ss work alone and compare answers in pairs, before feedback to the class.

Answers: **1** gave the performance of her life **2** persisted **3** due **4** dreads **5** dimmed **6** shivering **7** pervaded **8** visibly

3 stories

C Give Ss time to discuss the stories and think about the moral or 'message' in each one. Elicit their ideas.

Suggested answers: 'Performance of a lifetime?' ending 1; 'It pays to be honest' ending 2

GRAMMAR NARRATIVE TENSES

3A You could suggest that Ss use different ways of highlighting the four tenses, e.g. a circle for the past simple, a box for the past perfect simple, a wavy line for the past continuous and a straight line for the past perfect continuous (these could also be in different colours). Ss compare their answers in pairs. ***Stronger classes*** could also discuss why each verb tense is used.

Suggested answers: Many years ago a crowd gathered (past simple) outside the Paris Opera House to see a performance by one of the most famous opera singers of the time. Tickets had sold out (past perfect) weeks before, and opera fans had been looking forward (past perfect continuous) to this epic moment ever since the performance was announced. (past simple – passive). It was (past simple) a gorgeous spring evening, and everyone was wearing (past continuous) their finest clothes in celebration of the event.

B Ss read the rules alone, then underline the verb forms and check their answers with a partner. You could ask Ss what effect using the four different verb forms has on the story, i.e. adding more variety and making it more interesting to read.

Answers: **1** past simple **2** past continuous **3** past perfect simple **4** past perfect continuous

C Ask Ss to find and underline the numbered verbs. In pairs, ask Ss to match each verb to a rule, then discuss each example as a class.

Answers:
1 began = Rule 1
2 had never appeared = Rule 3
3 was driving = Rule 2
4 had been standing = Rule 4
5 was shivering = Rule 2
6 he'd finished = Rule 3
7 drove = Rule 1
8 was paying = Rule 2
9 remembered = Rule 1
10 had said = Rule 3

4A Remind Ss that the main verbs (which carry the meaning) are usually stressed and the auxiliary verbs (*be*, *do*, etc.) are not, so they are 'reduced'. You could look at the rest of the first sentence with the class, as an example.

B Play the recording, stopping after each sentence to check the answers. Play the recording a second time for Ss to say at the same time.

Answers:
1 The woman **had** (/ə/) **been** (/ɪ/) **standing** there for a long time and **was** (/ə/) **shivering** badly.
2 When she **was** (/ə/) **paying** for her meal, the old lady remembered what Steve Hunt **had** (/ə/) **said**.

▷ **LANGUAGEBANK 3.1** p132–133

You could use Ex A and B in class before attempting the more complex story in Ex 5A.

Answers:
A **1** 'd forgotten **2** was robbing **3** 'd been painting **4** 'd been using
B **1** ended **2** was working **3** heard **4** 'd been playing **5** ran **6** saw **7** joined **8** were searching **9** found **10** had been **11** had gone/went **12** was going **13** 'd heard **14** opened **15** 'd been sleeping

5A Ask Ss to read the whole text quickly without worrying about the gaps and find out why the king was disappointed with his present. Ss then work in pairs to complete the gaps.

Answers: **1** 'd never seen **2** had been training **3** was sitting **4** noticed **5** didn't see (*couldn't see* is also possible) **6** had been sitting **7** called **8** 'd tried **9** realised **10** was flying **11** cut **12** was sitting

B Ss discuss the possible moral of the story in pairs and how it could apply to their own life.

VOCABULARY SAYINGS

6A Put the first sentence *Every cloud has a silver lining.* on the board and ask Ss what they think it means (good things come out of bad things). Explain that this is a saying, i.e. a short, well-known statement that expresses an idea many people believe is true. Ask Ss to guess the meanings in pairs. Elicit their ideas.

B Ss match the sayings to their meanings. Elicit which one would match well to one of the stories. As a brief extension, you could ask Ss whether these phrases would translate directly into their own language. If not, ask if they have an equivalent expression.

Suggested answers: **1** c) **2** e) **3** b) **4** d) **5** a)
It pays to be honest: What goes around comes around – the man's generosity to the elderly woman was returned (in this case in an unusually coincidental way).

C Ask Ss to complete the conversations individually. When checking answers, ask pairs of Ss to read out loud parts A and B as you check.

Answers:
1 when in Rome do as the Romans do
2 Once bitten, twice shy.
3 What goes around comes around.
4 nothing ventured, nothing gained
5 every cloud has a silver lining

speakout TIP

Read the tip with the class and ask Ss why people only say the first part of a saying, i.e. they expect the listener to know it because the sayings are so well-known. Ask Ss to cross out the part they think people don't need to say.

Answers: It's enough to say … **1** when in Rome … **2** Once bitten … **3** What goes around … **4** nothing ventured … **5** every cloud …

SPEAKING

7A You could start by telling Ss a personal story that illustrates a saying, as a model. Before the lesson, prepare a list of key words to include in the story, as in Ex 7B. Tell the story, referring to your list occasionally. Ask Ss to guess the saying and show them the list of key words you used.

B Ss prepare their stories alone.

C Before you put Ss into groups you could remind them about listening 'actively', e.g. by showing interest/sympathy/surprise and commenting on the story as it develops. NB Tell Ss not to try to guess the saying until the person has finished telling the story.

WRITING A STORY

8A Focus Ss on the title and the picture and ask them to speculate on what happens in the story. Then give them a few minutes to read the story and answer the questions.

B Ss read the story and answer the questions alone, then discuss answers with a partner.

Answers:
1 The writer puts the same saying (or a version of it) in both the first and last paragraphs.
2 Paragraph 1 – past simple, past perfect simple, past perfect continuous, past continuous
3 Paragraphs 2 and 3 – all four past forms are used but the past simple is the dominant form in the section.
4 The writer expresses his feelings all through the story by using adverbs such as *stupidly* and by sometimes simply saying how he felt, e.g. *I was nervous* or his physical sensations, *my mouth was so dry I couldn't speak*.
5 He says what he learnt in the last paragraph.

9A Direct Ss to the first adverb (*stupidly*) as an example, then tell them to circle the rest as quickly as they can.

Answers: stupidly, naturally, Finally, awkwardly, Apparently, Unfortunately, politely, eventually

B Encourage Ss to look back at the adverbs in context to help them guess the meanings. Ss discuss answers in pairs before feedback with the class.

Answers: **1** stupidly **2** naturally **3** unfortunately **4** apparently **5** awkwardly **6** finally, eventually **7** politely

C Ss write the adverbs in the correct place in the table. Check the answers as a class. You could elicit any other words Ss can think of to include in the table.

Answers:
adverbs of manner: stupidly, awkwardly, politely
attitude markers: naturally, apparently, unfortunately
time markers: finally, eventually

speakout TIP

Give Ss time to read the tip then ask them where most of the adverbs occur in the story – mainly in the middle section where the writer is describing the action (adverbs of manner) and commenting on what happened (attitude markers). Explain that using too many adverbs (i.e. more than ten) will make the story awkward and unnatural.

10A Encourage Ss to make notes and do a rough first draft of their story. Monitor and help as necessary.

B Ss should proofread their own work for verb forms, spelling and adverbs. Encourage Ss to focus on just these three features. They could give it to a partner to check before writing the final draft (this could be done at home).

C These could be posted on the classroom walls and read by Ss during a break or during the week. Alternatively, if you have a LMS or forum you could post them on there. This would enable Ss to read more stories before voting.

▷ VOCABULARYBANK p150 Verbs used in stories

Ss complete the exercises in pairs without using a dictionary and using a process of logical deduction to help them guess those words they don't know. Feed back as a class or let Ss use bilingual and monolingual dictionaries to check anything they are not sure of.

If Ss speak the same language, it could be an interesting exercise to ask them to compare the metaphorical use of the verbs in Ex 1B with similar expressions in their own language.

Answers:
A **A** wander **B** gaze **C** whisper **D** crawl **E** sigh **F** yawn
B **1** sigh **2** yawned **3** crawled **4** whispered **5** wandered **6** gazed

Homework ideas

- Ss read a short story in English online, e.g. something like www.classicshots.com (correct at time of going to press) and report back in the next lesson.
- Ss write the story from the Warm up to the lesson (either the chain story, or the story of a favourite possession).
- Ss research the life of a famous person and make notes in English to bring to class and use in Lesson 3.2, Ex 8.
- **Language bank:** 3.1 Ex A–B, p133
- **Vocabulary bank:** p150
- **Workbook:** Ex 1–6, p18–19

A LIFE IN SIX WORDS

Introduction

Ss practise listening and speaking about regrets, using *I wish* and *If only* and related vocabulary. They also learn to use multi-word verbs in life stories.

SUPPLEMENTARY MATERIALS

Resource bank: p158 and p160

Ex 6B and **Ex 7C:** bring monolingual dictionaries for Ss to use.

Ex 8A: be prepared to tell a life story using some of the multi-word verbs.

Warm up

Tell Ss to close their books and write on the board: *Adjectives for stories.* Put Ss into small groups. Elicit one or two examples and then give them 2 mins to write as many adjectives to describe stories as possible. Elicit the words Ss think of and add them to the board. When doing Ex 1A, you could ask Ss to see if any of their adjectives are used in the sentences or if they can spot any synonyms.

VOCABULARY ADJECTIVES FOR STORIES

1A Brainstorm with Ss what they think are the main differences between spoken and written English. Ask Ss to look at the sentences with a partner and discuss which ones they think come from a conversation and which are from a written text. When getting feedback, ask Ss to give reasons and refer Ss to the ideas you discussed as a class earlier.

Suggested answers:

a conversation: sentences 1, 3, 4 and 7

a written text: sentences 2, 5, 6 and 8 (2 possibly a website of jokes and stories or a book blurb; 5 possibly a website caption for a news or video story; 6 possibly a film advert; 8 possibly a website caption for a news or video story or a book blurb)

B Elicit from Ss some common adjective endings, e.g. *-ing*, *-al*, *-ic*, *-ant*, etc. Then ask Ss to underline the adjectives in each sentence and match them to the definitions. Check the answers as a class.

Answers: **1** incredible **2** inspiring **3** hilarious **4** dramatic **5** remarkable **6** moving, poignant **7** intense

C Choose one of the adjectives and describe a news story and/or a film story that fits that adjective. Ask Ss to do the same in pairs with three of the adjectives.

D Put Ss into small groups and make sure they realise that when they are reading out their descriptions, they should not mention their adjective. The aim is for the group to guess the adjective. Check to see if some groups could not guess the adjective. If not, elicit the description and see if it needs changing.

LISTENING

2A Focus Ss on questions 1–3 and give them a few minutes to read the text about the radio programme. Put them into pairs to compare their answers and then conduct feedback with the whole class.

Suggested answers:

1 It could be about a baby that didn't survive, or a friendship that broke up before the writer had a chance to give the mother the baby shoes.
2 Larry Smith is an online magazine editor who is appearing on *Today* to talk about the six-word stories that people have contributed to his website.
3 It was a story that someone contributed.

B Give Ss time to read the sentences and predict the answers. Play the recording for Ss to check their answers.

Answers: **1** didn't expect **2** very intense about the challenge **3** their own life **4** regret and disappointment **5** tough

Unit 3 Recording 2

I = Interviewer L = Larry Smith

I: In the 1920s, Ernest Hemingway bet ten dollars that he could write a complete story in just six words. He wrote, 'For Sale: baby shoes, never worn.' He won the bet. An American online magazine has now used that to inspire its readers to write their life story in six words and they've been overwhelmed by the thousands who took up the challenge. They've published the best in a book which they've given the title of one of the submissions: *Not Quite What I Was Planning*. I asked the editor, Larry Smith, what made him think of the idea.

L: … so we thought, 'Let's ask our readers their six-word life story, a memoir' and see what happened. We really didn't know what would happen.

I: And what did happen?

L: It was incredible. In a couple of months we got 15,000 entries and I was just blown away. Funny, poignant – I really believe that everyone has a story and I was just so inspired by how serious and intense folks took the six-word memoir challenge.

I: OK, but before we look at the examples. It's one thing … because the Hemingway is a story but it's not a story of a life. That seems to be a bit of a challenge to fit that in six words.

L: Well, it's interesting because some folks clearly tried to tell a whole story of a life in six words, and you can tell, and other times they're telling a moment in their life, right at this moment, something that they're feeling right now. Or perhaps something that's been a thread throughout their lives.

I: Well give us some examples.

L: 'Wasn't born a redhead. Fixed that.' This woman took life under control. Whether she just always felt that her soul was a redheaded soul or simply at some point in life she was going to make a switch. She could have quit her job. She changed her hair colour.

I: But a lot of them are … quite sad or there's a sort of sense of regret or disappointment in a lot of them.

L: I didn't expect that. I thought people would come back with a lot of funny things, some playful things, plays on words … but those are really interesting reality. People really told us, 'It's tough out there.' 'Found true love. Married someone else.' 'Never should have bought that ring.'

C You could start by looking at the example and discussing with the class what happened in the person's life and whether they think it's a story of regret/disappointment or not. Then direct them to the other three stories and play the recording again. NB These stories are in the last part of the recording.

Answers: **1** what I was planning **2** a redhead. Fixed that **3** true love. Married someone else **4** should have bought that ring

D Ask Ss to look back at the adjectives in Ex 1A and to choose one to describe each story. Elicit Ss' choices. Tell Ss to discuss in their pairs what happens in stories 2–4, then to decide which story is the most interesting/the most positive/the saddest.

GRAMMAR *I WISH, IF ONLY*

3A You could do the first one as an example with the class. Vocabulary to check: *era* (period in history) and *gender* (sex).

Suggested answers:
1 when they were born, their social class and their gender
2 their career
3 probably where they ended up living
4 everything – they want another chance
5 their tendency to worry
6 probably a woman who wants to change her husband's behaviour

B Complete the first one with the class and establish that this is something the writer wants very much, but is unlikely to be able to change. Once Ss have matched the sentences, tell them to underline and label the verb forms that come after *I wish* and *If only*.

Answers: a) 4 b) 5 c) 3 d) 6 e) 2 f) 1

C You could write the rules on the board and invite Ss out to complete the gaps.

Answers: 1 a, b 2 c, e, f 3 d

D Ss could look at the sentences first and predict which words are stressed (point out that there are at least two in each sentence).

Answers: NB The main/strongest stress is on the last word in each sentence.
a) I wish I could do it all again.
b) I wish I weren't so anxious.
c) I wish I'd stayed where I was happy.
d) I wish he'd pay more attention to me.
e) If only I hadn't become a doctor.
f) If only I'd been born twenty years later.

Teaching tip

When you want Ss to practise saying a sentence with more than one stressed word in it, you can start by asking them to repeat just the stressed words a couple of times, so they get the rhythm of the sentence. Then they repeat the whole sentence, 'squashing' the unstressed words in between the stressed ones.
Example:
only – twenty – later
If only I'd been born twenty years later.

▷ **LANGUAGEBANK 3.2** p132–133

Ex A provides a useful check of the verb forms before Ss attempt the more challenging practice in Ex 4A. Ex B could be set for homework.

Answers:
A **1** liked **2** 'd hurry up **3** knew **4** 'd brought **5** didn't live **6** 'd met **7** were **8** could
B **1** lived **2** would come, weren't/wasn't wearing **3** knew, 'd remembered **4** wouldn't play/didn't play, 'd slept **5** 'd started **6** wouldn't bite

4A Direct Ss to the example and point out that they can't change the words given for the beginning of the new sentence. Ss can work alone or in pairs, then check with the whole class.

Answers:
1 I had a new laptop
2 I'd grown up in a large family / I hadn't grown up in a small family
3 I were/was more sociable / I weren't/wasn't so unsociable/ antisocial
4 my friend would speak louder/more loudly / my friend wouldn't speak so quietly
5 I could get to sleep earlier/before 2a.m.
6 I didn't lose my temper with people (so often)
7 I had my camera with me
8 I could cook (well/better)
9 it would stop raining
10 I'd spent more time with my grandfather

B You could demonstrate this by telling Ss which sentences you would tick and give an example of how you would change one of the others. Emphasise that Ss should not change the original 'stem' of the sentence. Give Ss a few minutes to work on their sentences alone.

C You could demonstrate this by choosing one student to say one of their sentences and eliciting examples of follow-up questions from the rest of the class.

SPEAKING

5A Tell Ss to discuss each story in turn, first saying what they think happened and then which one is the most powerful and why.

B Look at the first one together and elicit the word that has been left out (I). Then ask Ss to work in pairs to discuss other words left out or included.

Answers:
Writers can shorten their stories in different ways:
- they use only nouns, e.g. Blankets, books, bottles, books, blankets
- leave out 'I', e.g. (I) Love climbing those hills, (I) Found it.

C Write the following topics on the board to help generate ideas: *career, studies, skills, relationships, journeys, family, home, finances, possessions*. Circulate and help Ss with vocabulary that will enable them to 'condense' their ideas.

D Write the story *Wasted my whole life getting comfortable* on the board and elicit some examples of questions that Ss could ask the writer about it, e.g. *How did you get comfortable? What do you wish you'd done instead?* Then put Ss into groups of four to six and suggest that they each write their six-word story on a piece of paper so that everyone in the group can see it.

VOCABULARY PLUS MULTI-WORD VERBS

6A You could do the first part with the whole class. Write the four stories on the board and elicit from Ss where the multi-word verbs are (i.e. verbs with dependent 'particles': adverbs or prepositions). NB Ss will probably be familiar with the term phrasal verb, which is used in several learners' dictionaries. Give Ss a minute or two to match the meanings and compare answers with a partner.

Answers:
Story 1: turned up
Story 2: Gave up, took up
Story 3: Settled down
Story 4: Set up, ran out
a) take up **b)** run out **c)** turn up **d)** set up **e)** settle down **f)** give up

B Before putting Ss into pairs, use a simple example to check that they know what an object is, e.g. write on the board *Ditched the map, found better route* and ask Ss how many objects there are (*the map, better route*). Ss can look at their own monolingual dictionaries here and see how similar/different the *Longman Active Study Dictionary* is.

Answers: **1** run out **2** set up (something) **3** set (something) up **4** run out (of)

speakout TIP

Before Ss read the tip, elicit from them the kind of information that a dictionary gives you about multi-word verbs. Then put them in pairs to look at how the features are shown.

In the *Longman Active Study Dictionary* ...

1 ... if the verb has more than one meaning, these are numbered in bold.
2 ... any examples of language in use are given in italics.
3 ... to show that the verb and particle can be separated by an object, the abbreviation *sth* is put between them and there is a 'two-way' arrow.
4 ... if a verb can be followed by a preposition, this is indicated by a + sign and the preposition in bold.

7A Tell Ss to cover the text and look at the photo. If any of them recognise Maya Angelou, they could tell the class what they know. Otherwise, ask them to imagine what her life was like, what her job was, etc.

B Focus Ss on the four questions before they read the text (tell them not to worry about the verbs in bold at the moment). After Ss have read the text, they could discuss with a partner what they think of Angelou's life.

Answers:
1 No
2 writer, actress, cable car conductor, waitress, cook, singer, dancer, lecturer
3 the arts and politics
4 Suggested answer: She overcame great difficulties as a child and young woman, she did whatever it took to support her family, she achieved a great deal in different fields, particularly the arts and writing, and she had great courage and an appetite for life and expression.

C Remind Ss to use the context to help them work out the meaning of the verbs. Once they have matched the meanings and checked their answers with a partner, Ss could use monolingual dictionaries to check whether the verbs must be used with an object/can be used without an object and whether the verb can be separated from the particle.

Answers: **1** grow up **2** pick up **3** look up to **4** pass away **5** go on **6** go by **7** take on **8** stand for **9** drop out **10** be brought up

SPEAKING

8A You could start by telling a life story yourself, as a model. Point out to Ss that they need to know some details of the person's life in order to make the notes and use the multi-word verbs. If Ss researched a famous person for homework, they can use the information here. Ss should write notes rather than full sentences, so they sound natural when they tell the life story. Circulate and help Ss to use the multi-word verbs from Ex 6A and 7C appropriately.

B Make sure Ss realise that if they are talking about a famous person then they should not name the person as the other Ss have to guess who it is. If it is not a famous person then Ss should ask the person reading the description two follow-up questions.

▷ VOCABULARYBANK p150 Multi-word verbs

Ss decide on the answers to Ex 2A in pairs. Ex 2B could be done as pairwork or small group work. Check the answers as a class before completing the pronouns in Ex 2C.

Answers:
A a) between the main verb (*brought*) and the particle (*up*) or after the particle (*up*)
b) between the main verb (*brought*) and the particle (*up*)
C 1 Kieran wanted the job but they turned *him* down.
2 The shop had some great clothes but the loud music put *her* off.
3 Fifty people wanted to be extras in the film and the director took *them all* on.
4 Señor Almeida isn't here at the moment. Can you ring *him* back?
5 I finished the essay last night and gave *it* in this morning.
6 If I don't know new words, I just look *them* up in my electronic dictionary.
7 The sound of the doorbell at 2a.m. woke *us* up.
8 Is that a new coat? Anyway, take *it* off and hang *it* up here.

Homework ideas

- Ss write their life story from Ex 5C in exactly fifty words OR write the life story they told in Ex 8B.
- **Ex 5A:** Ss write a life story from one of the six-word stories using multi-word verbs.
- Ss bring one of their favourite books and another type of reading material that they like to talk about and use in Lesson 3.3, Ex 1B and Ex 7A.
- **Language bank:** 3.2 Ex A–B, p133
- **Vocabulary bank:** p150
- **Workbook:** Ex 1–6, p20–21

IT'S A GREAT READ!

Introduction

Ss practise speaking about their tastes in reading using phrases for expressing likes and dislikes. They also practise listening and learn to summarise a plot.

SUPPLEMENTARY MATERIALS

Resource bank: p161

Ex 1B: bring in a couple of examples of things you like to read.

Ex 7A: be prepared to tell Ss about the plot of a book you like and explain why they should read it.

Warm up

Tell Ss to cover Ex 1 and focus them on the photos. Ask them what types of reading material they can see, which ones they are familiar with, which appeal/don't appeal to them and why.

VOCABULARY READING GENRES

1A Do question 1 together as an example then put Ss into pairs. They can use monolingual dictionaries if necessary. Make sure Ss realise that the words can appear in more than one category.

Suggested answers:
1 blog, tweet, social media update, Wikipedia, website forum, online article
2 lyrics, poetry
3 blog, gossip magazine, biography, autobiography, blockbuster
4 biography, autobiography, manual, Wikipedia, website forum, online article
5 gossip magazine, manga, manual
6 novel, manga, blockbuster

B Demonstrate this by telling the class about things you like reading and showing them the reading material you've brought in. If Ss have brought their own reading materials, they can show them to their partner here. Note down any phrases Ss use to say why they like the material. Ask Ss to rewrite and improve these examples after Ex 5B.

2 Give Ss time to discuss the questions, then feed back as a class.

FUNCTION EXPRESSING LIKES AND DISLIKES

3A Ss can discuss what kind of books they are, where/when they're set, when they were published, etc.

B Suggest that Ss copy the table into their notebooks so they have more room to make notes in Ex 3C.

Answers:
The Hunger Games: Amy –; Beth ✓
The Kite Runner: Amy –; Carl ✓
Life of Pi: Amy –; Beth ✓; Carl ✗
Amy decides to take *The Hunger Games*.

Unit 3 Recording 4

C = Carl A = Amy B = Beth

C: So Amy, what time's your flight?
A: Oh it's at one.
C: Right.
A: It's really long as well about twelve hours.
C: Oh.
A: Listen I'm gonna need something to read I reckon, I need a good book. Have you got any ideas?
B: Yeah, actually yeah, you know *The Hunger Games*, have you ever read that?
A: No I don't think so.
B: Yeah, no it's really good, yeah, it sort of describes like this society in the future, you know about the government taking over and making these kids do a TV show, where they have to basically kill each other.
A: Ooh.
B: Yeah.
A: That sounds a bit violent for me.
B: Yeah it, yeah it is but it raises all sorts of you know really interesting questions about society. And the power of TV. I thought it was really great. I mean I'm a big fan of sci-fi novels anyway. But what I really liked about it was the main character, the girl.
A: Is that the one that's um played by Jennifer Lawrence in the film?
B: Yes, yeah, yeah, yeah and yeah I really like that character 'cos she's, you know, she's very brave and she's a survivor and she sort of stands for what she believes in and yeah I love her.
A: Yeah, no, it does sound quite good, but I don't really like sci-fi that much to be honest so, I don't think that's …
C: OK what about … ?
A: What else?
C: Can I suggest something else?
A: Yeah, yeah.
C: What about *The Kite Runner*, have you read that?
A: No I haven't actually.
C: Oh it's wonderful …
A: All right.
C: … it's just, it's a really moving story about two boys in Afghanistan and …
A: Oh, yes, yes, yes and doesn't one of them save someone's life or something?
C: Yes, I mean it goes through the years and it's so wonderful it really, I, I loved it. And the thing I love about it is the way it builds the whole story, you know and, and you get so involved with these characters that you, you just have to know what's gonna happen next.
B: Actually speaking of getting involved in characters, I really love *Life of Pi*, have you ever read that?
A: I've heard of it, but isn't that a bit weird, it's a bit of weird one isn't it about a …
B: Oh no I really enjoyed it.
A: … boy and a tiger in a boat or something but …
B: Yeah it's, it's very sort of, I think it has a deep and meaningful story behind it and I really like getting to know him and the fact that he loves these, you know this tiger and it is very fantasy.
A: It's not comedy then?
B: No, no.
C: No. I mean I did start it but I just I couldn't get into it I'm afraid.
A: I know it sounds …
C: I mean I can't stand books that sort of preach at you. And it felt to me that it was doing that, I …
A: Yeah.
C: … made me uncomfortable.
B: Yes.
A: Sounds a bit serious to me to be honest for a twelve-hour plane journey.
C: I'm not sure we've given any choices that have many laughs …
B: Yeah.
C: … to be honest have we?
B: No.
A: I don't know.
C: But actually there's a lot of warmth in *Kite Runner*, that's what I would say I mean. It's worth, worth trying you know, to stick with it.
A: Yeah – do you know what I think, no I think I might try *The Hunger Games* actually …
B: Yes!
A: … 'cos I think I've seen the trailer of the film and I, yeah it looks quite interesting.

C Emphasise that Ss only need to write notes, e.g. a couple of words or a phrase. Give them time to compare answers with a partner and help each other.

Answers:
1 *The Hunger Games*
Amy – a bit violent; doesn't like sci-fi so maybe not; it looks interesting (she's seen the trailer)
Beth ✓ good; raises interesting questions about society and the power of TV; likes/loves the main character – a survivor who stands for what she believes in
2 *The Kite Runner*
Amy – knows a little bit about the story – thinks one person saves someone else's life
Carl ✓ wonderful; a moving story; loves the way it builds the whole story; you get involved with the characters; you have to know what happens next
3 *Life of Pi*
Amy – a bit weird; about a boy and a tiger in a boat; sounds a bit serious for twelve-hour journey
Beth ✓ has a deep and meaningful story; likes getting to know the boy and the fact he loves the tiger
Carl ✗ started it but couldn't get into it; can't stand books that preach at him; made him feel uncomfortable

D Ss discuss their choices then share their ideas as a class and find out which is the most popular choice.

4A Ss should write the correct sentences in their notebooks so they can refer to them in the next two stages.

Answers:
1 I'm a big fan of sci-fi novels anyway.
2 What I really liked about it was the main character.
3 I don't really like sci-fi that much to be honest.
4 The thing I love about it is the way it builds the whole story.
5 I just couldn't get into it.
6 I can't stand books that sort of preach at you.

B Give Ss time to analyse the phrases in pairs, then conduct feedback with the whole class.

Answers:
1 I don't really like … that much.; I just couldn't get into it.; I can't stand …
2 The word order is different – it starts with *What I* + verb + *be* + key information to emphasise the main character.
3 The word order is different – it starts with *The thing I* + verb + *be* + key information to emphasise the way it builds the whole story.
4 1 I'm not a big fan of …
2 What I really hated/didn't like/liked least about it was …
3 I really like …
4 I thing I hate about it is the way it …
5 I really got into it.
6 I love/really like books that …

C Point out that several of the sentences have more than one main stress and remind Ss to look for the words that carry the meaning of the sentence. Play the recording, stopping after each sentence for Ss to check and repeat. Encourage Ss to use the stresses to help them sound convincingly positive or negative when they repeat the sentences.

Answers:
1 I'm a big fan of sci-fi novels anyway.
2 What I really liked about it was the main character.
3 I don't really like sci-fi that much to be honest.
4 The thing I love about it is the way it builds the whole story.
5 I just couldn't get into it.
6 I can't stand books that sort of preach at you.

5A Go through the example with the class, showing them that the words in brackets have been used unchanged and that the meaning of the new sentence is the same as the original. Ss work alone on the transformations.

Answers:
1 What I liked about *Atonement* were the characters.
2 I can't stand reading on my tablet (because it hurts my eyes).
3 I don't like (reading) detective stories that much.
4 I'm not really into blockbusters such as the *Bourne* series.
5 The thing I like about *Twelve Years a Slave* is the way it teaches you about history.
6 What I like best about Agatha Christie books are the plots.
7 I'm a big fan of Stieg Larsson.

B If you and Ss have brought in examples of favourite reading material, display these at the front of the class to prompt ideas. Give Ss time to write their sentences.

C Depending on your class size, you could do this task by a class vote and discussion or put Ss into smaller groups to discuss their ideas. Give Ss time to compare the different genres. Elicit their responses.

▷ **LANGUAGEBANK 3.3** p132–133

Show the class that the phrases are summarised in a table.

Answers:
1 I don't like opera *that much*.
2 I can't stand ~~on~~ depressing books like that one.
3 The thing I liked about it most ~~it~~ was the surprise ending.
4 *What* I love about Lee's films is that there's always a message.
5 I'm a big fan *of* historical novels.
6 What I like *about* her acting is that she brings something special to every role.
7 I *can't* get into classical music.
8 *The thing that* I hate about graffiti is that it's just ugly. / *What* I hate about graffiti is that it's just ugly.

LEARN TO SUMMARISE A PLOT

6A Ask Ss if any of them have read or heard of *Gone Girl*. Then tell them to read the summary and try to predict the missing words before they listen to the recording. In pairs, Ss discuss whether they would like to read the book or not. Elicit some reasons from Ss.

B Play the recording and ask Ss to complete the gaps. Check the answers as class.

Answers: **1** returns **2** finds **3** has disappeared **4** invade **5** decide **6** isn't **7** progresses **8** are forced **9** emerges

C Tell Ss to look through the summary at all the verbs that were missing and decide what they have in common. Direct them to questions 1–3.

Answers:
1 the present simple (sometimes in the passive) NB The present perfect could also be used.
2 Using present verb forms makes the plot more immediate, as if the reader/listener is experiencing as they read/listen.

SPEAKING

7A You could start by telling Ss about a book you like or a film you like that is adapted from a book. If Ss have brought in a favourite book, tell them to make notes about it and think about how to use it to illustrate what they're saying, e.g. to show the other Ss the main characters or the setting on the front cover. Give Ss some suggestions for phrases they can use, e.g.

1 *Has anyone read/heard of … by … ?*
2 *It's a thriller/romance/historical novel set in … (time/place). It's about … who …*
3 *The thing I really … / What I … / I'm really into …*
4 *I recommend it to anyone who … / You should definitely read it if you're a fan of …*

B Put Ss into small groups of three to five and tell them that their aim is to persuade the others to read their book.

Homework ideas

- Ss write an email to a friend recommending a book.
- **Language bank:** 3.3 Ex A, p133
- **Workbook:** Ex 1–3, p22

TESS

Introduction

Ss watch an extract from the BBC's serialisation of *Tess of the D'Urbervilles*, where Angel Clare carries Tess and her companions across a flooded path on the way to church. Ss then learn and practise how to describe and write about a favourite TV/film moment.

Warm up

Lead into the topic by brainstorming types of film and TV programme. Write them in two columns on the board, then put Ss into pairs to discuss which ones they like/don't like and why. Remind Ss of the phrases for describing likes and dislikes in the previous lesson.

Examples of films: *thriller, romance, comedy, costume/historical drama, action, science fiction*

Examples of TV programmes: *comedy series, soap opera, costume drama, documentary, reality show*

DVD PREVIEW

1 Direct Ss to the questions. Check that Ss understand that *set* (usually in the passive) refers to the place where (or time when) the story happens. Give Ss a minute or two to read the programme information and answer the questions.

Answers:
1 in rural Wessex, a semi-fictional area
2 They're all dairymaids and they're all in love with Angel Clare.
3 and **4** Students' predictions
5 No, because it's a 'tragic' story.

DVD VIEW

2A You could play the extract with no sound for the first viewing. Ss can tell quite a lot about how the women are feeling from their expressions and reactions (they could add some adjectives of their own, e.g. *jealous, agitated, contented*, etc.). Vocabulary to check: *eager* (wanting very much to do or have something), *thrilled* (pleased and excited) and *awkward* (embarrassed).

You could also ask Ss to imagine what each person is saying at certain points of the extracts and make a note of their predictions to compare with the dialogue when they watch the extract with sound.

Answers: **1** eager, pleased **2** nervous, awkward **3** excited, disappointed **4** anxious, happy

B Give Ss time to look through the quotes before you play the DVD again. You may need to play the extract a third time for Ss to confirm/change any answers they're unsure of.

Answers:
1 Tess. She means there's no need to be nervous about being carried by Angel.
2 Angel. He's commenting on the fact that Retty is much smaller and lighter than Marian.
3 Izzy. She wants to kiss Angel and asks Tess if she'd mind (because Tess is his 'favourite').
4 Angel. He's carried the other three women just so he can spend a few moments with Tess.
5 Angel. He means that he didn't expect to have this moment with Tess, not that he didn't expect the road to flood (as Tess suggests).

DVD 3 Tess of the D'Urbervilles

I = Izzy **M** = Marian **AC** = Angel Clare **R** = Retty **T** = Tess

I: We can't get there without walking through it.
M: That's that then, I'm going back to bed.
I: Marian, get back here, now.
AC: Good morning ladies, and how lovely you all look. Now I see the problem. Perhaps I can be of assistance. Who's first?
I: First for what, sir?
AC: I'll carry you across the water.
Don't go away.
R: I'm supposed to put my arms around his neck and put my face against his and feel his arms around me and put my face against his … I don't think I can.
T: There's nothing in it, Retty.
R: That's what you say. I think I'm going to burst.
M: Thank you, Mr Clare.
AC: Retty, a nice easy one this time.
I: I'm going to kiss him. I don't care what happens, I'm going to kiss him. You wouldn't mind would you if I tried? I know that you're his favourite and all.
T: Izzy.
I: But I've got to try, haven't I? I might never get another chance. How do I look? Do I look pretty? Tell me, Tess.
T: Very pretty, Iz.
I: Here I go. Wish me luck.
AC: What are you doing?
T: I think I can climb along the bank after all.
AC: Tess, no!
T: Really I'm quite all right.
AC: Tess!
T: And you must be so tired.
AC: I've undergone three quarters of the labour just for this moment.
T: They are much better women than I, all of them.
AC: Not to me.
T: I'm not too heavy?
AC: Compared to Marian you're like gossamer; you're a billow warmed by the sun.
T: That's very pretty, I seem like that to you.
AC: I didn't expect an event like this today.
T: Nor I. The water came up so quickly.
AC: That's not what I meant, at all.
Ladies.
M: Come on, we'll be late.
I: I was sure he was going to kiss me.

C Give Ss a few minutes to discuss the questions, then invite them to share their opinions with the class.

Suggested answers: Escapism: many people are fascinated by seeing how people lived in an apparently simpler and less stressful world, with wide divisions between gender roles and rich/poor, but without modern conveniences, technical and medical advances, etc. For many, the fascination is the costumes themselves: how attractive they make people look, how difficult they'd be to wear, etc.

speakout a favourite scene

3A If any Ss are familiar with *Fawlty Towers*, you could ask them to explain to the class what kind of programme it is, who the main characters are, etc. Otherwise, direct Ss to the questions and play the recording.

Answers:
1 Mrs Richards, an elderly female guest who complains a lot and is deaf.
2 Basil pretends to talk to Mrs Richards but he's miming, so she turns her hearing aid up. This happens twice and when it's at full volume he shouts at her and it's very loud.

Unit 3 Recording 7

Fawlty Towers. I absolutely love *Fawlty Towers*, I've seen this hundreds of times and it's my absolute favourite. It always makes me laugh – in fact, it makes me cry with laughter sometimes … can't get enough of it. And the main character, Basil Fawlty, played by John Cleese, is absolutely brilliant. It's like a lesson in comic acting; the more bad things that happen to this man the more we laugh.

My favourite scene is the scene with Mrs Richards and Basil Fawlty. And, it's very, very cleverly done. Mrs Richards wears a hearing aid and Basil Fawlty hates Mrs Richards – she's a terrible, grumpy, old, complaining customer who he really doesn't like. So he comes into the room and he mimes at her – so he moves his mouth but he doesn't make any sound – so that Mrs Richards turns up her hearing aid so that she can hear him.

And then he mimes again and he moves his mouth again not making any sound so she can't understand why she can't hear him, so she turns up her hearing aid again. And then once he's sure that her hearing aid is on full volume he shouts at her, 'Mrs Richards!' – of course which deafens her and, it's, it's, it's very, very funny and it's amazing because he gets his own back on her 'cos she's been awful to him, so, he, you know, he kind of wins in the end but, –

Oh it's just brilliant. If you've never seen it, you really should see it. There were very few episodes made. I think there were only – only ever one series, maybe eight episodes … something like that … I'm not entirely sure about that, but not very many made and, they're – they're really, really fantastic. Every one is absolutely priceless.

Optional extra activity

For ***weaker Ss*** who might struggle to understand exactly what happened, write the following on pieces of A4 paper and stick them on the board in the wrong order (or put them on slips of paper and give each pair of Ss a set).

Ss listen again and decide on the correct order:
- *Mrs Richards makes Basil Fawlty dislike her by being grumpy and complaining a lot.*
- *Basil goes into her room.*
- *He pretends to speak to her but he's miming.*
- *She thinks her hearing aid is turned down, so she turns it up.*
- *Basil mimes again.*
- *She turns her hearing aid up to full volume.*
- *Basil shouts at her.*

B First, go through the key phrases with the class and check the following: *absolute* is used for emphasis (it could also be for a negative opinion, e.g. *an absolute disaster*) and *send shivers up sb's spine*. Point out that where there are options in the phrases (e.g. *It always [makes me laugh/cry/sends shivers up my spine].*), Ss need to underline the option(s) they hear.

Answers: I've seen this (X) times and …; It's my absolute favourite.; It always [makes me laugh/cry/sends shivers up my spine].; It's like a lesson in [comic acting/timing/directing].; My favourite scene is [the one where/the scene with …]; It's very cleverly done.; If you've never seen it, you really should.

Optional extra activity

To give Ss more alternatives for the key phrases and more practice, write the following words on the board and ask Ss to decide which of the key phrases they fit into: *many, creatively, imaginatively, loads of, beautifully, lots of, one.*

Do some substitution drills by prompting Ss to change one word in the phrase when they repeat it, e.g.

T: *It's very cleverly done.*
Ss: *It's very cleverly done.*
T: *Creatively.*
Ss: *It's very creatively done.*

C Ss should only write notes for this so that they sound more natural when they're talking. Also, remind them to use the present tense to describe what happens and the present perfect if they need to explain what happened before that moment. Circulate and help as necessary.

D Encourage Ss to listen 'actively' while their partner is speaking, e.g. by saying *Uhuh, Yeah, Really? Oh no!* Ss could also work in groups of four to six to talk about their favourite moments, then decide which they'd most like to see of the other moments they heard about. Monitor the activity and note examples of good language use and problem areas to deal with in feedback.

writeback a description of a scene

4A Give Ss a minute or two to read the extract and complete the missing words. NB The film in English is called *Jaws* and not *Shark*, as it is in some languages.

Answers: Jaws, shark

B While Ss are writing, circulate and provide vocabulary, etc. but don't correct their work at this stage.

C You could either get Ss to swap their descriptions with a partner, or collect them in and stick them on the wall for Ss to walk round and read.

Homework ideas

- Ss could explore the BBC website for *Tess of the D'Urbervilles* (www.bbc.co.uk/tess (correct at the time of going to press)) and report back to the class.
- **Ex 4B:** Ss write a second, final draft of their description, having first checked it for accuracy.

LOOKBACK

Introduction

The aim of these activities is to provide revision and further practice of the language from the unit. You can also use them to assess Ss' ability to use the language, in which case you need to monitor but avoid helping them. You may feel that you don't need or have time to do all the activities. If so, you could allocate the activities that would be most beneficial for your Ss, or get individual Ss to decide which activities they'd like to do.

NARRATIVE TENSES

1A Start by asking Ss to read the text quickly and answer the question: *Does the man spend more time working on his house or his garden?* (his garden). Vocabulary to check: *keep yourself to yourself* (be private), *fall apart* (be in very bad condition) and *collapse* (fall down suddenly). Then Ss can work alone or with a partner to complete the gaps. You could also refer them to the Language bank on p132 to check the rules for narrative tenses.

Answers: **1** was **2** 'd lived/'d been living **3** was falling **4** hadn't painted **5** looked **6** walked **7** was always working **8** always said **9** was coming **10** 'd never walked **11** looked **12** saw **13** was watching **14** 'd been watching **15** came

B Give Ss a few minutes in pairs to brainstorm possible endings, then to write the one they like best. You could make this more challenging by giving them a specific number of words to use (e.g. thirty) or by telling them to include three different narrative tenses. Ss can read out their endings and the class votes on the best one.

SAYINGS

2A You could run this as a board race. Tell Ss to close their books and put them into two or three teams. Write the pairs of prompts on the board one at a time. One student from each team runs up to the board and tries to write the saying in full. Award a team point to the first student to write the saying accurately.

Answers:
1 Nothing ventured, nothing gained.
2 When in Rome do as the Romans do.
3 Once bitten, twice shy.
4 What goes around comes around.
5 Every cloud has a silver lining.

B Ss work alone on paraphrasing three sayings. Circulate and check that they don't use any of the words from the original sayings.

C Ss can work in pairs or small groups for this.

ADJECTIVES FOR STORIES

3A Ss work alone or with a partner to complete the stories.

Answers: **1** dramatic, intense, remarkable **2** hilarious, incredible **3** poignant, moving, inspiring

B Ss discuss which one they would most like to listen to. Elicit reasons for Ss' choices.

I WISH, IF ONLY

4A Do the first one as an example, then tell Ss to write the rest of the sentences in their notebooks. Point out that they need to think carefully about which other words to change in the original sentence.

Answers:
1 I had travelled more when I was younger.
2 my friends would really listen to me.
3 my partner liked the same kinds of music as me. (*would like* is wrong here because it's a state verb)
4 I had finished university.
5 would thank me for things/sometimes.
6 I could afford a new car.

B You could tell Ss to write their wish list on a separate piece of paper, so that they can pass it on to another student (see suggestion in Ex 4C below). Topics for Ss to use in their 'wish list' could be: studies, childhood, jobs, travel, family, friends, relationships, hobbies, appearance, health, etc.

C You could demonstrate this using two ***strong Ss*** in an open pair. Alternatively, for more written practice, you could collect in Ss' wish lists and redistribute them for another student to complete. Ss then have to guess whose wish list they were given.

EXPRESSING LIKES AND DISLIKES

5A You could run this as a competition. Tell Ss to close their books and put them into teams of three to five. Write the words in the box on the board, then display the sentences one at a time. Teams confer and put their hands up when they have an answer and you award points for correct answers. You could award extra points if Ss can finish the phrase convincingly.

Answers: **1** What **2** that **3** thing **4** get **5** fan **6** stand

B Ss should limit themselves to 8–10 items otherwise this activity will last too long. Encourage Ss to have at least three for each.

C You could start by giving an example of your own as a model for Ss. Write one book, film and band you know on the board. Use one of the expressions from Ex 5A to describe how you feel about one of them. Ask Ss to guess which one you are describing. Set the task for Ss.

6A If Ss were in teams for Ex 5A, they could continue to win points by putting the phrases into the past.

B You could start by giving an example of your own as a model for Ss. Tell them the name of the programme, what type of programme it was, what you liked/disliked, what other people in your family thought of it, etc. Emphasise that Ss should write notes rather than full sentences, so they sound more natural when they're speaking.

C Monitor this practice and make notes of good language use and areas for remedial work. In feedback, invite a few Ss to report back about their partner's TV programme, then give Ss some examples of their good use of language and errors for them to discuss and correct.

BBC interviews and worksheet

What was the last book you read?

This video looks at the topic of what people like reading.

OVERVIEW

4.1 OUT OF TIME

VOCABULARY | free time
READING | read about how our free time is changing
GRAMMAR | present and past habits
PRONUNCIATION | connected speech: contractions
SPEAKING | discuss how you use your time
WRITING | write an opinion essay; learn to use linkers

4.2 GREAT GETAWAYS

VOCABULARY | positive adjectives
PRONUNCIATION | word stress
LISTENING | listen to people talk about holidays
GRAMMAR | future forms
PRONUNCIATION | connected speech
SPEAKING | plan an alternative holiday
VOCABULARY *PLUS* | uncountable and plural nouns

4.3 HOW DOES IT WORK?

VOCABULARY | abilities
FUNCTION | describing procedures
LEARN TO | use mirror questions
PRONUNCIATION | stress and intonation: mirror questions
SPEAKING | describe procedures

4.4 THE HAPPINESS FORMULA BBC DVD

DVD | watch a BBC programme about happiness
speakout | a happiness survey
writeback | tips for being happy

4.5 LOOKBACK

Communicative revision activities

BBC INTERVIEWS

What's the perfect way to switch off?

This video looks at the topic of how we use our leisure time and explores the different things we might do in order to relax. Use this video at the start or end of Unit 4 or set it as homework.

OUT OF TIME

Introduction

Ss practise reading and speaking about present and past habits, using *used to*, *would*, frequency adverbs and *will*. They also learn how to use linkers in an opinion essay.

SUPPLEMENTARY MATERIALS

Ex 8B and **Ex 8C:** prepare copies of the opinion essay with the bold phrases blanked out.

Warm up

Lead into the topic by getting Ss to brainstorm the different things they spend their time doing in a week. Put Ss into small groups and ask them to discuss which ones they would like to spend more time on and which ones they would like to spend less time on. Elicit examples and reasons from the class. Draw a scale from 1 to 10 on the board. Next to 1 write: *I have lots of time and I'm very relaxed.* Next to 10 write: *I have no time and I'm really stressed.* Ask Ss to rate themselves on the scale and to compare it with a partner.

Teaching tip

Brainstorming involves getting Ss to think of as many examples/ideas as they can on a chosen topic, within a short time. Ss can work as a class, calling out ideas to be written on the board, or in pairs/small groups. It can be used as a warm up for a lesson, or to lead into an activity and can help you to assess Ss' knowledge of a specific area, e.g. vocabulary related to a particular topic.

VOCABULARY FREE TIME

1 If you didn't do the Warm up, you can give Ss a few minutes to discuss the questions in pairs or small groups. Alternatively, integrate these questions into the Warm up.

2A This section focuses Ss on verbs with multiple meanings. Do the first task with the whole class by asking them to match the verbs to a noun and then explain the meaning.

Answers: wind up an old clock, switch off a phone, focus on someone's face, recharge a phone, chill a drink

B Ss complete these sentences individually. Check the answers as a class.

Answers: **1** recharge **2** wind up **3** switch off **4** Chill **5** focus (your camera) on

C Explain that these verbs all can also have an informal or idiomatic meaning. Ask Ss to cover the definitions and to try to explain any of the idiomatic meanings they know (many will probably know *chill*). Ask Ss to match the verbs to their meanings. Check the answers as a class.

Answers: **1** chill (out) **2** focus on **3** recharge **4** wind up **5** switch off

D Books closed. Write these words on the board: *boring people*, *summer holiday*, *lazy Saturday*. Ask Ss which verbs could be used with these. Books open. Ask Ss to complete the sentences and check together.

Answers: **1** switch off **2** winds (me) up **3** recharge **4** chill (out) **5** focus on

E Ask Ss to discuss their opinions of the statements in Ex 2D.

READING

3A Ask Ss to read the headline and to predict the topics they think will be covered. Find out if Ss think they have more or less free time than their parents' generation and why.

B Ss quickly read the article and check their predictions. Ask Ss to look at the rankings in the article. In pairs, Ss should discuss whether these would be the same in their country. Elicit some examples from Ss where they think the statistics might be different in their country.

Answers: The article mentions shopping, the internet, housework and television.

C Ask Ss to read the article again to find support for these statements. This type of task is useful for opinion-based essays, and many exams, such as IELTS, contain these question types. Check the answers as a class.

Answers:
1 Not supported. The article doesn't say that people have less free time, only that they think they do.
2 Supported. 'go online in any location'
3 Not supported. The article says people spend more time watching TV than listening to music but doesn't mention any preference for these two activities.
4 Supported. 'Spending time on the internet ranked 4th in the 16–44 age range, but much lower among the 45-plus group.'
5 Not supported. The article doesn't mention attitudes towards work.
6 Not supported. The article doesn't mention internet use in relation to enjoyment.

4A Ask Ss to read the opinions and to discuss with a partner whether they agree or disagree with these statements. Next ask Ss to predict two things each expert might say on the topic. Elicit some predictions but do not confirm answers.

B Ask Student As to look on p159 to check their predictions and Student Bs to look on p160.

C Ss can work in pairs to discuss the questions and share the information they read. With ***weaker Ss*** it might be better to place them in groups of four. As they do this task, ask Ss to close their books, otherwise many have a tendency to simply read out loud.

Suggested answers:
Student A (Sandra McCullough)
1 People no longer know how to do nothing; they always want to be occupied in some way, therefore are drawn to the internet even when they would have real free time.
Student B (Gerald van Halen)
1 We define free-time activities differently now, and generalise a bit too much, considering for example all computer-based activities to be bad. Gerald thinks that if the activity is shared, it's good, even if it's an online game.

GRAMMAR PRESENT AND PAST HABITS

5A Elicit the parts of language to underline then put Ss into pairs to discuss the differences in meaning. For ***stronger classes*** you could write the phrases on the board and ask Ss to discuss the differences in meaning.

Answers: **1** used to have **2** would sit **3** are … always talking **4** 'll … play **5** usually watch

B Ask Ss to look at the rules and underline the correct alternative.

Answers: **a)** happened regularly in the past but not now **b)** activities **c)** simple, simple **d)** repeated, annoying **e)** activities, present

C This task looks at simple contractions in connected speech. With ***stronger Ss*** simply play the whole recording, with ***weaker Ss*** pause after each one. Check the answers as a class. Play the recording again and ask Ss to repeat the sentences.

Answers: **1** 'd **2** PS **3** 'll **4** PS **5** PS **6** 'd **7** 'll **8** PS

Unit 4 Recording 1

1 We'd sit around and watch TV.
2 We sit around and watch TV.
3 I'll make a coffee and check my email.
4 I make my coffee and check my email.
5 They play computer games.
6 They'd play computer games.
7 I'll phone her first thing every day.
8 I phone her first thing every day.

▷ LANGUAGEBANK 4.1 p134–135

Give Ss a few minutes to read through the rules and examples and ask you any questions. Ex A and B can be set for homework. Alternatively, you could see how well Ss do in the next stage (Ex 6A) and use one or both of them in class for further practice if needed.

Answers:
A **1** used to **2** 's always **3** 'd/used to **4** use to, always **5** 'd/used to **6** 'll/always, 'll **7** were always, 'd/used to **8** will
B **1** Mike is always coming up behind people and looking over their shoulders.
2 Where did you use to live?
3 I'm quite a spontaneous person and will often start conversations with strangers.
4 Pollution didn't use to be a rural problem, only an urban one.
5 In the 1960s the authorities would keep track of all their citizens' movements.
6 Peggy was always borrowing money and never paying it back.

6A Do the first one as an example, then Ss work alone on the rest. Use the Teaching tip to highlight some common errors.

Answers: **1** used **2** 'll **3** always **4** use **5** 'd
6 always/usually/normally/generally/typically – or any relevant frequency adverb **7** 'll **8** would **9** 'll
10 always/usually/normally/generally/typically – or any relevant frequency adverb

Teaching tip

1 Ss may assume that *used to* has a present form and say, e.g. *I use to play video games in the evening*. Point out that for present habits they need to use an adverb of frequency or *tend to*: *I often/tend to play video games in the evening.*
2 Ss may get confused between *would* for past habits and *would* in hypothetical statements, e.g. *During the holidays I'd play video games all day* and *I'd play video games all day if I could.* It's important to give examples in clear contexts so Ss can see the difference.

B Before putting Ss into groups, you could tell them to add two more sentences with their own reactions and comments. Circulate and help while Ss write these sentences. Then put Ss into groups of three or four to discuss the sentences.

SPEAKING

7A Ask Ss to look at the pie chart and to tell you what the person spends most and least time doing. Then ask Ss to discuss the three questions in pairs.

Answers: 1 and **2** Ss might comment on the man's time spent on work and social media being high, and the low amount of time spent with his son and in leisure activities with people.

B Ask Ss to draw their own pie chart for an average weekday. Before they start you might want to brainstorm other activities Ss do that are not in the example.

C Once Ss have drawn their pie charts, ask them to discuss the three questions in groups. Ask Ss to reflect on whether they think they have a balanced day or not.

WRITING AN OPINION ESSAY; LEARN TO USE LINKERS

8A Give Ss a few minutes to discuss the questions and make notes of their answers for feedback.

Suggested answers:
Possible 'meaningful' activities: fitness-related – sports, gym, exercise class, etc.; talking to friends; reading; volunteering; performance-related – acting, singing, dancing, etc.
Possible 'meaningless' activities: watching TV/DVDs/films; playing computer games; listening to music; texting; social networking; shopping

Optional extra activity

Tell Ss to close their books and give them a copy of the essay with the bold phrases blanked out. They will still be able to understand the overall meaning of the essay and decide if they agree with the writer, as in Ex 8B. Then ask Ss to think of some possible words/phrases to complete the gaps. This will help them to identify the purpose of each paragraph, as in Ex 8C. Finally, put the missing phrases on the board (in the wrong order) for them to compare with their own ideas and complete the gaps.

B After Ss have read the essay, put them into pairs to discuss which of the writer's points they agree/disagree with. Also ask them to comment on the style of the essay and establish that it is formal.

C Look at the first paragraph with the class and establish that the writer is introducing the topic and giving his/her point of view. Then give Ss a few minutes to discuss the other three paragraphs.

Answers:
Paragraph 1: introduces the topic and gives the writer's point of view
Paragraph 2: develops one side of the argument, giving examples of meaningless activities
Paragraph 3: develops the other side of the argument, giving examples of meaningful activities
Paragraph 4: gives a conclusion or summary and repeats the writer's point of view

D Ss can work alone or with a partner.

Answers: It seems to me that ...; I agree that ...; I feel that ...

9A While Ss are completing the table, copy it onto the board, so you can add all the phrases to it during this stage and the next one.

Answers: See answers to Ex 9B.

B You could do this with the whole class, inviting Ss up to the board to write the phrases in the correct column. Make sure Ss notice which linking words or phrases are followed by a comma.

Answers:

firstly to start with in the first place	furthermore in addition to this moreover	to conclude in conclusion to sum up
in contrast at the same time as opposed to this	for example for instance as an example	this shows this supports the view this proves

10A While Ss are making notes, be on hand to help with queries, e.g. about vocabulary.

B Group Ss who made notes on the same title together and give them time to exchange ideas and examples.

C Ss may not be used to the idea of writing a plan, so you could do an example on the board for the essay in Ex 8B, e.g. with notes and ideas for each paragraph. You could direct Ss to the speakout tip before they write their plan.

speakout TIP

Before you direct Ss to the tip, ask them how the opinion essay they read was organised, i.e. how many paragraphs there were and what the purpose was of each one. Then Ss can compare what they remembered with the information in the tip.

D Give Ss plenty of time to write their essay and check it. They could do this as homework if you don't have time in class. Remind Ss about the correction code from Unit 1 (p10). If there is time in class, Ss could also check their partner's essay.

Homework ideas

- **Ex 10A:** Ss choose another title and write the essay.
- **Language bank:** 4.1 Ex A–B, p135
- **Workbook:** Ex 1–6, p23–24

GREAT GETAWAYS

Introduction

Ss practise listening and speaking about alternative holidays using future forms and positive adjectives. They also learn to use uncountable and plural nouns.

SUPPLEMENTARY MATERIALS
Resource bank: p162, p164 and p165
Warm up: bring a selection of holiday brochures.
Ex 8C: bring monolingual dictionaries for Ss to use.

Warm up

If possible, bring in a few holiday brochures from your local travel agent (you only need to use the photos from these to generate ideas for holidays, so they don't need to be in English).

Either: Elicit types of holiday and write them on the board, e.g. *camping/skiing/walking/sailing/working/city/beach/flydrive/luxury/spa holiday*. Then put Ss into small groups to categorise the holidays according to criteria such as: *cheap/expensive, boring/interesting, stressful/relaxing*.

Or (if you have more time): Put the following prompts on the board: *Location? When? How long? Activities? What to take?* and give Ss a few minutes alone to imagine they have booked a holiday, answering the prompts. Then tell Ss they have a spare ticket for the holiday and they should try to persuade their partner to go with them. Their partner will need to give up their own planned holiday if they decide to go, so they will both need to be very persuasive! After a few minutes, conduct brief feedback to see who was persuaded. NB This activity should allow you to assess Ss' use of future forms. You could make notes of examples of good use of the forms and mistakes to use for discussion and correction after Ex 4D.

VOCABULARY POSITIVE ADJECTIVES

1A Ask Ss to write down the last place they went on holiday and three activities they did. Put Ss into pairs to tell each other whether they enjoyed the holiday or not. Lastly, get Ss to discuss how they found the holiday, why they chose it and whether they would go on holiday there again or not.

B Direct Ss to the photos and ask them if these are types of holidays they would enjoy. Give Ss a minute or two to answer the questions and then check as a class.

Answers:
1 Help out at a festival, Volunteer on a farm
2 Sail in the sun, Top 10 language holidays

2A Once Ss have underlined the adjectives and circled the nouns ask them whether they can think of any other collocations to describe places using these words. Elicit any examples from Ss.

Answers: classic destinations, delightful city, significant progress, breathtaking views, perfect opportunity, exceptional results, superb locations, stunning locations

speakout TIP

If you used the suggestion in Ex 2A to think of additional qualifications, you could then move on to talk about collocations that do not work. In ***monolingual classes***, you might want to share some of the typical mistakes Ss make with these collocations based on translation.

B This task shows Ss a number of common adjective-noun collocations. As an extension, you could ask Ss to translate these into their own language. Ask Ss whether these collocations translate directly into their own language or if a different collocation is used.

Answers: **1** perfect **2** classic **3** exceptional **4** delightful **5** significant **6** breathtaking, superb, stunning

C Ask Ss to match the adjectives to the stress patterns. In pairs, Ss should compare their answers before listening to the recording to check. Play the recording again to drill Ss' pronunciation.

Answers: **1** Oo perfect, classic, stunning **2** oO superb **3** Ooo breathtaking **4** oOo delightful **5** oOoo exceptional, significant

D If Ss are from the same country, encourage the partner to respond with agreement or disagreement after their partner has chosen a place. If they are from different countries, ask Ss to ask their partner a follow-up question about each place.

LISTENING

3A Tell Ss to read the adverts again and underline key words associated with each holiday. Such tasks are useful for many exam style questions. Play the recording and ask Ss to match each person to an advert.

Answers: **1** Volunteer on a farm **2** Alternative city breaks **3** Top 10 language holidays

Unit 4 Recording 3

Conversation 1

P = Penny S = Steve G = George

P: Hi, Steve. Come and sit down.
S: Thanks. Hi, Penny. Hi, George. Good to see you.
G: Hi.
P: Are you all packed now?
S: Yeah, all done. It was all a bit of a rush but I think I'm ready to go. I just hope I haven't forgotten anything.
P: When are you off?
S: The taxi's picking me up at seven tomorrow.
G: Where are you going?
S: France. On holiday, working on a farm there.
G: Work? Not my idea of a holiday!
S: Actually, I don't think it'll be too hard. They said they want me to work in the garden, not in the fields. They've got a big garden, and they need someone to look after it.
P: I didn't know you were interested in gardening.
S: I'm not, really, but apparently there might be some building work on the house. They're not sure yet. That's more my type of thing.
G: It still sounds like hard work. I wouldn't call it a holiday.
S: Well, I only have to work five hours a day and in exchange I get free board and lodging. So it's like a free holiday. Well, almost free.
P: I think it sounds great. Where are you going exactly?
S: It's in the centre of the country. Hold on a minute. I've got a photo on my phone. Yeah, here, look.
G: Ah, nice location!
P: It looks stunning.
S: Yeah, and this … is the local town.
G: So it's not all work?
S: No. I get lots of time off. I'm hoping to visit a few places at weekends and I'm going to Paris one weekend.
P: Yeah, I'm thinking of going over. A weekend in Paris sounds good to me.
G: Actually, looking at those photos I'm changing my mind. How did you find out about it?
S: On the internet – there are lots of sites. The one I looked at was …

Conversation 2

C = Customer Services Representative M = Man W = Woman

C: Yes, Sir?
M: Could you tell us what's happening with flight IB3056?
C: Flight IB3056 …
M: Yes, we've been waiting for over an hour and we've heard nothing. All it says on the screen is 'delayed'.
C: Erm, … I'm afraid the plane has been delayed coming in from Amsterdam, Sir. Bear with me a minute. I'll just check the latest information on the computer erm …
W: Thank you.
C: The plane is due to arrive at … er 10.30 … at the earliest.
M: But that's over three hours' time!
C: I'm sorry, Sir. And it's likely to be later than that.
M: This isn't good enough. We've only got a weekend and …
C: I'm sorry, Sir. There's nothing I can do.
W: And is there *any* way you could get us onto another flight? We're only going for two days and we've really been looking forward to it. It sounds as if we won't get to Seville till the afternoon.
C: I'm sorry, Madam. Our 9 o'clock flight to Seville is full.
W: What about another airline? Maybe we could transfer to another flight?
C: I'm really sorry, but that's not possible. It's not our policy except in an emergency.
M: This is an emergency!
W: Bill! Oh dear. Couldn't the airline at least pay for our breakfast?
C: Well, here are two vouchers for free coffee, courtesy of the airline.
W: Oh … thank you. Come on Bill, let's go and get some breakfast.
M: I can tell you, this is the last time I use your airline.
W: Come on, Bill.
M: This is the worst experience I've ever had …

Conversation 3

C = Chris J = Jan

C: Hi, Jan.
J: Oh, hi, Chris. When did you get back?
C: Last night. The plane got in at nine.
J: Welcome home!
C: Thanks.
J: So, how was it?
C: Brilliant. I had an absolutely amazing time.
J: And how's your Spanish?
C: Muy bien, gracias.
J: Sounds good to me. So tell me all about it.
C: Well, the family were lovely. Really hospitable. They made me feel at home straightaway. And incredibly generous. They even invited me out to a restaurant on my last night.
J: Yeah?
C: And Maria, who did the teaching, was very good, very patient. We spent a lot of time together going for walks along the lake – you know the town is on a big lake …
J: Yeah, I saw your photos on Facebook – they looked stunning, absolutely breathtaking.
C: … yeah, and we would chat or just sit around drinking limonada con soda and …
J: What's that?
C: Erm, that's freshly squeezed lemons and soda water. It's a typical drink there. But one week was really not enough.
J: So are you hoping to go back?
C: I'd love to. Maria's invited me and I might go back next summer but only if I can afford the flight. But I have a plan. I'm going to look for a new job, with more money.
J: Hey, are you free tomorrow for lunch? Why don't we meet up and you can tell me more about it?
C: Yeah, that would be great. Where shall we meet?

B Give Ss a few minutes to read through the questions and to try to answer any they can from memory. Play the recording again and check the answers as a class.

Answers:
1 most – building work, time off and a weekend trip to Paris; least – gardening
2 the holiday sounds more like work, (not my idea of a holiday); changes his mind – likes the photos
3 get them onto another flight; check another airline; give them a free breakfast
4 other flight is full; only transfers in emergencies; gives them free coffee vouchers
5 going out for dinner, going for walks, chatting, sitting and drinking lemonade
6 to go back; she needs to save up to afford the flight

GRAMMAR FUTURE FORMS

4A Ask Ss to read the conversations and to match them to a conversation in Ex 3A.

Answers:
From Conversation 1
1 Penny and Steve
2 George and Steve
3 Penny and Steve
From Conversation 2
4 Customer Services Representative
5 Customer Services Representative and male passenger
From Conversation 3
6 Chris and Jan

B Tell Ss to complete the gaps. They should think carefully about how definite the speakers are: do they refer to intentions, arrangements or just possibilities? Complete the first one with the class and establish that the present continuous is used because the speaker is referring to an arrangement. Ss can work alone and compare answers in pairs.

Answers:
1 is picking me up/is due to pick me up
NOT possible: *be going to*, *be likely to*, *might*, *will*
2 will be/is going to be/is likely to be
NOT possible: present continuous, *might*, *due to*
3 might be/is likely to be
NOT possible: *be going to*, present continuous, *be due to*, *will* – all too certain
4 'll (just) check
NOT possible: *be going to* – usually used when the plan is made before the moment of speaking. None of the other forms express a definite spontaneous decision.
5 is due to arrive
NOT possible: all others are too certain.
's likely to be
NOT possible: all others are too certain.
6 might go back
NOT possible: *be likely to* – isn't usually used for a personal intention. All others are too certain.
'm going to look for
NOT possible: present continuous implies an arrangement; *will* is unlikely for a general intention; *be due to* is for a schedule. The others are uncertain.

C Either tell Ss to look at the audio script on p167 or play the recording, stopping after each example to check the form the speaker used, but don't discuss the rules at this stage.

Answers: **1** 's picking (me) up **2** 'll be **3** might be
4 'll (just) check **5** is due to arrive, 's likely to be
6 might go back, 'm going to look for

D Look at the first rule with the class and point out that when the present continuous is used for a definite arrangement, a future time is usually mentioned (e.g. *seven tomorrow*). Although Ss should be familiar with these future forms, they may not have compared them all in this way before, so in class ensure that you pair Ss carefully to allow ***stronger Ss*** to help ***weaker ones***.

Answers:
Rule 1: The taxi's picking me up at seven tomorrow.
Rule 2: I'm going to look for a new job …
Rule 3: I'll just check the latest information on the computer.
Rule 4: I might go back next summer …
Rule 5: I don't think it'll be too hard.
Rule 6: The plane is due to arrive at 10.30 at the earliest.
Rule 7: And it's likely to be later than that.
Rule 8: … apparently there might be some building work on the house.

5A Books closed. Write the phonemic script of the non-connected versions on the board (a, a, b, a). Ask Ss to write these out in normal writing. Remove the phonemes from the board and set the task in the book. Ask Ss to read the natural version out loud.

B Play the recording to check and drill Ss on the pronunciation.

Answers: **1** b **2** b **3** a **4** b

▷ **LANGUAGEBANK 4.2** p134–135

There's a lot of information for Ss to take in here, so you may prefer to ask them to read it and do Ex A and B for homework.

Answers:
A **1** ~~will you come~~ **2** ~~I'm likely to do~~
3 ~~is the bus planning to leave~~ **4** might leave **5** ~~hoping to~~
6 ~~it's being~~ **7** ~~thinking~~ **8** ~~I'm seeing~~
B **1** might stay, 'll watch
2 Is (Sandra) going to be/Will (Sandra) be, 'll definitely go/'m definitely going
3 is due to arrive, likely to be delayed
4 is thinking of moving, 'll be
5 probably won't finish
6 might not see, 'll definitely see

6A You could do an example first, then Ss work alone or in pairs. In feedback, ask Ss which of the rules in Ex 4D each answer exemplifies.

Answers: **1** We're going **2** We'll probably **3** I'm meeting **4** I'm going to use **5** 'll rain **6** I'll stay **7** hoping to **8** I'm unlikely **9** to get **10** definitely won't

B Do an example and change one of the sentences so it is true for you first, e.g. *I'm going to Northern India on holiday this year. I booked a trekking holiday just after Christmas.* Then give Ss a few minutes to work alone on their sentences.

C Model this first by saying another sentence that is true about you and eliciting some examples from the class of follow-up questions they could ask, e.g.
On Saturday I'm taking my niece to the cinema.
What are you going to see?
How old is your niece?
Are you going in the morning or afternoon?
Put Ss into pairs and monitor the activity so you can provide feedback to the class afterwards on their use of the future forms.

SPEAKING

7A For ***weaker classes*** you may want to elicit some examples of questions Ss could ask for each bullet point, e.g. *What kinds of things do you like doing in your free time? When you go on holiday, do you like staying in a hotel, or do you prefer camping? Do you like self-catering accommodation? Do you like driving holidays, or do you prefer to go by train or bus? Do you like flying? What do you not like doing on holiday? How do you prefer to spend your time on holiday? How much do you want to spend on a holiday? Is luxury or a budget important to you?*
Remind Ss that they need to make notes of their partner's answers.

B Ask Ss to think of examples of alternative holidays from the lesson so far (they can look back at p47 if necessary) and any others they've heard of. Put Ss into new pairs, emphasising that they need to design two alternative holidays, one for each of their previous partners. Circulate and help, encouraging Ss to be creative with their designs.

C Before Ss return to their original partners, give them a few minutes to think about how they will present the holiday, including the use of future forms where appropriate, e.g. *Your train leaves at …, You're staying in …, You'll probably need to bring …* . Ss should make sure they include at least five different future forms. When Ss have finished, ask one or two to tell the class about the holiday their partner designed and what they think of it.

Optional extra activities
- Ss interview you in Ex 7A, then work in pairs to design an alternative holiday for you. Pairs then present their holidays and you choose the one you would like to go on.
- Elicit the names of some famous people that everyone in the class knows and write them on the board. Then write each one on a slip of paper and give each pair of Ss a name. They have to design an alternative holiday for that person. When they have finished, they present their holidays to the class, who guess which famous person they were given.

VOCABULARY PLUS UNCOUNTABLE AND PLURAL NOUNS

8A Focus Ss on the photo and discuss briefly with the class what they can see, where it might be, etc. Give Ss a minute to read the email then discuss the answer with the class.

Answers: Valerie likes the simplicity – she says 'I've realised that simpler is better' and her description emphasises this aspect of the place. (Ss might also mention some of the positives, e.g. friendly locals, horseback riding, that Valerie alludes to.)

B In pairs, Ss could think about the pros and cons of a holiday like this, then compare ideas as a class.

C Look at the examples with the class. If Ss have monolingual dictionaries, show them how the entries for *stairs* and *luggage* show that they are plural [plural] and uncountable [U] respectively. Ss can work with a partner to find the rest of the nouns.

Answers:
uncountable nouns: luggage, soap, cloth, wood, concrete, time
plural nouns: stairs, clothes, glasses, toiletries, outskirts, remains, cards, locals

9A Ss work alone or in pairs to correct the mistakes. They can use their dictionaries to check which nouns are uncountable or plural if they are not sure.

Answers: **1** informations **2** facilities **3** advices **4** How *much* **5** equipments **6** contents **7** means **8** scenery **9** remains **10** whereabouts

B You could put Ss into new pairs for this, or they could stand up and walk round the class, asking two or three different people the questions. Conduct feedback to find out how similar or different people's answers were.

▷ **VOCABULARYBANK** p151 Uncountable nouns

Let Ss work independently to complete the activities using a dictionary to check anything they are not sure of. Feed back as a class.

Answers:

A
1. The furniture was relatively inexpensive.
2. There is a lot of advice available to help with debt.
3. Is there any room left on the course?
4. Scientific research shows that obesity has doubled over the last decade.
5. The economic news from the World Bank is disturbing.
6. Chris has trouble hearing clearly.
7. What terrible weather!
8. The sports equipment is stored in that cupboard over there.
9. Is there any information available about the free trial?
10. Where is my luggage?

B a piece of ~~room~~ (we say *a bit of room*)
an item of ~~advice~~ (we say *a piece of advice*)
a bit of ~~transport~~ (we say *a means of transport*)

C a piece of clothing, equipment, advice, news, luggage, clothing, information, furniture
an item of information, research, news, furniture
a bit of information, room, research, advice, news, equipment, luggage, clothing

Homework ideas

- Ss imagine they are on their alternative holiday and write an email to a friend about it.
- **Language bank:** 4.2 Ex A–B, p135
- **Vocabulary bank:** p151
- **Workbook:** Ex 1–5, p25–26

HOW DOES IT WORK?

Introduction

Ss practise listening and speaking about games and abilities. They also learn to use mirror questions.

SUPPLEMENTARY MATERIALS

Resource bank: p163 and p166

Ex 3A and/or **Ex 5B:** if you are able to download/record extracts from some game shows to play in class, you could use these to prompt discussion in Ex 3A and/or for Ss to describe a game in Ex 5B.

Ex 6D: prepare definitions for extra practice of mirror questions.

Ex 7C: be prepared to describe one of the situations as a model for the class.

Warm up

Lead into the topic by playing 'Ten Questions'. Think of a game that Ss will know and tell them to ask you questions about it to find out what it is. The rules are that you can only answer with *yes* or *no* and if Ss haven't guessed the answer after ten questions, you win. If you have time, Ss can then play the game in small groups.

VOCABULARY ABILITIES

1 Write on the board the name of a game show that most Ss will have heard of and establish what a 'game show' is. Elicit a few more examples and put Ss into pairs (or small groups) to discuss the questions. Ss from the same country can compare which shows they like/dislike and Ss from different countries can describe shows to each other.

2A Ask Ss to use the phrases to complete the sentences. After you have checked the answers, ask Ss to match the abilities to the different game shows they discussed in Ex 1.

Answers: **1** know-how **2** understand human nature **3** a good sense of humour **4** cool-headed **5** in great shape **6** inventive **7** a sharp mind **8** good with (words/my hands, etc.)

B Put Ss into pairs and ask them to choose who is going to be A and who is going to be B. As Ss ask and answer the questions, listen for any good responses using the target language and elicit these in feedback. When Ss have finished, they swap roles.

C After Ss have done Ex 2B, go back to the game shows you brainstormed in the Warm up and in Ex 1 and elicit who would be best in the class at each game show.

FUNCTION DESCRIBING PROCEDURES

3A Focus Ss on the photos and tell them the names of the game shows (from left to right): *Would I lie to you?*, *Total Wipeout* and *Masterchef*. Elicit ideas from the class and write these on the board so that Ss can compare them to what they hear in the next stage.

B Tell Ss to listen and compare their ideas to the way the games are described. They should note down some 'key' words to help them.

Unit 4 Recording 5

Conversation 1

A: It's one of these games that involve lying and people trying to figure out if you're lying or not, but it's different and really funny.
B: I like that kind of thing. Are there teams or something?
A: Yeah, there are two teams with three celebs on each team.
B: Er … Three what?
A: Celebs. Celebrities.
B: Oh right.
A: There's a team captain on each team, actually the team captains are well-known comedians and they're on every show.
B: So each team has a comedian and two celebrities.
A: Exactly. The first thing they do is to tell a personal story. So a panellist tells a personal story …
B: Sorry, who tells a story?
A: A panellist. One of the people on one of the teams.
B: Oh, I see.
A: So they tell something about themselves, often something really embarrassing … Now it might be true or they might be lying. The key thing is to say something that's so unbelievable that it's hard to imagine it's true.
B: And then they vote?
A: Not right away. What happens next is the other team grills the storyteller …
B: Uh, they do what?
A: Grill him. Ask a lot of questions to try and find out if the person's lying.
B: Yeah, you can tell if someone's lying by how fast they answer.
A: Well, the panellists are usually very good at it. It's surprising how hard it is to guess. But for me the best thing is the humour, the joking around. It's really entertaining.
B: I'll bet I could figure out if they're lying.
A: Maybe. Anyway, after they've finished, the team that asked the questions decide if it was a lie or not. If they're right, they get a point.
B: What sort of things do they say?
A: Gosh, all sorts of things. One of my favourites was when a female panellist said she'd kissed one of the other panellists.
B: And was it true?
A: I'm not going to tell you. It's on TV tonight. We can watch and you can show me how great you are at saying if someone is lying.
B: Oh great …

Conversation 2

A: Oh, you must have seen it …
B: No, I've never even heard of it. How does it work?
A: Well, it sounds really stupid, but I'll try to describe it. It's basically a race over an obstacle course.
B: Uh … Over a what?
A: An obstacle course. There are lots of things that they have to climb over and balance on …
B: Oh, obstacle, got it.
A: … and if they fall off, they fall into water or mud.
B: Sounds dangerous.
A: It can be.
B: So what are the … obstacles like?
A: Well there are a lot of different ones. There's the Sweeper.
B: Sweeper, like a broom.
A: Yeah. Basically, the way it works is that twelve of the contestants stand on podiums over water …
B: They stand where?
A: On podiums. These tall columns, or blocks. Like little towers.
B: And is it hard to balance?
A: Well yes, mainly because of the Sweeper. It's a big arm really, and it turns around and around over the podiums. What you have to do is jump over the arm when it gets to you. Then you have to land on the podium without falling down.
B: And if they get knocked down?
A: They fall into the water. Sometimes quite dramatically. That's the thing I like best, those dramatic falls. The last one standing wins the round.
B: Sorry, they win what?
A: The round. That part of the competition.
B: Oh, so there are more obstacles.
A: Oh yeah. It's not just the Sweeper, there are lots of different types of obstacles. Tippy Tables, Teeter Totters, Dock Maze, Crazy Beams, Doughnuts.
B: Wow. Doughnuts. Crazy. And how do you win?
A: The point is to get round the course in the fastest time. The fastest person is the winner.
B: Sounds quite good fun.
A: The studio is amazing. They film it in BA. Imagine, the UK TV crew …
B: They film it where?
A: In BA. Buenos Aires. Argentina.
B: They fly to Argentina to film this?
A: Yeah, it's a big deal.
B: I'd like to see it.

C To allow space, Ss could write their answers in their notebooks while they listen. Give Ss a few minutes to compare their answers with a partner before feedback to the class.

Answers:
Conversation 1:
1 team
2 the aim for the team is to figure out if the storyteller is lying
3 the humour
Conversation 2:
1 individual
2 to go through an obstacle course fastest
3 when a contestant falls dramatically

4A Match the first pair as an example, then Ss work alone or in pairs on the rest. Ss could check their answers in the audio script.

Answers: 1 c) 2 g) 3 e) 4 a) 5 b) 6 d) 7 f)

B Ss can work on this in pairs and decide together which phrases are used for the functions in the list.

Answers: 1 phrase 7 2 phrases 1, 3, 4, 5 and 6 3 phrase 2

▷ LANGUAGEBANK 4.3 p134–135

Point out to the class that the phrases are summarised in the Language bank, with further useful examples for describing games and sports. If Ss are having trouble with the word order and/or remembering all the elements of each phrase, they could do Ex A in class.

Answers:
1 Basically the way it works is that
2 The first thing they do is
3 Then what the first player does is
4 The object is
5 The point is
6 What happens is that
7 The key thing is to

5A Tell Ss to read the description through quickly before they try to complete the gaps, so they have a general idea of the procedure described.

Answers: 1 way 2 is 3 first 4 do 5 What 6 next 7 they've 8 point/goal/aim 9 key/main

B While Ss write their notes, circulate and provide the vocabulary they need. If any Ss aren't confident about describing a game, pair them with Ss who are to help them make notes. You can move them to different groups for the next stage.

C Put Ss into groups of three or four and tell them that each person must finish describing their game/sport/show before the others guess what it is. Also encourage Ss to refer to their notes but look up and speak, rather than reading aloud. Monitor and make notes of good use of the phrases for describing procedures, as well as any problem areas, for feedback. When the groups have finished, you could ask which were the most difficult games/sports/shows to guess and why.

LEARN TO USE MIRROR QUESTIONS

6A Tell Ss they are going to read some extracts from the conversations they listened to about game shows. Ask them to look at B's questions and think about why and how they are used. Next, Ss underline the words that speaker A says that B does not understand the meaning of.

Answers: **1** celebs **2** a panellist **3** grills **4** (on) podiums

B Ask Ss to identify the words or phrases used to replace a noun and the ones used to replace a verb.

Answers:
what, who, where can replace a noun
do what replaces a verb

speakout TIP

Before directing Ss to the tip, discuss briefly why these 'mirror' questions could be useful for them, i.e. they can use them if they don't understand a word or phrase in a conversation, or if they didn't hear exactly what was said, e.g. on the phone. After Ss have read the tip, ask them if they have something similar in their own language(s), which helps the speaker to see what they need to repeat or explain.

C Ss should be able to predict where the stress goes. When Ss are repeating the questions, discourage them from making their intonation rise too abruptly on the question word as this will sound rude/aggressive. Instead, show them how to ask the question in a tentative way, with a gentle rise on the question word which will sound friendlier.

Answers: **1** Er … Three what? **2** Sorry, who tells a story? **3** Um, they do what? **4** They stand where?

D Point out to Ss that in three of the questions they only need one word to replace the phrase in bold. They could complete the gaps alone or together as a class.

Answers: **1** You have to do what **2** The first player writes what **3** You go where **4** The aim is to beat who/what

SPEAKING

7A Give Ss a few minutes to think about the situations and choose one.

B While Ss make notes, circulate and provide vocabulary they need.

C You could provide a model of the activity for Ss. Describe your procedure, including a few fairly obscure words/phrases, so that Ss have to stop you and ask mirror questions. You could run this as a competition, giving points to each pair or group who asks a good mirror question. While Ss are describing their procedures, monitor and make notes of good use of language and problem areas for praise and correction in feedback.

▷ VOCABULARYBANK p151 Sports and activities

Ex 2A, B and C extend Ss' vocabulary for talking about different kinds of sports. Before you start, you might want to go through some of the more specialised vocabulary, e.g. *tackle* (to try to take the ball from a player in the opposite team) and *shoot* (to try to score a goal by hitting, throwing, etc. the ball towards the goal). Ss work on the collocations in Ex 2A and match them with the photos in Ex 2B. During feedback, get Ss to talk about their experiences of playing any of these sports and to tell you which they might like to try in the future.

Ex 3A and B are concerned with sporting idioms. Let Ss do the matching in pairs and feed back as a class. Then ask Ss to try to find some examples of sporting idioms in their own language and translate them into English.

Answers:
2A **1** ~~win~~ **2** ~~beat~~ **3** ~~score~~ **4** ~~shoot~~ **5** ~~chess~~ **6** ~~athletics~~
2B **A** bounce a ball **B** do weight-training **C** let in a goal **D** tackle an opponent **E** play snooker **F** win a match
3A **1** e) **2** c) **3** d) **4** f) **5** b) **6** a)

Homework ideas

- **Ex 7A:** Ss write about another situation.
- **Language bank:** 4.3 Ex A, p135
- **Vocabulary bank:** p151
- **Workbook:** Ex 1–4, p27

THE HAPPINESS FORMULA

Introduction

Ss watch an extract from *The Happiness Formula*, a BBC series in which scientists investigate what makes people happy. Ss then learn and practise how to conduct a survey and write tips for being happy.

SUPPLEMENTARY MATERIALS

Ex 4A: write the 'ingredients' of happiness on ten pieces of A4 paper.

Warm up

Either: Write *Happiness is …* on the board and put Ss into pairs to write three endings that they both agree on. Conduct a brief feedback, so Ss can see how many ideas the class had in common.

Or: Write *Money can't make you happy …* on the board and give Ss 5 mins in pairs to think of as many ways to complete the sentence as they can. Elicit these to the board in feedback, then Ss can compare their ideas with the endings in Ex 1.

DVD PREVIEW

1 While Ss discuss the ways of completing the statement, encourage them to think of reasons and examples to support their opinions. Elicit some of their reasons and examples in feedback.

2 Give Ss a minute or two to read the information and to answer the first question. Then put Ss into pairs to think of theories and to predict what the scientists might say.

Answers: **1** money does not contribute to happiness

DVD VIEW

3A Emphasise that Ss should only try to get a general idea of what the scientist is saying, as they will watch the extract again to find more details.

Answers:
1 money does not contribute to happiness
2 The programme talks about two 'theories':
Research shows that in the UK, when average income is over £10,000 a year, additional income doesn't make people happier.
The problem of comparison: We become less happy when someone has something better than we have.
3 We should slow down and take more leisure time.

DVD 4 The Happiness Formula

N = Narrator ME = Mark Easton PK = Professor Daniel Kahneman I = Interviewee

N: We work, we buy, consume and die. We don't know why. The science of happiness says the answer is to rethink everything. The rat race: give it up. The rich: tax them. Holidays: take more. In short, change the way we live.

ME: New York City, capital of the consumerist world where status has a designer label sewn inside, but does happiness come in a gift-wrapped box? And if it doesn't, what on earth are we all doing?

PK: It's a fundamental fact in the happiness research: the standard of living has increased dramatically and, ah, happiness has increased not at all and in some cases has diminished slightly.

N: Put simply, the science shows that once average incomes are more than ten thousand pounds a year, extra income doesn't make people any happier.
The British fit this picture. Look at what's happened over the past half a century or more. Looking at 1950 to today, Britain has become much richer. But during the same period of time, happiness levels have hardly changed at all.
Consumerism promises happiness. But the science of happiness shows it can never work. One reason is that we are never satisfied with what we have.

ME: Scientists call it the problem of comparison. Imagine you've just got yourself a brand-new Mini. You're the only one on the street that's got one and you feel great. Then your neighbours drive up in two top-of-the-range BMWs. And suddenly your Mini just doesn't do it for you anymore. And that's the problem of comparison.

N: We are stuck in the rat race. In our search for happiness we work longer, commute further, to get richer, to buy more. And yet the science of happiness suggests we should do exactly the opposite.

I: If only we could learn as a society to slow down, we might all be able to become happier if we could all take more leisure together.

N: It is starting to happen. Politicians are realising that making people happy is as important as making people rich. The next task, though, is to convince us all to change the way we live.

B Check that Ss understand the term *rat race* (the pressured race to do well and get rich). Then play the recording again and check the answers as a class.

Suggested answers: **1** give it up **2** tax them **3** take more

C Give Ss time to read the extracts carefully before playing the DVD again. Point out that in most cases both options make sense, so they will only find out the right answer after listening. Play the recording and check the answers.

Answers:
1 box
2 dramatically, diminished
3 top-of-the-range, do it for you
4 commute, do exactly the opposite
5 convince

D Give Ss a few minutes to think about these questions before putting them into pairs.

speakout a happiness survey

4A Give Ss a few minutes to discuss the 'ingredients' and to select the ones most people consider important. In feedback, ask individuals to tell you whether they think they would also choose the same as most people or if they would choose differently.

Optional extra activity

Display the ten 'ingredients' on pieces of A4 paper on the board and invite the class to put them in order from the most to the least important. This can be done in pairs first, or as a whole class, with Ss coming up to move the pieces of paper on the board.

B Tell Ss to see what they have in common with the speaker. They can tick the topics in the box that the speaker mentions and underline the ones that are most important to him.

Answers:
He talks about cars, friendship, money and free time.
Free time and friendship are the most important for him.

Unit 4 Recording 7

W = Woman M = Man

W: Excuse me, hello, sorry to bother you, have you got a minute?
M: Ah, yeah, sure.
W: Do you mind if I ask you some questions? I'm just doing a survey on happiness.
M: Right.
W: I'll read out the questions to you and you can just tell me what you think, if that's OK.
M: Yeah, fine.
W: Great. Um, could you look at this list of five things so you've got, ah, number one car, then two is friendship, three good food, four money and five free time. So which two of these would you find it the most difficult to live without?
M: Which two, most difficult to live without?
W: Yes.
M: Ah, well, I couldn't live without friendship. I'm, I'm a very social animal I need, um, family and friends around me, so it can't be that one. Um – oh, no, sorry, that is, to live without … yes …
W: That's one.
M: That is one, so …
W: Then we just need one more.
M: … friendship is definitely one of them. Ah …
W: Yes, number two, OK.
M: Oh, that's difficult. Free time I don't have any anyway, ah, I could lose the car, I think that wouldn't be a problem. Um, do you know what …
W: How about money?
M: … sad as it is, it's probably money, because money actually …
W: Money, no, most people …
M: … you know leads to happiness in, in indirect ways I think.
W: OK, so I'm gonna put number two and number four for that one. And also, how happy would you say you are, on a scale of one to five, five being very happy?
M: Today or just generally?
W: I think generally.
M: Oh, generally OK, um, oh, ah, three or four, um – three and a half.
W: Ah.
M: Can I have half?
W: No.
M: Oh, OK. Um, well you've made me laugh, I'll have four.
W: Oh, lovely, I'll put you down for four. And what would you say is missing from your life, so what would make you happier?
M: Ah, probably, ah, working nearer to home?
W: OK.
M: That's, I think you know … just generally the time that would give me …
W: Right.
M: … with family.
W: So maybe it's free time then …
M: Yeah, yeah.
W: … more of that. OK that's lovely, thank you ever so much for taking part, really do appreciate it.
M: You're welcome.
W: OK, bye bye.

C Focus Ss on the phrases and give them time to read them through. Set the task for the listening and point out that where there are options in the phrases (e.g. *[Could I/Do you mind if I] ask you some questions?*), they need to underline the option(s) they hear.

Answers: [Could I/Do you mind if I] ask you some questions?; Which would you find the [easiest/hardest/most difficult] to live without?; What would you say is missing from your life?

5A You could suggest that Ss aim to include at least five of the key phrases. Also point out that they should try to make their survey different from the one they heard, e.g. they could change some of the 'ingredients' for happiness. Both Ss in the pairs should write out the survey in their notebooks because they will be talking to different people in the next stage.

B Ss should aim to talk to about three other people. They can either stand up and walk round the class, or they can work in groups of four, changing pairs until they have talked to the other three people in their group.

C Give Ss a few minutes to prepare to summarise their findings. You could suggest some phrases to use, e.g. *All three of the people I spoke to said …; Nobody thought that …; Only one person couldn't live without …; It was surprising that … .*
Invite a few individuals to read out their findings to the class.

writeback tips for being happy

6A Tell Ss to close their books and write *Don't read the news or watch TV* and *Get a pet* on the board. Ss discuss (as a whole class or in pairs) why these two tips would make people happier. Then direct them to the texts in Ex 6A. Were their ideas the same?

B Focus Ss on the box and tell them to copy the headings into their notebooks. With ***weaker Ss*** elicit one or two more ideas and write them on the board. Put Ss into pairs to work on their notes.

Optional extra activity

If any of your Ss are struggling to think of ideas, you could feed in some of the following: *learn a new skill, listen to music, take up a hobby, make some time for yourself, give yourself a 'treat', get rid of negative people, do some exercise, make a new friend, laugh, watch a funny TV programme.*

C Ss work alone to write their tips. Circulate and help as required, prompting Ss to correct their own mistakes as much as possible.

D Ss can pass the tips round the class, or stick them on the walls for everyone to walk round and read. Then ask individuals which tips they would try and why.

Homework ideas

- Ss write a list of tips for another topic, e.g. *How to be healthy/ How to find a good job/How to make new friends.*
- **Ex 5:** Ss write a report with the results of the survey they conducted. Suggest three paragraphs for the report:
  1 Introduction – the aim of the survey
  2 More details about what the survey contained and how many people were involved
  3 A summary of the findings.

LOOKBACK

Introduction

The aim of these activities is to provide revision and further practice of the language from the unit. You can also use them to assess Ss' ability to use the language, in which case you need to monitor but avoid helping them. You may feel that you don't need or have time to do all the activities. If so, you could allocate the activities that would be most beneficial for your Ss, or get individual Ss to decide which activities they'd like to do.

FREE TIME

1A Set this as an individual task.

Answers: 1 recharge 2 wound up 3 focus on 4 chill out 5 switch off 6 unwind

B Ask Ss to discuss their opinion of the advice. Elicit how they would change any of it to improve the advice.

PRESENT AND PAST HABITS

2A You could play this as a game. Put Ss into teams and give them enough time to correct the sentences and decide which sentence is correct. Ss should swap their sentences with another group and award marks as you read out the correct answers. Groups get 1 mark for a correct change and lose 1 mark for an incorrect change.

Answers: 1 I'd often *go* 2 are *always* thinking 3 I didn't *use* to 4 I *usually* get up 5 I'll *stay* 6 correct 7 *is* always sending 8 I *used to* believe

B Put Ss into groups to discuss which of the habits are good and which are bad. Conduct feedback with the class and find out which habits are most common in the class.

POSITIVE ADJECTIVES

3A You could run this as a board race with Ss in two or three teams. Tell Ss to close their books. Give each student in the team a number and write one of the phrases with the jumbled word in brackets on the board. As soon as a team has worked out the word, their number 1 runs to the board and writes it up. The team gets a point if it's correct. For the next phrase, the number 2 in each team runs up and so on.

Answers: 1 perfect 2 classic 3 breathtaking 4 superb 5 exceptional 6 significant 7 delightful 8 stunning

B Ss need to think of a place, person or thing for each phrase they choose. They then discuss their choices in pairs.

FUTURE FORMS

NB Ex 4 reviews predictions and Ex 5 reviews plans, intentions and arrangements. You may want to direct Ss to the relevant sections of the Language bank on p134 so they can review the rules before attempting each exercise.

4A Focus Ss on the headlines and check that they understand key vocabulary, e.g. *lifespan* (the length of time that someone will live), *exhausted* (all used) and *soars* (increases quickly). Ss discuss the questions in groups.

B Ss work alone to write their predictions, giving a reason for each one.

Suggested answers:
1 Italian will definitely never become a universal language.
2 The average lifespan is likely to increase to 100 years.
3 This will definitely never happen as more and more wars keep happening around the world.
4 This might happen, but other modes of transport are more likely to become expensive first.
5 The internet could be banned worldwide, but it's not likely to be.

5A You could elicit the first line of the first dialogue as an example, then Ss can work alone or with a partner to write the rest. Ss should write in their notebooks so they can use these prompts for oral practice in the next stage.

Answers:
1 **A:** What are you doing on Friday?
B: I might go to Julia's party or maybe I'll go to the cinema.
A: I'm going to Julia's party, so I'll give you a lift if you want.
B: Thanks. I'll phone you if I need a lift.
2 **A:** How are you planning to use your English in the future?
B: I'll probably try and/to get a job with/in an international company. How about you?
A: I'm hoping to get into an American university, but I'm unlikely to get my first choice.
B: I'm sure you will.
3 **A:** Hurry up or we'll miss the bus!
B: What time is it due?
A: It's due in two minutes. Leave your coat. You definitely won't need it today.
B: But it might rain. I'll take my umbrella just in case.

B Once Ss have finished practising the conversations, they could repeat them, making at least one change to each of Student A's and Student B's contributions, e.g.
A: *What are you doing after the lesson?*
B: *I might go straight home or maybe I'll go for a coffee.*
A: *I'll probably go for a coffee, so I might see you in the café.*
B: *OK. I'll see how I feel.*

In feedback, invite a few of the pairs to act out their new conversations.

DESCRIBING PROCEDURES

6A You could start by asking Ss what they think an Oyster Card is/does. If anyone has used one in London, they could explain how it works to the class or a partner.

Answers: 1 The 2 Basically 3 it works 4 happens 5 that 6 main thing 7 After

B Give Ss about 5 mins to write their tips. Then, before Ss compare their tips, remind them of the mirror questions on p51, which they can use to check anything they don't understand. Ss can work in small groups or stand up and walk round the room telling each other their tips. Monitor and make notes of good language use and problem areas for praise and correction in feedback.

Homework ideas

Workbook: Review 2, p28–31

BBC interviews and worksheet

What's the perfect way to switch off?

This video looks at the topic of how we use our leisure time and explores the different things we might do in order to relax.

OVERVIEW

5.1 BRIGHT IDEAS?

READING | read an article about the worst inventions ever
VOCABULARY | change
GRAMMAR | articles
PRONUNCIATION | weak forms and linking: *the*
SPEAKING | talk about inventions
VOCABULARY ***PLUS*** | compound nouns

5.2 CONSUMER CRAZY

LISTENING | listen to a programme about advertising
VOCABULARY | advertising collocations
GRAMMAR | real and hypothetical conditionals
PRONUNCIATION | sentence stress: conditionals
SPEAKING | describe adverts
WRITING | write a report; learn to make written comparisons

5.3 WHAT DO YOU THINK?

VOCABULARY | collocations with *idea*
FUNCTION | suggesting ideas
LEARN TO | show reservations
PRONUNCIATION | intonation: showing reservations
SPEAKING | take part in a brainstorming session

5.4 GENIUS BBC DVD

DVD | watch a BBC programme about presenting ideas
speakout | a presentation
writeback | a product review

5.5 LOOKBACK

Communicative revision activities

BBC INTERVIEWS

If you could start a business, what would it be?

This video looks at the topic of shopping and innovative products. Use this video at the start or end of Unit 5 or set it as homework.

BRIGHT IDEAS?

Introduction

Ss practise reading and speaking about inventions and change, using articles and vocabulary related to change. They also learn about compound nouns and practise weak forms and linking *the*.

SUPPLEMENTARY MATERIALS
Resource bank: p167 and p169
Ex 4A: prepare a handout with the complete sentences (see *Alternative approach*).
Ex 8C: bring monolingual dictionaries for Ss to use.

Warm up

Put Ss into small groups of three or four to discuss how the world has changed in the last fifty years/in their lifetimes. Write the following prompts on the board to guide their discussion: *communication, travel, work, leisure, food, health, home*. After a few minutes conduct feedback, asking each group to share their ideas.

READING

1 Books closed. Choose one invention yourself that you think has been particularly bad. Write it on the board and tell Ss your reasons for choosing this invention. Ask Ss to work in pairs and think of five other inventions. Elicit some examples and reasons from Ss.

2A Tell Ss to cover the article at the top of the page and focus only on the photos. Elicit some ideas from the class as to why fast food is one of the worst inventions and put Ss into pairs to write a reason for each invention. Then discuss Ss' ideas as a class.

B Ask Ss to check their predictions against the text. Briefly discuss with Ss whether they strongly agree or disagree with any of the choices.

C Give Ss time to read the article in more detail for this and to compare answers with a partner.

Answers:
1 T *Americans are the ultimate fast food eaters …*
2 NG It only says that reality TV started with *Candid Camera* (*Making its debut in 1948* with Candid Camera …) but we don't know how popular this programme was.
3 F *… men who smoke are twenty-two times, and women twelve times, more likely to develop lung cancer …*
4 T *… the modern car was initially the toy of the wealthy, but falling prices have made it a key part of family life.*
5 F *But a green* (i.e. alternative) *fuel is unlikely to take over from petrol soon …*
6 T *Nuclear power plants cost more to construct and operate than fossil fuel ones …*
7 NG The article doesn't talk about the dangers of mobile phones in relation to age.
8 F *Nuclear weapons were the worst offender …*

D Give Ss time to discuss this question. You could also extend the task by asking Ss to discuss: *What things would you add to the list? How would you change the order of the list?* Elicit answers for any of the questions you discuss.

VOCABULARY CHANGE

3A Ask Ss to briefly discuss in groups how each invention has changed people's lives. Elicit some ideas and then ask Ss to complete the sentences in the exercise.

Answers: 1 have 2 revolutionised 3 cause

B You could start by telling Ss to close their books and writing all the things that are mentioned in 1–8 on the board, i.e. *weather, the music business, the seasons, the economy, the environment, the holiday industry, education, equality*. Put Ss into pairs to discuss how these things have changed and what impact this has had on people. Ss then open their books and match the sentence halves.

Answers: **1** e) **2** g) **3** b) **4** h) **5** f) **6** c) **7** d) **8** a)

C Give Ss a few minutes to discuss the phrases in pairs and then ask them to match them to a category.

Answers:
1 react to change: *adapt to* + noun; *adjust to* + noun
2 make a positive change: *have a positive effect on* + noun/pronoun; *enabled* + noun/pronoun + infinitive with *to*
3 make a negative change: *have devastating effects on* + noun/pronoun; *cause/do harm to* + noun/pronoun; *cause damage to* + noun
4 make a big change: *revolutionise* + noun; *transform* + noun

D Put pairs of Ss together into groups of four or six. Ask Ss to decide on their own opinion individually before discussing them together.

GRAMMAR ARTICLES

4A Tell Ss to cover the article at the top of the page before they start this exercise. You could do number 1 as an example with the class, then put Ss into pairs to help each other complete the rest. For ***stronger classes***, once Ss have checked their answers with the text, tell them to discuss why the answer is *a(n), the* or (–) in each case.

Answers: **1** a, the **2** –, –, the **3** The, – , – **4** the, the, the, a

Alternative approach

For ***weaker classes***, or Ss who don't have an article system in their own language, omit Ex 4A. It may be too challenging if Ss are unsure of the rules of usage. Instead, give Ss the complete sentences on a handout, or write/display them on the board. Ask Ss to underline all the examples of articles in the sentences and, in pairs, discuss why each one is used. Then move on to Ex 4B.

B Complete the first rule as an example with the class and ask Ss for examples of the rule from the sentences in Ex 4A. Ss work on the rest of the rules alone or in pairs, finding examples for each one.

Answers: **1** a/an; a lawsuit, a key part (not the only key/important part of family life) **2** the; the fast food chain (mentioned before – McDonald's), The World Health Organization (unique) **3** – ; reality television (uncountable), British men (plural), women (plural) **4** – ; America **5** the; the late 1880s, the USA **6** the; the modern car, the wealthy

▷ LANGUAGEBANK 5.1 p136–137

The rules for using articles are presented in tabular form, which provide a concise record and may help visually oriented learners to clarify the differences. NB If your Ss still feel overwhelmed by the number of rules, tell them to ask themselves: 'Is it something new/something general/something we already know?' You could set Ex A for homework or for extra practice in class if Ss have had trouble with Ex 4.

Answers:
A **1** – **2** the **3** the **4** the **5** a **6** a **7** a **8** the **9** – **10** – **11** – **12** the **13** a **14** the **15** the **16** the **17** – **18** – **19** the (Normally with 'cinema' we use 'the'. It's possible here to use 'a' if we don't know which cinema is meant.) **20** the

5A Demonstrate the two different ways of pronouncing *the*, then put Ss into pairs and tell them to take turns to read the sentences aloud to each other and listen for the pronunciation of *the*. In the meantime, write the sentences on the board so that you can ask Ss to come out and circle/underline *the* in feedback. Play the recording and check the answers with the class. Ss could also repeat after the recording.

Answers:
1 The interesting thing is that many of (the) people who hate it are (the) ones who watch it.
2 The automobile has done less well since the economic crisis.
3 Those who voted for (the) car mentioned (the) harm it does to the environment as (the) biggest problem.
We tend to use /ðə/ before consonants and /ðiː/ before vowels.

B This task models how *the* is linked to words beginning with a vowel. Before playing the recording, you could ask Ss to predict which sound is used. Play the recording and check the answer.

Answer: /j/

6A Start by writing the title *Bicycle chosen as best invention* on the board and ask Ss to predict why people chose it. Ss read the text quickly (without worrying about the missing articles at this stage) to see if their predictions were correct. Then discuss briefly with the class what they found surprising in the text and whether they think the results would be the same in their countries.

B Ss then complete the gaps and compare answers in pairs before feedback with the class. Vocabulary to check: *innovation, harness* and *trail behind*.

Answers: **1** The **2** a **3** – **4** an **5** the **6** an **7** the **8** the **9** the **10** – **11** the **12** an

SPEAKING

7A Tell Ss they must choose one from each pair of items. They should not be allowed to choose both or neither. Setting the task in this way should generate more discussion. Hold a class vote on each pair and elicit some reasons in each case.

B This task requires Ss to consider perspectives other than their own, as Pair 2 is always going to have to disagree with Pair 1. Clarify with Ss that in this task they have to make counter arguments, whether they agree with them or not. If necessary, demonstrate with a group of four Ss, before Ss work in groups.

VOCABULARY PLUS COMPOUND NOUNS

8A Focus Ss on the pictures and give them a minute or two to discuss what each invention is for and which were the least successful.

B Ss read and complete the entries alone, then compare answers with a partner. Ss should not worry about the exact meaning of the words in bold at this stage.

Answers: **1** jet pack **2** wrist radio **3** bottle top **4** ring pull

C Ss match the definitions alone or in pairs. They could use monolingual dictionaries to check their answers.

Answers: **1** trade-off **2** outlook **3** breakdown **4** breakthrough **5** drawback, downside **6** outcome

9A Before Ss try to complete the gaps you could direct them back to the compound nouns in bold in Ex 8B and ask them how compound nouns are made. Then give Ss a few minutes to complete the information alone or with a partner.

Answers:
1 breakthrough/outlook/drawback/breakdown/outcome/downside
2 trade-off
3 breakthrough/trade-off/drawback/breakdown
4 outlook/outcome

B Emphasise that Ss only need to write the compound noun, not the complete sentence. They may need to listen again to check which part is stressed. Elicit where the stress usually falls (the first word in a compound noun is usually stressed).

Unit 5 Recording 3

1 There's been a breakthrough.
2 It's a trade-off between cost and safety.
3 The long-term outlook is very good.
4 The downside is I get paid less.
5 There's only one drawback.
6 There's been a breakdown in communications.
7 What was the outcome of the meeting?

C Direct Ss to the encyclopedia entries in Ex 8B and point out that each one is about two sentences long and contains at least two of the compound nouns they've studied. Put Ss into pairs to discuss and write their entries. Circulate and help as required.

D The entries could be stuck on the walls and Ss walk round guessing the inventions. In this way they see all the entries that the class has written.

▷ **VOCABULARYBANK** p152 Compound adjectives

Ex 1A and B move Ss on from looking at compound nouns to compound adjectives. Ss complete the exercises individually then compare the answers in pairs. In feedback, explain that whilst many compound adjectives are hyphenated, some have become single words, e.g. *waterproof*, *handheld*, and that this is something that tends to happen over time. However, in many cases, both the hyphenated and unhyphenated version of a compound adjective can be considered correct.

Answers:
A 1 c) 2 i) 3 j) 4 a) 5 d) 6 e) 7 g) 8 f) 9 h) 10 b)
B A energy-efficient light bulb
B hand-held/handheld GPS
C water-proof/waterproof watch
D pocket-sized camcorder
E eco-friendly detergent
F solar-powered torch

Homework ideas

- Ss find a short, fairly simple text (e.g. on the internet) describing an important invention and blank out ten or more articles. They bring the gapped text to the next lesson for their partner to complete.
- Ss write two paragraphs: one about what they consider to be the best invention and one about the worst invention of all time. They should aim to include at least two of the vocabulary items related to change and two compound nouns or adjectives.
- Ss do Ex 2A on Advertising on p152 (Vocabulary bank) in preparation for the next lesson, which is about advertising.
- **Language bank:** 5.1 Ex A, p137
- **Vocabulary bank:** p152
- **Workbook:** Ex 1–5, p32–33

CONSUMER CRAZY

Introduction

Ss practise listening and speaking about advertising using conditionals and related vocabulary. They also learn to make written comparisons and write a report.

SUPPLEMENTARY MATERIALS
Resource bank: p168 and p170
Warm up: bring in a variety of advertisements from glossy magazines.
Ex 1B: prepare A4-sized copies of the five questions in the questionnaire (see *Alternative approach*).

Warm up

Bring in a variety of magazine adverts.

Either: Put Ss into pairs or small groups and give each pair/group an advert to discuss: they should decide whether it's effective and why/why not, then share their ideas with the rest of the class in feedback.

Or: Display the adverts on the walls and ask Ss, working with a partner, to walk round discussing which advert they like best/least and why. Conduct feedback and see if there is a clear winner/loser.

LISTENING

1A Write the title of the questionnaire on the board and check that Ss understand *IQ* (intelligence quotient, or level). Tell Ss to discuss the questions in pairs and elicit some answers.

B Ask Ss to complete the questionnaire individually before comparing with a partner. Discuss Ss' ideas but do not reveal the answers at this point.

Alternative approach

To encourage more discussion during this activity, copy the questions (and question numbers) onto pieces of A4 paper or card. Tell Ss to write the numbers 1–5 in their notebooks so they can keep a record of their answers.

Either: Put Ss into five groups and give them one question each to discuss and make notes on, then on a signal from you they pass their question to the group on their right. This continues until they've answered all five questions.

Or: Display the questions on the board and Ss discuss them in pairs, making notes on their answers.

C Ss listen and confirm or change the notes they made in Ex 1B.

Answers:
1 at least a thousand each
2 above
3 **a)** blue **b)** green **c)** red **d)** yellow and orange
4 twenty-five percent
5 Monday and Tuesday between eleven and one o'clock

Unit 5 Recording 4

I = Interviewer J = Jake

I: Jake, you've been in advertising for what – thirty-five years? How have things changed over that time?
J: Well, there have been huge changes in *where* and *how* we advertise, but many of the basic principles of marketing are the same, for example, how consumers choose brands.
I: Can you give me an example?
J: Yes, let's imagine a coffee shop in a town centre somewhere,

anywhere, and it sells a thousand cups of coffee a day. Now, if another coffee shop opened next door …

I: … the first owner would be furious.

J: Don't be so sure. How many cups of coffee would each shop sell?

I: I don't know. Five hundred?

J: Logical, but no. They'd sell at least a thousand cups each.

I: Incredible. Why's that?

J: Choice makes people want things more. With one coffee shop, the question is, 'Shall I get a coffee or not?' but with two, the question becomes 'Which coffee shall I get?'

I: Fascinating. So what else hasn't changed?

J: Pricing is still important. People still like a bargain. But they also like to treat themselves.

I: What do you mean?

J: Well, supposing you wanted to sell a new brand of chocolate and your competitor's price was €2, what price would you set?

I: Mmm, I'd reduce the price. Maybe 1.80?

J: Why?

I: Because consumers want to save money.

J: True, to a certain extent. But experience shows that if the price is higher, people think your product is better.

I: So 2.50 would be better?

J: Indeed.

I: How about advertising a product? It's all video now, isn't it?

J: Well, not completely, but much more. One thing hasn't changed though, which is the way we respond to colour.

I: Oh, you mean like red means danger?

J: Yes, that kind of thing. We have built-in associations for every colour. Red is associated with energy, so it's good for energy drinks, cars, sports equipment and things like that. Green suggests safety, so it's often used for medical products. Apparently, yellow and orange stimulate the appetite, so they're used for food ads; blue on the other hand supresses the appetite, it's linked more to intellect and precision, so it's used to promote high-tech products.

I: And this … information is used in video adverts as well?

J: Sure. If a video advert goes viral, it'll get millions of views. And compared with TV, it's basically free. Your brand name will travel around the world provided the video goes viral.

I: And how can you ensure that?

J: You can't, but there are certain things that can help.

I: Such as?

J: Well about 25 percent of viewers will click off the video in the first 10 seconds. So you need to grab the viewer in the first 5 seconds.

I: Uh huh.

J: And you need to make the video memorable. I'll show you what I mean. I'll describe a video. You tell me the product.

I: OK.

J: Babies on roller skates dancing to hip-hop music.

I: Mineral water.

J: A gorilla playing drums to a famous pop song.

I: Chocolate. OK. I see your point. They were all quite bizarre.

J: Exactly, and memorable. People will click off unless the video is memorable. And millions of people shared them. And *that* didn't cost the advertiser anything. It's a great way to enter the market if you're a small business.

I: Yeah, I see. Any other guidelines?

J: Well, make it short. 15–60 seconds is good.

I: OK.

J: And it matters which day you post it. If you release the video at the weekend, you're dead.

I: But surely that's when people are free?

J: No, the best time is Monday and Tuesday, between eleven and one. Back at work, at their desks, bored.

I: Right. And what about the content?

J: Tell a story. Engage the viewer. For example …

D Give Ss a minute to read the questions and then play the recording again. Ask Ss to compare the answers with a partner.

Answers:
1 how people/consumers choose brands
2 It turns the decision to buy from a *yes/no* question into a *Which one?* question.
3 1 People like to save money, so they're attracted to lower prices.
  2 They also think that a higher price means higher quality, so when they want to 'treat' themselves, they buy the higher priced item.
4 1 Distribution of a viral video is free, and
  2 it can get millions of views if successful.
5 Five possible elements are mentioned, so any four of these:
  1 grab the viewer in the first 5 seconds
  2 make it memorable (or make it bizarre so that it's memorable)
  3 make it short (15–60 seconds)
  4 post it on a Monday or Tuesday, between 11a.m. and 1p.m.
  5 tell a story

E Ask Ss to work individually to write down the three most surprising things from the recording. In pairs, Ss compare their ideas.

VOCABULARY ADVERTISING COLLOCATIONS

2A Start by discussing with the class what different things advertisers can do to make sure consumers notice their product (e.g. invent a short phrase that people will remember, or an image that will remind people of the product, get someone famous to say they use it, etc.). Then direct Ss to the nouns in the box and ask them to complete the centre of each word web.

Answers: 1 a product **2** a price **3** a market

B Ask Ss to match the verbs in the box to the three nouns in the word webs. Check the answers as a class.

Answers: 1 promote, endorse **2** increase, reduce **3** dominate, see a gap in

C Ss should cover Ex 2A, or alternatively they could close their books and you could write the nouns on the board.

GRAMMAR REAL AND HYPOTHETICAL CONDITIONALS

3A Check that Ss understand the difference between *real* and *hypothetical*. Complete the first sentence as an example. Then ask Ss to work individually and decide which ones are real and which are hypothetical.

Answers: 1 real **2** real **3** real **4** real **5** hypothetical **6** hypothetical

B Do the first one as an example on the board and then set the task as individual work.

Answers:
1 Experience shows that if the price (is) higher, people <u>think</u> your product is better.
2 If a video (goes) viral, it <u>will get</u> millions of views.
3 People <u>will click off</u> unless the video (is) memorable.
4 Your brand name <u>will travel</u> around the world provided the video (goes) viral.
5 Supposing you (wanted) to sell a new brand of chocolate, … what price <u>would</u> you <u>set</u>?
6 If another coffee shop (opened) next door …, they'<u>d sell</u> at least a thousand cups each.

C Complete the first one as an example with the class then ask Ss to choose which words can replace *provided* and *supposing* in the sentences.

Answers:
Sentence 4: *provided* can be replaced with: *if, providing, on condition that, as long as*
Sentence 5: *Supposing* can be replaced with: *If, Providing, Suppose, Imagine, Let's say*

D Complete the first rule together and then ask Ss to work in pairs to complete the other rules. Check the answers together.

Answers:
1 **a)** present simple, present simple
b) present simple, (future with) *will*
2 past simple, *would* (+ infinitive without *to*)
3 **a)** unless
b) provided, providing, on condition that, as long as
c) supposing, suppose, imagine, let's say

4A You may need to play the recording twice for Ss to write down the complete sentences. Give them a minute or two to check what they've written with a partner.

Answers:
1 I'll buy it if you reduce the price.
2 I'd buy it if it weren't so expensive.
3 Suppose you had the money, which one would you buy?
4 I'll come as long as you let me pay.
5 You can't come in unless you're a member.

B Put Ss into pairs to underline the stressed words in each sentence, reminding them that the stress falls on the word which carries the meaning. You may need to play the recording one more time, stopping after each sentence for Ss to repeat and confirm their answers.

Answers: See the underlining in the answers in Ex 4A above.

speakout TIP

Read through the speakout tip with the class and ask Ss if they can 'complete' the conditional sentence in Bs reply, e.g. *Well, I'd take it if I were you*. Ask Ss why they think the speaker has omitted this, i.e. because it's obvious or implicit in the statement.

▷ LANGUAGEBANK 5.2 p136–137

Ss can read the grammar summary at home or in class. For a ***mixed-ability class***, you could give Ex A to ***weaker Ss*** and Ex B and C to ***stronger Ss***. Then give out answer keys for Ss to check their own work.

Answers:
A **1** 'll ask **2** offered **3** rains **4** would give **5** doesn't call **6** were **7** isn't **8** should take up
B **1** provided **2** unless **3** Supposing **4** Providing **5** unless **6** Imagine
C **1** you promise to keep it a secret
2 they don't pay our expenses
3 lost your job tomorrow
4 we don't have enough time
5 you don't stop being aggressive with me
6 met them in the street

5A Give Ss a few minutes to work in pairs and to think of ways of promoting a new product. Elicit some examples.

B To familiarise Ss with the concepts, tell them to read through the text quickly and answer these questions: *What is a vlogger?* (a person who blogs using video) *Do vloggers usually promote a product for free?* (No, they don't.). Find out if any Ss had put vlogger as one of their promotional ideas in Ex 5A.

C Ask Ss to choose the correct form of the verbs in each case. Tell Ss to think about the rules as they decide. Ask Ss to read the text out loud as you check.

Answers: **1** would **2** would **3** providing **4** will **5** as long as **6** will **7** goes **8** made **9** would **10** unless **11** won't **12** would

D If you have the facilities in your class, you could show one or two popular vloggers or blogs that Ss mentioned. As an extension, ask Ss to discuss the following questions: *Why do you think vloggers are popular? What topic would you like to vlog on? How do you know vloggers are telling the truth and not just trying to be popular?*

SPEAKING

6 You will need to pair As together and Bs together for the first part of this task. Monitor Ss' discussion before asking them to compare their predictions with the endings given on p161–162. Next ask Ss to work in A and B pairs and for each pair to tell their story to the other. After they have predicted the ending and discussed which one is more effective, hold a class vote to decide on the most effective.

Optional extra activities

- For Ss who enjoy acting:
  Put Ss into small groups to create a vlog, then give them time to practise acting it out. One student can be chosen to provide a 'voiceover', commenting on and explaining what's happening in the vlog. Ss then act out their vlog for the class.
- For Ss who enjoy being creative:
  Ss create a poster for their vlog, describing what happens and illustrating it with pictures. They then present their poster to the class. You will need to provide large sheets of paper, coloured pens, etc. for this option.

For both options, there can be a vote at the end to decide on the best concept for a vlog.

▷ VOCABULARYBANK p152 Advertising

Ex 2A and B consolidate and extend Ss' vocabulary for the topic of advertising. Ss should discuss and complete the two exercises in pairs, using a dictionary to check anything they are not sure about.

Answers:
A **1** commercials **2** slogans **3** makes **4** brand **5** trailer **6** logos **7** influence **8** jingle **9** campaigns **10** advertise **11** pop-ups **12** cold calls

Optional extra activity

For ***stronger classes***, ask Ss to choose an advert from the selection you brought into class for the Warm up. In small groups, Ss have to use as many words and expressions from the Vocabulary bank and the main unit to describe their advert as possible. Encourage Ss to add any extra information they know about the company and other adverts they have seen.

WRITING A REPORT; LEARN TO MAKE WRITTEN COMPARISONS

7A Tell Ss to cover the right-hand column of the page. Elicit some examples of gadgets, e.g. digital camera, MP3 player, mobile phone, watch, cordless headphones, video game console, then give Ss a few minutes to write their list of factors.

B Put Ss into groups to compare their lists and to say which factors they think are the most important.

8A Check that Ss understand the term *smartphone* (a mobile phone that can also send and receive email, browse the internet, etc.). Direct them to the list of factors on the left-hand side of the chart to compare with the list they made in the previous stage. Then give them a minute or two to answer the question.

Answers:
men: most important: useful/practical features;
least important: price
women: most important: fashionable; least important: size
teenagers: most important: my friends have the same;
least important: brand loyalty

B Once Ss have read the report they could work with a partner on the questions, then check their answers with the class.

Answers:
1 All except 'fashionable' (this only appears in the conclusion)
2 The student wrote that price is more important for men than for women, but the opposite is true.
3 1 Similarities; 2 Differences; 3 Teenagers

C Ask Ss to read the sentences and discuss whether they are true or false with a partner. Check the answers as a class.

Answers: 1 F 2 T 3 T 4 T

D Point out to Ss that a variety of phrases for comparing the different groups are used in the report, to avoid it becoming repetitive. Ss work alone finding the phrases, then compare answers in pairs.

Answers:
1 affect both groups more or less equally; there is no difference in; show only a slight variation
2 There are, however, significant differences in; far more important for x than for y; place greater importance on; showed an interesting contrast to
3 First of all,; For example,; However,; On the other hand,

9A Direct Ss to the chart and elicit the most obvious difference, i.e. the importance that teenagers place on friends having the same phone. Point out that Ss could use the phrase *far more important* for this point of contrast. Put Ss into pairs to note down four more points and choose appropriate phrases to use with them.

Suggested answers:
brand loyalty is the least important
price and fashionable are almost the same
friends have the same is the most important
most similar to men and women in relation to importance of size
most different from men in relation to useful/practical features and makes me look successful
most different from women in relation to brand loyalty

B Ss could work alone or help each other to write the paragraph about teenagers. Circulate and help them to use the phrases in Ex 8D accurately.

C Set this as a peer review task. Monitor and help.

Teaching tip

Peer review tasks tend to work best when modelled to Ss and when Ss have been given guidelines on what to do. Always set these tasks up to look at no more than three particular features, e.g. comparisons, structure and formality. Tell Ss to not focus on everything as too much feedback can be overwhelming. Instead suggest Ss pick out one good and one bad example of each factor they are looking at.

10 If you do not have time for this in class, you could set it as homework. Alternatively, Ss could complete a first draft in class and then write a final version for homework.

Homework ideas

- **Language bank:** 5.2 Ex A–B, p137
- **Vocabulary bank:** p152
- **Workbook:** Ex 1–6, p34–35

WHAT DO YOU THINK?

Introduction

Ss read about and practise brainstorming ideas, using phrases for suggesting ideas and related vocabulary. They also practise listening and learn to show reservations.

SUPPLEMENTARY MATERIALS
Resource bank: p171

Warm up

Ask Ss to close their books and put them into pairs. Tell them to discuss and make a list of as many ideas as they can for making sure they only speak English in class. After 3 mins, invite Ss to share their ideas and see which are the three most popular. NB This topic is also used in the Workbook, p36, Ex 1A: Ss could refer to the ideas there and see if there are any they didn't think of.

VOCABULARY COLLOCATIONS WITH *IDEA*

1A If you used the Warm up idea, elicit from Ss that this was an example of 'brainstorming'. Discuss the questions with the whole class, or give Ss a few minutes to discuss them in pairs first.

Suggested answers:
Brainstorming involves generating and writing down as many ideas as you can on a topic, usually with a group of people. It's used by companies, e.g. for problem solving, for developing/naming/marketing a new product, etc.

B Ask Ss to read the article and to check their ideas. In feedback, elicit which rule they think is wrong and why.

Answers:
Ss might offer various opinions and the teacher should be receptive to any they can justify. The conventions of brainstorming would say that Rule 5 is wrong. It should say: *Have a clear time limit. People often get their best ideas if they work under pressure.*

C Before Ss complete this task, write the word *idea* on the board. Ask Ss to think of one verb and one adjective that can collocate with this word. Set the task in the book.

Answers:
Verbs: come up with ideas, reject an idea, criticise an idea, get ideas, write an idea down, develop an idea
Adjectives: brilliant, predictable, bizarre, dreadful, unrealistic, best (good)

D Do the first one as an example with the class and then set this as individual work. Check the answers as a class.

Answers: **1** come up with **2** dreadful **3** reject **4** criticise **5** developing **6** bizarre **7** unrealistic **8** (a) predictable

E Choose one of the sentences from the list to tell the class your opinion on. Then put Ss into groups and ask them to do the same for the rest of the sentences. Elicit an opinion for each one.

FUNCTION SUGGESTING IDEAS

2A Introduce the topic, asking Ss why people don't walk as much nowadays and what can be done to encourage people to walk more. Then give them a few minutes in pairs to discuss and write down at least three ideas.

B Ss can underline any ideas that they thought of and add new ones to their list.

Answers: The ideas covered are: branding/get a sponsor, e.g. a shoe company; health benefits of walking; health problems, e.g. sitting down too long; close public transport for one day; video of people's feet; walking and talking (possibly viral video); charity campaign; use a celebrity

Unit 5 Recording 6

W1 = Woman 1 M1 = Man 1 W2 = Woman 2 M2 = Man 2

W1: OK people, so we're going to look for ways to get people walking more today and Ben's going to take notes.
M1: Right OK, I'm just gonna get a pen.
W1: Thank you. At this stage I think let's just get all our ideas down and we can discuss them later.
W2: Right, what I think, some sort of branding, we need a sponsor. Like, I don't know, a shoe company, for example.
W1: OK. Next idea.
M1: Well, I think walking is the easiest exercise anyone can take, and …
W1: Benefits of it?
M1: Yeah, the benefits of, of exercise you know and losing weight … keeping your heart healthy.
M2: And what about the other side of that, you know, scare people into thinking about what happens if you, if you sit down too much, if you don't, if you're not walking.
W1: Good.
M2: You know health problems and …
M1: Good idea.
M2: I tell you what, what about …
M1: Health.
M2: Could you, you know, I don't know, close public transport for a day, so everyone has to walk.
W2: That's good.
M1: So that's …
W1: That's really good.
M1: So what in a town, in the town centre you mean?
M2: Yeah, yeah.
M1: Yeah, that's a good idea.
W2: Hey, we're brainstorming!
M1: OK.
W1: Maybe a video showing just people's feet, so you've got walking and talking at the same time.
M1: Yeah – we could maybe, I know, incentivise people by raising money for charity.
All: Yes.
M1: Like distance covered, how many steps or …
W1: Have one more, one more.
M2: Well maybe get some celebrities involved.
W1: That's a great idea as well. Did you get all of that Ben?
M1: Yeah, so we've got, we've got um sponsorship, health in …
W1: Yes.
M1: … tied with that we've got scaring people, you know.
W1: Yes.
M1: We've got closing, um, public transport in the town.
W1: Yeah.
M2: Yeah.
M1: We've got a video.
W1: Online, the viral.
M1: Yeah the viral, yeah. And a charity campaign.
W1: Uh-huh.
M2: We're looking with …
M1: And, and oh yes celebrity, I didn't write that down.
W1: Celebrity, yeah OK brilliant, time's up and we've got some really great ideas, well done.

C Ss tick the three best ideas and compare their choices with a partner. While they listen, Ss cross off any ideas on their list that are rejected and write the reasons next to them. They circle the one that is chosen.

Answers:
They reject:
branding/get a sponsor – want a wider campaign; don't want the campaign linked to a particular company
health benefits of walking – a bit obvious; it's been done before, it's boring and expensive
health problems – people have been told about the dangers for years, not effective
close public transport for one day – unrealistic, transport companies wouldn't agree, they'd lose too much money
They chose a combination of:
video of people's feet and use a celebrity
The charity campaign is not discussed any further.

Unit 5 Recording 7

W1 = Woman 1 M2 = Man 2 M1 = Man 1 W2 = Woman 2

W1: OK, we're gonna look at the list and we've got all the ideas but we need to cut it down now. So I'm gonna put them up on the screen. And we'll start with the shoe company one, the sponsor, how do you feel about this idea?
M2: Well actually that could be a problem. I mean we want the campaign to be as wide as possible, don't we? So we don't want to link it just with one company, do we?
M1: Yeah, no that's a good point.
W2: That's true actually.
M1: Yeah, I mean my idea for example about pursuing the health angle.
M2: Yeah.
M1: I um. I mean we could get, we could get a TV doctor perhaps to make a programme about benefits of walking.
M2: Yeah, yeah.
W1: Nice.
M2: To be honest it wouldn't be my first choice, I have to say, I mean I, I like it.
W1: If you had the scientific angle to it, it could work.
W2: Yeah, it's a bit obvious maybe. D'you know what I mean it's kind of …
W1: What, been done?
W2: I think it has actually. I think it's a bit, a bit boring, I think the science thing's a bit boring. And actually that's quite a lot of money to …
M1: OK, fair enough.
W2: … to stick something on the telly.
W1: All right, so in that case would you consider the opposite idea of scaring people into it?
M1: Well frankly I don't think that will be effective. You know people have been told about the dangers of lack of exercise for years.
M2 Yeah, it's not a new thing, is it?
W1: All right then. How does the idea of closing public transport strike you?
W2: I don't think that's realistic to be honest with you. I don't, I don't think the train and bus companies would go for that.
W2: They'd lose so much money I just, just, I just think …
M1: To put it bluntly it …
W2: … disaster OK.
M1: … it wouldn't work.
W1: Because they'd just lose money.
W2: They'd lose too much money.
M2: Actually, I think we're on the wrong track here.
W2: Yeah?
M2: I mean I think it would be great if we could get celebrities to sort of promote walking generally, I think.
M1: That's not a bad idea at all. I think we should go for the feet idea.
W1: … with the video of the feet walking.
M1: That's right yeah.
M2: I mean I have to say at the moment I'm torn between the video and the celebrity. You know I think they're the best two ideas.
W1: All right, so with that in mind suppose we try combining the two ideas, our favourite ones. So we have the feet video but we have it so it's a celebrity.
M2: Famous feet!
All: Yeah, yeah.
M1: Famous feet! That's a good title for it as well.
W1: Oh and you could …
M2: Yeah, I like it.
M1: Famous feet.
W1: … have it as a competition.
M1: Yeah, brilliant!
W1: … so to guess whose feet that was for example.
W2: Yes.
M2: Yeah.
W1: So you have a shot of the feet walking, the person speaking and then you have to guess who it is …
M1: Sounds good to me.
W1: OK, let's go with that.

3A Give Ss a chance to look through the phrases first and try to predict/remember what was said. Ss could also copy the sentences into their notebooks to give themselves more space to complete the gaps. Play the recording again, then put Ss into pairs to compare their answers before group feedback.

Answers: **1** do you **2** you consider **3** strike you **4** would, could **5** go with **6** suppose we **7** go with

B Play the recording again and ask Ss to shadow read the suggestions as they listen.

Teaching tip

To help Ss to copy the stress and movement, you could exaggerate a model first and encourage Ss to imitate you. You can indicate that the phrase starts on a high pitch and gradually falls by using your hand. Point out to Ss that using a higher pitch is important because it makes the speaker sound interested/polite, whereas a low pitch can sound bored/rude.

C Ask Ss to complete these phrases with a partner and to check them in the audio script on p169.

Answers: **1** problem **2** choice **3** work **4** track **5** idea **6** torn

▷ LANGUAGEBANK 5.3 p136–137

Refer Ss to the tables in the Language bank so they can see the phrases for suggesting and reacting summarised. Ex A could be done in class as preparation before Ss move on to the flow chart on p63.

Answers:
A: What do you think about naming our language school *Tongues4U?*
B: That's a dreadful idea!
C: How do you feel about *Talk2Me?*
A: It doesn't grab me.
C: Would you consider *English246?*
B: I think we're on the wrong track here. All these numbers.
A: How does *Language Lab* sound?
B: Hmmm … Not bad.
C: I'm torn between *Language Lab* and *Lingo Lab.*
B: Let's go with *Language Lab* then.

4A Ss could brainstorm their own ideas for getting people to stop dropping litter before looking at the list here. Discuss briefly with the class which idea(s) they think is (are) best and why.

B Ss do not need to write the dialogue out in full, rather they should just use the flow chart as a prompt. Point out that they need to be careful with the verb forms in the phrases and refer them back to the Language bank if they need to check.

Suggested answers:
Possible dialogue though slight differences would be fine:
A: How do you feel about getting a celebrity to endorse the campaign?
B: That wouldn't be my first choice, I have to say.
A: How does the idea of increasing fines strike you?
B: It's been done before. I think we're on the wrong track. It would be great if we could use signs in the backs of cars.
A: That's predictable too. Would you consider bins with sound effects?
B: That's not a bad idea at all. I'm torn between that and using interesting signs in cars or other places.
A: Suppose we try combining the two ideas?
B: OK. It seems like the best suggestion.
A: Right, let's go with that.

C Ask Ss to change roles and note down two key words from each sentence before practising the conversation again. Monitor the practice and be prepared to give Ss feedback on their use of the phrases and their intonation.

LEARN TO SHOW RESERVATIONS

5A You may want to explain to Ss that a *reservation* in this context is a feeling of doubt about an idea. Put them into pairs to look at the comments.

Answers: 1 ✗ 2 ✗ 3 ✗ 4 ✗ 5 ✓

B Play the recording and ask Ss to fill in the missing words and phrases. Ask Ss to work in pairs to check their answers.

Answers: **1** Actually **2** To be honest **3** Frankly **4** To put it bluntly **5** I have to say

C Warn Ss that they should be careful how they use these comments. They will need to be especially careful with their intonation!

Answers: frankly, to put it bluntly

speakout TIP

Before directing Ss to the tip, you could tell them to read aloud to each other the negative comments in Ex 5A without the missing phrases and ask them what effect they have (i.e. they sound very direct and could offend the person who made the suggestion).

D Tell Ss to write a plus (+) or minus (–) sign next to the number when they hear the phrases.

Answers:
1 Well actually, I think it's … (+)
2 Well actually, I think it's … (–)
3 I have to say, I feel that … (–)
4 I have to say, I feel that … (+)
5 To be honest, it's quite … (–)
6 To be honest, it's quite … (+)

E Play the recording again, stopping after each phrase for Ss to repeat.

SPEAKING

6A Put Ss into groups of three to five for this. Tell them to select a topic and brainstorm ideas following the 'rules of brainstorming' they studied at the beginning of the lesson. Tell them to write down all the ideas they generate, but not to comment on them yet.

B Remind Ss to try to incorporate some of the phrases for suggesting ideas and showing reservations during the discussion and evaluation of the list of ideas. Monitor and note down examples of good language use and problem areas for feedback.

C Before Ss tell the class about their ideas, refer them back to the collocations with *idea* in Ex 1C and 1D and suggest they use one or two when explaining why they chose/rejected an idea, e.g. *We decided that it was a terrible idea …; At first it seemed like a crazy idea, but then we realised … .*

Optional extra activity

While each group is presenting their idea, other Ss write down a question they'd like to ask about it. Then, at the end of each presentation, allow a few minutes for questions 'from the floor'.

Homework ideas

- **Ex 4B** and **Ex 6A:** Ss write a conversation based on the flow chart in Ex 4B, using one of the topics from Ex 6A.
- **Language bank:** 5.3 Ex A, p137
- **Workbook:** Ex 1–3, p36

GENIUS

Introduction

Ss watch an extract from the BBC programme *Genius*, where people present ideas for new products or services and a celebrity guest decides if they are genius (very clever, brilliant). Ss then learn and practise how to present a business idea and write a product review.

SUPPLEMENTARY MATERIALS
Ex 5A: bring in examples of product reviews.

Warm up

Tell Ss to close their books and write the word *Genius* on the board. Ask Ss to define the word and to name three famous people they think are geniuses and the reasons why they think so.

DVD PREVIEW

1A Explain that the BBC programme they are going to watch is called *Genius* and give Ss a few minutes in pairs to discuss what they think the programme is about. Invite each pair to share their ideas with the class.

B Direct Ss to the statements, then give them a minute or two to read the text and decide in pairs if they're true or false.

Answers:
1 F Members of the public present their ideas.
2 T
3 F The celebrity guest decides which ideas are 'genius.'

DVD VIEW

2A Ask Ss to look at the photo and to elicit what they think it might be.

B Play the DVD and ask Ss to check their predictions. Ask Ss to discuss what they think of the idea. NB You could pause the DVD just after the 'piano choir' finishes singing and ask Ss to predict whether the idea will be judged 'genius' or not, then play the rest of the recording. They could also discuss what they think of the idea and whether they agree with the judge's decision.

Answers:
The idea is a 'piano choir' which is controlled by the keys of a piano. Each member of the choir is linked to a different key on the piano.
Added by the show: Each member of the choir holds a candle-shaped electric light, which is wired to the appropriate key on the piano; when the light goes on, the chorister sings their note.

DVD 5 Genius

DG = Dave Gorman DH = Dan Haythorn L = Laurie S = Stuart

DG: Hello, and welcome to *Genius*: a show all about you and your ideas. If you think you might be a genius, we can give you the chance to prove it: all you have to do is email us with your cleverest notion. We invite the people with the most potential to join us and it's here that we work out once and for all who really is a genius.
OK Stuart, let's see what you make of our final idea tonight. It comes from Dan Haythorn from North West London.
DH: Dear Genius, imagine hooking a piano keyboard up to a choir, so that each key caused a different chorister to sing that note. Someone playing the keyboard would then be essentially playing a choir. I've never seen this done before, and I would really like to.
DG: Would this, this choir … a person in the choir, a chorister, is that note. That's what they represent.
DH: Yeah, well each, note would, um, be assigned to a different chorister, so someone would be middle C, someone would be C sharp, etc., the length and breadth of the keyboard. And, you press that key – it would prompt them to sing that note.
DG: But it's not something an ordinary musician could ever own?
DH: No you couldn't have it at home, really no, not unless … not unless you happen to live with a choir of some sort.
DG: We obviously, we thought about doing it, in the studio and, and Thorin, our prop man, made an artist's impression of, of how he imagined it would look. He's imagining wires with lights from each key, to the choir, and we thought it was worthy of investigation so we have had a piano rigged up to lots of little candle lights. So if … if we can bring that in first of all …
Now just in case anyone thinks that this is just like a rehearsed thing and that this machine doesn't work, I think we're the perfect people to prove that this is … this is real. OK, you can see we've got the white keys, the black keys that correlate precisely with the white keys and the black keys on this piano. You don't mind if we do this, do you Laurie?
L: Ah, no.
DG: OK. After all we built it, I think we should. Just hit anything you like at random, a kind of …
What has he ever done to you?
And, well I think that you should maybe give it a go Laurie … you're, you're the man who knows.
L: Mm, yeah. Any particular style?
DG: I think we should go classical.
L: Something classical, OK. … Fantastic!
DG: Now apart from making Dan's dream come true, is this idea – Dan Haythorn and his piano choir – genius or not?
S: I think it's only begun to realise its potential. It's genius.

C Focus Ss on the sentences and play the DVD. Check the answers as a class.

Answers: **1** most potential, work out, make of **2** essentially, to **3** happen to **4** worthy of investigation **5** at random **6** give it a go

D Put Ss into pairs or small groups and tell them to think of at least one benefit and drawback for each of the ideas, as well as deciding on the most 'genius' idea. Conduct feedback with the whole class, to see if one idea emerges as the most popular.

Suggested answers:
Sell socks in threes:
Benefits – if a sock got lost in the wash, you'd still have a pair.
Drawbacks – you could end up with a lot of extra socks that you don't need.
'Democrobus':
Benefits – could cut down bus journeys because the bus wouldn't stop unnecessarily.
Drawbacks – time could be wasted discussing/arguing about where the bus should go.
Mini-elephants:
Benefits – they would eat less and cause less damage.
Drawbacks – there could be many other genetic weaknesses. It could damage eco-systems if they escape.
Food via pipes:
Benefits – would save a lot of time and effort.
Drawbacks – would have to be a soft or liquid consistency that could go through a pipe.

speakout a presentation

3A Put Ss into pairs and ask them to think of three reasons why Yummy Utensils might be a good invention. Hold an initial vote to decide whether Ss think it's genius or not.

B Play the recording and ask Ss to tick any reasons they wrote down that are the same. Ask Ss to summarise the reasons they heard. Hold a second vote to decide whether the idea is genius or not.

Answers:
Reasons: Environmentally friendly – compared with making plastic. They create no waste/rubbish as they dissolve in a few days. Fun – especially with kids. Good for you as made with vegetables.

Unit 5 Recording 11

W = Woman M = Man

W: We would like to introduce to you an idea that will change the way you eat: Yummy Utensils. As you can guess, we're talking about knives, forks and spoons that you can eat.
M: You'll never have to throw plastic knives, forks and spoons in the rubbish again. At the end of your lunch, after you finish eating, you simply eat your utensils, like this.
W: Yummy Utensils are made of a special vegetable and flour mixture, are strong enough to cut meat and pierce salad, but easy to digest after you chew them.
M: They're tasty, too – a bit like pretzels. Here, would you like to try one?
W: What makes our idea special is that it's not just practical, and it's not a simple gimmick.
M: No, Yummy Utensils are not just practical and fun, they're also environmentally friendly. Just think of all of the resources that go into making plastic utensils, which are just thrown into the rubbish and become a permanent part of the waste that we litter the planet with. Yummy Utensils are made from natural ingredients, using the same processes as are used to make bread products, and of course create no rubbish at all. Even if you don't eat your Yummy Utensils and throw them in the rubbish, they dissolve within days. So there's no damage to the environment.
W: We envisage this product being sold in supermarkets, in the same section where you buy picnic supplies. But don't be surprised if they're sold in the snack section – they taste better than some snack foods. And they're certainly better for you.
M: We think that Yummy Utensils will be a hit with families in particular, since they're the biggest consumers of disposable utensils.
W: And kids love having a fork or spoon they can eat. We've done some market testing and it was amazing how much the children enjoyed them.
M: In the future, we are planning to develop a sweetened version which will make Yummy Utensils the perfect dessert.
W: Thank you for your attention and we welcome any questions.

C Before you play the recording again, go through the key phrases with the class and check: *envisage* (imagine) and *differentiate oneself* (show a difference from). Point out that where there are options in the phrases (e.g. *We think that … will be a hit with [single people/families/…] in particular.*), Ss need to underline the option(s) they hear. Once you have checked the answers, drill the phrases and prompt Ss to substitute different alternatives from the box.

Answers:
We would like to introduce to you an idea that …; What makes our idea special is that it's not just … but it's also …; We envisage this product being sold [in supermarkets/on TV/via the internet/…].; We think that … will be a hit with [single people/families/…] in particular.; In the future, we are planning to develop a [business/lightweight/diet/…] version.

4A Put Ss into pairs and direct As and Bs to their list of business ideas. Give them a few minutes to read through their ideas then tell each other about them and choose one that they both like.

B Ss should aim to make their presentation about 2–3 mins long. They also need to give their product a 'catchy' name and think about how they could use visuals in the presentation, e.g. a picture of the product, a graph showing sales forecasts, etc. While Ss prepare, circulate and help with vocabulary, etc.

C Ss should decide which of them is going to start the presentation and at what point they're going to hand over to their partner, etc. Then put pairs together to help each other before they 'go public' with their presentations. Give Ss time in their pairs to make any changes to their notes.

D Encourage Ss who are listening to make a few notes on each product and write any questions they have for the presenters. Ss then decide on the product they like best and vote for it.

writeback a product review

5A In pairs Ss look at the review and discuss what they think of the product. Elicit how many stars they think it got.

Suggested answers: writer 1: five stars; writer 2: one star

B Ss highlight the features in the reviews. Check the answers as a class.

Answers: Both reviews include b), d) and e). The second review also includes a).

C Tell Ss to plan their own reviews and to look again at the models in the book. When Ss are writing their reviews, remind them not to visibly include any stars (they could mark them on the back of their review). The other Ss will have to guess how many stars it was given.

D Stick the reviews on the board or round the walls. Ask Ss to read them and guess how many stars each product review awarded the chosen product.

Homework ideas

Ss write a product review for another product from the lists they looked at in Ex 4A.

LOOKBACK

Introduction

The aim of these activities is to provide revision and further practice of the language from the unit. You can also use them to assess Ss' ability to use the language, in which case you need to monitor but avoid helping them. You may feel that you don't need or have time to do all the activities. If so, you could allocate the activities that would be most beneficial for your Ss, or get individual Ss to decide which activities they'd like to do.

CHANGE

1A Before you start this, ask Ss to close their books and, in pairs, make a list of as many words as they can for talking about change in both a positive and negative way. Then tell Ss to look at the exercise and see if they remembered all the words. Focus them on the example and give them a minute or two to rewrite the sentences.

Answers:
1 People with many talents can *adjust* to it well and tend to find a new job quickly.
2 It's *caused damage* to family relationships.
3 It's *had a positive effect on the quality of life of people in the developing world.*
4 It *revolutionised* the way people think about war.

B You could discuss sentence 1 with the class, then put Ss into pairs to discuss the other three.

Suggested answers:
1 losing your job/being made unemployed
2 TV, mobile phones, the internet
3 medicine, better crops, provision of water pumps/wells
4 news broadcasts, 24-hour news, photographs of war, blogs/forums/social media, a particular war film

ARTICLES

2A You could start by writing *basketball, windsurfing* and *Scrabble* on the board and asking Ss to tell you as much as they can about them. Then put Ss into pairs to complete the questions. You may want to refer Ss to the section on articles in the Language bank on p136 while they work on this.

Answers: **1** The **2** – **3** a **4** the **5** – **6** the **7** a **8** – **9** a **10** an **11** the **12** the **13** – **14** the **15** the **16** – **17** the **18** –

B Give Ss a few minutes to answer the questions. You could ask one student from each pair to come and write their five answers on the board before checking on p160 and see which pair(s) had the most correct answers.

Answers: **1** a) **2** b) **3** b) **4** c) **5** a)

ADVERTISING

3A You could run this as a competition in teams. When a team has the answer, they put up their hands and call out the missing vowels only. Then ask members of the team to tell you the complete words and give extra points for good pronunciation.

Answers: launch **1** break **2** gap **3** set **4** increase, reduce **5** promote **6** advertise **7** endorse

B Ss choose a product and answer the questions in pairs.

CONDITIONALS

4A Ask Ss to complete the sentences individually. When checking answers, ask Ss to explain the difference in the two responses from B each time.

Answers: **1** 'd, 'll **2** 'd, 'll **3** 'll, would **4** 're, wouldn't be

B Tell Ss to close their books and write the title *Seducing shoppers* on the board. Ask the class for ideas about what the text will say, then tell them to read the text quickly and see if they were right. Then give Ss a few minutes to choose the alternatives and compare answers in pairs. They could refer to the Language bank on p136 to check anything they're unsure of.

Answers: **1** Supposing **2** would **3** are **4** will put **5** provided **6** will put **7** saw **8** wouldn't **9** would be **10** unless

C Ss can discuss the question in pairs, then share their answers with the class.

SUGGESTING IDEAS

5A You could run this as a race. Put Ss into pairs and give each pair a copy of the conversation. As soon as a pair find and correct all the mistakes, they bring the exercise to you to check. Stop the race after two or three pairs have corrected the mistakes.

Answers:
A: It'*d* be great if we could have the class party at a four-star hotel.
B: That wouldn't be my *first* choice. How ~~much~~ do you feel about the school cafeteria?
C: The school cafeteria? To be honest, *it/that* wouldn't work. *How* does Pizza Rizza strike you?
B: That's *not* a bad idea at all.
A: Actually, I think we're on the wrong *track* here. I think we should go for somewhere nicer.
B: OK. *Suppose* we try the Four Seasons or the Hilton?
A: I'm *torn* between the two, but the Four Seasons is closer.
C: OK. Let's go with that.

B If you feel it will be too challenging for Ss to memorise the whole conversation, give them a copy of the conversation with key parts blanked out. Tell Ss to practise the conversation using the 'skeleton' to help them, e.g.
A: ________ we could have the class party at a four-star hotel.
B: That ________ choice. ________ the school cafeteria?
C: The school cafeteria? ________ it wouldn't work. ________ Pizza Rizza ________?
B: That's ________ at all.
A: Actually, I think we're ________. I think we should go for somewhere nicer.
B: OK. ________ the Four Seasons or the Hilton?
A: ________ the two, but the Four Seasons is closer.
C: OK. ________ that.

C Elicit some reasons why the class might decide to have a party, e.g. end of course, new Ss joining the class, Christmas, etc. Get the class to choose one of the reasons and tell them they're going to plan the party. Put Ss into groups and remind them to appoint someone to write their ideas down. Write the five categories they need to brainstorm on the board: *place, food, activities, music, dress.* Give them time to brainstorm all the categories.

Remind Ss to try to use some of the phrases for suggesting ideas. They can write the phrases on a piece of paper, then tick a phrase every time they manage to use it in the discussion.

BBC interviews and worksheet

If you could start a business, what would it be?

This video looks at the topic of shopping and innovative products.

OVERVIEW

6.1 THE TIME OF MY LIFE

SPEAKING | talk about the advantages and disadvantages of different ages
VOCABULARY | age
READING | read an article about early and late successes
GRAMMAR | modal verbs and related phrases
PRONUNCIATION | connected speech: elision
SPEAKING | discuss different ages and generations
VOCABULARY *PLUS* | word-building: prefixes

6.2 FUTURE ME

LISTENING | listen to a BBC programme about letters to your future self
GRAMMAR | future perfect and continuous
PRONUNCIATION | weak forms: auxiliaries
SPEAKING | talk about your future
VOCABULARY | optimism/pessimism
WRITING | an informal email; learn to focus on informal style

6.3 SO WHAT YOU'RE SAYING IS …

VOCABULARY | collocations
FUNCTION | persuading
PRONUNCIATION | intonation: persuading
LEARN TO | clarify ideas
SPEAKING | discuss the right age for different things

6.4 HOW TO LIVE TO 101 BBC DVD

DVD | watch a BBC programme about living longer
speakout | a debate
writeback | a forum comment

6.5 LOOKBACK

Communicative revision activities

BBC INTERVIEWS

What was the best period of your life?

This video encourages Ss to reflect on and discuss what they consider to be the best period or periods of their lives. Use this video at the start or end of Unit 6 or set it as homework.

THE TIME OF MY LIFE

Introduction

Ss practise reading and speaking about ages and generations using modal verbs and related phrases and vocabulary. They also learn about word building: prefixes.

SUPPLEMENTARY MATERIALS
Resource bank: p172 and p174
Warm up: prepare a handout with some sayings about age (see below).

Warm up

Either: Prepare a handout with sayings about age (collections of sayings can be found on the internet), e.g.

Age is an issue of mind over matter. If you don't mind, it doesn't matter. *Mark Twain*

Wrinkles should merely indicate where smiles have been. *Mark Twain*

Do not regret growing older. It is a privilege denied to many. *Author unknown*

Middle age is when your age starts to show around your middle. *Bob Hope*

Forty is the old age of youth; fifty the youth of old age. *Victor Hugo*

Growing old is mandatory; growing up is optional. *Chili Davis*

Youth is a disease from which we all recover. *Dorothy Fuldheim*

Thirty-five is when you finally get your head together and your body starts falling apart. *Caryn Leschen*

Put Ss into pairs to discuss what the sayings mean, which they agree with/like best, etc. then conduct feedback with the class.

Or: Put Ss into pairs and write *young*, *middle-aged* and *old* on the board. Ask them to:

1 decide on an age range for each group;
2 think of three adjectives they associate with each group.

Ss compare their ideas with the rest of the class in feedback. This will work best in a class where there is a range of ages and Ss will have different perceptions of what 'old' is, etc.

SPEAKING

1 Direct Ss to the box and discuss the advantages and disadvantages of being ten years old as a class. Then put Ss into pairs to discuss the rest.

VOCABULARY AGE

2A Focus Ss on the example and give them a few minutes to match the other phrases. Points to check in feedback: the phrases in 1–3 all need an appropriate possessive adjective; *maturity* is the noun from *mature* and is used with the verb *have*; *elderly* is more polite than *old*.

Answers: 1 f) 2 c) 3 a) 4 e) 5 h) 6 g) 7 b) 8 d)

B Put Ss into pairs to discuss the questions that interest them, then conduct feedback to find out where they agree/disagree. Monitor Ss' use of the vocabulary and help them with any pronunciation problems at this stage.

READING

3A Direct Ss to the title of the article and give them a few minutes to discuss what they think each phrase means. After Ss have checked their predictions against the first two paragraphs, elicit whether Ss can think of any early peakers or late bloomers.

Answers:
peak early – have success at an early age, and then lose it
late bloomer – someone who finds what they're good at and possibly has success in it relatively late in life

B Ss work in pairs and discuss their ideas, but do not read the text at this stage. Elicit some ideas for each one.

C Ss check their predictions against the text. Elicit the answers from the class.

Answers:
1 late bloomers: Ang Lee, Colonel Sanders, Cervantes; peaked early: Wang Yani, Nadia Comăneci, Jocelyn Lavin
2 sports ('Sports are particularly biased towards youth …')
3 Malcolm Gladwell is talking about the period before the late bloomer finds success, when they seem to be struggling and getting nowhere.
4 The article gives examples of:
- freedom: first when you're allowed to do things on your own in childhood, e.g. stay out late, take public transport alone, drive a car. Then when you're older and earning money, 'you don't have to worry about money for a nice holiday or a meal at a fancy restaurant'.
- obligation: the teenager who has to do her homework and come home before 10 o'clock.
- expectations: the 30-year-old who is obliged to work hard, doesn't feel successful, but meanwhile pretends he is successful because he feels it's expected.

4A Tell Ss to look at the sentence before and after each word and to use the context to guess the meaning. Elicit possible definitions for each.

B Ask Ss to check their ideas from Ex 4A by matching the words to the definitions. As an extension, allocate one word to each pair and ask them to write an example sentence on the topic of age using their given word. Elicit example sentences from the group.

Answers: **1** enterprise **2** ever-shifting **3** milestones **4** mediocrity **5** biased **6** pens **7** peers

C Depending on the issues raised in Ex 1, you could refer Ss back to some of these points for inspiration. The issues raised will probably vary depending on the age of your class, e.g. go to university, buy a house, get married, have children, retire, etc. and will often be very age dependent.

GRAMMAR MODAL VERBS AND RELATED PHRASES

5A Books closed. Write the sentences on the board without the modals and related phrases underlined. Ask Ss to identify the modals and phrases. Direct Ss to complete the table. While Ss work in pairs to complete the table, draw it on the board. You can then invite Ss to come up and add the verbs during feedback.

Answers:

obligation (strong)	*has to*	prohibition	*mustn't*
obligation (weak)	*should*	permission	*can*
lack of obligation	*don't have to*	ability/lack of ability	*can't*

B Some of these phrases, e.g. *be supposed to*, *be allowed to*, will probably be less familiar to Ss. Once they have decided on the best match to the rules, check the meaning and form.

Answers:
1 are able to – ability/lack of ability
2 be allowed to – permission
3 make someone – obligation (strong), let someone do – permission
4 be supposed to – obligation (weak) (often for something not fulfilled)
5 manage to – ability/lack of ability (usually when something is difficult)

6A Tell Ss to write the numbers 1–6 in their notebooks. Play the recording, stopping after each number to give Ss time to write.

Answers:
1 We must go home now.
2 I can't come to the party.
3 You don't have to do it.
4 You shouldn't listen to him.
5 We're supposed to speak English.
6 Are we allowed to use dictionaries?

B Ss may need to listen again in order to identify the sounds left out. To practise this, you could drill the complete sentences.

Answers: **1** must **2** can't **3** don't **4** shouldn't **5** supposed **6** allowed

▷ LANGUAGEBANK 6.1 p138–139

The Language bank has a summary of the present and past forms of all the modal verbs and related phrases. There is also a note about the use of *was/were able to* and *managed to* versus *could*. Ss could do Ex A and B for homework, or use Ex B for oral practice as a team game: display the sentences one at a time on the board and the first team to put their hands up and say the correct answer wins a point.

Answers:
A **1** had to **2** were supposed to **3** managed to **4** couldn't **5** made **6** able to **7** let **8** allowed to **9** have to **10** don't have to **11** can **12** ought to
B 1 I managed to fall asleep.
2 We had to stay for dinner.
3 He let me listen to my MP3 player.
4 He wasn't able to see anything.
5 She ought to leave before dark.
6 We were supposed to pay before going in (but we didn't).
7 Adults aren't allowed to enter this disco.
8 They made me change my passport photo.

Optional extra activity

To give Ss more practice in manipulating the present and past forms of the verbs orally, put Ss into pairs and give Student A and Student B a set of sentences each, e.g.

Student A

1 *I'm supposed to finish my work before I leave.*
2 *They're allowed to come with us.*
3 *We had to do lots of exams at school.*
4 *I can't afford a new car.*

Student B

1 *My brother never let me borrow his car.*
2 *Our teacher makes us work hard.*
3 *We didn't have to get up early.*
4 *He never manages to catch the early bus.*

Ss take turns to read out one of their sentences. Their partner repeats the sentence, changing it into the past or present as appropriate.

7A Ss work alone to complete the sentences. Make sure they understand that in some cases there is more than one possible answer.

Answers: **1** should/must, won't be able **2** couldn't/wasn't able to **3** let **4** was supposed to **5** make **6** manage **7** 'll be able to **8** don't have to

B You could demonstrate this first by changing one or two of the sentences to give your opinion. Once Ss have compared their answers, ask them to report back on opinions that they had in common with their partner and/or which of their partner's opinions they found the most interesting/surprising/amusing.

SPEAKING

8A Give Ss time alone to think about the three questions and make some notes for their answers. You may want to remind them to try to use the modal verbs and related phrases and the vocabulary related to age.

B Put Ss into groups of three to five to discuss the questions. Monitor and make notes on language areas for improvement in feedback.

Teaching tip

To use feedback time for teaching, rather than simply correction of errors that Ss made in the speaking activity, make a note of things Ss say that are not incorrect, but very simple, or awkward. In feedback write the phrase/sentence on the board and encourage Ss to improve it with more sophisticated English. You could prompt them by writing up an 'improved' version with gaps in it, e.g.

original sentence: *I think I'm a young adult, but old people think I'm a child.*

improvement: *I think of myself as a young adult, but people from older generations see me as a child.*

VOCABULARY PLUS WORD-BUILDING: PREFIXES

9A Give Ss a minute or two to add the negative prefixes and check answers with a partner. Don't confirm whether the answers are correct at this stage as Ss will hear the right answers in Ex 9B.

B Play the recording to check the answers. Play the recording a second time, asking Ss to repeat and to listen for the stress. With ***stronger groups***, you could also ask them to mark the stress as they listen and repeat.

Answers: **1** unrealistic **2** unpredictable, illogical **3** dissatisfied **4** unfamiliar **5** impatient **6** immortal **7** unwilling **8** misbehave **9** insecure, misinterpret **10** irrelevant, unhealthy
The prefixes are unstressed.

C Tell Ss to work individually and mark sentences with a Y for younger people or an O for older people if they think they relate more to one particular group. In pairs, Ss compare their choices and give reasons and support for each one.

speakout TIP

This task shows how negatives are shown in many dictionaries. Ask Ss to check the listings of any new words from Ex 9A.

10A Give Ss a few minutes to answer the questions alone. When they are ready, they can compare their answers with a partner. Check answers as a class and point out the use of hyphens, reminding Ss that even native speakers have problems with hyphen use because of their rather erratic nature.

Answers:
1 a) pre-war **b)** prehistory
2 a) post-war **b)** postgraduate
3 a) overtime **b)** overworked
4 a) underage **b)** underqualified

B This task can be set as a competition. Put Ss into small groups. Give Ss 2 mins to think of as many words as possible. After 2 mins find out which group has the most words and elicit their answers. Award one point for each correct word. Elicit any words the other groups had thought of.

▷ VOCABULARYBANK p153 Word-building: prefixes

Ex 1A, B and C give Ss more practice with word-building and enhance their awareness of the common patterns for the different parts of speech. Give them plenty of time to complete the tasks, using dictionaries to help, before feeding back as a class.

Answers:
A **1** micro **2** mega **3** multi **4** inter **5** bi **6** trans
B bilingual, bicycle, bimonthly
multilingual, multinational, multimedia, multitask, multi-storey
microchip, microwave, microphone, microscope
megaphone, megacity, megabyte
translate, transport, transit
international, interval, interview
C **1** multi-storey **2** intervals **3** transit **4** megaphone **5** interview **6** microscope **7** bimonthly **8** multilingual

Homework ideas

- Ss imagine they're taking a course in something new, e.g. dancing, cookery, pottery, another language. They write an email to a friend telling them about the course and what they *have to do/are supposed to do/can't do/aren't allowed to do* and what the teachers *make them do* in the lessons, for homework, etc.
- **Language bank:** 6.1 Ex A–B, p139
- **Vocabulary bank:** p153
- **Workbook:** Ex. 1–5, p37–38

FUTURE ME

Introduction

Ss practise listening and speaking about the future using the future perfect and future continuous and vocabulary related to optimism/pessimism. They also learn to write in an informal style.

SUPPLEMENTARY MATERIALS
Resource bank: p173 and p175
Ex 1A: be prepared to help Ss guess your four predictions for the year ahead.
Ex 7A: bring monolingual dictionaries for Ss to use.
Ex 9C: prepare a gapped copy of the formal email.

Warm up

Write this question on the board: *Do you feel optimistic or pessimistic about the future? Why?* Give Ss a few minutes to think about their answer, then invite them to share their answers in small groups or as a class. To help Ss to focus their ideas, you could also write the following prompts on the board: *work, health, transport, food, communication, energy, leisure time.*

LISTENING

1A Tell Ss you are thinking about your life over the next four years and write three sentence 'heads' on the board: *I'm definitely going to …; I might …; I hope …* . Give Ss clues so they can guess your answers. Give Ss a few minutes to think of their own answers.

B Ss either compare answers or do the same as above, i.e. write sentence 'heads' and help each other to complete the predictions by giving clues.

2 Once Ss have read the programme information, discuss the questions with the class.

Answer:
1 The website holds a letter you write and sends it to you on a date you pick.

3A Check that Ss understand the situation by asking: *How old is Laura? How old was she when she wrote the letter? Where was it during the time in between?* Tell them to listen and answer the questions.

Answer: 1 studies, relationship and family 2 romantic, optimistic

Unit 6 Recording 3

OK … so … Dear the future me, I hope this letter has found its way to you/me. As I write this, I am sixteen in year eleven; and as I read it, I am twenty. Wow! I will have changed so much. I can only guess what I will be like at twenty. I envisage myself at Oxford Uni, sitting … oh, this is embarrassing … sitting under a tree by the river in the college grounds. I think I'll be wearing something floaty and a bit indie, but I bet when I get this, it'll be raining.

I know, I'm a romantic. I hope that hasn't changed. My plans for myself in the following years are to find a man, someone good-looking, romantic and intelligent who shares my interests. Either way, I hope I'll have someone. I don't remember this … and then I think I'll have three children with long, brown hair and green eyes.

Well, I'll stop now even though I want to write everything I can down, but I'm running out of time. I hope I'm happy and hope this letter makes me feel good about who I was, or am, as I write this. Keep smiling, and while I can't really say bye, but good luck for the future and keep dreaming. Don't change too much, and be happy with who you are – I like who I am now more than any other time. Love, Laura.

B Give Ss time to look through the sentences. They may already have some ideas for the answers after listening for the first time. Check the answers as a class.

Answers:
1 … and *wearing* something floaty.
2 I know, I'm *a romantic*.
3 I hope I'll have ~~married~~ someone.
4 … with long, brown hair and *green* eyes.
5 … I *want* to write everything I can down, …
6 Don't *change* too much, …

C Ask Ss to predict Laura's answers. Vocabulary to check: *the way her life has turned out* (the way her life is now).

Answers: 1 shallow, unrealistic 2 very happy, ecstatic

Unit 6 Recording 4

It all seems really shallow looking back and reading what I thought I'd be doing or hoped I'd be doing. I think my sixteen-year-old self might have been disappointed with where I am, but because I, as my twenty-year-old self, have sort of grown up and matured. I'm absolutely ecstatic with where I am and it doesn't have to be this perfect sitting-by-a-lake kind of image.

GRAMMAR FUTURE PERFECT AND CONTINUOUS

4A Ss read and match the examples to the meanings. Check that Ss understand *in progress around the moment that she opens the letter* by asking: *Will it start raining when she gets the letter or before she gets it?* (before) *Will it stop raining?* (probably not).

Answers: 1 a) 2 b)

B For ***weaker classes*** write on the board: *be, past participle*, -ing *form, have*. Ss can choose from these.

Answers: 1 have, past participle 2 be, -*ing* form

C You could discuss these with the whole class. Elicit some other examples of state verbs, e.g. *like, have (possess), seem.*

Answers:
1 I'll own – *own* is a state verb and not usually used in the continuous form.
2 by – *I'll have finished by 12* = 'at some time before and no later than 12'; *I won't have finished until 12* = 'I expect to finish at 12 and no earlier.' (Notice that for this meaning we use a negative verb.)

D Demonstrate the task, using the sentences from Ex 4A, before you play the recording. Write the four sentences on the board and ask Ss to come up and mark the relevant parts.

Answers:
1 I'll have left home.
2 They won't have finished.
3 We'll be living in Spain.
4 It'll be snowing.

E Play the recording again and ask Ss to say the sentences at the same time as the speaker. As they are saying the sentences ask Ss to focus on the stressed words.

▷ LANGUAGEBANK 6.2 p138–139

Draw Ss' attention to the use of *by* with the future perfect, the use of the future continuous for something that will happen 'in the normal course of events', not as a result of a plan, and the use of adverbs and modal verbs with these future forms. If you want to use Ex A and B in class for practice, you could give half the class Ex A and the other half Ex B. Give Ss a key to check their answers when they've finished, then pair up As and Bs. Ss go through the exercise they've done and explain the answers to their partner.

Answers:
A 1 'll be watching, will have finished
2 'll probably be waiting, 'll have arrived
3 'll have eaten, 'll be dreaming
4 'll have decided, 'll be wishing
B 1 Will you *be* seeing Frank today?
2 Yes, could you tell him I *probably won't* have finished …
3 … this time tomorrow you'll *have finished* all your exams.
4 And you*'ll* be celebrating with your friends.
5 Will you *be using* your computer …
6 I might still *be* using it when you get back.

5A Give Ss a few minutes to work on the answers alone. You could do the first one as an example.

Answers:
1 you'll have received
2 will you be watching
3 you'll have fallen
4 will you still be studying, will you have passed
5 you will still like
6 will you be living

B Ss can work in pairs or walk round the class and ask each person they talk to two or three questions at random. Before Ss ask each other the questions, direct them to the phrases in the box and check that Ss understand the differences in meaning.

SPEAKING

6A Talk about yourself. Include one or two examples of the future perfect and continuous in your predictions, as well as adverbs such as *probably*, *definitely* and verbs such as *expect* and *hope*. Give Ss time to make notes.

B Ss work in pairs and note down any hopes/plans that they have in common.

C Draw a glass on the board then shade in half of it. Ask *Is the glass half full or half empty?* Discuss briefly with the class what the two different ways of looking at the glass mean. Tell Ss to use examples from Ex 6B to support their interpretation of themselves.

VOCABULARY OPTIMISM/PESSIMISM

7A Direct Ss to the quiz and give them time to read it and discuss the vocabulary in bold. Ss should use monolingual dictionaries to check their ideas.

B Do the first one as an example, then put Ss into pairs to complete the exercise.

Answers: 1 have mixed feelings about 2 look forward to 3 have your ups and downs 4 go nowhere 5 dread 6 fill you with despair 7 upbeat 8 look on the bright side

C Ss take turns to read out the quiz questions and make a note of each other's answers. They then read the analysis on p159 and discuss whether they agree with it or not.

▷ VOCABULARYBANK p153 Time idioms

Give Ss time to work through Ex 2A and B before comparing their answers in pairs. Let Ss check the time idioms in bold in their dictionaries if they have difficulty matching the idioms to the pictures in A. Check answers as a class.

Answers:
A 1 D 2 F 3 I 4 G 5 H 6 B 7 A 8 C 9 E
B **a)** kill an hour or two **b)** any time now **c)** in no time
d) drag your heels **e)** take your time **f)** time after time
g) cut something short **h)** in the nick of time
i) make up for lost time

WRITING AN INFORMAL EMAIL; LEARN TO FOCUS ON INFORMAL STYLE

8A Complete the sentence so that it is true for you. Ask Ss to predict how you have completed the sentence and then share your example. Ss complete it themselves and then elicit a few examples and find out if any Ss had the same ideas.

B Once Ss have read the emails, put them into pairs to discuss the differences in style.

Answers: Yes, she does. The first email is informal, while the second uses formal language.

C Point out that the numbered sentences fulfil a variety of functions. Ss discuss in pairs the function of each sentence.

Answers: **a)** 6 **b)** 3, 5, 7, 9 **c)** 1 **d)** 6 **e)** 4 **f)** 2, 8, 10

9A Write the first bold phrase (*delighted to receive*) on the board and ask Ss how they might say the same thing in a less formal way. Once you have elicited an example, ask Ss to do the same with the other phrases.

B Ask Ss to look at the phrases in the table. Ask Ss if any are the same or similar to the phrases they thought of in Ex 9A. Ss then complete the table.

Answers:
1 the perfect occasion to do so
2 regarding
3 I look forward to receiving further information
4 I would be interested to know
5 delighted to receive
6 I would like to accept the invitation
7 My preference would be for
8 Yours sincerely
9 I will inform you
10 I would be most grateful

C Ss can substitute the phrases from the table for those in the email. Alternatively, provide a blanked out email, ask Ss to close their books and see how many phrases they can complete from memory.

Suggested answer:
Dear Louise,
I was *happy to get* your email *about* the music festival, and *I'd love to come*. I've always wanted to visit Dublin, and this seems like *a great time for it*.
You asked me about concert choices but I didn't get the link. *It'd be great* if you could send it again. *I'd rather see* dance than music. *I'll let you know* about my specific choices once I see the programme.
Your cousin's flat sounds excellent. *Do you know* if it is in the city centre or on the outskirts?
I'll be able to stay for three days, and I will book a flight once I know the concert dates. *Can't wait to hear more* about it all.
All the best,
Corinna

10A Tell Ss to plan their reply before writing so that each paragraph has a particular focus. Monitor and provide help with structure and vocabulary. Remind Ss to use some of the informal expressions from Ex 9B.

B Ask Ss to check the organisation and informal style are accurate.

C This could be done in small groups. Alternatively, if you have time, post the replies around the room and allow Ss to read a number of replies before voting on the most excited reply.

Homework ideas

- Ask Ss to write a letter to their future self. You might want to limit the topics if you think your Ss could be sensitive about showing you this letter.
- **Language bank:** 6.2 Ex A–B, p139
- **Vocabulary bank:** p153
- **Workbook:** Ex 1–5, p39–40

SO WHAT YOU'RE SAYING IS …

Introduction

Ss listen to opinions and about persuasion and practise using phrases to persuade others. They also learn a range of collocations and how to clarify ideas when having a conversation.

SUPPLEMENTARY MATERIALS
Resource bank: p176

Warm up

Put Ss into small groups to brainstorm a list of things that they wanted to do/have as teenagers, but that their parents didn't let them (and why). Ss share their ideas as a class and discuss whether they now agree with their parents' point of view. If your Ss enjoy role-play, you could extend this by getting them to act out a situation in pairs: Student A is a teenager who is trying to persuade their parent to let them stay out late at a party; Student B is the parent who is insisting that they should be home at their normal time.

VOCABULARY COLLOCATIONS

1A Focus Ss on the example and explain or elicit that a collocation is a combination of words that are often used together and sound natural together. Ss can work on the exercise alone or in pairs. Vocabulary to check: *toddler* and *solo*.

If Ss find this relatively easy, you could direct them back to 3, 6, 7, 9 and 12 and ask them what preposition they'd need to add/change in order to make the other alternative correct.

Answers: **1** doing **2** owning **3** wearing (or *putting on*) **4** staying **5** getting **6** using (or *going on*) **7** having (or *signing up for*) **8** riding **9** babysitting (or *taking care of*) **10** travelling **11** staying **12** running (or *being in charge of*)

B Direct Ss to the photos and give them a minute or two to discuss them. They could also comment on how old they were when they did any of the things shown for the first time.

Answers: (from left to right) babysitting for a toddler; owning a smartphone; travelling solo; wearing make-up; riding a scooter

C You could give your own opinion about one of the activities as an example. Also remind Ss that they can use modal verbs to talk about this topic, e.g.
Children shouldn't … until they're at least …
I wasn't allowed to … until I was …
Parents shouldn't let children under the age of … have/get …
It's OK for a teenager to … but their parents need to …, etc.

D Use this feedback to find out which were the most 'controversial' activities.

FUNCTION PERSUADING

2A Make sure that Ss understand and are familiar with the context for the listening activity – a radio phone-in, where members of the general public phone to ask an expert for advice, or to give an opinion on a topic. Direct Ss to the list of activities in Ex 1A and play the recording whilst they tick the activities mentioned.

Answers: owning a smartphone, using social networking sites, getting your ears pierced

Unit 6 Recording 6

DJ = DJ E = Ed J = Julia D = Dan Z = Zara

DJ: And up next, it's time for 'Just tell me I'm wrong.' Today's topic: how young is too young or, perhaps more accurately, how old is old enough? We've received hundreds of calls, emails and text messages about the right age for a child to do all sorts of things, like have a smartphone. In fact our first caller asks about just that. His name is Ed. Go ahead, Ed. You're on.
E: Hi. My situation is that my eight-year-old kept asking for a smartphone, and eventually we bought her one a few months ago. Then, last week, I got a bill for over £200! I knew something like this would happen.
DJ: So basically you think she's too young for a phone?
E: Yeah, yeah, that's right.
DJ: Surely it's up to the parents to set guidelines.
E: So what you're saying is I should give her some rules?
DJ: Exactly. Right from the beginning. OK, thanks, Ed. Next caller is Julia. What's your question, Julia?
J: My question is about social networking sites. I don't let my daughter use them. She's only ten and I'm worried about online bullying.
DJ: So in other words, you're worried about kids being horrible to other kids.
J: Yeah. You hear so much about it nowadays.
DJ: That's a very good point. Online bullying is a serious problem … but isn't it better to talk it over with her? I'm sure they have lessons at school about how to stay safe online. She has to learn some time.
J: So what you mean is I'm being overprotective?
DJ: To be honest, yes. And if you try and stop her, she'll only find a way to go onto a social networking site in secret. And if she ends up in a bullying situation and you haven't prepared her, that could be much worse.
J: Oh dear… I'm sure you're right but it's not easy being a parent nowadays.
DJ: I agree. Thanks for your question, Julia. Let's go to our next caller. Dan, you're on.
D: Hi, my question's also about technology.
DJ: It seems like that's everyone's main worry. Anyway, go ahead Dan.
D: Well, my son, Seth, he's twelve and, up till recently he was a normal twelve-year-old, you know, he used to go out with his friends, play football with me, you know … we had a great relationship.
DJ: So, Dan, basically I'm guessing he doesn't want to spend so much time with you now and you feel a little bit …
D: Oh no, it's not that. It's just that he spends all his time on the computer now.
DJ: Surely that's just normal nowadays.
D: It's hard to say. Sometimes at the weekend he spends all day in his bedroom on social networking sites or playing video games. I don't think it's right. I mean for one thing, he never gets any exercise.
DJ: Don't you think it's just a stage he's going through? I used to spend hours in my bedroom listening to music when I was that age.
D: So what you mean is I should just relax and let him get on with it?
DJ: Yeah, he'll grow out of it. And you can't force him to go and play football if he doesn't want to.
D: I guess not. Thanks.
DJ: OK, our next caller is Zara. You're on.
Z: Um, I was wondering how you would deal with a thirteen-year-old wanting to get pierced ears?
DJ: Thirteen years old? Doesn't she simply want to be like her friends? I imagine a lot of them have pierced ears.
Z: Well … that's it. I'm not talking about a she.
DJ: Oh, in other words you're upset because your thirteen-year-old son wants to get his ears pierced.
Z: That's right.
DJ: Ah … so it's because he's a boy rather than his age?
Z: I suppose so.
DJ: Well, does he have friends who've got …

B Elicit from the class how many callers they hear (four) and tell Ss to copy the table into their notebooks so they have more space to make notes about the nature of each caller's problems and the advice that he/she is given.

Answers:
Caller 1:
Problem: 8-year-old daughter runs up mobile phone bill
DJ's opinion: parents should have set guidelines before giving her the phone
Caller 2:
Problem: mother doesn't let 10-year-old daughter use social networking sites, is worried about bullying
DJ's opinion: mother is being overprotective, should rather help daughter learn how to deal with bullying situations if they happen
Caller 3:
Problem: 12-year-old son spends too much time on the computer
DJ's opinion: let him, he'll grow out of it, it's normal these days
Caller 4:
Problem: 13-year-old son wants to have ears pierced
DJ's opinion: doesn't say, programme excerpt ends first

C Ss decide whether they agree with the DJ or what other advice they'd give. Conduct feedback with the whole class.

3A Tell Ss they're going to look at some of the language they heard in the phone in. Direct them to the four examples and ask them which two could be used to persuade someone to agree with your opinion (3 and 4). They may also be able to identify that 4 was said by the DJ on the recording. Then give them a minute or two to match the four examples to their meanings. Point out that 4 is a *negative* question, which starts with the auxiliary verb + *not/n't*.

Answers: 1 b) 2 a) 3 d) 4 c)

B You could do the first one as an example, then Ss work on the rest alone or with a partner.

C Play the recording for Ss to check their answers.

Answers: 1 Surely it's 2 Isn't 3 Surely that's 4 Don't you think 5 Doesn't she simply want

D Before playing the recording again, you could write one or two of the sentences on the board with arrows to show the intonation pattern. Play the recording again and ask Ss to repeat the sentences and copy the intonation.

Unit 6 Recording 7

1 Surely it's up to the parents to set guidelines.
2 Isn't it better to talk it over with her?
3 Surely that's just normal nowadays.
4 Don't you think it's just a stage he's going through?
5 Doesn't she simply want to be like her friends?

Teaching tip

The fall-rise used in these examples is a useful intonation pattern for Ss to learn because it will help them sound polite and interested, rather than too direct/abrupt (often the result of a rising tone) or bored (when there is little or no movement in pitch).

▷ LANGUAGEBANK 6.3 p138–139

Ss could do Ex A in class and practise the conversation in pairs before moving on to the more challenging practice in Ex 4A.

Answers:
1 Don't you agree that people should be able to start a family …
2 Clearly they're at …
3 But isn't it obvious that most 17-year-olds aren't …
4 … but doesn't it/that depend on the individual?
5 But surely they need (the) time to …
6 But isn't it a fact that in …
7 … but anyone can see that …

4A Remind Ss that in a 'gap year' young people often travel overseas and may work while they're away, either for a volunteer organisation or to fund their trip. Give Ss a few minutes to compare their opinions.

B Ss do not need to write the dialogue out in full, rather they should just use the flow chart as a prompt. Put Ss into pairs to practise the conversation then tell them to change roles. Monitor the practice and be prepared to give Ss feedback on their use of the phrases and their intonation.

Suggested answers:
Possible dialogue though slight differences would be fine:
A: Don't you think (that) everyone who finishes university should have a gap year?
B: I don't agree. Isn't it better to start working/work as soon as possible so that you (can) get work experience?
A: Yes, but doesn't a gap year give people a different kind of experience?
B: A gap year is just a long holiday. Surely a year working/a year's work is more useful?
A: I disagree. A year off gives people a chance to think about their career.
B: Haven't most 22-year-olds decided by that age?
A: Not always. People often end up in a job they hate. Anyway, surely it's worth trying?
B: I'm still not convinced. I think it's a waste of time.

Optional extra activity

Make the practice more challenging for ***stronger classes*** by removing some of the words in Student A's and Student B's prompts.

LEARN TO CLARIFY IDEAS

5A Establish that people ask for clarification to make sure they've understood the speaker's message.

Answers: So basically you think …; So what you're saying is …

B Ss work alone or with a partner to find the other phrases in the audio script. You may want to play the recording again so that Ss can focus on these phrases and how they're pronounced. Alternatively, provide the model yourself and get Ss to repeat the phrases, making sure that they sound friendly and polite.

Answers: So in other words, …; So what you mean is …

speakout TIP

Give Ss time to read the tip and check that they understand the idea of 'buying' time to think about what to say next. You could elicit other ways they know of doing this, e.g. saying *um, uhuh, I see, right.*

Optional extra activity

To give Ss practice in asking for clarification in other contexts, put them into pairs and tell them to choose one of the following situations:
1 *Give your partner directions to X.*
2 *Explain a recipe to your partner.*
3 *Explain to your partner what's involved in a certain job.*
Tell them that as they role-play the situation their partner should ask for clarification of anything they don't understand.

C Look at the example together as a class and then ask Ss to complete the other sentences using a paraphrase. Check the answers as a class.

Answers:
1 have to work
2 give elderly people more respect/respect elderly people more/ have more respect for elderly people
3 be/get punished
4 be/get paid as much as/more than men

D Put Ss into pairs of A and B. Ask Bs to cover the exercise and As to read out a statement from Ex 5C. Student B should try to clarify the ideas. They then swap roles. Ask one of the pairs to model their exchange to the class.

6A Give Ss plenty of time to think about and complete these statements. Circulate and be available to help them put their ideas into words.

B Point out that clarification often includes a paraphrase. Point out the example in Ex 5A of *guidelines* and *rules*. Give Ss time to paraphrase each other's ideas and help with synonyms where needed.

C Draw Ss' attention to the example and encourage them to continue the exchange beyond the first few lines. During the practice, monitor how effectively Ss ask for clarification and give them feedback on this. After Ss have practised this in pairs, choose one or two pairs to read out their sentences to the class. As they do this the rest of the class should try to write down the synonyms used.

SPEAKING

7A Begin by telling both Ss in the pair to write down as many points as they can in support of and against the opinions before choosing the best points. They should be able to generate more ideas this way and this will allow you to separate them to work with different Ss for the next stage of the activity.

B Put Ss into groups of three, making sure that they don't work with their partner from the previous stage. Explain that Ss are going to act out three calls to the radio phone-in show and each time they will take a different role: the DJ, the caller with a problem, or the caller who listens and gives their opinion. Direct Ss to their instructions and once they've read them, ask three Ss to start acting out the first situation in front of the class, to make sure that everyone understands what to do. If you want all the groups to move through the three situations at the same pace, use a signal (e.g. clap your hands or ring a bell) to stop them all and tell them to move on to the next one. Monitor and make notes so you can give Ss feedback on their language afterwards.

Optional extra activity

If you have access to recording facilities, record each group acting out one of the situations, then you can play the recordings for the class and give Ss 'live' feedback on their language.

Homework ideas

- If Ss have access to English-speaking radio and TV programmes, they listen to a phone-in or chat show and note down the ways of persuading and asking for clarification that the people use.
- **Language bank:** 6.3 Ex A, p139
- **Workbook:** Ex 1–3, p41

HOW TO LIVE TO 101

Introduction

Ss watch an extract from a BBC documentary about people on the Japanese island of Okinawa and the reasons why they live such long lives. Ss then learn and practise how to have a debate and write a forum comment.

SUPPLEMENTARY MATERIALS

Ex 2A: bring monolingual dictionaries for Ss to use.

Warm up

Put Ss into pairs and ask them to write a list of advantages and disadvantages of living to a very old age. Then invite Ss to share their ideas and see what they had in common.

DVD PREVIEW

1 Give Ss a few minutes to discuss the questions in pairs. Then invite them to share their answers with the class.

2A Focus Ss on the example and give them a minute or two to match the collocations. They can use monolingual dictionaries if necessary.

Answers: 1 f) 2 c) 3 a) 4 b) 5 h) 6 d) 7 e) 8 g)

Optional extra activity

To help Ss remember the collocations, tell them to cover the left-hand column in Ex 2A, then, working with a partner, try to remember the verb that goes with each of the nouns/adjectives on the right. Then they take turns to 'test' each other: one student closes their book and the other calls out the first part of a collocation for their partner to complete.

B Before putting Ss into pairs to discuss the factors, demonstrate that they'll need to use the verbs in the *-ing* form if they are the subject of the sentence, e.g. *Staying mentally active is very important.*

3 Focus Ss on the question and give them 1–2 mins to read the text. Vocabulary to check: *quest* (a long search for something that is difficult to find) and *stumble across* (discover something by chance).

Answers: Okinawa, Loma Linda and the mountains of Sardinia. People live longer in these places.

DVD VIEW

Culture notes

Okinawa island is part of Japan's southernmost prefecture (also called Okinawa) and is located southwest of mainland Japan. The islands which make up Okinawa Prefecture are also known as the Ryukyu Islands, named after the native culture, which is distinctly different from that of the rest of Japan in terms of language, cuisine, arts, etc.

The climate is subtropical, with temperatures barely falling below fifteen degrees in winter. The seas surrounding Okinawa's islands are considered among the world's most beautiful with coral reefs and abundant marine wildlife.

Towards the end of World War Two Okinawa became the stage of one of the war's bloodiest battles, when American troops invaded the islands. Okinawa remained under US administration until 1972 and several thousands of US military members remain stationed on the controversial US military bases on Okinawa Main Island today.

4A Tell Ss just to listen for the two reasons and that they will have a chance to watch the extract again to understand it in more detail.

Answers: eat different colour vegetables (rainbow diet); not overeat – eat until they're eighty percent full

DVD 6 Horizon: How to Live to 101

N = Narrator C = Craig Wilcox B = Bradley Wilcox

N: The remote island of Okinawa is home to one of the longest living communities in the world. In a population of only one million there are nine hundred people who are one hundred years or older, a percentage that's over four times higher than Britain and America. It's a place where age has a different meaning.
Where people like Mr Miyagi can expect to live well beyond his 92nd year.
Without thinking about the latest diet or lifestyle fad, Mr Miyagi has developed his own way of slowing the ageing process.
The Okinawans don't live the way they live in order to have a longer life. They don't think about the science of longevity.

C: Most of them couldn't care less what the scientists think – they just go about their business and live. They just happen to live a very long time.

N: The explanation for this extraordinary phenomenon begins in the most ordinary of places. Like every town in Okinawa the fruit and vegetable shop in Agimi lies at the heart of village life. It's here that Bradley and Craig believe the source of the Okinawa miracle can be traced.

C: Oh, look at that purple colour.

B: You see that purple? The purple really comes out more when you cook it. The key is to get a lot of vegetables that are very colourful, oranges, like these carrots here, dark greens and yellow vegetables. You might think of it as a rainbow diet.

N: For the past twenty years Bradley and Craig have been analysing the life-enhancing Okinawan ingredients.

C: Got reds here in the tomatoes, the peppers, you've got green peppers here.

N: They've identified a number of important properties that protect the Okinawans from disease. From the antioxidant-rich vegetables that protect against cell damage, to the high quantities of soya proteins.
In Ogimi, one-hundred-year-old Matsu is preparing a traditional Okinawan dish. When the food is served, one can observe the most important Okinawan tradition. It's the habit or custom of not eating too much, called hara hachi bu, literally, stomach eighty percent full.

C: The Okinawans developed also cultural habits over the years that appear to have health protective properties. They have a saying called 'hara hachi bu', eat until you're only eighty percent full.

N: In a typical day, Matsu only consumes around twelve hundred calories – about twenty percent less than most people in Britain and America.

C: In the West we're very much focused on getting more for our money, and one of the most popular things is all these all-you-can-eat restaurants. You go and you load up at the … at the, the all-you-can-eat restaurant and you, you walk away with this bloated feeling and you … you may have got your money's worth, but you probably didn't get your … your health's worth because what you're doing is just digging yourself into an early grave.

N: But for the time being, many of the secrets of long life can be learnt by observing the people who are healthy examples of active old age. The lessons of their lifestyles and traditions are there for us to learn, and it is up to us to follow them. If we don't, we may lose them forever.

B Pronoun referents such as these help to give a text, or extended speech, organisation. Point out that often, but not always, they refer back to a noun in one of the previous sentences. Give Ss time to discuss their ideas and then play the DVD again.

Answers:
1 the percentage of the population in Japan that is 100 or older
2 the science of longevity **3** at the fruit and vegetable shop
4 vegetables **5** the stomach **6** eat too much

C Ss should read the quotes from the DVD carefully before watching the extract again. Explain the differences in meaning between each of the words. Play the DVD again and check the answers.

Answers: 1 fad **2** phenomenon **3** properties **4** bloated

D Give Ss a few minutes to discuss the questions, then invite them to share their answers with the class. Ask *If you could go and live on Okinawa for a year, would you go? Why/Why not?*

speakout a debate

5A Check that Ss understand the idea of a debate: a formal discussion of a topic, where speakers take turns to give their points in favour of or against the topic and a vote is taken at the end to decide which side wins. You could start by eliciting an example of a point for or against the topic, then put Ss into pairs to write at least two more ideas for each side.

B Ss can make a few notes while they listen, then discuss in their pairs which speaker they agree with and whether any of their ideas were mentioned.

Unit 6 Recording 8

W = Woman M = Man

W: I'm going to speak against the statement: 'Employers should give preference to younger applicants when hiring.' The first point I'd like to make is that selecting a person for a job on the basis of their age is unfair. It's as bad as choosing someone because of their gender or race or religion. People should be selected for a job because of their abilities and suitability and not because they are a certain age. For example, if a sixty-year-old person is able, physically and mentally, to do a job they should be judged on the same basis as a thirty-year-old.

M: I would like to speak in favour of the statement. I would like to start off by saying that I fully support equal opportunities for people applying for a job. However, I would like to pick up on the point made by Sarah when she said 'if a person is able, physically and mentally, to do a job'. I think we need to be realistic here. As people age, this can affect their energy, their ability to react quickly and their memory. In some jobs it may be vital for people to have high levels of energy, for example in a creative industry such as advertising. Or people need to be able to react quickly, for instance if they're a lorry driver, or be able to concentrate for long periods of time if they're an airline pilot. It is simply a fact of life that, as we age, our mental and physical capabilities deteriorate and that, for certain jobs, younger people are better.

C First tell Ss to look through the phrases and decide what the purpose of each one is (the first two are for introducing your point, the other four are for referring back to a previous speaker's point). Then play the recording again for Ss to tick the phrases they hear. Point out that where there are options in the phrases (e.g. *In [answer/reply] to the point made by …*), they need to underline the option(s) they hear.

Answers: The first point I'd like to make is that …; I would like to start off by saying that …; I would like to pick up on the point made by …

6A To decide on the topic, you could ask for a show of hands for each one.

B Put Ss into pairs and make sure there are equal numbers in favour of and against the topic.

Alternative approach

Ss work together in groups of four to list the four (or more) points to support their position, then each member of the group takes one point to develop and speak about in the debate. Circulate and provide help with grammar and vocabulary as required. The groups should then spend some time practising making their points so they can make any corrections or improvements necessary before the debate. They also need to be prepared to pick up on points made by other speakers, either from their own group (which they can prepare) or from the opposing group (which they'll have to do 'on their feet').

C The debate can be conducted either by putting several 'for' and 'against' pairs together, or as a class. The latter would be more appropriate if your Ss need practice in public speaking in English. Ss from opposing sides take turns to stand up and make their points. At the end, Ss can vote for either side's arguments.

Teaching tip

You may feel that it's appropriate to give Ss individual feedback on their language use for an activity like a debate. Prepare individual feedback sheets (e.g. A5 size), with the name of the student at the top. Divide the sheet into two sections: one for good language use and one for corrections. You can then fill them in as each student is speaking and give them out after the debate.

writeback a forum comment

7A Give Ss a few minutes to read the comment. You could suggest they put a tick next to any points they agree with and a question mark or cross next to those they disagree with or have mixed feelings about. Invite a few Ss to share their opinions with the class.

B Ss number the parts and compare answers with a partner.

Answers: 1 c) **2** d) **3** b) **4** a)

C Ss can work on this alone or choose a topic with a partner and write the comment together. Encourage them to use the structure of the forum comment about children taking care of their parents as they get older.

D If you have time, these can be posted around the room. Under each comment Ss could write one or two sentences in response.

Homework ideas

- Ss write a forum comment on a topic from p74–75, e.g. whether a gap year is a good idea or not.
- Ss imagine that they are spending a year living on Okinawa and write home to a friend/relative, telling them about the place, the people, the food, the way of life, etc.

LOOKBACK

Introduction

The aim of these activities is to provide revision and further practice of the language from the unit. You can also use them to assess Ss' ability to use the language, in which case you need to monitor but avoid helping them. You may feel that you don't need or have time to do all the activities. If so, you could allocate the activities that would be most beneficial for your Ss, or get individual Ss to decide which activities they'd like to do.

AGE

1A You could run this as a board race. Tell Ss to close their books and put them into teams. Write/Display the sentences on the board one at a time. A member from each team races to the board to add the missing vowels and win points.

Answers: **1** elderly **2** in their prime **3** coming of age **4** for their age, their age **5** Age discrimination **6** Maturity

B You could start by telling the class your opinion about sentence 1 and invite them to agree/disagree with you. Then put Ss into pairs to discuss the rest. In feedback ask a few pairs to report back on which sentences they both agreed with and why.

MODAL VERBS AND RELATED PHRASES

2A Introduce the topic of amusement parks (Disneyland, etc.) and the people who work in them dressed as animals. Ask Ss whether they think it would be a good job or not and why. Tell Ss to read the text quickly and find three reasons why the writer doesn't like the job (*the costume is the worst, he can't see properly, the children annoy him*). Give Ss a few minutes to choose the correct alternatives and compare answers in pairs.

Answers: **1** makes **2** 'm not able **3** are allowed to **4** aren't supposed to **5** won't be able **6** don't have to **7** don't have to **8** managed to

B You could start by telling Ss about the worst job you've ever had and explain why, using at least three of the modal verbs and phrases, e.g. *I had to …; I wasn't allowed to …; I couldn't …*. Put Ss into pairs to choose a job and make a few notes about the reasons for their choice, using at least three modal verbs and related phrases. Ask the pairs to share their ideas and have a class vote on the worst job of all.

FUTURE PERFECT AND CONTINUOUS

3A Ss can work alone completing the sentences and compare answers with a partner.

Answers: **1** won't be sitting **2** will definitely have finished **3** 'll have arrived **4** will still be communicating **5** will have been replaced

B Tell Ss to give reasons for their answers, e.g. *That's not true because I'll be sitting here until 4.30.*

C Ss could either write one prediction for each of the topics given or five predictions for one of the topics.

D Pairs could choose the two most interesting predictions from their discussion to tell the rest of the class.

OPTIMISM/PESSIMISM

4A You could do this as a 'Listen and stop me' activity. Ss should close their books. Tell them you're going to read a story and if they hear you make a mistake with the vocabulary, they should shout *Stop!* and correct the mistake. Start reading the story and give the class one point each time they stop you in the correct place and another point if they can correct the mistake. Give yourself a point if Ss miss the mistake or if their correction is wrong.

Answers: had my *ups* and *downs*, had *mixed* feelings, look on the *bright* side, *upbeat*, looking *forward* to, dreaded, *going* nowhere, filled me ~~up~~ with despair

B Give Ss a few minutes to discuss what the student brought to class and why it made the teacher optimistic.

PERSUADING

5A You could run this as a race in pairs: the first pair to finish bring their books up to you to check. For ***stronger classes*** you could also tell Ss to cover the words in the box and work out the missing words themselves.

Answers:
A: Don't you *agree* that …
B: But *surely* …
A: Why? Anyone *can* see that …
B: But *shouldn't* …
A: So *what* you're saying is that …
B: But *isn't* it obvious that …
A: Well *clearly* …

B Tell Ss to close their books and put the answers from Ex 5A on the board as prompts for them to use while they practise the conversation.

C Leave the phrases from Ex 5A on the board for this speaking activity. Ss should spend a few minutes thinking about the topics and making notes before joining a partner to discuss them. If you want to extend the practice, you could swap the pairs around so that Ss are working with a new partner. Monitor and make notes of good language use and areas for remedial work. In feedback, invite a few Ss to tell the class whether their partner managed to persuade them to change their opinion about any of the topics, then give Ss some examples of their good use of language and errors for them to discuss and correct.

Homework ideas

Workbook: Review 3, p42–45

BBC interviews and worksheet

What was the best period of your life?

This video encourages Ss to reflect on and discuss what they consider to be the best period or periods of their lives.

OVERVIEW

7.1 TV GLOBETROTTERS

VOCABULARY | television
READING | read about TV with a global appeal
GRAMMAR | quantifiers
PRONUNCIATION | connected speech: linking
SPEAKING | talk about TV programmes
VOCABULARY ***PLUS*** | multi-word verbs

7.2 THE CAMERA NEVER LIES

LISTENING | listen to an expert talking about hoax photographs
GRAMMAR | reported speech
VOCABULARY | reporting verbs
PRONUNCIATION | word stress
SPEAKING | talk about celebrity and media
WRITING | a discursive essay; learn to use linkers of contrast

7.3 WHAT'S IN THE NEWS

VOCABULARY | the press
FUNCTION | adding emphasis
PRONUNCIATION | sentence stress
LEARN TO | make guesses
SPEAKING | express strong reactions

7.4 NEWS BUNDERS BBC DVD

DVD | watch a BBC programme about live news
speakout | a news story
writeback | a short summary

7.5 LOOKBACK

Communicative revision activities

BBC INTERVIEWS

What kind of news stories interest you?

This video encourages Ss to reflect on the kinds of news stories that they find the most interesting. Use this video at the start or end of Unit 7 or set it as homework.

TV GLOBETROTTERS

Introduction

Ss practise reading and speaking about television using quantifiers and related vocabulary. They also learn about multi-word verbs.

SUPPLEMENTARY MATERIALS
Resource bank: p177, p178 and p179
Ex 1A and **Ex 7C:** bring monolingual dictionaries for Ss to use.

Warm up

Either: Put Ss into pairs and give them 3 mins to brainstorm types of TV programme. Conduct feedback with the whole class and write a list on the board. Then tell Ss to write the headings *regularly/sometimes/never* in their notebooks and, working alone, put the programme types under the headings according to how often they watch them. They then compare answers in pairs or small groups.
Or: Write *Media* on the board and ask Ss what the term includes, i.e. television, radio, newspapers, magazines, the internet. Then put Ss into small groups to discuss which types of media they use most/least and why. Conduct feedback with the whole class.

VOCABULARY TELEVISION

1A Discuss the first pair of programmes with the class, as an example. Give Ss about 10 mins to discuss/look up the rest of the programme type pairs and make notes for feedback.

Suggested answers:
1 Both show real life: a wildlife programme features animals, plants, etc.; a reality show features people.
2 Both are dramas which involve a continuing story with the same set of characters: a costume drama is usually set in a historical context; a soap opera is set in a contemporary, modern context.
3 Both are comedies/funny: a sketch show has a lot of short comedy pieces; a sitcom is normally a single story and the stories connect in some way from episode to episode although each episode is self-contained.
4 Both are factual programmes: a documentary can be on any factual topic, e.g. scientific, historical, cultural, and is made from real footage; a docudrama is often about historical events and includes re-enacted sequences, i.e. sequences performed by actors but made to look real.
5 Both involve more than one programme: a series can be factual or, in a drama series, each episode is usually a different story, but with the same characters; a serial is a single story broken up into different episodes.
6 Both are exciting and often involve danger and facing and solving a problem: a thriller can be a combination of genres or types, it can include sci-fi, fantasy, detective, action type content, but it's always made to create excitement (or 'thrills'); a detective series usually focuses only on police work in connection with crime and as a series has the same characters with a different story every episode.
7 Both involve a competition between teams or individuals: a game show can have many formats, including a quiz format; a quiz is limited to question/answer formats.
8 Both are about real events/stories happening at the moment: a current affairs programme has feature stories about different topics in the news; the news is made up of shorter stories about the most current (immediate) events.

7 media

Alternative approach

To make this exercise less time consuming, give each pair of Ss one pair of programmes to discuss (or two, depending on the size of your class). Each pair then tells the class about their programmes in feedback, or you could split the pairs and have Ss in two groups telling each other their answers.

B You could start by telling the class which programmes you like the most/least and why.

READING

2A Tell Ss to cover the text and focus them on the photos. Explain that they need to match them with one of the programme types in Ex 1A. Some of the pictures may correspond with more than one possible programme genre. Avoid checking answers at this stage. Ss can wait to confirm their predictions when they read the article. Instead, conduct feedback with the class about what they imagine the programmes to be about and why they might be successful.

B Ask Ss to read the text and check their predictions.

Answers:
Natural World: visual content/cross-cultural appeal
Top Gear: the jokey relationship between the presenters; the challenges that feature in the programme
The Office: the programme has a romantic relationship between the two main characters at the centre
Sherlock: the interesting ('intriguing') relationships between the main characters
Strictly Come Dancing/Dancing with the Stars: nothing is singled out as the reason but the article lists all its features as the things people like: great dancing, celebrities, beautiful dresses, the music, the host (who is popular) and lots of viewer participation

C Look at the first sentence with the class and give Ss a minute or two to find the relevant phrase to show that it's false. When Ss have identified the rest of the phrases/sentences, put them in pairs to compare answers.

Answers:
1 Costume dramas and historical mini-series also seem to survive the transition to a different culture.
2 True, there are a large number of cars …
3 … a race between a supercar and a bullet train was another huge hit. (This means the race was very popular; it doesn't mean there was a crash.)
4 … and many people predicted *The Office* would flop because of … (flop = fail/be unsuccessful)
5 … because of its slightly strange British humour … Since then, this 'mockumentary' has become an international sensation … However, *The Office* is a sitcom with a heart …
6 … when the BBC decided to give him a makeover, there was a real risk of alienating fans of the much-loved classic tales.
7 … the long-awaited first episode of the third season was viewed almost seven million times in China only a couple of hours after it was initially aired in the UK.
8 Celebrity contestants with little or no experience of dancing pair up with professional dancers …

speakout TIP

After Ss have read the tip, you could write some expressions on the board and ask Ss to think of different ways of expressing a similar idea, e.g. *hilarious sitcom, a serious docudrama, a challenging quiz*, etc.

D Focus Ss on the example. Ss could work with a partner to match the rest of the meanings and check any they are unsure of in a dictionary.

Answers: **1** successes, hit **2** crazy, bizarre **3** global phenomenon, international sensation **4** pulled in, drawn in **5** broadcast, aired **6** resurrected, revitalised

E Ss could order the programmes from 1–5, starting with the one they'd most like to watch, then compare answers in pairs or small groups.

GRAMMAR QUANTIFIERS

3A Establish that quantifiers are words/phrases used with nouns to show quantity. Focus Ss on the first quantifier in bold in the first paragraph of the text (*quite a few*) and ask them which category it belongs to (*a moderate or small number/amount*), then give them time to find and categorise the rest and compare answers with a partner.

Answers:
all: *every, each* (*every* means all the people/things considered together; *each* means all the people/things considered separately, one at a time)
a lot: *quite a few, a large number of, many, a good deal of, plenty of*
a moderate or small number/amount: *several, few, little*
an additional one: *another*
zero: *no*

B Look at the first rule with the class, then put Ss into pairs to complete the rules.

Answers: **1** plural **2** uncountable **3** singular **4** plural, uncountable **5** singular

C Point out that *few* doesn't mean the same as *a few* and *little* doesn't mean the same as *a little*. Give Ss a minute or two to look at the sentences.

Answers: **1** not many **2** some **3** not much **4** some

▷ LANGUAGEBANK 7.1 p140–141

The table in the Language bank contains some extra quantifiers which you will need to check with Ss if you want them to do Ex A and B.
most = nearly all, e.g. most people, most of the people here
any = all, it doesn't matter which, e.g. I'll watch any reality show – I love them!
neither = not one or the other, e.g. neither politician could answer the question.
You could run Ex A as a competition in pairs. Read the text aloud for the class and when you reach a set of alternatives, the first pair to put their hands up with an answer is awarded a point if it's correct.

Answers:
A **1** a large number **2** each **3** both **4** some **5** either **6** Any **7** Very few **8** no **9** plenty of **10** Neither
B **1** very few **2** a little **3** A few **4** quite a few **5** very little **6** either **7** any **8** any **9** another **10** other

4A Tell Ss they are going to do a dictation exercise with five sentences. All the sentences will have quantifiers in them. Then play the recording, stopping briefly after each sentence for Ss to finish writing.

Answers: See answers to Ex 4B.

B Focus Ss on the example and show them that the sequence of sounds is consonant → vowel and that the *f* sounds like a *v* when it's followed by a vowel sound.

Answers:
1 All‿of‿us watch lots‿of TV.
2 Quite‿a few‿of‿us watch online.
3 A few‿of‿us prefer listening to the radio.
4 Both‿of‿us like wildlife programmes.
5 Neither‿of‿us enjoys detective stories.

C Encourage Ss to copy the tempo on the recording so they sound natural as they repeat the sentences.

Optional extra activity

Ask Ss where the consonant → vowel links are in *a good deal of* and *lots of* and ask them to write and practise an example sentence for each of these quantifiers.

5A Ss can work in pairs to correct the sentences. You could do the first one with the class as an example.

Answers:
1 I watch very few sports programmes.
2 Every programme has/All (the) programmes have a commercial break every ten minutes.
3 The weekend schedules usually include a few/several talent shows, at least three or four.
4 I like every programme/all programmes/any programme about hospitals or emergencies.
5 I once spent quite a few days watching a box set of the series *24*.
6 I think a great deal/a lot/lots of TV has been dumbed down.
7 We have plenty of detective shows; we don't need more.
8 I think a little/some news is OK but not 24-hour news non-stop.

B You could demonstrate this first by changing one or two of the sentences to make them true for you/your country.

C Put Ss into pairs and tell them to make a note of any points that they have in common.

D In feedback, encourage Ss to tell the class some of the things they have in common, using *We both (think) …*, *Neither of us thinks …*, etc.

Optional extra activity

Ss write one or two paragraphs about 'must-see' programmes in their countries, incorporating vocabulary from Ex 1A and Ex 2D and quantifiers. Circulate and help Ss to 'proofread' and correct their work, if necessary writing a second draft. The descriptions can then be put on the walls round the classroom for other Ss to read and decide which programmes they'd like to watch. If Ss are from the same country, they write the descriptions without naming the programmes and the other Ss have to guess which programmes are being described.

SPEAKING

6A Ss work in pairs and discuss the questions.

B Give Ss a few minutes to read the statements and to decide on their opinion.

C Groups should spend a few minutes discussing their opinions. Before eliciting feedback, tell Ss to summarise their opinions, using quantifiers where possible, e.g. *Quite a few of us …*, *Only a few of us …*, *None of us …*, *Most of us …*, *We all …*, etc. Ss share their ideas with the whole class.

VOCABULARY PLUS MULTI-WORD VERBS

7A Tell Ss to read the quotes and decide which programme they think the quotes come from.

Answers: 1 Top Gear 2 Natural World 3 World News 4 Dancing with the Stars 5 Sherlock 6 The Office

B You could identify the first multi-word verb in quote 1 as an example with the class. Working with a partner, Ss should find and underline the other multi-word verbs.

Answers: 1 brought out, take back 2 come across, put up with 3 turned out 4 takes (me) back, brings out 5 comes across, turns out 6 put (me) up

C Focus Ss on the example and remind them to use the context when trying to work out the meaning of the verbs. Ss work alone for a few minutes and compare answers in pairs. Ask Ss to decide whether each verb takes an object or not (transitive or intransitive) and whether the verb and particle can be separated. They could use dictionaries to help with this. Ss then add *sth* (*something*) or *sb* (*somebody*) into the possible sentences.

Answers: (words in brackets commonly go with the multi-word verbs)
1 bring sth out 2 bring out sth 3 put up with sth 4 put sb up 5 come across sth 6 come across (as) 7 take sb back (to) 8 take sth back 9 turn out 10 turn out

Teaching tip

Show Ss how to check in a monolingual dictionary whether a verb is transitive or intransitive and separable or inseparable. The symbols are usually *[T]* for transitive and *[I]* for intransitive and a separable verb is shown with an object and a two-way arrow between the verb and particle: *bring sth ↔ out*.

8A Tell Ss to cover the exercises above before completing this task. Alternatively, you could display the sentences on the board with Ss' books closed.

Answers: 1 back 2 across 3 up 4 out 5 out 6 out 7 across 8 out 9 up 10 back

B In pairs, Ss ask and answer the questions. Elicit one or two answers for each question.

▷ VOCABULARYBANK p154 Multi-word verbs

Ex 1A introduces some new multi-word verbs which can have different meanings. Let Ss work in pairs to read the pairs of sentences and deduce the two different meanings of the verbs in bold. Allow them to check their ideas in a dictionary to help complete the table in Ex 1B.

Answers:
A 1 raise 2 mention 3 delaying 4 causing me not to like 5 reject 6 lower the heat 7 stopped working 8 not continuing 9 hired 10 competed against 11 started to drive 12 left
B a) take on b) turn down c) pull out d) put off e) bring up f) break down

Homework ideas

- Ss write about their family's or friends' attitude to the radio and newspapers, using quantifiers, e.g. *Quite a few people in my family listen to the radio in the car. Very few of my friends read a newspaper from cover to cover.*, etc.
- **Language bank:** 7.1 Ex A–B, p141
- **Vocabulary bank:** p154
- **Workbook:** Ex 1–5, p46–47

THE CAMERA NEVER LIES

Introduction

Ss practise listening to and speaking about the news, using reported speech and reporting verbs. They also learn to use linkers of contrast and write a discursive essay.

SUPPLEMENTARY MATERIALS
Resource bank: p180

Warm up

Tell Ss to close their books and write on the board the title *The camera never lies*. Brainstorm some ideas with the class about what the phrase means. If Ss mention the idea of someone trying to make people believe a picture that isn't true, pre-teach *hoax*.

LISTENING

1A Check that Ss understand the idea of a *hoax* and a *composite photo*, i.e. when two or more photos are combined. Discuss the photos with the whole class or put Ss into pairs to discuss them.

B Tell Ss just to listen for whether the photo is a hoax or not and play the recording.

Answers: **A** real **B** hoax **C** hoax

Unit 7 Recording 2

P = Presenter **H** = Hoaxer

P: Welcome to *Insight*, where the topic for the day is hoaxes, specifically photo hoaxes. It was extremely difficult to get someone who produces hoax photos, a hoaxer, to agree to appear on the show, and it was only on condition that we promise to keep his identity secret. So, I'd like to welcome my guest to the show.
H: Thank you.
P: For starters, can you explain why you want to remain anonymous?
H: Two reasons really. I suppose, one is mystery. What I mean is a good hoax photo is more powerful if people don't know where it came from. If people knew I'd produced the photo, the effect would be lost.
P: Fair enough. And the other reason?
H: Well, it's a fact that hoaxers often use photographs taken by someone else, and often without permission, and the original photographer could sue us.
P: So basically, you're playing it safe then.
H: Yeah, you could put it that way.
P: OK. Now I asked you before the show if you'd ever earned money for your hoax work, and you said that you often work with the police and detectives. What exactly do you do for the police?
H: Well, when a politician, for example, appears in a published photograph in any … embarrassing situation, say accepting money … sometimes the police ask me to look at it. Then, if I decide if the photograph is a hoax, they see if they can find out who did it.
P: Right. OK, well, let's look at some photographs that we found on the internet – some hoaxes; some not. Talk us through the photographs if you would.
H: So, this photo of a bike in a tree *looks* like a hoax simply because it's such an unusual image. Also, it *looks* a bit like a composite photo …
P: What's a composite photo?
H: When you combine two or more photos, that's a composite. In this case, it would be very easy to put a picture of the two halves of the bike over a photo of a tree. In fact, this would be a very easy hoax photo to put together.
P: So what you're saying is, it isn't real.
H: No, it actually *is* real. I wasn't sure myself, but I found out it was near Seattle, Washington. So I asked a friend who lives there, and he told me he'd seen it with his own eyes a number of years before. Apparently, there are many different legends about how it got there.
P: Well, I thought that one was definitely a hoax. Let's look at the next one. This one could be real. A man hanging on the landing gear of a jet plane is such an extraordinary sight, maybe that's why it looks a bit fake.
H: Well, even if you'd never seen such a thing, common sense would tell you that a man couldn't survive even the landing. The wind would pull him off.
P: Then it IS a hoax photo.
H: Yes, a classic composite photo. Not badly put together, though.
P: Remarkable. Now this next one could be real, sharks swimming through a flooded suburb. I remember seeing this on the internet after one of those big hurricanes.
H: Ha, you've probably seen lots of photos like this, and maybe this exact one.
P: Why? Why's it funny?
H: I'm ninety-nine percent sure this is a hoax simply because it's a cliché – yet another photo of sharks swimming where they shouldn't be! Look on the internet and you'll find plenty of hoax photos of sharks.
P: And that's it? Is there a technical reason why you know its a hoax?
H: Well, yes. The water next to the fins isn't right. The surface of the water would break differently if there really were sharks there. Look closely.
P: I see. You know, it seems like a lot of work. Why do people do it? It can't be for the money.
H: I dunno. I can only speak for myself and to be honest I'm thrilled when people believe one of my photos.
P: Because they want to believe it?
H: Well, yes. Maybe we all like to believe something really unusual could be true.

C Give Ss a minute or two to look at the statements and see if they know any of the answers, from listening the first time. Make sure Ss understand that in some cases both options may be correct. Play the recording again, then Ss compare their answers in pairs. Vocabulary to check: *sue* (to make a legal claim against someone, especially for a sum of money, because you have been harmed in some way).

Answers: **1** a) and b) **2** a) **3** a) **4** b) **5** a) and b) **6** b)

D Ss tick the statements they agree with and discuss their opinions in pairs for a couple of minutes, then share their opinions as a class.

Optional extra activity

Bring in some descriptions of famous hoaxes for Ss to read. These can be found on the internet, e.g. at www.museumofhoaxes.com – Top 100 April Fool's Day hoaxes (correct at the time of going to press). Ss discuss which hoax they liked best, which was the most unbelievable, etc.

GRAMMAR REPORTED SPEECH

2A This should be revision for Ss, so you could go through these sentences with the whole class.

Answers: **a)** 2, 3 **b)** 4 **c)** 1

B Ss could work in pairs on this.

Answers:
1 'Have you ever earned money for your hoax work?'
2 'I saw it with my own eyes a number of years ago.'
3 'I often work with the police.'
4 'Could you look at it?'

C You could look at the first rule with the whole class then put Ss into pairs.

Answers:
Rule 1: past
Rule 2: sentence 3, still true
Rule 3: an affirmative statement
Rule 4: infinitive with *to*

Optional extra activity

Put some more sentences from the interview on the board or on a handout and ask Ss to change them from direct to reported speech, or vice versa, e.g.

1 Hoaxers often use photographs taken by someone else.
He said that hoaxers often use photographs taken by someone else.
2 I asked a friend who lives there and he told me he'd seen it with his own eyes.
I saw it with my own eyes.
3 Why's it funny?
She asked him why it was funny.

▷ LANGUAGEBANK 7.2 p140–141

If Ss seemed unsure of the rules in Ex 2C, give them time to read through the Language bank in class. Otherwise, tell them to read the section for homework. You could give Ss Ex B for extra practice in class. ***Stronger classes*** could do it as a race in pairs, or as a 'listen and stop me' activity, where you read the story aloud and Ss stop you when they hear a mistake and correct it.

Answers:
A **1** where I'd been all day
2 what I'd been watching on TV the night before
3 if I'd washed my hands for dinner
4 if I'd got any homework for the next day
5 if I was going to help her with the housework that weekend
B I was eighteen when I went for my first job interview, at a photo laboratory. The manager asked me *to* take a seat and then asked *(me) what my name was* and I was so nervous that I told him I *didn't* understand the question. Then he wanted to know *if I had* any plant experience; I *told him that/said that* I had done some work in my grandmother's garden. He laughed and said that by 'plant' he had meant 'factory', not 'trees and flowers'. I felt terribly embarrassed and simply told him that I *had* never worked in a factory. He had my file of photos and he asked *me to talk* about them. I was so nervous that I dropped them all on the floor! Then he asked me if I *had* any referees; I thought he meant the kind of referees they have in a football match, so I told him that I didn't play team sports but that I had been doing long-distance running for years. I was sure that I'd messed up the interview, but then he enquired when I *could* start! He wanted *me to start* the following Monday!

3A In pairs Ss should match the sentences to the presenter or the hoaxer. Afterwards, Ss can check their answers against the audio script.

Answers: **1** P **2** P **3** P **4** H **5** P **6** H

B Give Ss time to write out the sentences in their notebooks, before putting them in pairs to compare answers.

Answers:
1 She asked him to explain why he wanted to remain anonymous.
2 She asked him what exactly he did for the police.
3 She asked him to talk them through the photos.
4 He said he hadn't been sure himself but he found out it was near Seattle, Washington.
5 She asked if there was a technical reason why he knew it was a hoax.
6 He said he was thrilled when people believed one of his photos.

VOCABULARY REPORTING VERBS

4A Give Ss a minute or two to read the news story or ask one of the Ss to read it out loud. Then ask Ss to discuss with a partner whether they think Les Brown is telling the truth or not. Hold a vote to decide and elicit one or two reasons.

B Ask Ss to check their predictions against the update. Ask Ss whether they have heard of any similar stories and elicit any details Ss remember.

C Display the texts and underline the first reporting verb as an example. Give Ss a minute to underline the rest. Check the answers as a class.

Answers: accused, denies, promised, refused, admitted, persuaded, warned, apologised, agreed

D Ask Ss to find a verb in one of the texts that is followed by the *-ing* form. Put Ss into pairs to complete the rest of the table.

Answers:
1 *-ing* form: deny, admit
2 preposition + *-ing* form: apologise for doing sth
3 object + preposition + *-ing* form: accuse sb of doing sth
4 infinitive: promise, refuse, agree
5 object + infinitive: persuade sb to do sth, warn sb to do sth

5A Do the first one as an example with the class and then set the task for individual work. Ask Ss to compare their answers in pairs and then check as a class.

Answers:
1 *-ing* form: suggest
4 infinitive: threaten, offer
5 object + infinitive: tell sb to do sth, invite sb to do sth, advise sb to do sth, remind sb to do sth

B Ask Ss to mark where they think the stress is on each word and then play the recording for Ss to check. Drill the correct stress with the class.

Answers:
Stress on the first syllable: promise, threaten, offer, warn, tell
Stress on the second syllable: deny, admit, suggest, apologise, accuse, refuse, agree, persuade, invite, advise, remind

C Complete the first one as an example on the board. Set the rest as individual work and pairwork checking.

Answers: **1** of not taking **2** not to talk **3** not to lie
4 for not telling (*for not having told* is also possible) **5** not to do

6A Ask Ss to read through the situations quickly and decide which they would find the most difficult to deal with. Discuss their answers briefly as a class and put them in pairs to complete the questions. Vocabulary to check: *betray* (hurt someone who trusts you), *bonus* (extra money above your basic salary – usually for good work) and *take credit for* (accept praise for something even if it wasn't your hard work).

Answers:
1 **a)** to pay **b)** doing (*having done* is also possible) **c)** for acting (*for having acted* is also possible)
2 **a)** of betraying **b)** to believe **c)** writing, never to do
3 **a)** to take **b)** to go **c)** for not keeping
4 **a)** to do **b)** asking **c)** to report

B Ss should note down each other's answers and see where they agree. You could also encourage Ss to write an extra answer for any of the situations where they would react differently and share these with the class in feedback.

SPEAKING

7A Ask Ss to read the statements and explain any difficult words. Vocabulary to check: *manipulation* (a change to something), *idealised* (perfect) and *public figures* (not ordinary members of the public but well-known people). Ss choose two statements and for each one write down a reason for and a reason against with a partner and think of examples to support their ideas.

B After Ss work in groups, elicit a reason for and against for each statement from the class.

WRITING A DISCURSIVE ESSAY; LEARN TO USE LINKERS OF CONTRAST

8A If there are any stories concerning celebrities currently in the news, you could bring in some news headlines and/or photos and put them on the board for Ss to discuss what they know about the story, what they think of the celebrity involved, etc. Ss then read the essay and discuss their reaction in small groups.

Answer: The essay is about topic 3: 'The media should be free to examine the lives of public figures.'

B Before Ss underline the correct alternatives, you could ask them to decide on the purpose of each paragraph with a partner. Then they can do the exercise to check their ideas.

Answers: **1** explains why the topic is of interest **2** for **3** against **4** gives the writer's

9A While Ss circle the linkers, write up the four sentences on the board so you can highlight them in the next stage.

Answers: **1** despite **2** While **3** Although **4** However

B Give Ss a few minutes to discuss the questions. You could also ask them which of the linkers can go at the beginning or in the middle of the sentence.

Answers:
1 a comma
2 an *-ing* form (e.g. *despite knowing*)
3 The main clauses are:
sentence 1 – Celebrities invite publicity …
sentence 2 – … others never want or plan for it.
sentence 3 – … often they are more interested in selling a sensational story.
4 the subordinate clause

C Ss work on this alone and compare answers in pairs.

Answers:
1 Some celebrities are good role models for young people. However, others set a negative example. / Although some celebrities are good role models for young people, others set a negative example.
2 Despite the fact that anonymously published internet news is unreliable, many people rely on it as a main source of information. OR Despite anonymously published internet news being unreliable, … OR Despite the unreliability of anonymously published internet news, … / While anonymously published internet news is unreliable, many people rely on it as a main source of information.
3 While false reports of celebrity deaths are common, some people still believe them. / False reports of celebrity deaths are common. However, some people still believe them.
4 Although the scandal damaged his reputation, he still has millions of fans. / Despite the scandal damaging his reputation, he still has millions of fans. OR Despite the fact that the scandal damaged his reputation, … OR Despite the damage that the scandal did to his reputation, …

10A Ss could decide on a topic in pairs and brainstorm some ideas, then work alone to write notes for each paragraph.

B Ss write a first draft in class, then read their partner's work and give them some feedback. Ss write a final draft for homework.

Homework ideas

- **Language bank:** 7.2 Ex A–B, p141
- **Workbook:** Ex 1–5, p48–49

WHAT'S IN THE NEWS?

Introduction

Ss practise listening and speaking about the press using phrases for adding emphasis. They also learn to make guesses.

SUPPLEMENTARY MATERIALS

Resource bank: p181

Ex 1A: bring examples of tabloid and broadsheet newspapers.

Warm up

Tell Ss to close their books and put the title *What's in the news?* on the board. Put Ss into groups of three to five to discuss stories that have been in the news for the past few days and make a list of the topics. Write a list on the board.

VOCABULARY THE PRESS

1A Ss keep their books closed. Write the headline of the article on the board and check that they understand *tabloids* (newspapers that have a small page size and don't have much 'serious' news). If you have brought in some tabloid and broadsheet newspapers, show Ss the difference. Ask the class which topics they think are the most popular. Give Ss a minute or two to read the article quickly and check their predictions.

B With ***stronger classes*** direct Ss to the words in bold and ask them to discuss what they mean in pairs. Then they can do the matching task and check their ideas. Pronunciation to check: *feature*, *biased* and *sensationalism*.

Answers: **1** tabloid **2** editorial page **3** feature **4** biased **5** supplement **6** sensationalism **7** edition **8** circulation

C Give Ss a few minutes to discuss the questions. Find out which sections of the paper are the most/least popular.

▷ **VOCABULARYBANK** p154 Parts of a news website

This exercise revises and extends the vocabulary for talking about the press in the context of a news website. Let Ss work independently to label the diagram of the website and check their answers in pairs. Feed back as a class.

Answers: (from top to bottom, left column then right column) 8, 1, 4, 2, 7, 3, 9, 5, 10, 6

FUNCTION ADDING EMPHASIS

2A Give Ss a couple of minutes to discuss the headlines, then ask different pairs to talk about each headline in feedback.

B Ss should note down just the letter of each headline in the order that they hear them.

Answers: **1** E **2** A **3** C

Unit 7 Recording 4

W = Woman M = Man

Conversation 1

W: Wow!
M: What's that?
W: It's this story. Listen to this. 'A woman used a wooden soup ladle to save her husband from attack by a tiger.'
M: What? A ladle?
W: Well, her husband was being attacked by a tiger.
M: Where was this?
W: In Malaysia. Apparently, her husband had just gone into the forest. She saw the tiger attack him and grabbed the first thing she could find, which was a wooden soup ladle. And she just charged at the animal yelling at the top of her voice and bashing its head.
M: And it didn't attack her?
W: No. The amazing thing is that the tiger ran off.
M: Wow, there's no way I'd do that!
W: Not even for me?
M: Not even for you! You're the one who's always telling me to stop.
W: Stop what?
M: Stop helping people so much.
W: I didn't mean to stop helping *me*!

Conversation 2

W: Hey, Mike. Did you buy a lottery ticket?
M: No, why?
W: Well, you want to be careful. It says here that some store clerks are taking the winnings. You know when customers take in a winning ticket and they have to check it in the store …
M: Yeah …
W: Well, these guys have been telling customers that they didn't win and then they take the winning tickets for themselves.
M: That's so wrong! Suppose it was, like, a big amount?
W: One of the tickets was for $1,000 and the …
M: That's totally outrageous!
W: Yeah. Exactly.
M: So, how did they find out?
W: The police did some undercover investigations at convenience stores. And … yeah, one of them was for $1,000 and the …
M: Hey, maybe we won something …
W: In your dreams. You don't buy lottery tickets anyway.
M: That's true.
W: But it's weird that the customers didn't notice, isn't it? That's more surprising than the actual theft.
M: Yeah. I do think they should do something about it.
W: Who?
M: The lottery companies.
W: They *are* doing something about it. They're going to install machines so you can check your own numbers.
M: That *is* a good idea.

Conversation 3

M: That's extraordinary!
W: What is?
M: This story about the baby in China.
W: What happened?
M: It's about a baby and apparently it climbed out onto a window ledge on the second floor. Oh there's a video … And, oh look, you can see these people underneath just holding out their arms because they know it's going to fall. And there are some people putting cardboard down to try and break the fall. Wow!
W: Let me see. Wow! Look at that man! How on earth did he catch it?
M: 'Just human instinct,' that's what one man said.
W: What a catch! That's such an amazing thing!
M: It's lucky the men noticed the baby.
W: Yeah, I suppose they saw some movement.
M: Or maybe they heard something.
W: What's that? The woman's bringing something.
M: It's hard to say but it looks like a cushion.
W: Yeah, it could be a sofa cushion.
M: I guess they thought the baby might fall on it.
W: That must be the luckiest baby alive.
M: Absolutely incredible. Let me see again.

C Tell Ss to listen for one surprising fact in each story. Give them time to compare answers with a partner.

Answers:
1 That the tiger ran off and didn't attack the woman.
2 That the customers didn't notice.
3 That the man caught the baby.

3A Underline the first one together as an example and then set the rest as pairwork.

Answers:
1 The amazing thing is that the tiger ran off.
2 Wow, there's no way I'd do that!
3 You're the one who's always telling me to stop.
4 That is so wrong!
5 That's totally outrageous!
6 I do think they should do something about it.
7 That *is* a good idea.
8 How on earth did he catch it?
9 That's such an amazing thing!
10 Absolutely incredible!

B This task focuses Ss on some of the linguistic features and rules used to add emphasis. Give Ss time to discuss these in pairs and then check answers as a class.

Answers:
1 *So* is followed by adjective/adverb, *such* is followed by (*a/an*) + (adjective) + noun.
2 *Do* is not normally used with the present simple affirmative. It is used here to emphasise an opinion.
3 Any adverb that can be used with an ungradable/extreme adjective, e.g. *really, completely, just, quite*. *Very* can't be used.
4 It adds *the one who's* to emphasise the person.
5 *on earth*, e.g. *What/Why/Where/Who on earth ... ?*

C Establish that a word used on its own to add emphasis (e.g. *absolutely*) will always be stressed and in a phrase the stress will be on the 'content' words, e.g. *amazing* in sentence 1. Encourage Ss to copy the speakers' intonation.

Unit 7 Recording 5

1 The amazing thing is that the tiger ran off.
2 Wow, there's no way I'd do that!
3 You're the one who's always telling me to stop.
4 That is so wrong!
5 That's totally outrageous!
6 I do think they should do something about it.
7 That is a good idea.
8 How on earth did he catch it?
9 That's such an amazing thing!
10 Absolutely incredible!

speakout TIP

Give Ss time to read the tip and then read out the first sentence using very exaggerated stress and intonation. Ask Ss to do the same with the other sentences.

▷ LANGUAGEBANK 7.3 p140–141

Ss look at Ex 3A again and try to categorise the different ways of adding emphasis. Direct them to the Language bank to check their ideas.

Answers:
A: What *on earth's* the matter? You look terrible!
B: I've just seen Marco with Claudia. I'm *so* furious, I can hardly speak.
A: That's *totally* crazy. I'm sure there's a mistake. Why don't you call him?
B: *There's no way I'm* going to phone him.
A: But Marco's *such* a great guy and you're *so* good together.
B: Well you can be (*really*) sure that Claudia's (*really*) going to regret it.
A: I *do* hope you're not going to do anything stupid.
B: You*'re the one who* told me to fight for him. I'm just following your advice.

4A Ss work alone or with a partner to rewrite the sentences.

Answers:
1 **A:** I'm *so* angry with you. Why didn't you tell me about the party?
B: But I *did tell* you. A few minutes ago.
A: That's *really* helpful! How am I supposed to get ready in time?
B: But you*'re the one who* said you never want to go to parties.
2 **A:** Dave's good-looking but she's *absolutely* crazy about Will.
B: *The sad thing is*, Dave adores her.
A: Yeah and he's really kind; *such* a nice man.
B: What *on earth* shall I say if he asks me about Will?
3 **A:** I'm quitting my job. It's *so* badly paid and it's *such* hard work.
B: I *do* think you'll regret it.
A: You*'re the one who always says* I should do what I want.
B: But *there's no way you should* just quit.

B Circulate and help Ss to use the phrases for emphasis accurately in their conversations.

C You could suggest that Ss write one or two key words in their notebooks from each of A's and B's lines to act as prompts to help them remember the conversation.

LEARN TO MAKE GUESSES

5A Encourage Ss to complete the sentences with anything that is grammatically correct and makes sense.

Answers: 1 suppose 2 maybe 3 hard 4 looks 5 could 6 guess 7 must

B Put Ss into pairs to look at the words. Check the answers as a class.

Answers: 1 imagine 2 perhaps 3 difficult 4 seems 5 might 6 think 7 's surely (~~be~~)

6A Play the sound effect for Ss to listen and write down two ideas.

B Explain that the prompts are there to help Ss discuss their opinions. Check the answers and then allow Ss some time to compare their answers for Ex 6A in pairs.

Suggested answers:
A: What do you think it is?
B: It's hard to say but it might be (your first idea).
A: I think it sounds like (your first idea).
B: I suppose it could be (another idea).
A: Or perhaps it's (another idea).
B: Well, I think it's (final decision).

C Pause the recording after each sound and give Ss time in pairs to practise the conversation in Ex 6B. You could encourage ***stronger classes*** to refer to the past in the conversation, e.g. *What do you think it was?* etc.

SPEAKING

7A Give Ss a few minutes to think of the top five for each category. Elicit some ideas but do not let Ss check the answers yet.

B Go through the instructions for the activity, reminding Ss they can use phrases for emphasis when they react to the correct answers. Then put Ss into groups of four and give them time to read their information before working in groups.

Homework ideas

- **Ex 2:** Ss write dialogues about headlines B, D and F using phrases for adding emphasis, as in audio script 7.4.
- **Language bank:** 7.3 Ex A, p141
- **Vocabulary bank:** p154
- **Workbook:** Ex 1–4, p50

NEWS BLUNDERS

Introduction

Ss watch an extract from a BBC programme about TV news out-takes. Ss then learn and practise how to retell a news story and write a short summary.

SUPPLEMENTARY MATERIALS

Ex 3C: If you think your Ss may have difficulty coming up with a news story, you could find a couple in advance by looking at a news site with some global or quirky stories or some interesting stories you have found locally.

Warm up

Start by eliciting some jobs involved in making the TV news, e.g. producer, researcher, newsreader (also newscaster and anchorman/woman in the USA), weatherperson, camera operator. Conduct feedback with the class.

DVD PREVIEW

1A Put Ss into pairs to discuss the questions. After eliciting their answers you could tell Ss about any TV blunders you have found particularly funny.

B To familiarise Ss with the programme information, ask them to read it quickly and find out why mistakes on TV news programmes happen more often nowadays and how many types of mistakes there are.

Answers:
1 Because there is 24-hour rolling news now.
2 Four: newsreaders stumbling over their words, technical hiccups, microphones malfunctioning, the wrong guest being brought into the studio for an interview.

C Put Ss into pairs to match the words/phrases and definitions. Check the answers as a class.

Answers: **1** stumbling over their words **2** strike **3** technical hiccups **4** rolling **5** blunders **6** malfunctioning

DVD VIEW

2A Explain to Ss that they will see seven blunders in total and ask them to write the numbers 1–7 in their notebooks so they can make notes about each one. They could use a tick for blunders they found funny, a cross for those they didn't find funny and a question mark for the ones they didn't understand. They should also write down a few key words to help them remember what happened each time. Ss then compare answers in pairs and help each other with any blunders they didn't understand.

B You could play the first blunder and check that Ss understand what happened. Then play the rest of the recording and give Ss time to compare answers.

Answers:
Malfunctioning equipment – 1
People stumbling over their words – 2, 3
The wrong guest in an interview – 5, 6, 7
An accident on a live programme – 4

DVD 7 The Funny Side of the News

I1 = Interviewer 1 N = Newsreader R = Rob Ri = Riz
V = Voiceover NO = Nicholas Owen LEP = Look East presenter
FB = Fiona Bruce TB = Tanya Beckett WG1 = Wrong guest 1
SR = Sophie Raworth WG2 = Wrong guest 2 I2 = Interviewer 2
GG = Guy Goma KB = Kevin Bakhurst GP = GMTV presenter

I1: Mark Pragnal is Managing Director of the Centre for Economic and Business Research. Uh, Mark, are you there? We've lost you.
N: And there'll be live coverage on the BBC of the Democratic convention in New York in just in … under ten minutes, that's in about, ah, ten minutes.
R: And that is all the business news for the moment. Riz.
Ri: Thank you very much Rob. I'm back with a look at the, ah, headweather … with the headlines after a look at the weather with Rob McElweather.
V: News. Everybody's got an opinion about it: there's too much of it; it's on at the wrong time; it's too serious; it's too fluffy; it's too short; it's too tall. And most of all, it's live.
NO: So if it starts going wrong, you're going to see it, and probably enjoy it at the same time.
LEP: And finally, my thanks to Hugh Smith of Holt and Kay Coulson of Fordham Heath, Colchester for sending me these little and large bottles with, ah, impossible nails and screws through pieces of wood to further tantalise my brain on how they did it … oh … ah!
FB: The thing about rolling news is that you have to fill an awful lot of time, and things are changing around you and you won't necessarily be that clear about, you know, you know you've got to interview about three or four guests, the order of them might change – you're not quite sure who it's gonna be …
V: And 24-hour rolling news has created a new category. The right interview with the wrong guest.
TB: Managing Director of Internet at NTL, Jerry Rust joins me now. What's gone wrong? What's gone wrong in, ah, in your offer?
WG1: I'm afraid this is not what I'm talking about, I'm not …
TB: I'm afraid we obviously have the wrong guest here. That's, ah, deeply embarrassing for us.
SR: The Head of the NUT's Education Department is John Bangs. He's in our …
WG2: Ah you've got the wrong …
SR: … Central London Studio … he was in our Central London Studio but he seems to have disappeared so hopefully we shall go back to him later on!
V: But the undisputed champion of the Wrong Guest division is the BBC News 24 incident involving the charming but inappropriate Guy Goma.
I2: So what does this all mean for the industry and the growth of music online? Well Guy Kewney is the Editor of the technology website, ah, News Wireless. Hello, good morning to you.
GG: Good morning.
I2: Were you surprised by this, ah, verdict today?
GG: I'm very surprised to see … this verdict to … to come on me, because I wasn't expecting that.
KB: It was an item in one of the business slots on News 24, and the Business Producer went downstairs to reception and said, ah … 'Is Guy here for BBC News?', and Guy Goma put his hand up … There were two Guys there, ah, but the wrong Guy put his hand up first and came upstairs and as you know he was here for a, he was here for an interview but it wasn't for an interview for News 24, it was an interview for a job.
GP: The Sun headline is 'Big Bluffer', we find the Beeb news … Beeb news show's accidental 'expert' …
V: And for a while, Guy Goma found himself living the celebrity lifestyle. But anyway, it goes to show just how much the public love a good news blunder.

C Direct Ss to the extracts and give them a minute or two to predict/remember the missing words.

Answers:
1 wrong
2 thing, is
3 embarrassing (*deeply* means *extremely* and also collocates with *worrying* and *involved*)
4 champion, involving
5 show (*It goes to show* is a common spoken phrase used when an experience proves something to be true)

D Give Ss a few minutes to discuss the question, then ask one or two pairs to tell the class their answer and explain why they chose that incident.

Optional extra activity

Play the DVD again and ask Ss to make notes about exactly what happened in Guy Goma's case (including the fact that he became a minor celebrity for a while afterwards). Ss then role-play either an interview between Guy Goma and a reporter about his story, or the conversation between Guy Goma and a friend or family member after the incident.

speakout a news story

3A Before Ss look at the exercise, use the pictures to pre-teach *paper clip*, *snow globe* and *door knob*. Then ask Ss in pairs to decide how these three objects could be connected in a story and discuss their ideas as a class. Introduce the story and explain that *swap* and *trade* both mean to exchange something with someone so that you each get what you want. Tell Ss to number the items from 2–6 and play the recording. Check answers with the class and ask Ss what they thought of the story.

Answers: 1 a paper clip **2** a pen shaped like a fish **3** a door knob **4** a snow globe **5** a part in a film **6** a house

Unit 7 Recording 8

M = Man W = Woman

M: Did you hear this story in the news about this guy that swapped a paper clip for a house?
W: No.
M: It sounds a bit out there but apparently what happened was he started … he was at his desk looking for a job or phoning up about jobs …
W: Yeah.
M: … and, um, he saw a paper clip on his desk and he thought, I wonder what I can do with this paper clip – whether I can swap it for something.
W: Oh.
M: Anyway, so he got onto the internet and he made this website – I think it's called the-red-paper-clip dot com.
W: Right.
M: And he put this, this on the internet, photographs it, puts it on and sees if anyone wants to swap something with him.
W: And did, did anything happen?
M: Yeah, so first of all, I don't remember all the details but as I recall two Vancouver women, um, took up the first challenge and they swapped the paper clip with, I think it was a pen shaped like a fish they had found …
W: Random.
M: Yeah – they had found on a camping trip, yeah random. But he meets up with all these people he doesn't just send the things. And so then from that, I believe, this guy in Seattle wanted the pen and, swapped it for a door knob. And the door knob, was swapped for something to do with camping, …
W: Oh so he kept trading up each time.
M: Yeah he kept trading, trading up so and then that was swapped for a beer keg I think. Apparently what happened was all these

people were … the same sort of thought patterns as him and they wanted to sort of meet up and it was about a social event as well.
W: Ah.
M: Anyway, the next thing he got was a snow globe and, according to the report, it said a film director wanted it and said he'd swap it for a part in his film. And then this town decided, they had this house in this town and that they would swap the house for a part in this film.
W: No! So he went all the way from the red paper clip to getting a house.
M: … a house. And my impression was that he, he was just crazy at the beginning but he, he ended up having this – I'm not sure how good the house was but, well, yeah.
W: Well, better than a paper clip.
M: I know basically that's what happened.
W: Wow!

B Give Ss a minute or two to look through the key phrases before you play the recording again. At this point you may want to check: *It sounds a bit out there* (unconventional, eccentric) and *random* (without any particular reason, aim or pattern). Point out that where there are options in the phrases (e.g. *Did you [hear this story/ seen the news] about … ?*), they need to underline the option(s) they hear.

Answers: Did you [hear this story/see the news] about … ?; Apparently what happened was …; According to [the report/the guy on the news] …; Anyway, so he…; I don't remember all the details, but …

C If you have brought in news stories for Ss, distribute these among the class for them to refer to. Get Ss to work alone on their story. Be available to help with vocabulary, etc.

D Ss work in groups of three to five. Remind those listening to use words/phrases to show they're interested and to take notes. After they've all told their stories, Ss discuss which story was the most interesting/the funniest/the weirdest, etc. then tell the rest of the class what they decided.

writeback a short summary

4A Give Ss a minute to read the article and identify the item it mentions which was not in the recording.

Answers: 1 a neon sign

B Ask Ss to complete the tasks individually. Check the answers and explain that these features all make a text more varied and help with the cohesion.

Answers:
1. There are five possibilities: A Canadian man, Bored blogger, the 26-year-old, paper clip owner, homeowner
2. trading/exchanging; objects/items
3. step by step: emphasises the time taken in small stages; larger and larger: again emphasises the progression. The use of two comparatives is common as a way of emphasising.

C Use the suggested answer below to show the first words that could be cut. Tell Ss to work individually and cut the text to 45 words. Ask Ss to compare their cuts with a partner.

Suggested answer: A Canadian man has made headlines by trading a paper clip for a house. Bored blogger Kyle Macdonald started by exchanging small objects – ~~a pen, a door knob, a neon sign~~ – but ~~step by step the 26-year-old~~ built up to items of larger ~~and larger~~ value, and after one year his journey from paper clip owner to homeowner was over.

D In class Ss write the first draft of their summary.

E Put Ss into pairs. They take turns to read their articles aloud and decide if their partner's summary is the same story they told in Ex 3D and if it is an accurate summary.

Optional extra activity

To further practise shortening summaries, Ss could exchange their summaries with a partner. Each person should try to cut 15 words from their partner's summary.

Homework ideas

- **Ex 3D:** Ss write another summary of one of their stories.
- Ss research redpaperclip.com (correct at the time of going to press) on the internet and report back on their findings in the next lesson.

LOOKBACK

Introduction

The aim of these activities is to provide revision and further practice of the language from the unit. You can also use them to assess Ss' ability to use the language, in which case you need to monitor but avoid helping them. You may feel that you don't need or have time to do all the activities. If so, you could allocate the activities that would be most beneficial for your Ss, or get individual Ss to decide which activities they'd like to do.

TELEVISION

1A You could set a time limit – for example 2 mins – for Ss to find the fifteen different types of TV programme in the wordsnake, working either alone or in pairs, before feeding back as a class.

Answers: sketch show, sitcom, the news, costume drama, quiz, serial, documentary, detective series, game show, current affairs programme, soap opera, reality show, thriller, wildlife programme, docudrama

B You could set a time limit for this, e.g. 3 mins, and see which pair has written down the most examples for each category.

Suggested answers:
laugh – sketch show, sitcom, reality show, game show
learn something – documentary, quiz, current affairs programme, docudrama
just relax and watch real people – game show, reality show
catch up on the news – the news, current affairs programme
test your knowledge – quiz

QUANTIFIERS

2A You could do the first sentence as an example, then give Ss a few minutes in pairs to do the rest. Remind Ss to look carefully at the verb forms used (singular or plural) and that the sentences are about just two people.

Answers: **1** Both **2** Neither **3** quite a few of **4** a little **5** hardly any **6** Neither **7** every **8** another **9** several **10** a few

B Ask two Ss to demonstrate the example and point out that if the answer is not the same for both of them, they need to say *One of us (enjoys spending time in airports), but the other (doesn't).* Choose a few Ss to tell the class some of their answers in feedback. You could extend this by asking Ss to choose a famous celebrity couple, or a movie/cartoon couple and tell them to change the sentences as if they are answering for that couple. The idea is to produce some amusing answers!

REPORTED SPEECH

3A You could do the first sentence as an example with the class. Ss work alone and compare answers with a partner.

Answers:
1. Last week, an interviewer asked me what my biggest weakness was.
2. The other day, a complete stranger walked up to me and asked what I had been doing lately.
3. Once, I was trying on trousers and the shop assistant asked if I would like/wanted to try a bigger size.
4. Every day, my flatmate asks me to do the dishes and then says he/she'll do them next time.
5. At the end of a first date, the girl asked me when I wanted to get married.
6. At 3a.m., my phone rang and the caller asked if I was sleeping.

B You could start by telling Ss which question would make you feel the most uncomfortable and why. Then put Ss into small groups to explain their choices. You could extend this by asking Ss to imagine that someone did actually ask them the questions and tell their group how they replied, e.g. (for question 1) *I told him I didn't have any weaknesses!*

REPORTING VERBS

4A Focus Ss on the example and put them in pairs to help each other with the rest of the exercise.

Answers: **1** to help **2** making **3** to lend **4** to pay **5** for being **6** to quit **7** of being **8** to do

B Encourage Ss to read out the questions to each other, focusing on appropriate stress and intonation. For ***weaker classes*** you may want to drill the questions first. To extend this, ask Ss to choose two questions each to ask other people in the class, then to stand up and walk round asking the questions and making a note of the answers they get. Ss then go back to their original pairs and report the answers to their partner, e.g. *Everyone said they'd always apologise for being late. One person said he'd refused to pay a bill: it was in a restaurant – his pizza was burnt!*

ADDING EMPHASIS

5A You could run this as a race in pairs: as soon as a pair has finished the exercise they bring their books up to you to check.

Answers: **1** ~~so~~ **2** ~~so~~ **3** ~~very~~ **4** ~~the~~ **5** ~~that's~~ **6** ~~she~~ **7** ~~such~~ **8** ~~that~~ (the first one)

B You could demonstrate this first by taking the role of Student A yourself and asking a strong student to take the role of Student B, e.g.

You: *There's no way that I'd ever borrow money from a friend.*
Student B: *What makes you say that?*
You: *Well, it's embarrassing if they don't pay you back.*
Student B: *How do you mean?*
You: *You know, you don't want to ask them for the money in case they've forgotten, or …*

After Ss have practised in pairs for a few minutes they could report some of the conversations back to the class, e.g. *My partner told me her hometown's a boring place because there's nowhere to go out at night. When I asked her what she meant by that, she said there were some cafés and pubs, but no clubs.*

BBC interviews and worksheet

What kind of news stories interest you?

This video encourages Ss to reflect on the kinds of news stories that they find the most interesting.

OVERVIEW

8.1 IT'S A TOUGH CALL

READING | read three articles about life-changing decisions
VOCABULARY | collocations: decisions
GRAMMAR | past and mixed conditionals
PRONUNCIATION | connected speech: weak forms
SPEAKING | talk about a difficult decision you've made
VOCABULARY *PLUS* | compound adjectives

8.2 FAIR SHARE

SPEAKING | talk about values and behaviour
VOCABULARY | values
LISTENING | listen to an experiment about fairness
GRAMMAR | *-ing* form and infinitive
PRONUNCIATION | connected speech: intrusive /w/
WRITING | an informal article; learn to use linkers of purpose

8.3 HAVE YOU GOT A MINUTE?

VOCABULARY | behaviour
FUNCTION | handling an awkward situation
PRONUNCIATION | sentence stress and intonation
LEARN TO | soften a message
SPEAKING | deal with awkward situations

8.4 THE HUMAN ANIMAL BBC DVD

DVD | watch a BBC documentary about body language
speakout | advice for a visitor
writeback | cross-cultural article

8.5 LOOKBACK

Communicative revision activities

BBC INTERVIEWS

What kind of behaviour gets on your nerves?

This video looks at different kinds of irritating behaviour and our reactions to them. Use this video at the start or end of Unit 8 or set it as homework.

IT'S A TOUGH CALL

Introduction

Ss practise reading and speaking about decisions they've made using conditionals and related collocations.

SUPPLEMENTARY MATERIALS
Resource bank: p182 and p184
Ex 1B and **Ex 7A:** bring monolingual dictionaries for SS to use for the *Optional extra activity* and when preparing to talk about a difficult decision.

Warm up

Ask the class for an example of an important decision that a person may have to make in their life, then put Ss into pairs to make a list of examples. Write the examples on the board in feedback and discuss with the class which they think are the most difficult decisions to make.

Examples of decisions: *whether to go to university or not and which one to go to/what subject to study; what career path to take; whether to change jobs; what car/house to buy; what town/country to live in; whether to get married/have children/get divorced; what to do about problems in a friendship/relationship.*

READING

1A Direct Ss to the photos and write the headlines on the board to avoid Ss getting distracted by the texts. Ss discuss what happened in pairs and agree on two sentences to give the details of the situation and describe what happened for each article.

B Give Ss about 5 mins to read the articles and discuss how accurate their predictions were with their partners.

Optional extra activity

In order to check some key items of vocabulary from the texts and to encourage further prediction, write the following words on the board and ask Ss to decide which article they're from:
thrift, lumpy, stashed, deposit slip, gust, tracks, stroller, heartbroken, allegedly, surveillance
Encourage Ss to use monolingual dictionaries to check the meaning of unfamiliar words.

C Ask the class to identify all the people in the articles, even if they don't know their names, then look at the example together. Either individually or in pairs, Ss think about who might have said each sentence.

Suggested answers:
1 Delroy Simmonds
2 Anne McQuinn's father, or her uncle
3 the widow
4 the woman whose baby Delroy Simmonds saved
5 Sergeant Tom Landers or another police officer
6 Reese Werkhoven
7 Gerry Comber/Anne McQuinn's father
8 one of the three roommates

D Ss discuss which decision was hardest and what they would have done. When eliciting their answers, you could hold a class vote on some of the possibilities. For example, find out how many of the Ss would have kept the money.

VOCABULARY COLLOCATIONS: DECISIONS

2A You could start by writing the following on the board (Ss should have their books closed) and asking Ss to think of a suitable verb for each gap:

1 ________ a decision
2 ________ your principles (strong ideas about what's right or wrong)
3 ________ a situation

Add any acceptable suggestions that Ss give you to the board, then give them a minute or two to complete the word webs in their books. They should use monolingual dictionaries to check any verbs they're unsure of.

Answers: put off a decision, go against your principles, assess a situation

B Ss draw lines to match the words with a similar meaning and then check their answers with a partner. With ***stronger Ss*** do not check their answers until after Ex 2C. With ***weaker Ss*** check the answers before setting Ex 2C.

Answers: put off – postpone; reach – arrive at; follow – stick to; go against – betray; evaluate – assess; explore – look into

C Look at the first definition with the class and establish that the two missing verbs have the same meaning. Point out that two collocations match each definition, although there may be some difference between them in the level of formality, e.g. *postpone* versus *put off*, *betray* versus *go against*, *stick to* versus *follow*. Pronunciation to check: *postpone* and *betray*.

Answers:
1 arrive at, reach a decision
2 postpone, put off a decision
3 follow, stick to your principles
4 go against, betray your principles
5 explore, look into a situation
6 evaluate, assess a situation

Optional extra activity

For personalised practice, write the following sentence heads on the board for Ss to complete with verbs from Ex 2A and their own ideas:

1 I often find it easier to ________ a decision than to …
2 I would only ________ my principles if …
3 It's easier to ________ a difficult situation if …

Ss then compare and discuss their answers in pairs or small groups.

3A Give Ss a minute or two to read through the extracts from the web forum and decide which decision is more difficult and why. Discuss this briefly with the class, then give Ss a few minutes to complete the texts.

Answers: **1** evaluated/assessed **2** go against/betray **3** arrived at/reached **4** look into/explore **5** stick to/follow **6** put off/postponed

B Give Ss a few minutes to discuss the situations and the questions.

GRAMMAR PAST AND MIXED CONDITIONALS

4A Ss at this level should be familiar with the concept of past conditionals, but may not be confident in referring to the past and present in the same sentence. Start by asking Ss which newspaper stories each of the four sentences refers to. Then, while Ss underline the verbs, write/display the sentences on the board so you can highlight the verbs and later label them with the answers to Ex 4B.

Answers:
1 I think if any of us had used it, it would have felt really wrong.
2 If that had happened to me, I might not have jumped.
3 I would have done the same thing.
4 If he hadn't jumped down there, the baby wouldn't be alive.

B Look at the first sentence with the class and establish that it refers to a hypothetical situation. Put Ss into pairs to do the rest of the exercise.

Answers:
1 All four sentences are hypothetical because the condition is always in the past so can't be changed.
2 1–3 refer to the past; 4 refers to the past and the present
3 The conditional (*if*) clause is often not used if the condition is understood or obvious. Another example from text 2 in Ex 1B: 'Anybody would have done the same.'

C Tell Ss to look back at the example sentences in Ex 4A to help them with this. For ***stronger classes*** suggest that Ss cover the words in the box and try to complete the rules from their own knowledge first. When you've checked their answers, ask Ss to look again at the sentences in Ex 4A and reverse the order of the clauses in sentences 1, 2 and 4. Elicit/Point out that when the main clause is at the beginning of the sentence, like this, a comma in the middle is not necessary. You could also drill these sentences at this stage, showing Ss that when they pause briefly on the comma, their pitch shouldn't drop.

Answers:
1 past perfect
2 **a)** modal + *have* + past participle
b) modal + infinitive

5 Direct Ss to the phonemic script and see if they can predict the matches first. Play the recording and ask Ss what happens to the *h* in *have* (it disappears). Then play the recording again for Ss to repeat the sentences.

Answers: **1** d) **2** a) **3** c) **4** b)

▷ LANGUAGEBANK 8.1 p142–143

Ss could read the notes and do Ex A and B for homework.

Answers:
A 1 a) 2 b) 3 a) 4 a) 5 b)
B 1 If Beth had studied, she could have passed the exam.
2 If you had invited me to the party, I would have come. OR I would have come to the party if you had invited me.
3 If Ludmila hadn't lost all her money on the stock market, she would be rich now. OR Ludmila would be rich now if she hadn't lost all her money on the stock market.
4 If Greg had been travelling fast, he might have hit the motorcyclist. OR Greg might have hit the motorcyclist if he had been travelling fast.
5 If they hadn't stopped the fire, it could have destroyed most of the building. OR The fire could have destroyed most of the building if they hadn't stopped it.
6 The plant wouldn't have died if you had watered it. OR If you had watered the plant, it wouldn't have died.
7 Mei-li couldn't have afforded a new car if she hadn't just won some money. OR If Mei-li hadn't just won some money, she couldn't have afforded a new car.
8 If we hadn't been working together in Tokyo, we wouldn't be married now. OR We wouldn't be married now if we hadn't been working together in Tokyo.

6 Start by asking Ss to read the three situations. Ask Ss to discuss with a partner which person had the most difficult decision to make. Ss complete the gaps alone and check answers in pairs.

Answers:
1 **a)** had been, wouldn't have needed
b) would/might/could be, had left
2 **a)** could have died, had taken
b) wouldn't/couldn't have done
3 **a)** would have felt, had done
b) hadn't saved, might never have recovered

SPEAKING

7A Ss should make some notes about two of the situations so they can answer the questions in Ex 7B. Ss could use monolingual dictionaries to help develop their responses.

B You could start by talking about a difficult situation that you were in. Invite different Ss to ask you questions 1–5 and answer them, incorporating some conditionals and some collocations in your answers.

Optional extra activity

Ss think of a famous person, e.g. a politician, a footballer, an actor, who's been in the news because of a difficult situation they've been in. Ss can 'be' the famous person, answering the questions in Ex 7B as if the situation happened to them.

VOCABULARY PLUS COMPOUND ADJECTIVES

8A Complete the first one on the board as an example. In pairs, Ss complete the other two. Check the answers as a class.

Answers:
1 a widow who is 91 years old
2 $4,000 in bills which are wrapped in bubble wrap
3 a daughter who robbed a bank

B After setting and checking this task, you could also focus Ss' attention on the use of relative pronouns in the rewritten sentences.

Answers: 1 bubble-wrapped 2 bank-robbing 3 91-year-old

speakout TIP

Ask Ss to look at the compound adjectives in Ex 8A and to find one that matches the rule in the speakout tip. To extend the practice with this, Ss could write example sentences using quantity compound nouns.

C Write the first one on the board as an example and then set the rest for individual work. Ask Ss to check their answers in pairs and then confirm the answers as a class.

Answers: 1 three-day-old baby 2 hand-made clothes 3 15-metre-high wall 4 life-changing moment 5 long-running TV series 6 five-year-long course 7 well-qualified 8 time-consuming activity

9A Ss complete the gaps with compound nouns using the information in brackets. Check the answers as a class.

Answers: 1 twelve-year-old 2 non-smoking 3 two-month 4 odd-sounding 5 solar-powered 6 twenty-storey

B Choose one of the sentences to give your own opinion on and briefly discuss this with the class. Set the rest of the task for individual work followed by pairwork discussion.

▷ VOCABULARYBANK p155

Compound adjectives for describing people

Without looking at the box in Ex A, ask Ss to describe one of the people to their partner. Then ask Ss to complete the labels using the words from the box. Ask Ss whether they used any of the collocations when they described the people. Ss could either complete Ex B in pairs or for homework.

Answers:
A 1 curly-haired 2 brown-eyed 3 sun-tanned 4 dark-haired 5 broad-shouldered 6 tight-fitting jeans 7 high-heeled shoes 8 brand-new dress
B straight-haired, fair-haired, loose-fitting jeans

Homework ideas

- **Language bank:** 8.1 Ex A–B, p143
- **Vocabulary bank:** p155
- **Workbook:** Ex 1–6, p51–52

FAIR SHARE

Introduction

Ss practise listening and speaking about values and fairness using *-ing* forms and infinitives and vocabulary related to values. They also learn to use linkers of purpose and write an informal article.

SUPPLEMENTARY MATERIALS
Resource bank: p185
Ex 2B: bring monolingual dictionaries for Ss to use.

Warm up

Write these situations on the board. In pairs, Ss discuss whether they think the person is being fair or not.
A man decides to buy a house his friend wanted to buy. He gets it by offering more money.
An employee doesn't get a pay rise just because the boss doesn't like him.
The parents of a boy stop his pocket money for a month because he comes home late once.
Elicit some responses from Ss.

SPEAKING

1A Ask Ss to read the instructions for the games and discuss what they think each one shows about a person's behaviour. Elicit some responses from the class.

B Ss complete the gaps individually. Make sure Ss understand that the amounts in the first two gaps must add up to £10.

C In pairs, Ss compare their amounts for each game. Ask the whole class to try to get into groups where people gave similar amounts. In their groups Ss discuss the questions together.

VOCABULARY VALUES

2A Look at the example with the class. Highlight how the phrase *even though you don't have to* gives them the clue that it matches to the word *fairness*. Ss match the two halves of the sentences in pairs. When checking the answers, ask each pair to read one half of the sentence out loud each and then check everyone agrees. Elicit which words or phrases helped them to match each one.

Answers: 1 d) 2 f) 3 b) 4 c) 5 e) 6 a)

B Ss may want to check some of the vocabulary in their dictionaries before doing this task. Allow Ss time to match the words to the definitions and to compare their answers with a partner.

Answers: 1 generosity 2 aggression 3 equality 4 control, power 5 fairness, justice 6 greed

C Explain that some phrases can match both games. Once Ss have matched each phrase to a game, elicit their choices and ask them to explain their answers.

Suggested answers:
1 both
2 Dictator Game (some could argue that this is true for either game)
3 Dictator Game
4 Dictator Game
5 both
6 Dictator Game

LISTENING

3A Tell Ss they will hear two people playing The Ultimatum Game. Point out that in the first half of the recording someone is explaining the game to Dominic and Heather. Pause the recording after Dominic says *I would quite like all of it* and ask Ss whether they think he will keep all of it. Play the rest of the recording and ask Ss to answer the questions.

Answers:
1 Dominic offered £5.
2 Yes, she did.
3 It's not fair to offer less, and he doesn't think she would have taken it.
4 It was kind and generous, and it was an equal split.
5 Heather wouldn't have accepted less than £5.

Unit 8 Recording 2

M = Man **D** = Dominic **H** = Heather

M: OK, Dominic and Heather we're going to play a game.
D: Oh.
H: Ahem.
M: Its, it's an experiment. Um what I'm gonna do is – hang on I'm just gonna get it out of my pocket. I'm going to give you, Dominic, £10.
D: OK, can I keep it?
M: OK – for now. And you have to decide how much you're going to offer Heather.
D: OK.
M: And if Heather accepts, then you divide the money as agreed. You get some and she gets some.
D: Right.
M: But, if Heather rejects your offer and she doesn't like the way you've split the £10 …
D: Ahem.
M: … then I get the £10 back and neither of you get anything.
H: Um.
D: Ah, OK.
H: OK.
M: Could you understand?
D: Yeah, I think so.
H: Yeah.
M: Are you sure?
H: Yeah.
D: So I basically have to choose how much money I'm going to offer Heather.
M: Yeah.
H: And then …
D: And if she's happy with it …
H: I decide if I want it or not.
M: That's right, OK?
H: OK?
D: So …
M: Right there you go.
D: Thank you, that's for me. That's a lot of money, I would quite like all of it. Uh, do I just say it now, out loud?
M: Yeah.
D: OK, uh I'm going to offer you £5.
M: Um.
H: Go on then, I'll accept that.
D: Yeah.
H: Yeah, I will yeah.
D: Great so we get a five, fiver each.
M: You do indeed and I, and I lose £10.
D: Yeah, that was worth it.
M: OK, so I mean that's really interesting. Why, why Dominic did you decide on that split?
D: Um, I guess, if I offered any less, I didn't think you'd take it.
H: No.
D: So I thought this way.
M: But why, why, why would you?
D: Um, because it's, it's not fair, you know 'cos this isn't any more my money than it is hers really, just 'cos it's a game, you've given it to me.

M: Interesting.
D: Um it, it was.
M: And why, why did you accept?
H: Um, because I felt that it was equal you know an, an equal split, um, I thought it was very kind and yeah generous to give me half.
D: Uh.
M: OK and um, OK then – here's an interesting question. Heather, in your mind what would have …
H: Um …
M: been the lowest amount?
D: Ahem.
H: It act –
M: that you would have accepted?
H: It actually would have been £5 because I think any lower than that and I'd have felt sort of you know.
D: Hard done by.
M: Very interesting.
H: Hard done by, yeah, is the word, yeah.
M: Thanks guys, cheers.

B Tell Ss to discuss their reaction to the recording and to make a prediction on The Dictator Game. Elicit reasons for Ss' predictions.

C Play the recording and ask Ss to answer the questions. Check the answers and find out whether anyone predicted how they would behave accurately.

Answers:
1 Dominic offered £1 and kept £9.
2 He gave £1 to show he's not heartless. But it was easier to keep most for himself, so he did.
3 She feels hard done by, cheated.

Unit 8 Recording 3

M = Man D = Dominic H = Heather

M: OK guys, uh we're gonna play another game now.
D: Um.
M: It's called The Dictator Game. And, uh, I think I'm gonna be very out of pocket by the end of the day.
D: More money?
M: Yeah. Another £10.
D: Oh a ten.
M: And, I'm gonna give it to you again.
D: Thank you.
M: But this time – instead of making an offer which you can, you Heather can accept or reject …
D: OK.
M: You have to accept it.
D: Ah.
M: So Dominic …
D: OK.
H: OK.
D: I have the power.
M: It's your decision. You have the power. It's your decision.
D: Um, OK so I just say it out loud?
M: Yeah.
D: Uh, the offer I'm going to give you this time is £1 and that means £9 will be for me.
M: OK.
H: Well then I accept that 'cos I have no choice.
D: You have no choice.
M: You have no choice. But, but the question here is how do you feel, how do you feel about that?
H: Yeah I feel a bit hard done by, to be honest. I feel a bit cheated really, um.
M: His fairness, from last time has all disappeared.
H: Yeah, um.
D: Um I guess I gave you £1 to still show that I'm, you know, not heartless.
H: Ahem.
D: Uh, you know so, you know I want to keep all of it, but um I guess with the offer of being able to have more, without the choice.
H: Um.
D: Um, it sort of, it was easier for me, to say, I won't feel so guilty, I don't feel.
H: Yeah tempting, isn't it?
D: Feel a bit guilty now, but no I just thought – is, there's no option for her so I might as well keep more of it.

D Give Ss a few minutes to discuss the questions in groups. As an extension Ss could play the games using imaginary money.

GRAMMAR *-ING* FORM AND INFINITIVE

4A Focus Ss on the example. Ss can work in pairs and help each other with this. Suggest that if they're not sure of an answer, they could read the sentence aloud, trying out the different forms, to see which one 'sounds' right.

Answers: **1** to respond **2** thinking **3** being **4** to think **5** to act **6** to impress **7** to be seen **8** to act **9** sharing **10** keep **11** have **12** share **13** having **14** cooperate **15** exploiting

B Tell Ss to underline the thing that surprises them the most and to compare it with a partner. After Ss have decided whether they agree or disagree with the last sentence, ask them to get into groups with other Ss who have the same opinion. In their groups Ss should think of three reasons why they agree/disagree with the statement. Elicit some answers.

C Check that Ss understand the terms *infinitive*, *infinitive + to* and *-ing form* by writing *go*, *to go* and *going* on the board and asking them which is which.

Answers:

	-ing* form, infinitive or infinitive + *to	**example**
after a preposition	*-ing* form	2, 13
to express purpose	infinitive + *to*	6
after *let someone* or *make someone*	infinitive	11
as part of a semi-fixed phrase, e.g. *It's important/easy* and *the chance*	infinitive + *to*	5, 7, 8
as a subject or object (or part of one of these)	*-ing* form	3
after modal verbs	infinitive	10, 12
after certain verbs e.g. *enjoy, avoid, imagine*	*-ing* form	9, 15
after certain verbs e.g. *want, would like, tend*	infinitive + *to*	1, 4
after *had better, would rather*	infinitive	14

▷ LANGUAGEBANK 8.2 p142–143

Direct Ss to the Language bank in class if you think they'll benefit from seeing more examples of the uses of *-ing* and the infinitive. You could do Ex A as a team competition: write/display the sentences one at a time on the board for teams to discuss: to liven this up, when they're ready with the answer, the team members could make a sound like a 'buzzer' that people press, e.g. in a televised competition.

Answers:

A
1 It's no use *explaining* – you never listen anyway.
2 There's no point in *going* to bed now – we have to get up in an hour.
3 Do you expect *me to know* all the answers?
4 *Listening* to your MP3 player during class is rude.
5 My parents never let me ~~to~~ stay out past 8 o'clock.
6 We all look forward to *seeing* you in person.
7 You'd better ~~to~~ get ready – the taxi's arriving in ten minutes.
8 The trip was a good opportunity *to practise* speaking English.
9 They're used to *speaking* English with each other even though they're both Japanese.
10 I phoned the station *to ask* about departure times.

B
1 Have you considered becoming a doctor?
2 I've managed to pass my driving test – after three tries.
3 My mother taught me to type without looking.
4 We avoided talking to each other all through the party.
5 Jorge expects to finish the painting by the end of the week.
6 My computer keeps freezing whenever I hit the delete button.
7 Could you remind me to lock the door, Jan?

5A This exercise shows Ss that because the form of the modal verbs *must* and *can* doesn't change, they need to use an appropriate form of *have to* and *be able to* for expressing obligation and ability. Direct Ss to the example and remind them about the rules in Ex 4C. After Ss have had a minute or two to discuss their answers, play the recording.

Answers:
1 I don't want to have to refuse.
2 I hate having to argue to get my way.
3 I don't seem to be able to stand up for myself.
4 I enjoy being able to offer people help.

B Play the recording, stopping after each sentence for Ss to mark the pronunciation of *to*.

Answers:
1 to /tə/ have; to /tə/ refuse
2 to /tu:w/ argue; to /tə/ get
3 to /tə/ be; to /tə/ stand
4 to /tu:w/ offer

C As Ss listen again, ask them to read the sentences and to try to work out a rule from the patterns. Check the answer as a class. Then play the recording again for Ss to repeat.

Answer:
When a vowel sound follows *to*, the /w/ sound is needed to link the vowels, so *to* is pronounced /tu:w/. Before consonants it's normally pronounced in the weak form /tə/.

6A Ask Ss to cross out the incorrect forms in each sentence. Vocabulary to check: *just* (fair, right in the situation). Check the answers as a class.

Answers:
1 ~~being/to be~~/be
2 ~~working/to work~~/work
3 cheating/~~to cheat/cheat~~
4 losing/~~to lose/lose~~
5 ~~being/to be~~/be
6 ~~earning~~/to earn/~~earn~~
7 ~~giving~~/to give/~~give~~, ~~receiving~~/to receive/~~receive~~
8 Being/~~To be/Be~~, being/~~to be/be~~

B Give Ss a minute or two to decide which ones they agree with and which ones they disagree with.

C In groups, Ss discuss their reactions to the statements. In addition to finding out who they agreed with most, you could find out which statement it was hardest to agree on.

speakout TIP

It's important for Ss to record language in chunks rather than simply learning individual words. This will give Ss patterns they can replicate accurately. Ask Ss to write sentences using the phrases in the tip box and elicit some examples.

WRITING AN INFORMAL ARTICLE; LEARN TO USE LINKERS OF PURPOSE

7A Tell Ss to cover the article and look at the three titles. Elicit some ideas about the possible content of an article with each of the titles. Then Ss read the article and choose the title.

Answer: c) Change the things you can

B Ss underline the correct alternatives and then explain their reasons to a partner. Alternatively, simply elicit the reasons from individual Ss.

Answers:
1 student magazine (because it's informal in tone and style)
2 give advice (the author offers ideas on how best to behave in different situations)
3 beginning

C Look at the first guideline with the class, establishing that there is a personal example in the third and fourth paragraphs. Put Ss into pairs to work through the rest.

Answers:
1 T *I've often made that mistake and lived to regret it.; That's how I managed to get a promotion recently after a long fight for justice.; For example, once someone bumped into my car and drove away, and I couldn't really do anything about it …*
2 T There are eight examples of *you* in the first paragraph; *you, me, I* and *my* are all used several times throughout the article.
3 F Examples come throughout the text, e.g. *it's* and *you're* in the second paragraph; *it's, Don't, that'll, I've* and *That's* in the third paragraph.
4 T The tone is generally conversational, e.g. *Do you hate it when people treat you unfairly?; I've often made that mistake and lived to regret it.; That's how I managed to …; For example, once someone bumped into my car and …*, etc.
5 T Examples in the article include *First of all, Second* and *Finally.*
6 T *Do you hate it when people treat you unfairly?*
7 F Examples in the article include *miss out on* and *stand up for.*
8 F There are no examples of the passive in the article.

8A Before you refer Ss to the article, write the linkers of purpose on the board and elicit what all of the words have in common (they explain why someone does something). Ss then write down the patterns following each word.

Answers:
1 **a)** so as to, in order to, to **b)** so that, because **c)** for
2 so as to, in order to
3 in order not to, so as not to

B Explain that Ss are going to practise using the patterns from Ex 8A in this task. Do the first one as an example and then set the rest for individual work.

Answers:
1. A good leader treats everyone equally so that everyone feels valued.
2. When I'm upset I usually phone my sister for a chat.
3. It's important to check everyone in a team reaches a decision together so as not to leave anyone/someone behind.
4. In a good relationship, it's important to sit down together from time to time to make sure everything is OK.
5. Sleep on it because your brain will continue working overnight and you'll wake up knowing what to do.
6. In a family, it's good to have a list of tasks for each person in order not to give anyone the feeling they are doing more than their fair share.

9A Choose one of the topics to brainstorm as a class and write it on the board. Spend a few minutes brainstorming it together. Next ask Ss to brainstorm one or two more in pairs.

B As Ss write their articles, monitor and help with ideas and structures. Once Ss have finished, ask them to exchange their articles with a partner. They should each underline examples of informal words and phrases and linkers of purpose. They should also make one suggestion to improve their partner's article.

Homework ideas

- **Ex 9A:** Ss write another article from the list.
- **Language bank:** 8.2 Ex A–B, p143
- **Workbook:** Ex 1–5, p53–54

HAVE YOU GOT A MINUTE?

Introduction

Ss practise listening and speaking about awkward situations using phrases for handling awkward situations and vocabulary related to behaviour. They also learn to soften a message.

SUPPLEMENTARY MATERIALS

Resource bank: p183 and p186

Ex 1A: bring monolingual dictionaries for Ss to use.

speakout tip: give Ss some dialogues to add fillers to.

Warm up

You could start by telling Ss about an awkward situation (real or invented) that you found yourself in, e.g. a friend borrowed something (a book, an item of clothing) and returned it damaged. Elicit some more examples of awkward situations from the class and ask Ss how it's best to behave when dealing with a situation like this. Ss may say you need to be tactful/honest/direct, etc.

VOCABULARY BEHAVIOUR

1A You could do the first one as an example with the class. Pronunciation to check: *supportive*, *unhelpful*, *diplomatic*, *tactful*, *sensitive*, *sensible*, *confrontational*, *collaborative*, *aggressive*, *assertive*, *direct* and *focused*. Ss could check the stress on the words in their dictionaries.

Answers:
1 D *Supportive* and *unhelpful* are near opposites.
2 S Both mean you try to avoid hurting feelings or making people upset when you communicate with them.
3 D *Sensitive* means you are easy to hurt or that you understand what other people feel and care about their feelings. *Sensible* means you make good, rational decisions.
4 D These are near opposites. If you are *confrontational*, you like a fight, if you are *collaborative*, you like to work with others.
5 D *Aggressive* is negative and means you push too much in any situation. *Assertive* is more positive and means you have the confidence to give your point of view, for instance.
6 S These are similar. If someone is *direct*, they say what they mean clearly. If someone is *focused*, they are clear about what they want to say and are able to say it clearly.

B Give Ss a few minutes in pairs to try making opposites and saying them aloud to see if they 'sound' correct.

Answers:
1 supportive – unsupportive; unhelpful – helpful
2 diplomatic – undiplomatic; tactful – tactless
3 sensitive – insensitive; sensible – senseless
4 confrontational – unconfrontational; collaborative – uncollaborative (These opposites exist but are not common.)
5 aggressive – non-aggressive; assertive – unassertive
6 direct – indirect; focused – unfocused

C Focus Ss on the example and put them into pairs to discuss the situations.

Suggested answers:
breaking bad news: sensitive, tactful, focused
a friend is down: supportive, sensitive
making a complaint: diplomatic, assertive, direct
working on a project: supportive, diplomatic, collaborative, focused
driving or cycling: sensible, focused
sort out a problem: tactful, sensitive

▷ VOCABULARYBANK p155 **Behaviour idioms**

Ask Ss to look at the pictures and without using the words in the box to describe what they can see. Then ask Ss to match the idioms to the pictures. Set Ex 2C and D for homework.

Answers:
A **A** talk behind sb's back **B** walk all over sb **C** lock horns with sb **D** (be) a shoulder to cry on **E** not lift a finger **F** give sb a helping hand
B positive: be always there for sb, go out of one's way to do sth, (be) a shoulder to cry on, give sb a helping hand
negative: talk behind sb's back, walk all over sb, not lift a finger, lock horns with sb
C **1** give (anyone a) helping hand **2** lift a finger **3** shoulder to cry on **4** talking behind (my) back **5** lock horns with **6** is always there **7** go out of (his) way **8** walk all over
D **1** be always there for sb **2** go out of one's way to do sth **3** lock horns with sb **4** give sb a helping hand **5** (be) a shoulder to cry on **6** talk behind sb's back **7** walk all over sb **8** not lift a finger

FUNCTION HANDLING AN AWKWARD SITUATION

2A Direct Ss to the photos and ask them what the awkward situation might be in each case. They then look at the three situations together and match the photos. Put Ss into pairs to discuss how to handle the situations.

Answers: 1 A 2 B 3 C

B Give Ss a few minutes to read and discuss the tips. Ask Ss to discuss the following questions: *Which do you agree/disagree with? Would you add anything to the list?* All the tips are valid, so they may agree with them all. You could ask them which they feel are the most/least important.

3A Give Ss 1–2 mins to read the statements then play the recording.

Answers:
1 F She borrows small amounts each time but they add up to quite a lot.
2 F Next week, after she's been paid.
3 T He says that she's said she'll pay him back before.
4 F He suggests she pays back however much she can afford each week.

Unit 8 Recording 5

J = Jim L = Liz

J: Here's your coffee.
L: Thanks, Jim. Oh, I needed that.
J: No problem. Hey, Liz, there's something I've been meaning to talk to you about.
L: Oh yeah?
J: It's just that … well … you know you borrowed some money from me last week?
L: Oh, right. It was €10, wasn't it? … I don't actually have that on me at the moment.
J: It's not that, it's … well … I hope you don't take this the wrong way, but, um …
L: Right.
J: It's just that this isn't the first time I've lent you money and, er, well you haven't paid it back. I mean, I know it's not a lot, just small amounts each time but it kind of adds up quite quickly … I dunno. Do you know what I mean?
L: Yeah . Sorry. I didn't realise. I know I'm terrible with money. I just forget. Look, I promise I'll give it back, but could you wait a week? Until I get paid.

J: Well, actually, you've said that once before. I don't want you to get the wrong idea, but … it, you know, never happened. And it makes things slightly awkward. It makes me feel just a bit annoyed. Do you see where I'm coming from?
L: Oh. Yeah. I suppose so.
J: Look, I've got a suggestion. I'd feel better if we could work out how much is owed and then you could pay me back a little each week, you know, however much you can afford. How does that sound?
L: Yeah, yeah. That sounds reasonable.
J: OK, great so …

B Refer Ss back to the tips in Ex 2B then play the recording again.

Answers: He follows all the tips. He says clearly at the beginning why he wants to talk to her. He's specific, reminding her that she said she'd pay it back later once before and telling her that he feels annoyed. He doesn't say what anyone else thinks. He gives her space by asking 'Do you know what I mean?' He suggests a solution.

4A Once Ss have completed the phrases with their own ideas, either direct them to the audio script or play the recording again, for them to check.

Answers:
1 meaning (= intending, thinking about)
2 just (*It's just that* … 'softens' the message)
3 take
4 what
5 sound

B Give Ss a minute or two to read the sentences aloud and think about the stress and intonation, then play the recording.

Answers:
1 There's something I've been meaning to talk to you about.
2 I hope you don't take this the wrong way, but …
3 I don't want you to get the wrong idea, but …
The first phrase goes down as it is a completed statement. The other two phrases go up because they are unfinished.

C Ss could practise saying the phrases to each other and comment on whether they sound tactful or confrontational.

▷ LANGUAGEBANK 8.3 p142–143

Ss could do Ex A before moving on to the more challenging practice in Ex 5 on p99. Once Ss have completed the conversation, they could practise acting it out, making sure they sound appropriately diplomatic/focused, etc.

Answers:
A 1 c) 2 f) 3 b) 4 e) 5 a)

5 Tell Ss to read through the prompts quickly and match the situation with the appropriate photo (*the girl talking on the phone with the woman looking exasperated in the background*). Ss do not need to write the dialogue out in full, rather they should just use the flow chart as a prompt.

Suggested answers:
Possible dialogue though slight differences would be fine:
A: Alex, there's something I've been meaning to talk to you about.
B: Yeah. What's up?
A: Well, look I don't want you to get the wrong idea but …
B: But what?
A: It's just I'm very busy and you're always on the phone.
B: Oh, right.
A: It's quite annoying. Do you know what I mean?
B: I'm sorry, I wasn't thinking.
A: I've got a suggestion. Why don't you ask your friends to call your mobile instead of our land line?
B: You mean I should use the phone in a different room?
A: That's right. How does that sound?
B: That seems reasonable. I'm really very sorry.
A: No problem. Forget it.

LEARN TO SOFTEN A MESSAGE

6A Tell Ss they're going to hear some extracts from the conversation between Jim and Liz again and give them a minute to read through the sentences. Ask Ss to discuss the words they could add to soften the message.

B Explain that the extra words or sounds they'll hear make the speaker sound more tactful and less confrontational. Play the recording and ask Ss to add any extra words or sounds they hear.

Unit 8 Recording 7

1 It's not that, it's … I hope you don't take this the wrong way, but … um … it's just that this isn't the first time I've lent you money and, er, well you haven't paid it back. I mean, I know it's not a lot, just small amounts each time but it kind of adds up quite quickly … I don't know. Do you know what I mean?
2 Well, actually, you've said that once before. I don't want you to get the wrong idea, but … it, you know, never happened. And it makes things slightly awkward. I mean … It makes me feel just a bit annoyed. Do you see where I'm coming from?

speakout TIP

Before Ss look at the tip, ask them to look back at Ex 6B and decide which words are used instead of a pause and which are used in front of an adjective to soften the message.

Optional extra activity

For more practice in adding fillers to a conversation, give Ss some four- to six-line dialogues (on a handout or written on the board) and ask them to add fillers.
The following situations should naturally generate the need for pauses/getting thinking time and softening the message:
an invitation to dinner/a party/an event (the person inviting is nervous), e.g.
A: I was (kind of) wondering if you're (I mean) free on Saturday?
B: I think so, yes.
A: (Well, um) There's a jazz (kind of) festival in town in the afternoon. Would you like to (um) go?
B: That sounds great, I'd love to.
giving directions (the person giving directions is unsure of the exact route)
making an excuse for being late (the listener is quite annoyed with the late arrival)

SPEAKING

7A Give Ss time to think how they'd start each conversation. They could also think of a solution that one of the people in each situation could offer.

B Ss should take a minute or two to think about which phrases they can use in the conversation and when/how they might need to 'soften' their message. Monitor and note down examples of the phrases and fillers Ss use, for feedback later.

C Put Ss into new pairs and give them a minute to prepare as in Ex 7B. Monitor as above. If you have access to recording facilities, you could record some of the role-plays, then play back the recordings for Ss to analyse, e.g. if Ss didn't use many fillers, ask them to identify places where they could have used them.

8 Give Ss a few minutes to note down a few ideas for each topic and then ask them to work with other Ss. In groups, Ss should try to agree on a list of the three most annoying habits in each context.

Homework ideas

- **Ex 7A:** Ss write conversations for the situations they didn't practise in class.
- **Language bank:** 8.3 Ex A, p143
- **Workbook:** Ex 1–3, p55

THE HUMAN ANIMAL

Introduction

Ss watch an extract from a BBC programme about human behaviour. Ss then learn and practise how to give advice to a visitor and write a cross-cultural article.

Warm up

Tell Ss to close their books. Put them into pairs or small groups and ask them to think of as many ways as they can of greeting someone, both verbal and non-verbal. These could be from their own country, or from other countries they've visited or heard about. Circulate and provide vocabulary as required. In feedback, take the opportunity to review this and pre-teach other vocabulary that will help Ss with the DVD viewing tasks and the discussion of gestures in other countries, such as: *shake hands, kiss (on the cheek/hand), hold/clasp (someone's hand/arm), hold your palms/hands out/up, hug, bow, rub (noses), slap (on the back)*.

DVD PREVIEW

1A Give Ss a few minutes to compare their list from the Warm up with the list here. Ss should demonstrate the gestures they know to a partner. Mime each gesture to your class and ask them to number each one as you do it. Check Ss have numbered them in the right order.

B Explain that different gestures can mean different things in different countries. Ask Ss to explain what these gestures mean in their own countries. If you have a ***multilingual class***, you could elicit any other gestures common in Ss' countries that are not in the list in Ex 1A and get them to explain the meaning of the gestures to each other.

2 Ask Ss to read the text and to correct the sentences. Check the answers as a class.

Answers:

1 Desmond Morris observed human behaviour in the way that a bird-watcher might.
2 He classified human behaviour, not words.
3 It took him many years (we don't know how many). Sixty refers to the number of countries he travelled to.
4 The programme looks at greeting and gestures, not at sign language.

DVD VIEW

3A Ss discuss the questions in pairs, then demonstrate the gestures in feedback.

B Establish that Ss will see lots of different handshakes and ways of saying *You're crazy*. They don't need to explain them all, just the ones they find most interesting.

DVD 8 The Human Animal

DM = Desmond Morris

DM: Back in the late 1960s I was sitting in this very restaurant on the island of Malta talking to my publisher. I drew his attention to the fact that over the other side of the road there were two men who were gesticulating in a particular way. The way they were holding their palms to one side was fascinating me and he said, 'You know, you look at people the way that a bird-watcher looks at birds' and I said, 'Yeah, I suppose you could call me a "man watcher".'
As soon as I said it, it was as if I'd fired a starting gun on a major new project, one that was to engross me for many years to come and take me to over sixty different countries. I was going to do for actions what dictionary makers had done for words. I began making huge charts naming every facial expression, every gesticulation, every movement, every posture. I kept at it for month after month.

One of the first problems I encountered was that even the simplest human action, such as the handshake, has countless variations. Sometimes it's reduced to a mere palm touch, as with these Masai elders in East Africa. But in other countries it becomes more elaborate. In Mali in West Africa the hand shaker briefly touches his own forearm as the palms clasp.

In Morocco the hand shakers kiss one another's hands at the same time as clasping them. And in Turkey, these Kurdish farmers have taken this simple action and converted it into what amounts to a minor ritual. It's the local rule that they can't start bargaining until they're shaking hands and they have to keep on doing so until the deal is struck.

The essential feature of hand shaking is that it's an egalitarian act. Regardless of their social standing, the two people involved are momentarily performing identical actions.

Despite their variations, all these greetings have one thing in common: they're all fine-tuned to the precise context in which they occur.

Because a single message is given in a different way in different countries. The crazy sign: how do you say to somebody, 'You're crazy'? Well, here in Rome you do this, but, in England I would probably do this – the temple screw saying 'he's got a screw loose' – or I might say 'his brain is going round and round', or I might, tap my head saying, 'what does he think he's got inside his skull?' In some countries you do it with two hands; it varies from place to place and, if you go to Japan you have to be careful because if you do it this way it means 'he's intelligent', you have to do it in an anticlockwise direction in Japan if you want to say that somebody is crazy. So, all over the world the same message is given in a slightly different way.

C Give Ss time to match the gestures to the people and places before playing the DVD again.

Answers: Shaking hands: **1** d) **2** c) **3** a) **4** b)
Saying you're crazy: **1** c) **2** a), d) **3** b)

D Play the DVD again and ask Ss to underline the correct alternative. Ask Ss to explain the meaning of the words used and the words not used to check they understand the difference.

Answers: 1 drew, gesticulating **2** engross me
3 expression, posture **4** variations **5** egalitarian
6 fine-tuned to, context

speakout advice for a visitor

4A Before Ss listen to the recording, write *the USA* on the board. Find out if anyone has ever visited there. If they have, elicit what advice they would give someone going. If no Ss have been, ask them to list three things they would like to know before going. Play the recording and discuss as a class anything that surprised Ss.

Unit 8 Recording 8

OK, here are some things that I think would be useful if you're visiting the States, especially if you're coming here to do business.

So first of all, with names. When you first meet someone, it's considered good manners to use a title along with their surname, you know like Mr Smith or Ms Jones, and so on. But the funny thing is that in fact people will in most cases want to use first names, you know be on a first-name basis, like 'Hey call me Bob' and all that. That might not be comfortable for you but in fact if you stick to a more formal Mr Smith sort of thing, it's not going to be comfortable for them. I also think that once they know your name you'll find people use it a lot, so they'll say it periodically in a conversation. If you're not used to it, it can seem strange at first.

Now with meeting people for the first time … It's pretty normal for people to shake hands, or at least guys do. Women usually do, certainly in business, but not always. On the whole, Americans tend to avoid greetings that involve hugging and other close physical contact, except with family members and friends. Having said that, don't be surprised if someone gives you a hug the first time you meet them, either as a hello or a goodbye. You sort of have to keep your eyes open and try to anticipate what they'll do.

When people sit down, like in a meeting, people like to get comfortable, so people cross their legs with one ankle on the other knee. I know this is rude in some countries but it's normal here. That reminds me, if you're chatting with someone in an office, standing up, they might sit on a desk, which I know is a big no-no in places like Japan. Other gestures? Well, if an American wants to show agreement, they'll sometimes give the thumbs up sign or they'll make a circle out of their thumb and index finger. Don't be offended if in your culture this isn't polite. It just means 'A OK' in the States.

Last of all, timing: punctuality is very important for business occasions and it's unacceptable to be late, and if you are late it will be appreciated if you let your contact know if you are going to be late. It's the same for social occasions, you need to arrive on time.

Of course, having said all this, it's important to remember that the United States is huge and there's a lot of variety in what's acceptable in different places. Anyway, I hope this advice helps.

B Give Ss time to read through the key phrases. Tell Ss to tick the ones they hear. Point out that where there are options in the phrases (e.g. *It's considered [good/bad] manners to …*), they need to underline the option(s) they hear. In feedback you could drill some of the phrases or put Ss into pairs to practise saying the phrases to each other.

Answers: It's considered [good/bad] manners to …; If you're not used to it, it can seem strange at first.; Having said that, don't be surprised if …; It's [unacceptable/perfectly acceptable] to …

C Give Ss time to make notes and circulate and provide help as necessary. Remind Ss to incorporate some of the key phrases where appropriate. Ss could practise their advice in pairs or groups.

D Put Ss into different groups to present their advice to each other. Monitor and make notes of good language use and problems for discussion and correction in feedback.

writeback cross-cultural article

5A Tell Ss to read the short article and tell each other which aspects from Ex 4C it covers.

Answers: Greetings; Personal space, eye contact, posture, voice; Special gestures

B If your class are all from the same country, you could discuss this question as a class. If you have a ***multilingual class***, put Ss into mixed nationality groups and then hold a feedback session.

C Using their notes from Ex 4C and the model in Ex 5A, Ss should write a short article covering one or two topics. Monitor and provide support as necessary.

D If your Ss are from different countries, pair them together with someone from another country, as this will allow more discussion. If they are from the same country, Ss could discuss whether they agree with each other's advice or not.

Optional extra activity

Ss research a country they would like to visit and find out cultural advice for people going there. They should write down three or four of the most important tips they find. In class, Ss should share the countries they chose and the advice they found.

Homework ideas

Ss write some tips for people visiting their country, telling them about important gestures and their meaning.

LOOKBACK

Introduction

The aim of these activities is to provide revision and further practice of the language from the unit. You can also use them to assess Ss' ability to use the language, in which case you need to monitor but avoid helping them. You may feel that you don't need or have time to do all the activities. If so, you could allocate the activities that would be most beneficial for your Ss, or get individual Ss to decide which activities they'd like to do.

COLLOCATIONS

1 Ss can work on this in pairs.

Answers: 1 evaluate, postpone 2 stick to, go against 3 explore, putting off 4 assess, arrive at

PAST AND MIXED CONDITIONALS

2A You could start by writing just the beginnings of the three sentences on the board and asking Ss to complete them so that they are true for them. Then direct them to the exercise, so they can compare the endings given there.

Answers:
1 **a)** might have studied **b)** wouldn't have gone **c)** wouldn't be
2 **a)** would have taken **b)** would have found **c)** would have chosen
3 **a)** would be **b)** spend **c)** have ended up

B Ss choose one answer each from a), b) or c).

C Ss should explain to each other why they chose the answer in each case.

Optional extra activity

Ask Ss to think of ideas to substitute the following in each of the three sentences:

1 studying English (e.g. *going to the gym, working for (name of company), wearing glasses, (cookery) lessons*)
2 live in a different country (e.g. *start my own business, travel for six months, take a year off, meet someone famous*)
3 computers (e.g. *cars, mobile phones, fridges*)

They then write their own endings and compare ideas in groups.

VALUES

3A You could run this as a competition between two teams. Write/Display the sentences on the board one at a time and give teams time to confer. They put up their hands when they're ready, then call out just the missing vowels in the correct order (you could give a point for every correct letter and take away a point for any incorrect letter).

Answers: 1 fairness, equality 2 aggression 3 generosity, control 4 power, justice 5 greed

B If Ss are in teams, they could ask these questions in open pairs. A student from one team chooses a student from the opposing team and asks them the question. Points can be given for good pronunciation, interesting answers, etc.

-ING FORM AND INFINITIVE

4A You may want to let Ss refer to the Language bank on p142 while they're doing this exercise. You could make this a race: as soon as a pair has finished the exercise they bring their books up to you to check.

Answers: 1 travelling 2 to learn, hearing 3 to be 4 to do 5 Riding 6 making 7 being able to watch 8 Having to wear

B You could start by giving one or two examples about yourself, as a model for Ss. Give Ss a few minutes to work on this alone.

C Demonstrate this by saying one of the sentences that is true for you and inviting Ss to ask you at least three different follow-up questions, e.g.

T: *Cooking is one of my favourite ways of relaxing.*
S1: *Really? Why's that?*
T: *Because I like being creative.*
S2: *What kinds of dishes do you like cooking?*
T: *I love cooking desserts and cakes.*
S3: *Do you know how to make cheesecake?*
T: *Yes – would you like a recipe?* etc.

Ss could stand up and walk round the class reading and responding to their statements.

HANDLING AN AWKWARD SITUATION

5A You could start by putting Ss into pairs, directing them to the three situations in Ex 5B and asking them to rank them in order from most to least awkward. In feedback discuss their reasons for ranking them as they did and ask them what solutions they'd suggest. Ss could then correct the sentences in pairs, or in teams, as a competition. Write the corrected sentences on the board for Ss to refer to in Ex 5B.

Answers:
1 Excuse me, Wendy. Do *you* have a *moment*?
2 There's *something* I've *been* meaning to talk to you about.
3 Look, I *don't* want you to get the *wrong* idea, but …
4 It's *just that* I've noticed that …
5 I'*d* feel *better* if …
6 How *would* you *feel* about that?

B After Ss have practised one situation, choose two or three pairs to act out their conversations for the class and give them some positive and constructive feedback. Then ask Ss to change roles for the next situation and choose different pairs to act out for the class afterwards. Repeat the process for the final situation.

Homework ideas

Workbook: Review 4, p56–59

BBC interviews and worksheet

What kind of behaviour gets on your nerves?

This video looks at different kinds of irritating behaviour and our reactions to them.

OVERVIEW

9.1 WITNESS

VOCABULARY | crime
READING | read an article about memory
GRAMMAR | *-ing* form and infinitive
PRONUNCIATION | connected speech: elision
SPEAKING | discuss how good a witness you are
VOCABULARY ***PLUS*** | dependent prepositions

9.2 SCAM

VOCABULARY | synonyms
LISTENING | listen to people talking about getting tricked
GRAMMAR | past modals of deduction
PRONUNCIATION | connected speech: past modals
SPEAKING | speculate about scams
WRITING | a 'how to' leaflet; learn to avoid repetition

9.3 IT'S AN EMERGENCY!

SPEAKING | talk about emergency situations
VOCABULARY | incidents
FUNCTION | reporting an incident
PRONUNCIATION | sentence stress
LEARN TO | rephrase
SPEAKING | talk about a burglary

9.4 SURVIVAL BBC DVD

DVD | watch a BBC programme about a sea rescue
speakout | agreeing priorities
writeback | an escape story

9.5 LOOKBACK

Communicative revision activities

BBC INTERVIEWS

Do you have any phobias?

This video extends the unit topic to deal with the issue of phobias and the irrational fear people have of certain situations, activities, things, animals or people. Use this video at the start or end of Unit 9 or set it as homework.

WITNESS

Introduction

Ss practise reading and speaking about memory and being a witness using the *-ing* form and infinitive and vocabulary related to crime.

SUPPLEMENTARY MATERIALS
Resource bank: p187, p188 and p189
Ex 1C and **Ex 7C:** bring monolingual dictionaries for Ss to use.

Warm up

Put Ss into pairs and direct them to the two photos on p104–105. Tell Student A to look at the photo on the left and Student B to look at the photo on the right. Give Ss a minute to look at their photo and try to remember as many details as possible. After a minute, tell Ss to take it in turns to close their books and to test their partner on their memory of the photo. Ss can then report back to the class about how good their partner's memory was.

VOCABULARY CRIME

1A You could start by brainstorming different types of crime with the class (Ss close their books). To prompt Ss give them categories, such as crimes which involve:

1 damaging something
2 taking something which isn't yours
3 harming a person
4 getting money from someone

Ss then discuss which ones are the most common where they live. Elicit a response.

B Put Ss into pairs to complete the newspaper extracts. Pronunciation to check: *kidnapping, vandalism, identity theft, bribery, counterfeiting, arson* and *shoplifting.*

Answers: **1** arson **2** hacking **3** shoplifting **4** stalking **5** kidnapping **6** Bribery **7** vandalism **8** counterfeiting **9** identity theft **10** mugging

C First suggest that Ss draw a table with eleven rows and three columns, to write their answers in. Put Ss into pairs, emphasising that they should try to help each other work out the answers and only use a dictionary for those they're really unsure of. Check answers as a class and ask Ss to share any other crime vocabulary they thought of.

Answers:

crime	person	verb
arson	arsonist	to commit arson
hacking	hacker	to hack into sth
shoplifting	shoplifter	to shoplift
stalking	stalker	to stalk
kidnapping	kidnapper	to kidnap
bribery	–	to bribe
vandalism	vandal	to vandalise
counterfeiting	counterfeiter	to counterfeit
identity theft	thief	to steal someone's identity
mugging	mugger	to mug

D Ss discuss the questions in groups and feed back to the class.

9 trouble

READING

2A If you did the Warm up, you could extend Ex 2A by asking *What tricks do you know for remembering PIN numbers, passwords or people's names?* You could also do an example for the second question by telling Ss about a technique you have for remembering passwords, PIN numbers, etc., if you have one.

B Give Ss 2–3 mins to read through the article quickly and find the information.

Answers:
1 Seeing a video of the bus exploding in the 2005 terrorist attacks in London.
2 Seeing a white van or truck leaving several of the crime scenes during sniper attacks in the Washington DC area in 2002.

Culture notes

The Washington sniper attacks took place during three weeks in October 2002 in Washington, D.C., Maryland and Virginia. Ten people were killed and three others critically injured in a series of shootings. At first thought to be the work of a single sniper, it was later found that two men were responsible.

The London bombings (also known as 7/7) were a series of coordinated suicide attacks on London's public transport system during the morning rush hour of 7th July 2005. At 08.50 three bombs exploded within fifty seconds of each other on three London Underground trains, a fourth exploding an hour later at 09.47 on a double-decker bus in Tavistock Square. The explosive devices were packed into rucksacks and detonated by the bombers themselves, all four of whom died. 52 other people were killed and around 700 were injured.

C You could do the first one as an example and establish that *witness testimony still plays an important part in court cases* is the key phrase to underline. Give Ss time to go through the article carefully and mark the statements true or false.

Ss compare answers in pairs before feedback with the class. Vocabulary to check: *DNA tests* (tests that can prove the identity of a person by studying some of their DNA, which is unique for each individual), *testimony* (what a witness says in court) and *flee* (to run away).

Answers:
1 F 'Even in these days of DNA tests and other forensic techniques, witness testimony still plays an important part in court cases.'
2 F '… forty percent of people claimed to have seen this nonexistent footage.' *but* 'Some even went on to describe what happened in vivid detail.' (i.e. some of the forty percent)
3 T 'In many cases, an unreliable memory is not a problem. It just means we forget to send a birthday card …'
4 T 'In 1998, an American study calculated that in ninety-five percent of felony cases – the more serious crimes – witness evidence (in other words, people's memories) was the only evidence heard in court.'
5 F '… witnesses reported seeing a white van or truck fleeing several of the crime scenes.'
6 T 'In twenty percent of cases they pointed to a volunteer.'

D Focus Ss on the example and establish that *it* refers back to the noun *recollection*. When Ss have finished the exercise, explain that this use of pronouns can help them to understand a text when they're reading and also be useful for them to use in their writing to structure the text and avoid repeating the nouns.

Answers:
1 Most of us have some recollection of the 2005 terrorist attacks in London. **It** could well be a mental image of …
2 But what about CCTV footage? Do you remember seeing a video of the bus exploding? What can you see in **that** video?
3 Well, the truth is, you shouldn't be able to see anything in your mind's eye because **such** CCTV footage simply doesn't exist.
4 Many of us think we have a good memory. After all, **it's** got us through the occasional exam.
5 In many cases, an unreliable memory is not a problem. **It** just means we forget …
6 When **they** were caught, the sniper suspects were actually driving a blue car.

E Ask Ss to find the answer individually and to then compare and discuss in pairs. Finally, Ss can discuss the question about their ability as a witness. Ask one student who thinks they would be a good witness to explain why.

Answer: The author blames the over-reliance on witness memories that are often inaccurate.

GRAMMAR -*ING* FORM AND INFINITIVE

3A You could write the sentences on the board and go through them with the whole class, or put Ss into pairs to discuss them first.

Answers: 1 seeing **2** to describe **3** to send

B If you have a ***mixed-ability class***, try to ensure that ***stronger Ss*** are paired with ***weaker*** ones for this activity. Monitor the pairwork closely so you can help any pairs who are struggling. You may want to go straight on to Ex 3C if Ss have coped well with identifying the differences in pairs.

Answers:
1 **a)** I remembered, then I set the alarm. It was my responsibility to set the alarm.
b) I remember now that I thought then that the building seemed very quiet.
2 **a)** I forgot that I needed to buy the tickets, so I didn't do it.
b) I'll always remember the concert that I saw.
3 **a)** Henri stopped first because he wanted to drink some coffee. He stopped and then he drank.
b) He didn't continue driving.
4 **a)** Billy finished the training and later became a famous dancer.
b) Billy continued practising every day.
5 **a)** He made an effort to recall her name.
b) He experimented by going through the alphabet to help him remember.
6 **a)** We're sorry that we have to give this bad news.
b) I'm sorry I spent so much money on the ticket.

C You could do the first one with the class as an example, then put Ss into pairs to match the rest.

Answers: 1 b) **2** a) **3** b) **4** a) **5** a) **6** b) **7** b) **8** a) **9** a) **10** b) **11** b) **12** a)

4 Play the recording and ask Ss to cross out letters at word endings that are not pronounced. Once you've played the recording for Ss to check and repeat, ask them what the missing letters have in common. (When /d/ or /t/ follow each other the first sound disappears. This is also true when /t/ follows /t/ and when /d/ follows /d/, e.g. *I remembered doing it.*)

Answers:
1 I remembere~~d~~ to lock up.
2 Sorry, I forg~~ot~~ to bring it.
3 We stopp~~ed~~ to have something to eat.
4 I tri~~ed~~ to phone you but you weren't answering.
5 We reg~~ret~~ to inform you that the train is delayed by approximately half an hour.

▷ LANGUAGEBANK 9.1 p144–145

Direct Ss to the Language bank for further examples of the verbs which have a different meaning when followed by *-ing* or an infinitive, as well as a list of verbs which can be followed by *-ing* or an infinitive with no difference in meaning. You could do Ex A in class: put Ss into pairs and tell Student A to cover the right-hand column and Student B to cover the left-hand column. Student A reads a sentence beginning at random and Student B listens and chooses the correct ending. Then both Ss cover the right-hand column and try to remember the ending of each sentence.

Answers:
A **1** b) **2** a) **3** a) **4** b) **5** a) **6** b) **7** b) **8** a) **9** b) **10** a)
B **1** to get (*getting* is also possible but the *-ing* form is not used so much in the negative) **2** to investigate **3** seeing **4** to intervene **5** doing **6** to take **7** to tell **8** not coming forward **9** to identify **10** to do **11** helping/to help **12** being

5A Focus Ss on the example and give them a few minutes to work on the questions alone or with a partner.

Answers: **1** to get **2** to buy **3** to help **4** witnessing **5** doing **6** thinking **7** to take **8** to become **9** writing **10** to inform **11** studying **12** hiding

B Help Ss to sound natural by focusing on the linking at the beginning of some of the questions and drilling them, e.g. *Have you ever …, Do you ever/always …, Has anyone …, How long do you … .*
You could then demonstrate the idea of follow-up questions by inviting Ss to ask you one of the questions and answering it, then eliciting two or three examples of follow-up questions that they could ask.

SPEAKING

6A Give Ss a few minutes to read the situations and think about what they would have done and why. Make sure they understand that they should consider questions a)–c) for each situation and make notes of the answers to use in the discussion activity.

B Put Ss into groups of three to five to discuss the situations, nominating one person to keep a record of the questions they agreed/disagreed on. In feedback, encourage Ss to summarise some of their group's answers, e.g. *We'd all …, None of us would …, Most of us said we'd … .*
You could also have a brief discussion about which group's answers were surprising/predictable, etc.

VOCABULARY PLUS DEPENDENT PREPOSITIONS

7A Encourage Ss to read the headlines out to each other and see which prepositions 'sound' correct.

Answers: **1** with stealing **2** of taking **3** for selling

B Focus Ss on the example and establish that the present perfect is commonly used to introduce news stories, before details of time, place, etc. are added using past forms. Elicit the full forms of the other two headlines from the class and write them on the board.

Answers:
1 A fake police officer has been charged with stealing a £600 necklace. Passive
2 A woman has accused a con artist of taking her bag and PIN. Active
3 A gang has been arrested for selling one car nine times. Passive

C Encourage Ss to work together and help each other before checking in a dictionary.

Answers: **1** of accessing **2** for cheating **3** for causing **4** of becoming **5** for employing **6** from travelling **7** for saving **8** from being eaten **9** of murdering **10** from drowning

8A You could start by giving Ss an example as a model, e.g. *A fourteen-year-old student is facing a four-mile walk to school every day after being banned from travelling by train for a year. Judi Leigh, who goes to Maryfield High School, was caught on CCTV camera spraying graffiti on the wall of her local station for the third time in a month. The teenager claims that it is a case of mistaken identity.*

B Combine pairs into groups of four and ask Ss to take turns reading out their articles and choosing the correct headline.

▷ VOCABULARYBANK p156 Dependent prepositions

Ex 1 gives Ss more practice in using dependent prepositions in the context of newspaper headlines. You could write the prepositions *about, in, for* and *from* up on the board to give them some extra help. Let them work independently to try to complete the headlines, then check their answers in pairs.

Answers:
1 for **2** from **3** for **4** about/of **5** from **6** for **7** about **8** in **9** from **10** for

Homework ideas

- Ss look through a newspaper or the news on the internet and write a summary of the types of crime that were reported, e.g. *There were two stories about vandalism in my local paper – in one story the vandals …, in the other they vandalised … .*
- **Language bank:** 9.1 Ex A–B, p145
- **Vocabulary bank:** p156
- **Workbook:** Ex 1–5, p60–61

SCAM

Introduction

Ss practise listening and speaking about scams using past modals of deduction and synonyms. They also learn to avoid repetition in writing and write a 'how to' leaflet.

SUPPLEMENTARY MATERIALS
Resource bank: p190
Warm up: prepare sets of slips with vocabulary to review/preview.

Warm up

Write the following on separate slips of paper: *mug, fake, counterfeit, bribe, rob, a scam, shoplifting, identity theft, hacker*. Put Ss into groups of four to six and give each group a set of slips. Demonstrate that Ss should put the slips face down in a pile in front of them and take turns to turn over a slip and define the word for the rest of the group. Whoever guesses the word keeps the slip. If a student doesn't or can't define the word or nobody can guess it, the slip is put to the bottom of the pile. The winner is the person with the most slips. Any words left in the pile can then be looked at and discussed by the group.

VOCABULARY SYNONYMS

1A If Ss have trouble thinking of an example, tell them about *phishing*: you get an official-looking email from your bank telling you the information on your account is outdated and providing a link to a page where you can update your information. The link will take you to a webpage that looks identical to the reputable site, but which has been set up by a scammer to collect your personal information.

B Direct Ss to the infographic on the right. Ask Ss what the function of an infographic is (to give a quick very visual overview of information on a topic). Put Ss into pairs to read the information and answer the questions. After a few minutes, invite Ss to share their answers with the class.

Answer: 2 The Shoulder Surf, The Fake Police Officer and Escalator Jam can be done by one person. The other two need at least two people working together.

C Focus Ss on the example and give them a few minutes to match the rest, working alone or in pairs.

Answers:
1 pretend to be, pose as
2 deceive, fool
3 distract, divert someone's attention (from sth)
4 snatch, grab
5 be taken in (by), fall for
6 switch (sth with sth), swap (sth for sth else)

NB Although these verbs and phrases are used as synonyms in this context, it's worth pointing out to Ss other contexts where some of them can be used:

pretend to be = behave as if something is true: *pretend to be asleep, pretend you didn't hear*

switch = change from one thing to another: *He's switched jobs.; She can switch from Italian to English easily.*

grab = take hold of something suddenly: *She grabbed my arm when she heard the scream.*

swap = exchange: *Let's swap phone numbers.*

speakout TIP

Before Ss read the tip, ask them why it's important to learn synonyms. Give them a minute or two to read the suggestions and to rewrite the sentences.

Suggested answer: Yesterday was very pleasant. I had a good meal at an excellent restaurant with some lovely people.

You could discuss with the class which way(s) of learning synonyms they've tried and suggest that they try one new one when they next read or write something.

LISTENING

2A Direct Ss back to the infographic and tell them to listen for which two of the five scams the people talk about.

Answers: The Tourist Photo, The Fake Police Officer

Unit 9 Recording 2

Conversation 1
L = Lise J = Jeff

L: So what happened was, I was sitting in a café and this young couple – they looked like tourists – asked me to take a photo of them. And I took their photo, and they thanked me and left and then I looked at my seat and realised my handbag had gone, with my mobile, wallet, credit card, keys, everything.
J: No! What did you do?
L: Well, there was a guy on the next table and he saw I was really upset and I explained about the bag and he asked me which bank I was with and he said he worked for that bank and gave me a phone number and let me use his mobile to phone them and stop my credit card.
J: And you believed him?
L: Yeah, I mean I was in a real panic. I was really grateful for his help. Anyway, I phoned the number and talked to a woman from 'the bank' and gave her my name and address and my account number.
J: She sounded genuine?
L: Yeah, completely. I could hear the sounds of the call centre behind her. And she asked me to key in my PIN on the phone and she said they'd stop my card.
J: Wow. And you did? You punched in your PIN?
L: Yeah, unfortunately.
J: So it was a double scam. They got your bag and your bank account details.
L: I felt so stupid.
J: So who actually took your bag?
L: Well, it can't have been the young couple because I was looking at them all the time I was taking the photo. Their job was just to distract me. So it must have been stolen when I was taking the photo.
J: Was it the guy at the next table, then? The fake banker?
L: I think so. He must have taken my bag when I wasn't looking. Then he could have hidden it in his case or maybe he gave it to another member of the gang.
J: And then he gave you a fake phone number to call the bank.
L: Yeah, and they probably used a recording of a call centre so that it sounded like the real bank.

Conversation 2
D = Dan I = Ingrid

D: I was badly tricked a few years ago when I was working in a jewellery shop.
I: You never told me about that. What happened?
D: Well, this woman came in and was looking at necklaces. She was young, attractive, well dressed, and then a guy came in shortly afterwards and he was just looking around. But then the woman went to pay for a very expensive necklace that she'd picked out, and when she was counting out the money onto the counter, the guy grabbed her, flashed his police ID and said he was arresting her for paying with counterfeit money.

I: Fake money! Wow!
D: So he took the cash and the necklace as evidence, wrote down his contact details, and promised me he'd bring the necklace back by the end of the day. I didn't suspect anything. Then he took the woman away, presumably to book her at the police station.
I: And he didn't come back?
D: No, and stupid me, I didn't even begin to suspect anything until it was closing time, so then I phoned the police and they had no idea what I was talking about. That was it, end of story.
I: How much was the necklace worth?
D: £600. And my boss took it out of my salary. That's why I quit.
I: So the police ID was a fake.
D: Must have been. I just didn't check it.
I: And wait a second, was the woman a real customer?
D: No, the woman must have been working with the guy. She couldn't have been a real customer or she wouldn't have gone with him …
I: But she might have had fake money.
D: I really don't think so.
I: Talk about an ingenious scam …

B Give Ss time to read through the statements and to try to complete them with a partner. Play the recording again for Ss to check.

Answers:
1 asking her to take a photo of them.
2 he said he worked for a bank, he let her use his mobile, she was in a panic and grateful for the help.
3 she could hear sounds of the call centre; the man supposedly worked for the bank and she believed he had phoned the bank.
4 getting her to key/punch it in on the man's mobile.
5 a police officer.
6 paying with counterfeit money.
7 the necklace, the cash and the woman.
8 bring the necklace back.

3 Ss can work in pairs or small groups. Give them a few minutes to discuss the questions, then get feedback from the whole class.

GRAMMAR PAST MODALS OF DEDUCTION

4A For ***stronger classes***, first tell Ss to cover meanings a)–c) and discuss in pairs the different meanings of sentences 1–7.

Answers: 1 c) 2 a) 3 a) 4 b) 5 a) 6 c) 7 b)

Check that Ss understand the idea of speculating or making a deduction, i.e. if you're less than 100 percent sure (e.g. *He took my bag.* = I know this, it's a fact.).

B While Ss complete the rules, write them on the board so that Ss can come out and complete the gaps in feedback.

Answers:
1 *must/could/might/can't/couldn't* + *have* + past participle
2 modal + *have* + *been* + *-ing*
3 modal + *have* + *been* + past participle

5A You could focus Ss on the phonemic script and see if they can predict how the past modals are pronounced, before you play the recording.

B Play the recording and ask Ss to repeat the phrases as they listen.

Unit 9 Recording 4

1 It must have been great!
2 It could have been me!
3 It might have been him!
4 It couldn't have been worse!
5 She can't have been there!

▷ LANGUAGEBANK 9.2 p144–145

Direct Ss to the Language bank for examples of the past modals of deduction in different contexts. You could use Ex A and B in class for some controlled practice before going on to Ex 6A. Put Ss into pairs and either allocate an exercise to each pair or ask them to choose one (Ex B is more challenging, so direct ***stronger Ss*** to this one). When Ss have finished, provide them with an answer key to check their answers, then put them together with a pair who did the other exercise and tell them to swap answers.

Answers:
A 1 Jenna might have phoned while we were out.
2 He can't/couldn't have heard you.
3 The thieves might/could/may have got in through the window.
4 I realised I couldn't have saved the document.
5 It must have hurt a lot.
6 Her plane might/could/may have been delayed.
7 I must have made a mistake.
8 She can't/couldn't have been trying hard enough.
B 1 must have cost
2 might/could/may have switched off
3 must have been working
4 might/could/may have been thinking
5 can't/couldn't have looked
6 might/could/may have been told

6A You could start by telling Ss to read through the two accounts quickly and decide which scam is the most ingenious. Then give them a minute or two to complete the gaps and compare answers in pairs.

Answers: 1 might/could/may have dropped 2 might/could/may have fallen 3 must have pulled 4 can't have been 5 must have been 6 must have been working

B Put Ss into pairs to discuss which of the scams would be most likely to fool them.

SPEAKING

7A Explain to Ss that they're going to read about a scam and that they should add a few details to it and practise telling it so that it sounds as if the scam happened to them. They should also try and work out how the scam worked by thinking about the questions under the story. Put Ss into two groups, As and Bs and give them time to practise and discuss their story.

B Pair Ss up so you have one from group A and one from group B in each pair. Student B tells Student A their story without looking at the text, then they speculate together about how the scam was done, using the questions for guidance. Remind Ss to use past modals here. Monitor and note down some examples of good use of the past modals and any problems for feedback later.

C Student A tells Student B their story without looking at the text, then they speculate together about how the scam was done, using the questions for guidance.

D Finally, direct the class to the answers on p161.

WRITING A 'HOW TO' LEAFLET; LEARN TO AVOID REPETITION

8A Ask the class for some examples of problems people can have when they visit an unfamiliar city, e.g. with transport – catching the right bus, getting a reliable taxi driver; with shops – being charged more than the real price, being given the wrong change, etc. Elicit some advice for dealing with the problems.

B Establish that a *leaflet* is a small piece of printed paper containing information, advertising, advice, etc. As they read, Ss could put a tick in the margin next to ideas they discussed and a cross next to the ones they didn't think of. You could invite them to comment on how useful they think the advice is.

C Put Ss into pairs and give them a minute or two to look at how the information is organised and made to 'stand out' in the leaflet before they complete the guidelines.

Answers: **1** title **2** sections, subheading **3** fonts, underlining **4** bullet points **5** contracted

9A First check with Ss how many verbs in bold there are in the leaflet (eleven). Ss work alone and compare answers in pairs.

Answers:
1 Never (take), Always (ask)
2 Make sure you (carry), Be sure to (keep), Be particularly careful to (cover), Try to (check), Take time to (look)
3 Phone, Keep, Use, Book

B Direct Ss back to the phrases with verbs in bold to help them complete the rules.

Answers: **1** never **2 a)** sure **b)** sure **c)** careful **d)** to **e)** time

Optional extra activity

Ss look through the leaflet again for more useful language. Ask Ss to find examples with:
1 *Be careful* and *Take care* and highlight the pattern *Be careful/ Take care when* verb + *-ing.*
2 *may* – e.g. *you may find yourself …, you may find that …, (x) may happen, (y) may have been done*

These patterns are often used to describe the possible problems before explaining how to avoid them.

10 Ss could work in pairs and brainstorm ideas for one of the topics, then write a first draft individually. They then swap their first drafts and, using the checklists in Ex 8C and 9B, give each other feedback. Ss can then write a final draft in class or for homework. The finished leaflets can be displayed round the room or passed round for others to read.

Homework ideas

- **Ex 10:** Ss write another 'how to' leaflet.
- **Language bank:** 9.2 Ex A–B, p145
- **Workbook:** Ex 1–5, p62–63

IT'S AN EMERGENCY!

Introduction

Ss practise listening and speaking about reporting an incident, using appropriate phrases and vocabulary for describing incidents. They also learn to rephrase when their listener doesn't understand.

SUPPLEMENTARY MATERIALS
Resource bank: p191
Ex 5: prepare role cards (see *Alternative approach*).

Warm up

Tell Ss to close their books and write the title *It's an emergency!* on the board. Put Ss into pairs and give them one minute to brainstorm reasons for calling the emergency services, e.g. you've seen a car accident, someone in your family is very ill, you've been robbed, some friends went out in a boat and haven't returned, a building nearby is on fire, etc. Conduct feedback with the class.

SPEAKING

1A Choose two Ss to explain what they can see in each picture. In pairs, Ss discuss what they would do in each situation. Elicit some responses from the class.

B If you did the Warm up, you could ask Ss to look back at their ideas in that section. Ss could choose the three they think are most important to call the emergency services. Elicit some responses for the three questions.

VOCABULARY INCIDENTS

2A For ***stronger classes***, tell Ss to cover the box and try to think of an appropriate verb to put in each gap.

Answers: **1** got stuck **2** is on fire **3** knocked (it) over **4** broken down **5** been stolen **6** fallen off **7** locked (myself) out **8** got knocked out **9** run over **10** been robbed

B Focus Ss on the example and put them into pairs to discuss the other sentences.

Suggested answers:
1. security department in a bank; What's your name? Do you know your account number?
2. fire service; What's the address? Is anyone in the house?
3. ambulance; Where are you? Is anyone injured?
4. vehicle recovery; Where are you exactly? Do you have vehicle recovery membership?
5. police; Did you see who did it? Can you come into the police station and report it?
6. ambulance; What's your address? Is he conscious?
7. locksmith, police; What's your address? Is anyone in the house, for example a child?
8. ambulance; How do you feel now? What's your address?
9. vet; Is the cat bleeding? Can you pick it up and bring it in?
10. receptionist at gym; What did the bag look like? Did you see anyone suspicious?

▷ **VOCABULARYBANK** p156 Cars and accidents

These two activities in the Vocabulary bank expand Ss' vocabulary for describing car accidents and incidents with motor vehicles. Ss can work in pairs to label the diagram of the car for Ex 2, using a dictionary if necessary to help them with anything they are not sure of. In feedback, check pronunciation and word stress of any new items.

Before attempting Ex 3, check the meaning of *skid* (to slip), *collide with* (to hit something violently), *pull out* (to start moving onto a road or a different part of a road) and *swerve* (to change direction suddenly). Ss work in pairs to match the correct verb phrases with the images.

Answers:
2 **1** J **2** D **3** A **4** B **5** C **6** H **7** K **8** F **9** L **10** E **11** G **12** F
3 **1** skidded **2** swerved **3** overtook **4** exceeded the speed limit **5** scratched **6** collided with **7** pullêd out **8** drove the wrong way

FUNCTION REPORTING AN INCIDENT

3A Tell Ss to make a few brief notes about what happened and that they'll be able to listen for more detail the next time.

Answer: He was robbed by a man posing as a jogger in the park.

Unit 9 Recording 5

P = Police officer A = Alain

P: Hello, police. Can I help you?
A: Yes, I'd like to report a crime. I've been robbed.
P: I'm very sorry to hear that, Sir. OK, I'll need to take a statement.
A: A statement?
P: To write down some details, if that's all right.
A: Yes, sure.
P: Could you give me your name please, Sir?
A: Alain Girard.
P: Right. That's Jirard with a J?
A: No, G and it's Alain spelled A-l-a-i-n.
P: Right, Mr Girard. Could you tell me exactly when the incident happened?
A: Just now. About an hour ago.
P: Could you be more precise?
A: Excuse me?
P: Could you give me the exact time?
A: I think at 2.50 or 2.55.
P: That's about 2.50 on 7th June. And where did it happen?
A: Park Avenue.
P: Can you pinpoint the exact location?
A: Pinpoint?
P: Tell me exactly where.
A: Oh. It was near the entrance to the park. Just about fifty metres inside.
P: OK. Could you tell me what happened?
A: I was walking out of the park and a man was running towards me and he hit into me hard.
P: He collided with you?
A: Yes and he said 'sorry' and something else, then before I realised what had happened, he had run on. It was only about thirty seconds later that I realised my wallet had gone and that he must have taken it when he hit me, collided with me.
P: But did it cross your mind that it wasn't just an accident?
A: No, it never occurred to me that he'd done it on purpose.
P: Did you run after him?
A: No, my mind just went blank and I stood there not knowing what to do.
P: But you were OK? Not hurt?
A: No, just very shocked.
P: OK. Could you tell me exactly what your wallet looked like and what was in it?

A: It's brown, leather and it has my credit card and about €250 and …
P: Hold on a minute, credit card … about €250, yes?
A: And a photo of my girlfriend.
P: OK. So you saw the man. Can you give me a description?
A: Erm, about twenty, white, quite tall. And he was wearing a sweater, grey colour with a … you know … erm, something you put over your head …
P: A hood? He was wearing a hoodie?
A: Yes, that's the word. So I didn't see his face, not clearly. But he looked as if he was just out jogging, you know, he was wearing some sort of dark trousers, for running or for the gym.
P: Tracksuit bottoms?
A: Yeah. I can't remember anything else, it all happened so quickly.
P: So that's a tall white male, about twenty, wearing a grey hoodie and dark tracksuit bottoms?
A: That's right.
P: And did he have any other distinguishing marks or features?
A: Sorry?
P: Anything special or different from normal? For example, a scar on his face or anything like that?
A: No, he just seemed like a normal guy, out running. Nothing special. Except …
P: Yes?
A: He reminded me a bit of that actor, Vin Diesel. But younger. Do you know who I mean?
P: Vin Diesel, yeah. I'll put it down. And you said he said something to you.
A: Yeah, but I didn't catch what he said. It was too quick.
P: Right, one last question and then I'll take your contact details. Were there any other people in the vicinity?
A: Vicinity?
P: In the surrounding area – nearby. Any witnesses who saw what had happened?
A: No, there was no one nearby, in the … vicinity.
P: Right, now I just need to take your contact details, Mr Girard and I can also give you a phone number to ring if …

B Give Ss a minute or two to look through the report and check *incident* (an event, often unusual, versus accident, something that is not planned), *serial number* (a number put on an item by the manufacturer), *ethnicity* (ethnic group) and *distinguishing marks or features* (something that makes you look different/stand out, e.g. a scar). Play the recording, pausing after each of the longer sections to ensure that Ss have time to write their notes.

Answers:
Name: Alain Girard
Date and time of incident: *2.50, 7th June*
Location of incident: *Park Avenue, near the entrance to the park, 50 metres inside*
Description of incident (what exactly happened?): *Robbery. Victim was walking out of the park when a man ran into him and stole his wallet.*
Description of stolen or damaged property or vehicle (serial number, bank card type, value of property, colour, make, model of car, etc.): *wallet, brown leather with credit card, €250 and photo of girlfriend*
Description of suspect or offender (age, sex, ethnicity, build, clothing, distinguishing marks or features, etc.): *Tall white male, about twenty, wearing dark tracksuit bottoms and a grey hoodie. Looked like Vin Diesel.*
Witnesses: *none*
Contact details: –

4A Ss could complete the phrases in pencil so they can make any necessary changes when they listen to the recording. They could also refer to the audio script for a final check of their answers. Check that Ss understand *Did it cross your mind … ?* (Did you think … ?), *It never occurred to me* (I never thought), *My mind went blank* (I couldn't think of anything) and *I didn't catch* (I didn't hear/understand).

Answers: **1** Before, had happened **2** only, later that, had gone **3** cross, mind **4** occurred, that **5** blank **6** as if **7** all happened **8** seemed like **9** reminded, of **10** catch

B Look at the first sentence with the class, as an example, then put Ss into pairs.

Answers:
a) 6, 8, 9 **b)** 1, 2, 7
Phrases 3, 4, 5, 10 all refer to something else, they describe the victim's reaction.

C Ss could practise saying the sentences to each other at natural speed and listening for the 'content' words, i.e. those that carry the important information.

Teaching tip
When you play the recording again for Ss to repeat, you could divide the class into smaller groups of about six and nominate groups at random to repeat each sentence. This will add more variety, rather than having the whole class chorus all ten sentences.

Unit 9 Recording 6

1 Before I realised what had happened, he had run on.
2 It was only about thirty seconds later that I realised my wallet had gone.
3 But did it cross your mind that it wasn't just an accident?
4 It never occurred to me that he'd done it on purpose.
5 My mind just went blank.
6 He looked as if he was just out jogging.
7 It all happened so quickly.
8 He just seemed like a normal guy.
9 He reminded me a bit of that actor.
10 I didn't catch what he said. It was too quick.

▷ LANGUAGEBANK 9.3 p144–145

Direct Ss to the summaries of the different types of phrase on p144. You could drill some of the alternatives for each phrase that were not on the recording, e.g. *It was only much later that I remembered …, He looked like a student., I didn't catch the car number plate.* Ss could do Ex A before moving on to the more challenging practice in Ex 5 on p111. Once Ss have completed the conversation, they could practise acting it out.

Answers:
1 It never crossed my mind until I saw the picture on *Crimebeat* on TV.
2 It occurred to me then that I should contact you.
3 I saw him near the factory. He looked as if he was taking photos of the building.
4 When he saw me he left quickly and he looked guilty.
5 It was only later that I realised that there was something strange about how he left.
6 I don't know. It just seemed quite strange but then I didn't think any more about it till I saw the programme.

5 Tell Ss to read through the instructions and prompts quickly and answer these questions: *What was stolen? Where? Who might have stolen it?* Ss do not need to write the dialogue out in full, rather they should just use the flow chart as a prompt.

Alternative approach

To allow Ss to be a little more creative, use role cards instead of the flow chart, e.g.

Student A

You're the police officer. Someone calls to report a stolen item. Find out:

1 What was stolen, when and where.
2 Whether the victim knows who stole the item or suspects anyone.

Student B

1 You're the caller. Your bag was stolen from the changing room in a shop.
2 You were trying on clothes. You left the bag to go out and show your friend the clothes.
3 You saw another woman in the changing room. She looked a bit like your boyfriend's ex-girlfriend.

Ss act out the conversation, they then could refer to the flow chart and compare the sequence of questions and answers to their ideas.

Alternatively, half the class use role cards and half use the flow chart. They act out their conversations and compare them.

6 In pairs, Ss choose one of the incidents in Ex 2A and create a dialogue together. Ss should use the flow chart as guidance. Ask one or two pairs to act out their dialogue to the class.

LEARN TO REPHRASE

7A Check that Ss understand *rephrase* (saying the same thing using more familiar words, so it's clearer) and give them a minute or two to find the examples. You could also ask Ss what the caller does when he doesn't understand (he says *Excuse me?* or repeats the word that was unfamiliar: *Pinpoint?*).

Answers:
1 Could you give me the exact time? (= rephrasing of *Could you be more precise?*)
2 Tell me exactly where. (= rephrasing of *Can you pinpoint the exact location?*)

B Point out that sometimes the police officer rephrases what the caller said and gives him the correct word for what he was trying to say. Ss then work in pairs to match the words and phrases.

C When Ss have checked their answers, you could ask them what new words the caller learnt from this conversation (*collided, hoodie, tracksuit bottoms*) and direct them to the speakout tip.

Answers: 1 d) 2 e) 3 c) 4 b) 5 a)

speakout TIP

Read the tip with the class and point out that the use of rephrasing helped the conversation to 'flow' more smoothly for both the caller and the police officer.

Optional extra activity

For more practice in rephrasing, write the following questions on the board:

Do you remember what you were doing *prior to the incident?* (5)
Was *there any damage to the vehicle?* (4)
Are any of *the occupants* trapped inside? (2)
Is it *causing an obstruction?* (3)
Does he *appear to be in a stable condition?* (6)
Has the machine *malfunctioned?* (1)
Does anyone have a *spare* key? (7)
Do you have any idea who *nicked* it? (10)
Is there anyone *in the vicinity* who could help you? (8)
Did you *take down* the number plate? (9)

Put Ss into pairs and tell them to match the questions to the situations in Ex 2A (suggested answers given in brackets), then rephrase the parts in italics using more familiar vocabulary (they can use dictionaries to check). The pairs then act out some of the phone calls and the person answering the call rephrases the questions to help the caller understand.

SPEAKING

8A Direct Ss to their pictures and make sure they keep them hidden from each other. Student A should spend a few minutes thinking how to explain the route that the burglar took to get into the house and Student B how they got out of the house. If there are words they don't know, they need to paraphrase them.

B Tell Ss that Student B needs to draw the burglar's route in with Student A's help.

C Ss reverse roles and Student A draws the burglar's escape route. At the end they can show each other their pictures. Monitor and write down examples of good use of rephrasing for feedback.

Homework ideas

- Ss write an email to a friend about an incident that happened to them, who they reported it to, what happened in the end, etc.
- **Language bank:** 9.3 Ex A, p145
- **Vocabulary bank:** p156
- **Workbook:** Ex 1–3, p64

SURVIVAL

Introduction

Ss watch an extract from a BBC programme about people being rescued from a sinking cruise liner. Ss then learn and practise how to negotiate choices for a difficult or dangerous situation and write an escape story.

Warm up

Direct Ss to the photos and discuss what they can see.

Ask questions to elicit key vocabulary for the lesson, e.g.
Why's the helicopter there? (to rescue people from the sea/a ship)
What's the person wearing? (a safety harness)
What's happening to him/her? (He's/She's being airlifted.)
What's the weather like? (There's a gale./There are gale force winds.)
How would you feel if you were on board a ship in this weather? (worried/scared that it might sink)

DVD PREVIEW

1A Put Ss into pairs and give them a few minutes to discuss the questions, then share their answers with the class.

Suggested answers:
1 panic, scream, cry, freeze, try to do something/escape
2 luck, planning, knowledge of the situation, the ability to stay calm, good problem-solving skills
3 the ability to stay calm, good problem-solving skills

B Direct Ss to the questions and give them a minute or two to find the answers in the text.

Answer: It mentions planning ahead, how the brain reacts and luck.

DVD VIEW

2A Play the DVD without pausing. Vocabulary to check: *tunnel vision* (ability to focus on only one aim). Check the answer as a class. You could discuss with Ss when they think tunnel vision might be useful.

Answer: He experienced tunnel vision and remained focused on his survival, rather than panicking or freezing.

DVD 9 Horizon: How to survive a disaster

V = Voiceover N = Newsreader P = Paul Barney
PS = Professor Silke

V: On 28th September 1994, the car ferry *Estonia* was making a routine crossing from Tallinn to Stockholm. At 1.12a.m., while many of her passengers were asleep, water was seen breaching the car deck. Within forty minutes, the ship would sink. In that time, each of the 989 passengers and crew would face life or death trying to escape. Amongst them was Paul Barney.
N: Paul Barney's decision not to spend extra money on booking a cabin well below the waterline aboard the *Estonia* almost certainly saved his life. Instead he slept in the cafeteria near the top of the ship and was able to make his escape when the vessel listed, took on water and turned on her side. With a dozen other survivors who'd scrambled aboard an upturned life raft, Mr Barney watched the *Estonia* sink.
PB (1994): It was just like … It was something out of a film. The moon had suddenly come out and everything was calm and it was all lights and then this … the boat was … disappeared … in a sort of red smoky haze, and er, and then the, then the real storm moved in.
PB (today): One of the questions people ask me loads is whether you were scared on board the ship and I say to them really that there was, there was no time to be scared, there was literally no time. Your, your main focus is getting off the ship.
V: As the *Estonia* rolled on her side, Paul became trapped in the cafeteria.
PB: There was a point when all the chairs and tables and ashtrays and everything in the cafeteria suddenly went and slid in one, one go.
V: In the final moments before the *Estonia* sank, Paul clambered up pipework on the ceiling, and out onto the upturned hull of the ship. From there, he scrambled aboard the last remaining life raft.
PB: It was a very scary place to be because you never knew whether the next wave was going to wash you away from the life raft. You never knew when your last moment was coming.
V: Of the 989 passengers and crew on board, just 137 survived. Whilst Paul's escape may appear miraculous, the key to his survival could be the changes that occurred in his mind.
PB: From the moment I realised that there was something wrong with the ship, I got a strong sense of tunnel vision, which sort of concentrated my mind on, on making the decisions that I needed. I'm purely thinking of what's going to save me here.
PS: Initially our body is preparing for action and our brain is focusing on whatever the threat or danger is, and it's focusing on that to the exclusion of everything else. Literally people describe it as looking through a tunnel. That is a good thing, that is a positive thing, and that's exactly what you want.
V: Some passengers did nothing to save their own lives.
PB: One of the things I remember clearly is the, is the water actually coming into the cafeteria and, and seeing lots of people around just frozen to the spot and I could never really understand why they weren't doing anything to save themselves. There seemed to be plenty of opportunity to escape yet they were just rooted to the spot.
V: We all hope our instinct for survival would preserve us in a disaster. But the truth is relatively few of us will cope well.

B Give Ss a few minutes to read the statements before playing the DVD again. Vocabulary to check: *waterline* (the height of the water against the boat) and *life raft* (a small boat for rescuing people). Check the answers as a class.

Answers: 1 F 2 T 3 F 4 T 5 F 6 T 7 F

C Give Ss time to read through the extracts carefully and predict the missing words before playing the DVD again.

Answers: **1** to be scared **2** wash you away **3** save me (here) **4** of everything else **5** frozen to the

D Put Ss into pairs to discuss the questions for a few minutes, then continue the discussion as a class.

speakout agreeing priorities

3A Tell Ss to look through the list and check they understand what all the items are. While they listen, Ss should make brief notes about why an item is rejected/kept.

Answers:
lighter – rejected: can't start a fire on a raft, not a priority to cook a hot meal, just survive
blanket – kept: keep warm, use as a towel, protect you from the sun
hand mirror – mentioned but no decision made

Unit 9 Recording 8

W1 = Woman 1 **M** = Man **W2** = Woman 2

W1: So, we really need to decide then what it is we get rid of and what is absolutely essential to keep on the life raft, I think that's probably the most important thing, isn't it?
M: I'm sure it's easy to get rid of a few things, isn't it?
W2: Like what?
M: Well, I'm not sure about the lighter. I mean, we can't really start a fire on a raft, can we?
W2: No.
W1: I suppose it depends on what the life raft is made out of, doesn't it?
M: Yeah, but it's not exactly top priority to be able to cook a hot meal, you know, when you really just need to survive.
W1: So no lighter?
M and W2: OK.
W1: OK. So what do you think is important?
W2: I'd say that a blanket is essential.
W1: Interesting choice. What for?
W2: Well, you can use it for a lot of different things. To keep you warm obviously, but you can use a blanket as a towel if you get wet.
W1: If you fall in the water?
W2: ... for example. And a blanket can protect you from the sun.
M: That hadn't occurred to me. OK, I'm convinced. So what else?
W1: Well I can't see the point of taking the hand mirror, can you?
M: Actually, I can. Because if ...

B Ss look through the key phrases before listening again. Ss should tick the phrases they hear. Point out that where there are options in the phrases (e.g. *It depends on [what/whether] ..., doesn't it?*), they need to underline the option(s) they hear. Vocabulary to check: *priority/prioritise* (the most important thing/ put in order of importance), *essential/vital/crucial* (very important) and *dehydrate* (lose water from your body). When Ss have checked their answers, highlight the use of the *-ing* form in *I can't see the point of ...* and *to [prevent/keep/protect] you from ...* .

Answers: It depends on [what/whether] ..., doesn't it?; It's (not) a top priority to be able to ...; I'd say that ... is/are [essential/vital/ crucial]; ... to keep you [warm/dry/alive],; ... to prevent/keep/ protect] you from [the sun/dehydrating/getting ...]; [It/That] hadn't occurred to me.; I can't see the point of [taking/choosing] ...

C Circulate and help while Ss make notes on their six items. Encourage Ss to incorporate some of the key phrases and to practise talking about their items on their own before joining a group in the next stage.

D Put Ss into groups of four or five and explain that the goal is to agree on six items. A spokesperson for each group could then read out the list to the class and see what they all have in common. Monitor and note down good examples of language use, particularly the key phrases and any problems, for discussion and correction later.

writeback an escape story

4A You could start by writing the title *A lucky escape* on the board and check Ss understand that in the following exercises they should use the given words in the order they appear in the boxes. Direct Ss to the word string in the box (they should cover the story in Ex 4B) and either put them into pairs to invent a story, or elicit one round the class, inviting one student at a time to add more to the story, using the next word in the string.

B Ss read the story and discuss the answers to the questions in pairs.

Answers: The man's tent caught fire while he was sleeping inside, and a friend threw soup on the fire, which made it possible for the man to get out.

C Ss could choose a word string in pairs and brainstorm ideas for the story before writing a first draft, then exchange stories and make any suggestions for improvements.

D Ss' stories can be put round the walls of the classroom for others to read and comment on.

Homework ideas

Ex 4C: Ss write another 'lucky escape' story using the word string they did not use in class.

LOOKBACK

Introduction

The aim of these activities is to provide revision and further practice of the language from the unit. You can also use them to assess Ss' ability to use the language, in which case you need to monitor but avoid helping them. You may feel that you don't need or have time to do all the activities. If so, you could allocate the activities that would be most beneficial for your Ss, or get individual Ss to decide which activities they'd like to do.

CRIME

1A You could divide the class into teams for this and set a time limit. The team who has the most crimes on their list when time is up wins points.

Answers: (from p104 – Ss may think of others) arson, bribery, counterfeiting, hacking, kidnapping, identity theft, mugging, shoplifting, stalking, vandalism

B Ss can stay in their teams for this and do it as a board race. Read out the descriptions one at a time (Ss should have their books closed so they can't look ahead) and as soon as a team thinks of the answer, one member runs up and writes the crime(s) on the board. Points can be awarded for correct answers, but deducted for incorrect spelling.

Answers: **1** arson, vandalism **2** kidnapping, mugging, stalking **3** counterfeiting, hacking, identity theft **4** bribery **5** shoplifting

C Put Ss into pairs or small groups to discuss this and the reasons why those crimes are more often in the news.

-ING FORM AND INFINITIVE

2A You could start by either asking Ss to read through the article quickly and think of a suitable title for it, or putting Ss into pairs to brainstorm advice they'd give to someone who'd been mugged, then read the article to see if their ideas are mentioned.

Answers: **1** doing **2** to check **3** being **4** to find **5** shaking **6** drinking **7** to phone **8** seeing **9** to do **10** doing

B Ss discuss their opinions of the article in pairs and/or as a class. They could then go on to write a similar article (using *-ing* forms and infinitives) for someone whose house has been broken into.

SYNONYMS

3A Give Ss a few minutes to rewrite the questions. They could also practise saying the questions at natural speed in preparation for the pairwork in Ex 3B.

Answers: **1** distract you **2** grab **3** to pose as **4** deceiving **5** fallen for **6** switch

B Encourage Ss to ask follow-up questions after their partners have answered. You could demonstrate this by inviting Ss to ask you one or two of the questions first.

PAST MODALS OF DEDUCTION

4A You could start by reading out the situations to the class (with their books closed) and encourage them to make guesses about what happened using modals of deduction. Then direct Ss to the options and give them a minute or two to rewrite them.

Answers:
1 a) The man must have moved recently.
b) His friends might/could/may have sent mail to the old address.
c) The postman can't/couldn't have delivered the letters.
2 a) She might/could/may have been practising in an empty concert hall.
b) She must have been deaf, so no one clapped.
c) The audience can't/couldn't have liked the music.

B Encourage the class to think of two more explanations for each situation before they read the solutions on p162, e.g. *someone else must have taken the letters; the lock on his post box might have been broken, so they fell out and blew away; the pianist must have asked the audience not to clap for some reason; it might have been in a country where the custom is not to clap*, etc.

REPORTING AN INCIDENT

5A For ***stronger classes***, you could tell Ss to cover the box and try to remember the appropriate words for the gaps first, then check with the words in the box.

Answers: **1** occurred **2** reminded **3** realised **4** went **5** happened **6** didn't catch **7** happened **8** crossed **9** if **10** like

B You could start by looking at one of the incidents with the whole class as an example and elicit some ideas about how to use the sentences. Then put Ss into pairs to work on a different incident and circulate to help with language as required.

C You may want to refer Ss back to the flow chart on p111 before they start the role-play. Monitor and make notes of good language use and problems for feedback and correction.

BBC interviews and worksheet

Do you have any phobias?

This video extends the unit topic to deal with the issue of phobias and the irrational fear people have of certain situations, activities, things, animals or people.

OVERVIEW

10.1 MOVING EXPERIENCES

VOCABULARY | adjectives to describe films
LISTENING | listen to people talk about films
GRAMMAR | relative clauses
PRONUNCIATION | intonation: relative clauses
SPEAKING | talk about a film you never get bored with
WRITING | a review; learn to use adverb + past participle combinations

10.2 POPULAR CULTURE

READING | read answers to popular culture questions
GRAMMAR | participle clauses
VOCABULARY | the arts
PRONUNCIATION | word stress
SPEAKING | talk about popular culture and arts experiences
VOCABULARY *PLUS* | two-part phrases
PRONUNCIATION | connected speech

10.3 ON THE LEFT ...

SPEAKING | talk about places of interest in your town or city
FUNCTION | giving a tour
PRONUNCIATION | intonation in comments
VOCABULARY | dimensions
LEARN TO | express estimates
SPEAKING | show a visitor around part of your town

10.4 THE PEOPLE'S PALACE BBC DVD

DVD | watch a BBC programme about an innovative building
speakout | a town project
writeback | a work of art

10.5 LOOKBACK

Communicative revision activities

BBC INTERVIEWS

What area of the Arts do you enjoy?

This video encourages Ss to reflect on the areas of art and culture that they enjoy the most. Use this video at the start or end of Unit 10 or set it as homework.

MOVING EXPERIENCES

Introduction

Ss practise listening and speaking about films using relative clauses and adjectives for describing films. They also learn to write a review and use adverb + past participle combinations for description.

SUPPLEMENTARY MATERIALS
Resource bank: p192 and p194
Ex 1D: bring monolingual dictionaries for Ss to use.

Warm up

Brainstorm types of film. Put Ss into pairs and give them 2 mins to make a list of as many types of film as they can. Ask Ss to think of one film title for each genre they thought of.

VOCABULARY ADJECTIVES TO DESCRIBE FILMS

1A Direct Ss to the photos and give them a minute or two to decide which film genre is shown in each photo (*action film, romantic comedy*) and discuss which types of film they like/don't like and why.

B Elicit some ideas for the first sentence. At this stage, do not confirm the answers.

C Look at the first one together as an example. Check the answers as a class.

Answers: **1** j) **2** a) **3** b) **4** f) **5** c), h) **6** i) **7** g) **8** d) **9** e)

D In pairs, ask Ss to match the adjectives to their synonym or near-synonym. Ss may need to use dictionaries at this stage. Check the answers as a class.

Answers:
hilarious – hysterical
moving, poignant – touching
offensive – controversial (However, *offensive* is completely negative while *controversial* means it's offensive to some people.)
superb, stunning – outstanding
dramatic, intense – gripping, full of suspense

2A Put Ss into groups of three to five and give them a minute or two to write down ten to fifteen films they all know.

B Focus Ss on the example and check how many of the adjectives from Ex 1C and D are used by Student A in the description. Then emphasise that each of the other Ss in the group should ask a *yes/no* question before anyone can guess the film.

10 culture

LISTENING

3A Put Ss into groups and ask them to tell each other the title of their favourite film. Elicit one or two examples and then play the recording.

Suggested answer: The film is *Speed*. He likes it because it's tense, gripping and full of suspense.

Unit 10 Recording 1

W = Woman M = Man

W: So come on then, favourite movie of all time.
M: I would have to say, 'cos I love action films, uh, that it would be *Speed* – have you ever seen that?
W: *Speed*?
M: Yeah it's with Keanu Reeves and Sandra Bullock.
W: Oh, I like her.
M: She's very good isn't she? So yeah, I just love any kind of action film. And I remember watching it when I was really young and watching it with my dad. And it's the sort of, like, a family-friendly action film, because it's not too violent, it's not too gory but it's just really tense. And I remember just like watching it, we had a cushion, me and my dad, and I was just like what's gonna happen next? Have you seen it?
W: No! I haven't I, I think I've seen bits of it, like trailers and things but …
M: OK, it's … erm …
W: No, I knew she was in it.
M: Yeah, so basically, he, there's a baddy in it, as every action film has a good baddy, and he's got no thumb. I remember that, that was like a memorable bit of it, he had no thumb. And so they sort of highjack this … this bus. And it's set that it can only drive at a certain speed – hence the name. And so it's just basically driving through, through the city and it can't stop otherwise there's a bomb and it's gonna blow it up. So, and there's a, Keanu Reeves he's, he's the goody, he's a policeman. And he's … he jumps on board the bus to try and stop this bomb from going off. And, it's just all the different characters on the bus. It's just really …
W: The whole film is on the bus?
M: Yeah and, but it's, it's, well not at the beginning, it sort of goes onto the bus. But it's just I remember it being so tense and gripping, 'cos you just didn't know what was gonna happen. You didn't know.
W: It sounds really uncomfortable to watch, was it not?
M: It … it's … I just like that kind of that feeling of like pure suspense 'cos you just have no idea if it's gonna end well or not. And it did end very well. You have to watch it.
W: Well yeah, as long as there's, you know, a point when you can relax, 'cos I don't like feeling like that the whole way through a movie, anxiety.
M: Yeah, because you know when it's like driving along, and it, 'cos I think it has to stay at fifty miles per hour. And so if there's, driving along a motorway and it's, there's traffic and stuff you have to change the route and things, so you just don't know where it's gonna go.
W: Oh, OK.
M: And then they get to a bridge that's, hasn't finished being built. So you're not sure how they're gonna get over the bridge and stuff like that. So there's lots of moments where you just think, I have no clue what's gonna happen.
W: Good stunts?
M: Very good, and I heard that he did all his stunts himself, Keanu Reeves.
W: Yes, they always say that.
M: He likes a bit of action, doesn't he? So, and I think it always helps to have a very good heroine in a film and she's, she's beautiful, don't you think?
W: Yes, I love her. I think she's very funny, but tell me there's some comedy in there.
M: There's not a huge amount of comedy. It's one of your traditional sort of American blockbuster action films. So yeah but it's, it's just, it's – there's not many action films with comedy in though are there?
W: I think that's why I don't watch them.
M: Oh really?
W: Yeah.
M: What's your sort of, your favourite type of film?
W: I don't like to feel uncomfortable, so it's just comedy.
M: Watch *Speed*.
W: Mm, um OK.

B Give Ss a moment to read through the points and to make notes on anything they remember, then play the recording again.

Answers:
1 It's tense without being too violent or gory.
2 He's missing a thumb.
3 The bus has to keep going above a particular speed (fifty miles per hour), or it will blow up.
4 She thinks it sounds uncomfortable to watch.
5 Keanu Reeves jumping onto the bus; the bus driving in traffic; the bus going onto a bridge that's being built.
6 Keanu Reeves did his own stunts.
7 She's beautiful.
8 She prefers comedies.

C In pairs, Ss discuss the questions. There are in fact quite a few action comedies, so Ss may mention the series *Kick Ass*, *Men in Black* and *Night at the Museum*.

4A Give Ss a few minutes to make notes about the film they choose. Circulate and help with vocabulary as necessary.

B Put Ss into pairs to tell each other about their films.

C You could extend this task by asking Ss to describe the film without naming it and asking the other Ss to guess the name of the film.

GRAMMAR RELATIVE CLAUSES

5A For ***weaker classes***, you may want to start by eliciting what each pronoun is used for, i.e. *who* – people, *which* – things, *whose* – belonging to, *where* – place, *when* – time.

Answers: **1** which **2** who **3** who **4** whose **5** which **6** which **7** which **8** where **9** which **10** when **11** which **12** whose

B Go through each item with the class eliciting if *that* can be used and if the pronoun can be omitted but do not explain the reasons for this yet.

Answers:
That can be used in sentences 1, 3, 5 and 10.
The relative pronoun can be omitted in sentences 3, 5 and 10.

C Using the forum messages from Ex 5A, ask Ss to choose the correct options to complete the rules. When checking the answers, ask Ss to point out the examples in the text that helped them.

Answers: **1** essential, extra **2** defining **3** object **4** end, before, (b) **5** Which **6** non-defining

6A Ask Ss to quickly read the forum message and identify the film (*Twilight*). If Ss have seen the film, ask them to raise their hand. While Ss put in the commas, you could write the extract on the board so you can focus Ss on the intonation in the next stage.

Answers: It's a film which appeals to the teenage market and centres on the relationship between Bella, who has just arrived in town, and her mysterious classmate Edward, whose family seems to have a strange secret. When Bella discovers Edward's true identify, which happens about a third of the way through the film, she has a big decision to make, a decision which will change her entire life.

B Play the recording a couple of times for Ss to hear the lower pitch on the non-defining clauses. Tell Ss that the drop in pitch is a way of indicating the commas round the extra information.

Answer: They are spoken in a lower voice (or pitch) than the rest of the sentence.

C Encourage Ss to read along as they listen, copying the intonation and rhythm as closely as possible.

▷ LANGUAGEBANK 10.1 p146–147

Give Ss time to read through the rules and examples carefully, particularly if they found Ex 5A challenging. To give Ss controlled practice, they could do Ex A and B in class.

Answers:

A
1. The man who/that is marrying Suzanne is very lucky.
2. The house where I used to live burnt down yesterday. / The house I used to live in burnt down yesterday.
3. Pablo Picasso, whose father was also an artist, spent his early childhood in Malaga.
4. The moment I realised I wanted to be an actor was the most important moment of my life.
5. The holiday I enjoyed most was in Canada. / The holiday I most enjoyed was in Canada.
6. Usain Bolt, who was the first man to win six gold Olympic medals in sprinting, is a global superstar.
7. When I was a student, I lived with a guy whose hobby was fixing motorbikes.
8. This is the sort of occasion when you should make a speech.

B
1. It was the house which I spent my childhood *in*. / It was the house *in* which I spent my childhood. (more formal)
2. It was a lesson which I'll always be grateful *for*. / It was a lesson *for* which I'll always be grateful. (more formal)
3. She's definitely the woman *with* whom he wants to spend the rest of his life.
4. The cinema I most often go *to* is the Odeon in the town centre.
5. Funnily enough, it was the planning which we spent the most time *on*. / Funnily enough, it was the planning *on* which we spent the most time. (more formal)
6. He was an athlete *for*/*to* whom success came as naturally as his speed.
7. He was a friend I could always depend *on*.
8. You're the person who we always turn *to* when a speech is needed.

7 Complete the first one as an example on the board and then set the rest of the task as individual work. Check the answers as a class.

Suggested answers:
1. The main role is played by Chiwetel Ejiofor, whose portrayal of Solomon Northup earned him several awards.
2. Megastar Chris Hemworth, whose career got its biggest boost from his role in *Thor*, gives an emotional performance in his latest film.
3. *Invictus* is a story about leadership and forgiveness at a critical period when Nelson Mandela had just become president of South Africa.
4. The film *Star Trek* was based on a popular TV series in which William Shatner played the role of Captain Kirk. / The film *Star Trek*, in which William Shatner played the role of Captain Kirk, was based on a popular TV series.
5. The film, which was directed by Sam Mendes, was Daniel Craig's third outing as James Bond. / The film, which was Daniel Craig's third outing as James Bond, was directed by Sam Mendes.
6. Adrian Brody shot to fame after starring in *The Pianist*, for which he won the Best Actor Oscar. (written, more formal) / Adrian Brody shot to fame after starring in *The Pianist*, which he won the Best Actor Oscar for. (spoken, more informal)
7. *Lost in Translation* takes place in a Tokyo hotel, where/in which the two main characters meet and form an unusual bond.
8. *The Hurt Locker* is a war film directed by Kathryn Bigelow, for whom the choice of Jordan as the filming location was important.

SPEAKING

8A Complete some of the sentences so that they are true for you as an example. Ss complete the sentences, working alone.

B First, elicit some examples of appropriate follow-up questions, e.g.

A: *My favourite actress is Toni Colette, who was in* Japanese Story *and* Muriel's Wedding.
B: *Really? What's so special about her?*
A: *Well, she always plays different characters, she's not typecast.*

Ss report back to the class about their partner's answers and share anything they found in common.

WRITING A REVIEW; LEARN TO USE ADVERB + PAST PARTICIPLE COMBINATIONS

9A Start by directing Ss to the picture and asking if anyone has seen the film and what they thought of it, or what they know about it. Put Ss into pairs to discuss the questions.

Answers:

2. to help people decide if they want to see a film
3. plot summary, actors' names, recommendation, setting of the film, reviewer's opinion of different elements (You don't usually find a description of the film's ending because people don't want to know that before they see the film, nor the ticket prices because they vary from cinema to cinema.)

B Ask Ss to read the review and decide whether they would like to watch the film or not. If Ss have already seen the film, ask whether they agree with the reviewer or not.

C Elicit the topic of the first paragraph as an example with Ss and then set the rest as individual work. Check the answers as a class.

Answers: **1** setting of the film, actors' names **2** plot summary **3** reviewer's opinion of different elements **4** recommendation

10A Direct Ss to the third paragraph and give them time to find two adverbs followed by past participles.

Answers: skilfully directed, convincingly acted

B Put Ss into pairs to complete the phrases. Suggest that they try saying the combinations to see if they sound correct.

Answers:
1. skilfully/sensitively/poignantly
2. convincingly/skilfully/sensitively/poignantly
3. widely/overwhelmingly/highly
4. harshly/widely/overwhelmingly/heavily

11A Ss can work alone or with a partner who's chosen the same film.

B While Ss write their first draft, make a note of any common problems, so that you can give some feedback on these before Ss write their final draft in Ex 11D.

C Before exchanging reviews, Ss could write (on a separate piece of paper) a star rating for the film. The person reading their review should then guess how many stars they gave it and check with them when they hand it back.

D Ss can write their final draft in class or for homework.

Homework ideas

- Ss write a review of a play, concert or CD.
- **Language bank:** 10.1 Ex A–B, p147
- **Workbook:** Ex 1–5, p65–66

POPULAR CULTURE

Introduction

Ss practise reading and speaking about popular culture using participle clauses, vocabulary related to the Arts and two-part phrases.

SUPPLEMENTARY MATERIALS

Resource bank: p193 and p195

Ex 4B: bring monolingual dictionaries for Ss to use.

Ex 4B: prepare a copy of vocabulary definitions (see *Optional extra activity*).

Ex 5A: be prepared to answer one of the questions yourself, using some words/phrases from the unit so far.

Warm up

Lead into the topic by putting the title *Popular culture* on the board and discussing with Ss what it means to them.

READING

1A Ss could discuss the photos in pairs or as a class. In feedback ask if any of them have experience of performing.

B Ask Ss to discuss these questions in pairs and to make notes on their answers.

C Student As turn to p163 and Student Bs read the text on this page. Ask Ss to check the questions from Ex 1B that their text answers and their predictions.

Answers:

Student A: In order the questions are 4, 2, 7 and 6.
Student B: In order the questions are 3, 8, 1 and 5.

D Emphasise that Ss should summarise the answers in a maximum of five words.

E Put Ss into pairs and tell them to cover their text before using their notes to summarise their answers for their partner. When Ss have heard all the answers, they could discuss which ones they found most interesting/surprising/predictable, etc. and share their ideas with the class.

GRAMMAR PARTICIPLE CLAUSES

2A Tell Ss to read the article quickly and find the answers to the questions.

Answers:

The article mentions registering in hotels as a situation where celebrities use fake names.

Alotta Warmheart sounds like 'a lot of warm heart'.

Ross Vegas sounds like 'Las Vegas'.

George Clooney's fake name is the name of another star who doesn't look anything like him.

B In pairs, Ss answer the questions. Rather than checking them all at the end, check each one as Ss complete it.

Answers:

1 All of them.
2 1 who/that are registered at hotels under their real name
  2 who/that are trying to take their pictures
  3 who/that are taking selfies
  4 which/that involve wordplay
  5 who were/got married in 2000 but were/got divorced five years later
  6 which/that was used by George Clooney
3 present participle (*-ing* form) or past participle

C Ask Ss to underline the participle clauses and check they have underlined the correct parts. Then ask Ss to complete the rules.

Answers:

1 b) Names <u>involving wordplay</u> are common.
2 b) The people <u>working in the hotel</u> thought the name was funny.
3 b) The hotel, <u>built in the 1980s and regularly used by film stars</u>, is famous.

Rule 1: present Rule 2: past

speakout TIP

Before Ss read the tip, direct them back to the text in Ex 2A and ask them why they think it's a good idea to use participle clauses (they help you avoid repetition and make your writing more economical and 'polished'). Read the tip with the class and elicit how to improve the sentence *I couldn't concentrate on the concert because there were so many people who took photos.* (*I couldn't concentrate on the concert because so many people were taking photos.*)

▷ LANGUAGEBANK 10.2 p146–147

Give Ss time to read through the rules and examples. You could use Ex A in class for a short controlled practice activity. Ss could do Ex B for homework.

Answers:

A 1 worn 2 waiting 3 deleted 4 injured 5 brought up 6 taking

B 1 The taxi almost drove over a man lying in the street.
  2 *Sunflowers*, painted by Van Gogh, is one of the most popular paintings ever.
  3 The army, led by Napoleon, advanced towards the hill.
  4 I don't know the people living next door to me.
  5 I used to like block-busters involving lots of action.
  6 The apartments overlooking Central Park are the most expensive.
  7 Some factories forced to close during the recession still haven't reopened.
  8 Many people think that the Taj Mahal, built in the seventeenth century, is the most beautiful building in the world.

3A Do the first sentence as an example. Ss work alone or with a partner on the rest of the sentences.

Answers:

1 People taking photos should ask their subjects' permission first.
2 Films based on books are disappointing.
3 It's great to see rock stars in their sixties still playing concerts.
4 Architecture designed in the 1960s is generally quite ugly and ought to be pulled down.
5 Photos of people posing for the camera don't work as well as spontaneous pictures.
6 Film and TV stars appearing in the theatre attract huge audiences.
7 Jokes involving racial stereotypes are not funny.
8 Photographers using software to enhance their photos were justifiably banned from entering a national competition last month.

B You could give your opinion on the first sentence as an example and invite Ss to agree/disagree. Then put Ss into pairs to discuss the sentences, or ask Ss to walk round the room choosing sentences at random to discuss with different people. Conduct feedback with the whole class and find out if there are any sentences that everyone agrees with.

VOCABULARY THE ARTS

4A Tell Ss they're going to read three forum comments about the same singer. Give them a couple of minutes to read and underline the adjectives which reveal the writer's attitude. They should then decide whether the overall tone of each comment is positive, negative or mixed and mark it ✓, ✗ or – accordingly.

Answers: 1 ✓ 2 ✗ 3 –

B Look at *creating a stir* with the class as an example. Establish that, from the context, the meaning is positive and ask Ss what other meanings of *stir* they know, i.e. to mix something up or cause strong feelings. Put Ss into pairs to discuss the rest and check in their dictionaries.

Answers:
to create a stir: to cause a feeling of excitement (or sometimes annoyance)
ground-breaking: using new ideas, innovative
rave reviews: strong praise for a new performer, music, film, play, etc.
a sell-out: a performance, sports event, etc. for which all the tickets have been sold
must-see: (informal) something that is so good, exciting or interesting that you think people should see it
hype: noun [U] (informal) publicity – when something is talked about a lot on TV, in the newspapers, online, etc. to make it seem good or important
a letdown: (informal) something that disappoints you because it is not as good as you expected
a flop: a film, show, plan or product that is not successful
mainstream: the most usual ideas or ways of doing something which are accepted by most people
alternative: different from what is usual or accepted

Optional extra activity

Put Ss into pairs and give a copy of the answers above to Student A who 'tests' Student B by reading out a definition and asking him/her for the correct word. They then swap roles, e.g.
A: *Something that disappoints you because it's not as good as you expected.*
B: *A letdown?*
A: *Correct!*

C Ss practise saying the words individually first and mark the stress. They then listen and check their answers. Repeat the recording for Ss to listen and repeat.

Answers:
1 She's certainly creating a stir …
2 … her ground-breaking mix of rap and folk.
3 … she got those rave reviews in the press …
4 … each performance has been a sell-out …
5 … it's the must-see performance of the year.
6 … after all the hype surrounding her concerts …
7 … the concert was a real letdown!
8 It was a complete flop …
9 I just hope she doesn't go mainstream …
10 … all the other alternative artists.

D Ask Ss to write their forum entries on a separate piece of paper so they can be passed round the class for other Ss to look at.

E Ss pass their entry to the person on their right, who reads it and passes it on, etc. If a student is interested in a performance, they could write any questions they have about it on the piece of paper underneath the forum entry for the writer to answer when they get the entry back. Or, if a student has seen the same performance, they could write a further comment, saying whether they agree (as in the examples in Ex 4A). Make sure everyone gets their original entry back and give Ss the opportunity to answer questions/reply to comments written on their entries.

▷ VOCABULARYBANK p157 Music

Ex 1 and 2 revise and extend Ss' vocabulary for talking about musical instruments, phrases and idioms. For Ex 1, let Ss work individually or in pairs to label the musical instruments before feeding back as a class. During feedback, extend the discussion into Ex 1B and find out which Ss in the class play instruments or which they would like to learn.

Answers:
1A 1 E 2 J 3 I 4 L 5 C 6 H 7 F 8 K 9 D 10 B 11 G 12 A
2 1 c) 2 d) 3 e) 4 a) 5 g) 6 h) 7 f) 8 b)

SPEAKING

5A You could start by answering one of the questions yourself, as a model. Then give Ss time to look through the unit for language they could use in their answers and write down some key phrases to prompt them in the next stage.

B Put Ss into pairs and encourage them to listen 'actively' to each other while they're talking about their experiences, e.g. by asking questions, commenting on what their partner says, showing interest/surprise, etc.

C Group Ss so they're not with their partners from the previous stage. Tell the listeners in each group to make a note of any questions they want to ask while each person is making their recommendation and remind them to ask their questions when everyone has spoken. Monitor the group work and note down examples of good language use and problems for discussion and correction later. Conduct feedback, asking Ss to tell the rest of the class which thing/person they would most like to go to see/hear and why.

VOCABULARY PLUS TWO-PART PHRASES

6A Focus Ss on the example sentences and give them a minute or two to discuss what the two-part phrases mean.

B Refer Ss to the dictionary entries, pointing out that a good dictionary will always have an example sentence to help them understand the meaning, as well as a definition. You could also ask Ss if they've come across any other two-part phrases like these and whether they have similar phrases in their own language.

7A To help Ss match the pairs, point out that they often contain two opposite ideas, or repeat the same word/idea. Ss could work on this in pairs, saying the combinations to each other to see if they sound plausible.

B When Ss have checked their answers, play the recording again and tell them to listen to the way *and* is 'squashed' between the two words so that it seems to become part of the first word in the pair.

Answers: ups and downs sick and tired (of) on and on peace and quiet leaps and bounds pros and cons rough and ready through and through now and then give and take

8A Ss could start by reading the sentences together and predicting where some of the more 'literal' word pairs might go. Then they read their definitions and examples and complete only the five sentences for their five word pairs.

B Monitor closely and help Ss sort out any confusion, e.g. if they've both put their word pair in the same sentence, refer them back to their dictionary definitions and examples to work out which one doesn't fit.

Answers: **1** peace and quiet **2** now and then **3** through and through **4** sick and tired **5** leaps and bounds **6** ups and downs **7** on and on **8** give and take **9** pros and cons **10** rough and ready

C Give Ss a few minutes to change the sentences so that they are true for themselves. After Ss have compared in pairs, elicit which ones they agreed on.

▷ VOCABULARYBANK p157 Two-part phrases

Ex 3A and B introduce Ss to more two-part phrases which are commonly used in spoken English. Let Ss work in pairs to try to complete both exercises, avoiding the use of dictionaries if possible. Feed back as a class. If Ss are enjoying the topic, ask them if they can find equivalent expressions in their own language.

Answers:
A **1** later **2** leave **3** swim **4** take **5** nothing **6** death **7** miss **8** another
B **a)** 2 **b)** 5 **c)** 4 **d)** 7 **e)** 1 **f)** 8 **g)** 3 **h)** 6

Optional extra activity

Tell Ss you're going to ask them for some pieces of information, which they should write in random order on a clean page in their notebooks. Tell them to write down:
a place you'd go to get some peace and quiet
somewhere you used to go a lot but now you only go to every now and then
a book or film that you'll never get sick and tired of
a book or film that goes on and on for too long
someone who's an animal lover through and through
someone whose English has improved in leaps and bounds
a band whose songs are a bit rough and ready
a band whose music you listen to on and off
Ss then show each other what they've written and guess what each piece of information means, e.g.
'War and peace'– Is that a book that you'll never get sick and tired of?
That's right!

Homework ideas

- **Language bank:** 10.2 Ex A–B, p147
- **Vocabulary bank:** p157
- **Workbook:** Ex 1–5, p67–68

ON YOUR LEFT ...

Introduction

Ss practise listening to and giving a tour, using appropriate phrases. They also learn vocabulary for giving dimensions and how to express estimates.

SUPPLEMENTARY MATERIALS
Resource bank: p196
Ex 3B: Prepare sets of cards for a matching activity (see *Optional extra activity*).

Warm up

Ss should have their books closed. Tell them to write down the names of two cities they've visited and three places of interest to see in each city. Ss then either work in groups or stand up and walk round the classroom, telling each other about the cities and places they've chosen, with reasons for their choices. Conduct feedback, asking Ss which cities sounded most appealing to them.

SPEAKING

1 Put Ss into pairs and give them a few minutes to discuss the questions.

FUNCTION GIVING A TOUR

2A Direct Ss to the photos and elicit what they know about each place and find out whether anyone has been to each one or not.

B Tell Ss to write the letters from the photos (A–F) in order as they listen.

Answers: 1 C 2 B 3 A 4 D 5 F 6 E

Unit 10 Recording 5

Conversation 1

W = Woman M = Man

W: So here we are in Greenwich Village.
M: It looks very different from the rest of New York.
W: Yeah, the streets are quite narrow and the buildings aren't as high.
M: It does look quite village-like.
W: Yeah, but it's quite big. It extends out west that way to the Hudson River, north above Washington Square. We'll go up there in a bit.
M: And you lived here?
W: When I first came to New York, yeah. In an apartment just around the corner, on West Third Street. Actually, you can see the building over there.
M: Near The Blue Note Jazz Club?
W: Yeah.
M: I've heard of The Blue Note.
W: It's pretty famous. There are some great jazz clubs around the neighbourhood and that's one of the best. We can see a show there one night if you want.
M: That'd be great.
W: Now up here on the left is the Café Reggio. It's where I used to hang out and read when I wasn't working.
M: Looks good.
W: Their cappuccino is great. The story goes that the original owner brought cappuccino to America. You can see the original cappuccino machine inside.
M: Cool. We could stop and have a coffee.
W: Maybe a bit later? Let's head over to Washington Square Park and then circle back.
M: OK – lead the way!

W: A lot of these clubs we're walking by have a real history. As I'm sure you know, Greenwich Village has always been a centre of artistic life – very bohemian. It's always attracted famous writers, dancers and poets. And in the sixties, it was a big part of the folk music scene: Simon and Garfunkel, Joni Mitchell, Bob Dylan, you know.
M: Before my time! Now what's this?
W: This is Washington Square Park. We'll walk into the park on this side. Can you play chess?
M: A bit, yeah.
W: Any of these guys here would be happy to challenge you to a game of chess. They're here all day, every day.
M: Maybe next time – I'm not that good! What's the arch over there? It looks like the Arc de Triomphe in Paris.
W: Well it should, that's the Washington Square arch. It was modelled on the Arc de Triomphe and built in 1889 to celebrate the hundredth anniversary of the inauguration of George Washington as president.
M: Could we sit down a second? I need a break.
W: Why don't we retrace our steps and go back to the Café Reggio?
M: Sounds good. I could really do with a coffee. Oh and I have to ...

Conversation 2

M1 = Man 1 W = Woman M2 = Man 2

M1: So, this is Radcliffe Square.
W: Wow! Is this right in the centre then?
M1: Pretty much.
M2: What's that?
M1: Hold on. Let's just get off our bikes ... Right, so that building in front of us is the Bodleian, named after the founder – Thomas Bodley. Believe it or not, despite the fact that it's circular, it's actually a library.
W: Cool!
M1: Yeah, it gets a copy of every book published in the UK.
M2: Who can use it?
M1: Any student at the university. Of course, each college also has its own library – you know the university's divided into colleges, right?
M2: Right. How many colleges are there?
M1: Just under forty. Well, thirty-eight to be exact.
W: So that means thirty-eight libraries?!
M1: Mm but they're not all as big as the Bodleian. Anyway, we'll need to get back on our bikes for the next bit ...

M1: Can you hear me if I talk as we cycle along?
M2: Yeah.
W: OK, but don't go too fast. I'm not very steady on this thing!
M1: So, here's the famous Bridge of Sighs, connecting two sides of Hertford College.
M2: I've seen the original.
M1: What, of the bridge? In Italy, you mean?
M2: Ja, it's in Venice. Beautiful.
M1: OK. We'll go past New College and then onto the High Street.
M2: Is that New College there?
M1: Yep.
W: How 'new' is new?
M1: Roughly 1370.
W: You're kidding!
M1: No, really! Interestingly, the oldest college was actually only founded a hundred or so years earlier! Uh-oh, watch out on this corner ... That's the 'Schools'. It's where the students take their exams. Apparently, the biggest room can seat somewhere in the region of 500 students although I haven't seen it myself. Anyway, we're turning right here. The street's cobbled, so be careful.
M2: How many students are there at the university in total?
M1: To be honest, it depends. In term time, you'd probably get upwards of 20,000.
M2: Many international students?
M1: Some, but most are from the UK. We'll finish by cycling down this way to Christ Church. We can actually go inside if we're quick. It's well worth a visit.
M2: Christ Church is another college?
M1: Yeah, the biggest and probably the most famous. Have you seen any of the Harry Potter films?
M2: No ...
W: I have!
M1: Oh, well, you'll recognise the Great Hall. It's where they have the feasts in Hogwarts School. You know the bit when Harry ...

C You could suggest that Ss copy the list of places into their notebooks so they have more space to write notes about them. Give Ss time to compare answers in pairs, adding anything they missed to their own information. You may want to play the recording again, for Ss to 'fill out' their notes.

Answers:
1 The Blue Note Jazz Club: It's famous; it's one of the best jazz clubs in the neighbourhood.
2 The Café Reggio: The first owner brought cappuccino to the USA, the original cappuccino machine is there.
3 Greenwich Village in general: It's a centre of artistic life and attracts writers, dancers, poets; it was a big part of the 60s folk music scene.
4 Washington Square Park: People play chess there every day. The arch was modelled on the Arc de Triomphe in Paris and was built in 1889 to celebrate the 100th anniversary of the inauguration of George Washington.
5 The Bodleian Library: Named after founder Thomas Bodley, the Bodleian is a (circular) library, which has a copy of every book published in the UK; any student at the university can use it.
6 The Oxford colleges: There are 38 Oxford colleges.
7 The Bridge of Sighs: It connects the two sides of Hertford College; is modelled on a bridge in Venice.
8 New College: The college was founded in 1370.
9 The 'Schools': Students take their exams there; biggest room can seat 500 students.
10 Christ Church College: It's the biggest and most famous college at Oxford; famous from the Harry Potter films.

3A Put Ss into pairs to work on the answers.

B Give Ss a time limit for checking their answers, so they don't get too distracted by the long audio script. Check that Ss understand *head over to* (go in that direction) and *retrace our/your steps* (go back the way we/you came).

Answers: **1** head **2** circle **3** retrace **4** modelled **5** celebrate **6** named **7** founder **8** As **9** know **10** Interestingly **11** Apparently **12** worth

Optional extra activity

To give Ss controlled practice of some of the key phrases from the recording, prepare sets of sixteen cards (one set for each pair of Ss) with the following 'half 'phrases:
1 head | over to
2 circle | back*
3 retrace | our steps
4 modelled | on
5 built | to celebrate
6 named | after
7 well worth | a visit
8 as I'm sure | you know

Ss first match the phrases, then take turns to turn over one card from each pair and 'test' each other.

**head back* is also possible

C Play the recording and encourage Ss to copy the intonation pattern. You could model the same words with falling intonation, to show Ss that this sounds off-putting, whereas the fall-rise is used by the speaker to keep the listener engaged, as well as sounding enthusiastic.

▷ LANGUAGEBANK 10.3 p146–147

Direct Ss to the summaries of the different types of phrase on p146. Draw Ss' attention to the phrases which are not in Ex 3, i.e. *Supposedly, Strangely, Believe it or not* (under 'commenting on facts') and *to commemorate, in honour of, burnt down/destroyed/rebuilt/restored* (under 'giving facts') and drill them briefly to make sure Ss can pronounce them. Ss could do Ex A for controlled practice: once they've corrected the conversation, they could act it out, paying attention to their intonation.

Answers:
1 **A:** So here we are at Margit Island, named *after* a nun whose father was once king.
A: Yeah, interesting*ly* at one time it was three islands and only used by people who had land here.
2 **A:** *Supposedly* these caves run for miles.
A: The story *goes* that when there was an invasion, the local people hid in these tunnels
3 **A:** That's the Vajdahunyad Castle. It was modelled *on/after* a castle in Transylvania.
A: It was built for the city's millennium exhibition in 1896, to *commemorate* the one thousand-year anniversary of the founding of the state.
4 **A:** Let's retrace our *steps* to Castle Hill.
A: Exactly and the museum is well *worth* a visit.

4A Before Ss look at the prompts, ask them which three places they'd go to if they were visiting Paris. Then tell them to read through the prompts quickly and find out if any of those places are mentioned. Give Ss a few minutes to write out the conversation in their notebooks, leaving the prompts 'clean' for them to use later for spoken practice.

Answers:
1 Let's head over to the cathedral, Notre Dame.
2 Yes, it's well worth visiting it.
3 Yes, it was modelled on a famous Roman arch.
4 To celebrate one of Napoleon's great victories.
5 So here we are at the Eiffel Tower, named after its designer, Gustave Eiffel.
6 Yeah, apparently it can sway six to seven centimetres in the wind!

B Ss should only look at the prompts, not read aloud from their notebooks. Monitor the practice and note down any problems for correction in feedback.

VOCABULARY DIMENSIONS

5 You could start by eliciting ways of asking about dimensions that Ss already know, using adjectives (*How high/long/wide/deep is … ?*) and *get* + comparative (*get longer/narrower/wider/deeper/shorter*), then focus on the first question and elicit *height*. Ss could then use monolingual dictionaries to help them find the rest of the nouns and verbs.

Answers: **1** height **2** length **3** widen **4** thickness **5** narrows **6** breadth, depth **7** enlarge **8** shorten

Optional extra activity

Draw the table below on the board (without some or all of the words in italics, depending on how well you think your Ss will cope with it) for Ss to copy and ask them to complete it.

adjective	noun	verb
high	*height*	*raise*
long	*length*	*lengthen*
wide	*width*	*widen*
thick	*thickness*	*thicken*
narrow	*narrowness*	*narrow*
broad	*breadth*	*broaden*
deep	*depth*	*deepen*
large	*size*	*enlarge*
short	*shortness*	*shorten*

LEARN TO EXPRESS ESTIMATES

6A Give Ss a minute or two to find the examples, working alone or with a partner.

Answers: **1** just under **2** roughly, or so **3** somewhere in the region of **4** upwards of

B Tell Ss to think about whether the phrases express the idea of 'more than' or 'less than' a given number to help them decide with which expressions they might be replaced.

Answers:
1 fewer than – just under
2 more than – upwards of
3 about/around/approximately – roughly, or so, somewhere in the region of

C Before you play the recording, tell Ss to work in pairs and read aloud the two alternatives for each answer, so they familiarise themselves with the numbers. Explain that they will have to decide which of the two options corresponds to the information that they will hear in the audio.

Answers: **1** b) **2** b) **3** a) **4** a) **5** a) **6** b)

Unit 10 Recording 7

1 It's roughly 1,500 metres in length.
2 There are upwards of 35 corridors.
3 It's just under 1,200 metres above sea level.
4 It's somewhere in the region of 715 km.
5 It's two metres or so at its thickest point and then it narrows.
6 You get approximately 370 to the euro.

D Give Ss time to think about and note down their estimates alone first, then put them into pairs to read out their estimates in turn and agree/disagree, e.g.

A: *I'd say there are roughly 450 students in our school.*
B: *I reckon it's upwards of 500.*

Conduct feedback, inviting the class to compare their estimates.

SPEAKING

7A Give Ss time to make notes about what the tour of their town or city would include and to think about how to incorporate some of the language from Ex 3–6. If Ss are from different countries, they can work alone on their tours. If Ss are studying away from home, they may want to design a tour of the city where they're staying. Circulate and provide help as required.

B Put Ss into new pairs and monitor the 'tours', noting down examples of good language use and problems for discussion and correction later.

Alternative approach

You may want to ask Ss to finish preparing their tours at home so they can research some facts about the places they've included and find some photos/maps, etc. that they can use to bring the tour to life. Ss then bring what they've found to the next lesson and give their tours.

Homework ideas

- Ss imagine they're visiting a city and write an email to a friend telling them about some of the important sights.
- **Language bank:** 10.3 Ex A, p147
- **Workbook:** Ex 1–3, p69

THE PEOPLE'S PALACE

Introduction

Ss watch an extract from a BBC programme about the biggest public library in Europe. Ss then learn and practise how to discuss the pros and cons of ideas for a town project and write about a work of art.

Warm up

Ss should have their books closed. Ask the class to think about the following question: *If you could have the biggest or best facility in your town, what would it be?* You could write some ideas on the board for Ss to consider, e.g. library, shopping centre, ice rink, park, cinema, theatre, museum, etc. Put Ss into pairs to describe and discuss their choices, then invite the class to share their ideas.

DVD PREVIEW

1A Check the following vocabulary: *makes a bold statement* (is impressive and often unusual), *fresh* (original), *pleasing on the eye* (attractive to look at), *elaborate* (very detailed) and *unsightly* (ugly). As you check the meaning, ask Ss to name a building in their town that matches the meaning of the word. Then ask Ss to describe the new library to a partner and to answer the questions that follow. Elicit answers to the questions.

B Focus Ss on the three statements and give them a minute or two to discuss which ones they think will appear in the DVD. Vocabulary to check: *budget cuts* (less money to spend) and *breed* (generation or version).

DVD VIEW

2A Play the DVD and ask Ss to check their predictions to Ex 1B as they watch.

Answers: Sentences 2 and 3 are covered in the DVD. (Sentence 1 is only partly covered. The reporter talks to local people and the designer of the building but doesn't speak to any celebrities.)

DVD 10 The Culture Show

V = Voiceover **FH** = Francine Houben **TD** = Tom Dyckhoff
M/W/C = Various local residents

V: People from every walk of life have come in their thousands and from right across the city and beyond.
They've come for the opening of a new building and a very special one at that. At a time when many libraries across Britain face budget cuts and closure, Birmingham is opening the biggest public library in Europe.
Birmingham is not a city that people associate with attractive architecture. It's been described as a godless concrete urban hell. So it wants a new, brighter image, and the City Council of Birmingham is regenerating the city centre. The new library is part of the rebranding.
So it's goodbye to sixties concrete …
… and hello to the latest in design. Such as the 2010Q Building, with its jigsaw-like shaped panels. And this crazy department store building, with its surface of aluminium disks.
And now, the new library. It's no surprise that its design also makes a bold statement. First impressions?
M: First impression? Ooh no.
W: I think it's quite unique and I quite like it.
M: Not very pleasing on the eye I don't think.
W: I love it I think it looks really fresh, modern.
M: I just think it's too busy to look at. There's just too much going on.
V: Francine Houben is the design force behind the building. How did she go about reflecting the character of the city and its people?
FH: I feel it's a very young and energetic city. And it's very colourful. So the idea is that it's really made for all these people. Bold and delicate at the same time, that's the way we tried to make the building.
V: And what about the circles on the outside?
FH: We started with this idea, that's the heritage of the proud industrial city, with the steel industry. It's also bringing unity, it's a kind of bringing everybody together, because … That's why I called it a People's Palace.
V: So how do the taxpayers of Birmingham feel about public money, nearly 200 million pounds, being spent on such an elaborate design for a library?
W: I think any investment of money put into libraries at the moment is fantastic.
M: And in a time of economic austerity, what a bold step to take. Wonderful stuff!
C: I think it's cool.
M: I think they could've done something better with the money.
V: Inside the new library there's 35,000 square metres of space spread across ten floors, including cafés, auditoriums and even roof gardens. How did the designer combine the different roles of a library in one building?
FH: I think what is nowadays so essential that as many ways of studying and learning. There's a lot of people, students, they want to be individual but be part of a bigger collective.
TD: That's interesting.
FH: We made all our study places so you can sit here together on this table or you can have your little own private room or …
… you can sit here on what we call the 'façade bench', being very individual, at the same time dreaming, or maybe talking to someone who's next to you.
V: And finally the day has come for the people to test out their new library.
So what do the people think of their new space?
W: Lovely. Yes, I think it's done Birmingham proud.
M: It's brilliant, yeah, I really like it, it's very user-friendly.
W: Oh it's beautiful. I think it's so amazing. I love this especially. I love this outside bit with the balcony. It's really relaxing.
M: It's just a nice place to come and just chill out. And it's so big you can be here all day.
V: So all in all, the People's Palace seems to be the right name for this great new building.

B Give Ss time to read through the questions and discuss possible answers in pairs. Check the meaning of *regenerating* (renewing or bringing to life again). Play the DVD again for Ss to check their answers.

Answers:
1 Why: Birmingham has a bad reputation for its architecture and wants a new image.
How: by putting up buildings with unusual and modern designs.
2 She describes the city and its people as young, energetic, colourful, bold and delicate. She says they tried to make the building bold and delicate at the same time.
3 Because it brings unity, brings everybody together.
4 There are cafés, auditoriums and roof gardens. The clip also shows a variety of sitting areas.
5 It's a long bench facing the window. You can dream or chat to someone next to you.
6 Specifically, a man calls it 'user-friendly', a woman mentions the outside area with the balcony, and a man says it's a good place to relax and to spend the day because it's so big.

C Give Ss time to read the sentences. At this stage do not explain the difference between *austerity* and *strictness*, otherwise the answer will be obvious. Play the DVD again. When checking the answers, explain that *austerity* relates to cutting or controlling spending and that *strictness* usually means controlling behaviour.

Answers: **1** heritage **2** investment **3** austerity **4** individual **5** user-friendly **6** especially, bit

3 Ss work in pairs to discuss the statements.

speakout a town project

4A Give Ss a minute or two to look through the list and check they understand what all the projects are: *a theatre workshop* (a space where people can practise any skills related to the theatre, such as acting, dancing, stage lighting, etc.), *state-of-the-art* (using the most modern designs, materials, etc.), *a multiplex* (a cinema with several screens) and *a botanical garden* (a large public garden where different types of plants are grown for scientific study). While Ss listen, they should also make brief notes about why each person likes the particular project they have chosen to support.

Answers:
Tim: state-of-the-art multiplex – most beneficial, would bring jobs, provide entertainment for young people.
Sarah: botanical garden – good for different age groups, also blind people and those with disabilities; education centre good for young people.
Nigel: theatre workshop space – to stop young people getting bored and hanging around: will motivate them, parents will come to performances. Could be multi-purpose, e.g. has sprung floor for dance classes, etc.

Unit 10 Recording 8

S = Sarah T = Tim N = Nigel

S: Right, well, we have our shortlist for the new feature that we're going to put into the town centre, which one gets your vote, Tim?
T: I'm really in favour of the – the state-of-the-art multiplex cinema. I think that it would be most useful and beneficial for the community. I think it will be used a great deal, I think it would bring jobs to the area, and I think it would provide entertainment and activities for young people.
N: The only thing that would concern me though is that that's going to be very, very expensive.
T: Um hm.
S: I mean, I personally would prefer the botanical garden.
T: Oh.
S: Because I think that that will satisfy the needs of many different age groups. I think it would be very good for wheelchairs, for … for blind people, for people with disabilities, there would be areas that would be excellent for young people, and lots of learning opportunities in the education centre. And we know from past experience that the older age group certainly enjoy gardens.
T: The only thing that would concern me on that is that you mention youth, but I don't think that you're going to get as many young people involved in a botanical garden. I think if it was interactive then it would be … but just as a thing that was showing I'm, I'm not so sure.
N: Well, I don't want to harp on about costs again but we have to consider the maintenance of this botanical garden. There are very high maintenance costs involved.
S: Oh, so, Nigel what, what would you prefer?
N: Well, my vote would go to the theatre workshop space for young people. And I know we said we don't want to discriminate against any … we don't want to leave out certain members of our society, but I think we've got a problem in this town about kids getting bored, hanging around on street corners, they need something to do and a theatre workshop space is going to get them … it's going to give them a routine, it's going to give them a motivation, and then when they do their shows, they're bringing along their grandparents, their parents, I feel it's very inclusive.
T: Can you see the older generation wanting it, liking it?
N: I think the older generation want to be sure that kids aren't hanging about the streets with nothing to do.
S: And could that theatre workshop space be used for other things as well?
N: Absolutely.
S: Could it be used for meetings, for other sections of society?
N: … Aerobics … there's going to be a sprung wooden floor so there'll be dance classes, yoga, pilates, multi-purpose …

B Ss look through the key phrases before listening again. Ss should tick the phrases they hear. Point out that where there are options in the phrases (e.g. *I think that it would be [beneficial for the community/popular/ …].*), they need to underline the option(s) they hear. Once Ss have listened again and checked their answers, they could look at the audio script and underline three or four more phrases that they think would be useful.

Answers: I'm really in favour of the …; I think that it would be [beneficial for the community/popular/ …].; The only thing that would concern me though is that …; We have to consider [costs/maintenance/ …]; Can you see the [older/younger] generation [using/liking] it?

5A Give Ss time to choose and discuss two projects and make notes to show how their projects fulfil the three criteria given. They should also think about how to incorporate the key phrases when presenting their ideas in the next stage. NB If Ss are from different towns/cities and are studying away from home, they could choose a project for the town or city where they're studying. Circulate and provide help and advice with language as required.

B Put Ss into groups of four to six to discuss and agree on one project. Monitor and note down good examples of language use, particularly the key phrases and any problems, for discussion and correction later.

C You could ask one student from each group to act as spokesperson, or ask each student from each group to present one aspect of their chosen project.

writeback a work of art

6A Give Ss time to read about the competition, then elicit some more ideas for works of art, buildings, rooms, etc. that Ss could write about. Ss make notes about what they would choose and why, then compare their ideas in pairs.

B When Ss have ticked the things in the box that the writer mentions, they could also look at the purpose of each paragraph, i.e. 1 what/where it is and why the writer likes it; 2 who made it; 3 a summarising comment.

Answers: setting (valley in southern France), when it was made (21st century), size (2500 metres long), who made it (a French engineer and a British architect), why he/she likes it (it's 'graceful', 'breathtaking to behold' and looking at it gives him/her 'a sense of calm')

C Encourage Ss to use the ideas in the box in Ex 6B and any of their own ideas. Ss write their competition entry.

D Ss could swap with a partner and comment on the accuracy of the language, how persuasive the entry is, etc. Ss then display their entries around the class and vote on the best place to visit.

Homework ideas

Ss write a second draft of their competition entry taking into account their partner's feedback.

LOOKBACK

Introduction

The aim of these activities is to provide revision and further practice of the language from the unit. You can also use them to assess Ss' ability to use the language, in which case you need to monitor but avoid helping them. You may feel that you don't need or have time to do all the activities. If so, you could allocate the activities that would be most beneficial for your Ss, or get individual Ss to decide which activities they'd like to do.

ADJECTIVES

1A You could run this as a game of 'Backs to the board'. Put Ss into two teams and ask one volunteer from each team to come and sit with their back to the board. Write an adjective from p116 on the board: the rest of the team has to give their volunteer clues to help them guess the word and the first one to do this wins their team a point. A new volunteer from each team comes up and the game continues.

B Ss complete the comments alone or with a partner.

Answers: 1 moving/touching 2 hysterical/hilarious 3 gripping (brilliant, electrifying and unforgettable are also possible) 4 controversial

C Ss could write their comments with a gap for the adjective, then pass them to the next pair to complete.

RELATIVE CLAUSES

2A Ss can work on this alone or with a partner.

Answers: 1 whose 2 where 3 that 4 where 5 whom 6 which

B Elicit some examples of how to change the first sentence, e.g. *A person whose main interests include reading detective novels/ playing computer games/photography/cooking.*
Also point out that in sentence 3, the sentence could read *someone that knows* ***how to*** *speak English/play the guitar really well/ cook, etc.*
Ss work alone to change the sentences.

C Direct Ss to the example and put them into groups of three or four, or ask them to stand up and walk round the class, talking to at least three other Ss. Conduct feedback with the class about the most useful/interesting information they found out.

PARTICIPLE CLAUSES

3A You could run this as a competition with Ss in teams of four to six. Ask each team to choose a sound which they can use as a 'buzzer' when they're ready to answer a question. Display the questions one at a time on the board. Ss 'buzz' to answer and are given one point for a correct participle and a further point for a correct answer to the question (you could also deduct points for Ss shouting out answers rather than 'buzzing').

Answers: 1 standing, made 2 started, known 3 played, involving, taking 4 crowned, defeated 5 awarded 6 living, using, called 7 consisting, rolled 8 written, featuring

B Ss can work either in pairs or individually to answer the questions in the quiz.

C Feed back on the answers as a class or let Ss check their answers on their own on p163.

Answers: 1 Sydney Opera House 2 Apple Inc. 3 squash 4 Napoleon Bonaparte 5 Oscar 6 the Inuit 7 sushi (makizushi) 8 *Hamlet*

Optional extra activity

Ss work in pairs and write their own trivia quiz of four or five questions. Each question should contain at least two participle clauses. When Ss have written their quizzes, they can either put them round the walls or leave them on a piece of paper on their desks for other pairs to walk round and try to answer. In feedback, Ss could comment on the best/most challenging questions.

THE ARTS

4 Ss could work on this in pairs. You could run it as a race, asking the first pair to finish to bring their answers up to you to check.

Answers: 1 flop 2 rave 3 creating a stir 4 ground-breaking 5 sell-out 6 letdown 7 hype 8 must-see 9 mainstream 10 alternative

Optional extra activity

Ss write four descriptions of performers, shows, CDs, exhibitions, celebrities, etc. using at least one of the words related to the Arts in each sentence, e.g. *There was a lot of hype surrounding this film, but when it came out, most people thought it was a real letdown.* Ss read out their sentences to a partner, who has to guess what they're describing.

GIVING A TOUR

5A For ***stronger classes***, you could tell Ss to cover the box and try to decide what words are missing from the sentences first, then check with the words in the box.

Answers:
1 It *was* built in the 17th century by Shah Jahan in *honour* of his wife. As *you* may know, it's made of white marble and it is well *worth* a visit. (The Taj Mahal)
2 It was *named* after its designer and was built in 1889. The *story* goes that many Parisians hated it because it was too modern. (The Eiffel Tower)
3 Parts of it were *rebuilt* many times. Believe *it* or not, millions of Chinese died in its construction. (The Great Wall of China)

B Ss can work in pairs to write their sentences, using at least two of the phrases from p122–123 in each sentence.

C You could do this with the whole class, or put Ss into groups of six to eight. One pair reads out their sentences and the others make guesses. The pair who guesses first wins a point, but every wrong guess gives the pair who wrote the sentences a point.

Homework ideas

Workbook: Review 5, p70–73

BBC interviews and worksheet

What area of the Arts do you enjoy?

This video encourages Ss to reflect on the areas of art and culture that they enjoy the most.

PAGE	UNIT	PHOTOCOPIABLE	LANGUAGE POINT	TIME
147	1	**Happy flatmates**	**Vocabulary: personality** • review vocabulary for describing personality • practise speaking skills by describing people	20 mins
148	1	**How do I feel?**	**Vocabulary: describing feelings** • review vocabulary for describing feelings • practise adjective/noun word building	25 mins
149	1	**Good cop, bad cop**	**Grammar: indirect questions** • practise forming indirect questions • practise speaking skills in interviews	40 mins
150	1	**Talk about ...**	**Grammar: present perfect** • review the present perfect and contrast it with the past simple • personalised fluent speaking practice	45 mins
151	1	**How can I help you?**	**Functional language: polite enquiries** • practise functional language for making and managing enquiries	25 mins
152	2	**Scrambled issues**	**Vocabulary: issues** • review vocabulary for issues • free speaking practice on issues	45 mins
153	2	**You're on camera**	**Vocabulary: surveillance** • review vocabulary for surveillance • practise speaking skills by discussing surveillance	25 mins
154	2	**It's a perfect world**	**Grammar: present perfect simple and continuous** • practise using the present perfect simple or continuous according to context	25 mins
155	2	**A brief history of energy drinks**	**Grammar: the passive** • practise forming questions in the passive • review different passive tense forms	25 mins
156	2	**Big issues**	**Functional language: opinions** • practise giving opinions and supporting them with reasons and examples	40 mins
157	3	**What's my saying?**	**Vocabulary: sayings** • review sayings from Lesson 3.1 • practise speaking skills by telling an anecdote	35 mins
158	3	**Change it!**	**Vocabulary *plus*: multi-word verbs** • review the multi-word verbs from Lesson 3.2	25 mins
159	3	**Past consequences**	**Grammar: narrative tenses** • practise using narrative tenses • guided sentence writing	35 mins
160	3	**Spiralling regret**	**Grammar: *I wish, if only*** • practise with *I wish, if only* • free speaking practice talking about regrets	35 mins
161	3	**Literary critics**	**Functional language: expressing likes and dislikes** • practise expressing likes and dislikes • review language for describing books	35 mins
162	4	**Noun maze**	**Vocabulary *plus*: uncountable and plural nouns** • review uncountable and plural nouns • practise choosing correct forms by playing a game	15 mins
163	4	**I'm good at something**	**Vocabulary: abilities** • review vocabulary for talking about abilities	20 mins
164	4	**Then and now**	**Grammar: present and past habits and future forms** • practise a range of verb forms for habits and the future by completing sentences	35 mins
165	4	**Questions of the future**	**Grammar: future forms** • practise a range of future forms by answering questions	40 mins
166	4	**The new football**	**Functional language: describing procedures** • practise describing procedures • practise mirror questions	45 mins
167	5	**Compound snap**	**Vocabulary *plus*: compound nouns** • review compound nouns in the context of invention and innovation	25 mins
168	5	**Product, price, market**	**Vocabulary: advertising collocations** • review vocabulary for advertising • practise speaking skills by defining words	25 mins
169	5	**Ahead of its time**	**Grammar: articles** • review the use of articles	25 mins
170	5	**Conditional dominoes**	**Grammar: real and hypothetical conditionals** • review conditional structures • practise speaking skills by discussing and evaluating conditional statements	30 mins

Photocopiable activities index

PAGE	UNIT	PHOTOCOPIABLE	LANGUAGE POINT	TIME
171	5	**Campaign competition**	**Functional language: suggesting ideas** • practise functional language for suggesting ideas and showing reservations	45 mins
172	6	**Tell the group**	**Vocabulary: age** • practise word-building with prefixes • practise speaking skills in free discussion	30 mins
173	6	**Coffee machine chat**	**Vocabulary: optimism/pessimism** • review and practise vocabulary for expressing optimism and pessimism	25 mins
174	6	**Off the beaten track**	**Grammar: modal verbs and related phrases** • practise using a range of modal verbs • practise speaking skills in the context of trip planning	40 mins
175	6	**Futurologist forum**	**Grammar: future perfect and continuous** • review and practise future perfect and continuous	35 mins
176	6	**It's debatable**	**Functional language: persuading and clarifying ideas** • practise persuading and asking for clarification in a debate	45 mins
177	7	**What's my programme?**	**Vocabulary: television** • recycle vocabulary for TV programmes • practise speaking skills by defining words	25 mins
178	7	**Multi-word verb reformulation**	**Vocabulary *plus*: multi-word verbs** • review multi-word verbs from Lesson 7.1	25 mins
179	7	**Quantifier dice**	**Grammar: quantifiers** • practise using quantifiers with a range of nouns	30 mins
180	7	**AWOL**	**Grammar: reported speech** • practise reporting direct speech • practise speaking skills in the context of a meeting	20 mins
181	7	**Hold the front page**	**Functional language: adding emphasis** • practise adding emphasis and making guesses in free speaking in the context of news stories	40 mins
182	8	**Collocation dilemmas**	**Vocabulary: collocations: decisions** • review verb/noun collocations from Lesson 8.1 in the context of dilemmas	45 mins
183	8	**It's how you say it**	**Vocabulary: behaviour** • practise using vocabulary connected with behaviour	25 mins
184	8	**Conditional fox and hounds**	**Grammar: past and mixed conditionals** • practise hypothetical conditionals in a free speaking activity	40 mins
185	8	**Bad behaviour**	**Grammar: *-ing* form and infinitive** • review use of *-ing* form and infinitive • practise speaking skills in discussion and decision making	25 mins
186	8	**Don't take this the wrong way**	**Functional language: handling an awkward situation** • practise softening a message • practise dealing with a difficult situation	40 mins
187	9	**What's my punishment?**	**Vocabulary: crime** • review collocations for crime • practise speaking skills in free discussion	40 mins
188	9	**Noughts and crosses**	**Vocabulary *plus*: dependent prepositions** • review and recycle dependent prepositions	40 mins
189	9	**Verb form bingo**	**Grammar: *-ing* form and infinitive** • practise the correct use of *-ing* forms and infinitives after certain verbs	25 mins
190	9	**Deduction blocks**	**Grammar: modals of deduction** • practise using modals of deduction	35 mins
191	9	**Tell me what you saw**	**Functional language: reporting an incident** • practise functional language for describing an incident	45 mins
192	10	**I wouldn't recommend it!**	**Vocabulary: adjectives to describe films** • review adjectives to describe films	25 mins
193	10	**Two-part phrase game**	**Vocabulary *plus*: two-part phrases** • practise using two-part phrases in context	30 mins
194	10	**Relative clause quiz**	**Grammar: relative clauses** • practise distinguishing between defining and non-defining relative clauses	40 mins
195	10	**Change and discuss**	**Grammar: participle clauses** • practise forming and using participle clauses	35 mins
196	10	**Top tours**	**Functional language: giving a tour** • practise the functional language for giving a tour	40 mins

Student A

1 Housemate name	2 Housemate name	3 Housemate name	4 Housemate name	5 Housemate name
Personality	**Personality**	**Personality**	**Personality**	**Personality**
1.	1.	1.	1.	1.
2.	2.	2.	2.	2.

Housemate names
- Sam
- Josh
- Gemma
- Lucy
- Sara

Personality
- a people person
- a computer geek
- keep yourself to yourself
- witty
- down-to-earth
- a good laugh
- spontaneous
- a morning person

- **(Start)** Josh thinks Sam's glasses make him look like a computer geek, and he really is one!
- Lucy is always realistic about things.
- The two male housemates are next to each other.
- The quick minded housemate who makes people laugh is next to the housemate who keeps himself to himself.
- The housemate who's fun to be with is standing up.
- Josh is a people person and next to Gemma.
- The female computer geek housemate is next to the housemate that rarely hesitates.
- The housemate who is bright and cheerful first thing is between a male and female housemate.

Student B

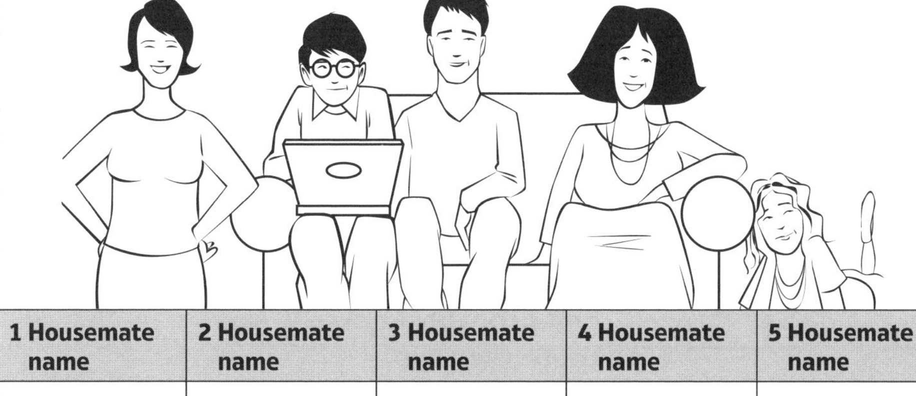

1 Housemate name	2 Housemate name	3 Housemate name	4 Housemate name	5 Housemate name
Personality	**Personality**	**Personality**	**Personality**	**Personality**
1.	1.	1.	1.	1.
2.	2.	2.	2.	2.

Housemate names
- Sam
- Josh
- Gemma
- Lucy
- Sara

Personality
- a people person
- a computer geek
- keep yourself to yourself
- witty
- down-to-earth
- a good laugh
- spontaneous
- a morning person

- The housemate who keeps herself to herself is not sitting on the sofa.
- All the housemates think the person lying on the floor is a computer geek.
- The male housemate who is obsessed with computers is next to the housemate who's a good laugh.
- The down-to-earth housemate hates Sara and is as far away from her as possible.
- The housemate who likes mornings is next to the housemate who keeps herself to herself.
- The witty housemate is in the middle.
- The spontaneous housemate is next to the sociable person.
- The introverted male housemate is next to Lucy.

HOW DO I FEEL?

Vocabulary: describing feelings

I've been saving money to do this for three years and tomorrow I'm finally going to set off on my trip round the world. *How do I feel?* **thrilled**	**I've just won $5m on the lottery. I can give up my job and do anything I want!** *What's the feeling?* **thrilling**	**I am a visitor at the home of a couple who argue all the time. They keep asking me to take sides.** *How do I feel?* **awkward**	**I'm meeting my partner's parents for the first time and making conversation is difficult.** *What's the feeling?* **awkwardness**
People keep asking me for my autograph. *How do I feel?* **admired**	**People think Messi is the best football player in the world.** *What's the feeling?* **admiration**	**My brother has broken my smartphone.** *How do I feel?* **angry**	**The shop won't refund my money.** *What's the feeling?* **anger**
My teenage son didn't come home last night and he always calls if he's going to be late. *How do I feel?* **anxious**	**I need to catch a connecting flight and my flight is delayed.** *What's the feeling?* **anxiety**	**My team lost the final.** *How do I feel?* **disappointed**	**The world champion fell over and missed winning an ice-skating medal at the Olympics.** *What's the feeling?* **disappointment**
I still can't find a parking space. I've been looking for over half an hour. *How do I feel?* **frustrated**	**I've got lots of urgent emails waiting for me, but my internet connection is down.** *What's the feeling?* **frustration**	**I'm about to give a presentation to fifty people I've never met. They are all experts in the field and probably know more than me.** *How do I feel?* **nervous**	**I am going to ask my partner if he/she wants to marry me. I don't know what he/she is going to say.** *What's the feeling?* **nervousness**
I slapped my friend on the back and told him to hurry up, but when he turned round I saw it was a stranger. *How do I feel?* **embarrassed**	**I am going to introduce my colleague to the new boss, but I just can't remember her name.** *What's the feeling?* **embarrassment**	**I lost my wallet and spent one hour looking for it. I've just found it in my coat pocket.** *How do I feel?* **relieved**	**Your friends were on a plane that crashed. You've just found out nobody was injured.** *What's the feeling?* **relief**

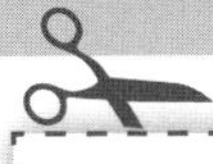

Good cop

You are a detective investigating the theft of five priceless works of art from the Metropolitan National Gallery of Art. There was no sign of the thief/thieves breaking into the building and you suspect the Director of the gallery may be involved. The Director is a highly respected and famous art expert and has been Director for over twenty years. There are rumours about him/her illegally selling valuable paintings to rich private collectors, but they may not be true and he/she may be completely innocent. You are going to interview him/her and you need to:

- find out what he/she was doing on the night the paintings were stolen
- search his/her house(s)
- access his/her bank accounts
- close the gallery for at least four days
- check his/her personal emails
- look at CCTV footage from the gallery
- ask about the rumours.

Remember:
The Director is a very important person and you are worried about wrongly accusing someone so respected and well-known. Therefore be as polite and as diplomatic as possible and only ask him/her indirect questions. Your partner is not going to be so polite and you need to make any direct questions your partner asks into indirect ones.

Bad cop

You are a detective investigating the theft of five priceless works of art from the Metropolitan National Gallery of Art. There was no sign of the thief/thieves breaking into the building and you suspect the Director of the gallery may be involved. The Director is a highly respected and famous art expert and has been Director for over twenty years. There are rumours about him/her illegally selling valuable paintings to rich private collectors, but they may not be true and he/she may be completely innocent. You are going to interview him/her and you need to:

- find out what he/she was doing on the night the paintings were stolen
- search his/her house(s)
- access his/her bank accounts
- close the gallery for at least four days
- check his/her personal emails
- look at CCTV footage from the gallery
- ask about the rumours.

Remember:
The Director is a very important person but you don't care. You think he/she is highly suspicious and believe he/she is using his/her good reputation to hide criminal activity. You don't care about seeming rude and you are going to only ask the Director direct questions.

Gallery director

You are the Director of the Metropolitan National Gallery of Art. You have been Director for over twenty years and you are a famous and respected art expert. You are friends with many rich and powerful people. However, you are deeply dishonest and greedy. You arranged for five priceless paintings from your gallery to be stolen and sold to wealthy private collectors. They paid you $200m for the paintings. This money was paid into your Swiss bank account. You supplied the thieves with the keys and alarm codes. The paintings have already left the country. The police are going to interview you. You are a very private person and dislike the police, but of course you need to be helpful and convince them that you are not involved in the thefts.

TALK ABOUT …

Grammar: present perfect

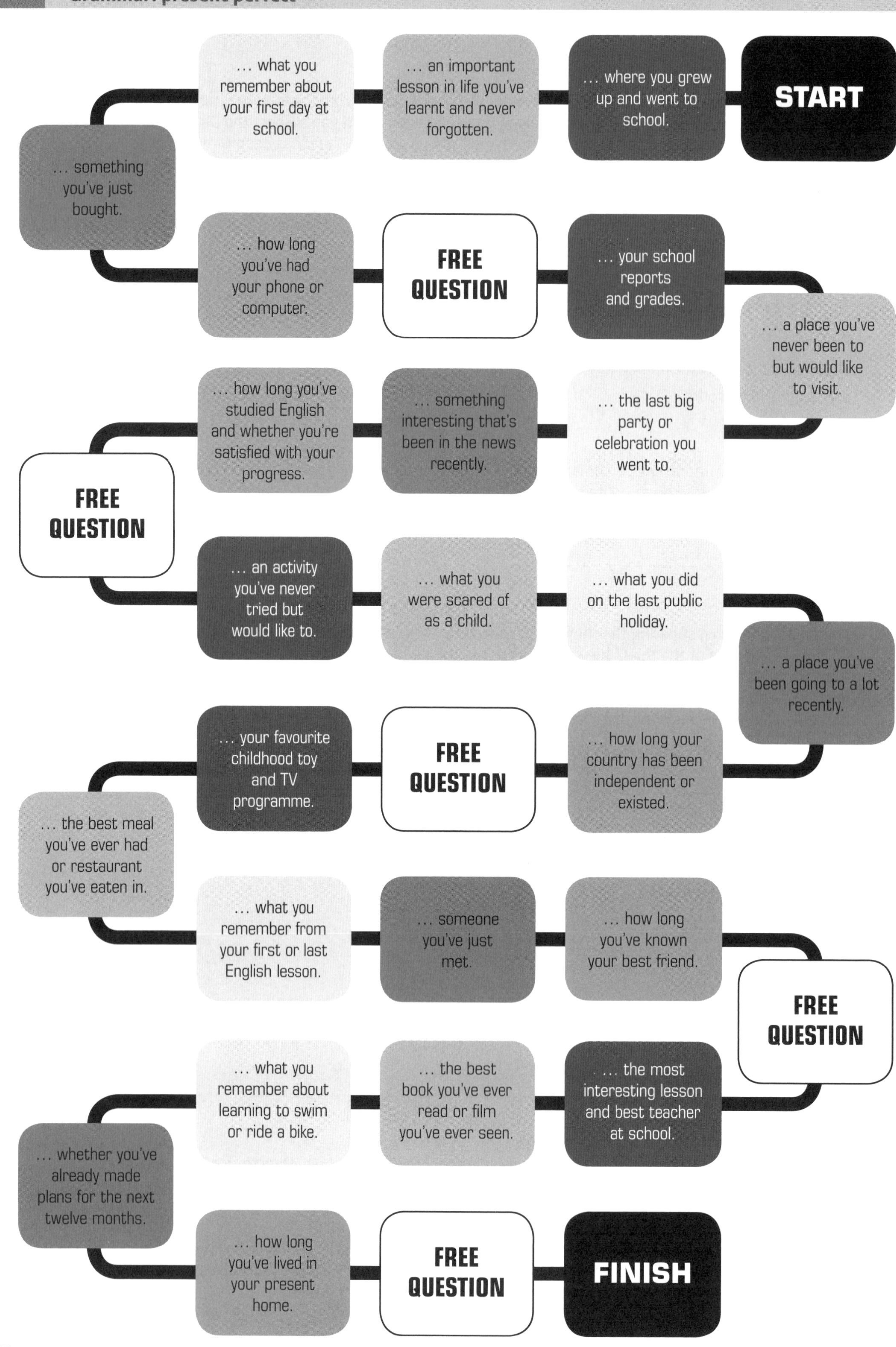
START
… where you grew up and went to school.
… an important lesson in life you've learnt and never forgotten.
… what you remember about your first day at school.
… something you've just bought.
… how long you've had your phone or computer.
FREE QUESTION
… your school reports and grades.
… a place you've never been to but would like to visit.
… the last big party or celebration you went to.
… something interesting that's been in the news recently.
… how long you've studied English and whether you're satisfied with your progress.
FREE QUESTION
… an activity you've never tried but would like to.
… what you were scared of as a child.
… what you did on the last public holiday.
… a place you've been going to a lot recently.
… how long your country has been independent or existed.
FREE QUESTION
… your favourite childhood toy and TV programme.
… the best meal you've ever had or restaurant you've eaten in.
… what you remember from your first or last English lesson.
… someone you've just met.
… how long you've known your best friend.
FREE QUESTION
… the most interesting lesson and best teacher at school.
… the best book you've ever read or film you've ever seen.
… what you remember about learning to swim or ride a bike.
… whether you've already made plans for the next twelve months.
… how long you've lived in your present home.
FREE QUESTION
FINISH

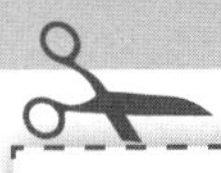

Student A – Making enquiries

There is a power cut on your street and you have had no electricity for twelve hours. You phoned the power company just after it happened and were told to phone back later in the day after they had investigated the problem. You are now phoning for a second time.

- Find out when the power will be switched on again.
- Find out what the problem was and if it will happen again.
- Find out why there are not any engineers working on the problem now (there were some this morning).
- Find out what compensation you can expect to receive.
- Explain how inconvenient it has been and how unhappy you are with the situation.

Phone Customer Service now!

Student A – Managing enquiries

You work in the customer service department of a national bank, CTB. You deal with customer complaints and problems.
A customer is going to phone you regarding a cloned cash card. Their money was stolen but the bank has not refunded it yet.

- Ask for personal and bank account details as well as security passwords.
- Apologise that the computer system is really slow today.
- Explain that the customer has not received a refund because the bank has not received a police crime reference number yet.
- Explain refunds take a minimum of ten working days.
- Explain customers should not normally have to pay overdraft charges in these circumstances. You can ask your supervisor to refund the charges immediately.

Start the conversation with: *Hello, this is CTB. This is* (name) *speaking. How can I help you?*

Student B – Managing enquiries

You work in the customer service department of a national power company, EGON Power.
A customer experiencing a power cut is going to phone you for the second time about the problem.

- Ask for their personal details and account number.
- Apologise for the fact that the computer system is really slow today.
- Explain that the problem is complex and will take up to three days to repair as special equipment is needed.
- Explain that engineers only work for eight hours and then another team arrives.
- Compensation is paid after thirty-six hours with no power.

Start the conversation with: *Hello, this is EGON Power, I'm* (name). *How can I help you?*

Student B – Making enquiries

Your cash card was cloned and over $1500 was taken from your account. The bank accepted it was not your fault and promised to refund the money. Three weeks later they have not done this and you are now paying overdraft charges.

- Explain the situation to the customer service representative.
- Find out why the money has not been refunded and when you will receive it.
- Explain that you have already given the bank the police crime reference number.
- Explain that you need money desperately as you have to pay your rent this week.
- Find out why you are paying overdraft charges. It is not your fault that your account is overdrawn.

Phone Customer Service now!

Vocabulary: issues

Scrambled Issue	Unscrambled Issue	Idea one	Idea two	Idea three
tbed	*debt*	*Educate children at school about how to manage their money.*	*Banks should only lend money to people who can definitely pay it back.*	*Governments should provide loans with low interest rates to help poor people.*
unollipot				
nempynutlome				
tertes icemr				
mesenseslosh				
hogrutd				
grud sueba				
tecodmis eniclove				
eyostib				

Councillor A

You are a local councillor and your town has a number of problems:

1 Motorists drive too fast through the narrow streets.
2 Vandalism and drunkenness are a problem in the town centre. Families and elderly people keep away.
3 Attacks by dangerous dogs are becoming more common.
4 Gangs are selling illegal fake goods in the town centre.

You believe ways to deal with the issues are:

- to install cameras to act as a deterrent but also help the police keep track of trouble-makers and catch wanted criminals.
- to microchip all dogs so the owners of dangerous ones are registered. They can be easily identified and their details handed over to the police.
- to install CCTV in the town centre so the gangs selling fake goods will move out of the town. You believe their presence encourages others to break the law.

Councillor B

You are a local councillor and your town has a number of problems:

1 Motorists drive too fast through the narrow streets.
2 Vandalism and drunkenness are a problem in the town centre. Families and elderly people keep away.
3 Attacks by dangerous dogs are becoming more common.
4 Gangs are selling illegal fake goods in the town centre.

You believe ways to deal with the issues are:

- not to install CCTV. You believe our surveillance society is not only an invasion of privacy but very expensive. The money could be spent on more police and other towns with CCTV still have these problems.
- not to microchip dogs, as only responsible owners would do this and not the owners of the dangerous dogs.
- not to worry about the people selling fake goods. You don't see the harm in people selling a few fake handbags and sunglasses.

Councillor C

You are a local councillor and your town has a number of problems:

1 Motorists drive too fast through the narrow streets.
2 Vandalism and drunkenness are a problem in the town centre. Families and elderly people keep away.
3 Attacks by dangerous dogs are becoming more common.
4 Gangs are selling illegal fake goods in the town centre.

You believe ways to deal with the issues are:

- to install surveillance cameras. You believe that if you are a law-abiding citizen and you have done nothing wrong then it doesn't matter that your every move is monitored and logged.
- to use number plate recognition technology to discourage known criminals, some of whom are selling the fake goods, from entering the town.
- to install speed cameras. The evidence that they reduce accidents and make streets safer and nicer places to be is overwhelming.

Councillor D

You are a local councillor and your town has a number of problems:

1 Motorists drive too fast through the narrow streets.
2 Vandalism and drunkenness are a problem in the town centre. Families and elderly people keep away.
3 Attacks by dangerous dogs are becoming more common.
4 Gangs are selling illegal fake goods in the town centre.

You believe ways to deal with the issues are:

- not to install speed cameras. You believe they cause accidents by people slowing down quickly before them and speeding up after them. The money they make is not spent on improving roads.
- not to install CCTV. It is rare for police to actually look at it for minor crimes like drunkenness and vandalism.
- to encourage citizens to be more responsible and use their camera phones if they see someone committing a crime. You believe this would make individuals more accountable for their actions.

Grammar: present perfect simple and continuous

Student A	Student B	Student C
1 I feel emotional and I'm crying. **2** I love the cinema. **I've just seen a sad film.**	**1** I'm crying but I don't feel emotional. **2** I'm cooking. **I've been chopping onions.**	**1** I don't have any money left. **2** Now I can drive anywhere I want to go. **I've bought a new car.**
1 We're at the theatre. **2** My partner looks angry and we can't go in. **I've forgotten the tickets.**	**1** I feel sick. **2** There are five chocolate bar wrappers on the floor. **I've eaten five bars of chocolate.**	**1** I'm at the doctor's. **2** I always wake up in the night. I feel exhausted. **I haven't been sleeping well.**
1 I'm completely wet. **2** I didn't take an umbrella with me. **I've been walking in the rain.**	**1** I'm celebrating with my partner. **2** I met him/her fifty years ago. **I've been married for fifty years.**	**1** I'm in pain and my body is red all over. **2** I was at the beach. **I've been sunbathing.**
1 My boss is angry with me. **2** I find it difficult to get up in the morning. **I've been arriving late for work.**	**1** I'm playing football. **2** All my team-mates are running towards me. **I've just scored a goal.**	**1** I'm really anxious. **2** It had my credit cards and cash in it. **I've lost my wallet.**
1 I'm really happy I passed. **2** I'm in a bar with all my friends. **I've been celebrating.**	**1** I used to have a beautiful garden. **2** All the plants are dead. **I haven't been watering my plants.**	**1** Jean is my best friend. **2** We became friends when we were children. **I've known Jean since we were children.**
1 I really, really like tennis. **2** I first played tennis when I was thirteen. **I've loved tennis since I was thirteen.**	**1** I'm tired and really hot. **2** I was at the gym. **I've been working out.**	1 I'm heavier than I was. 2 I can't stop going to the kitchen. **I've been eating too much.**

Student A

Although Irn-Bru from Scotland has never been marketed as [1]____________________, it can claim to be the first. Called Iron Brew at the time, it was first sold in 1901. In Japan, energy drinks have been produced for over fifty years starting with the release of Lipovitan in the 1960s. A lot of Japanese energy drinks do not look like soft drinks at all and are sold in [2]____________________. These energy drinks are known as 'genki drinks' and are aimed at [3]____________________.

Lucozade Energy, first sold in 1929, was originally introduced as a hospital drink for 'aiding the recovery'. However, by the early 1980s it had become an energy drink and was promoted as a [4]'____________________'.

The first drink designed to improve the performance of sports stars was Gatorade. It was invented in the 1960s for the University of Florida football team, the Gators, hence its name. It was designed to aid [5]____________________. Gatorade is considered to be safer than many energy drinks and is known more as a sports drink.

[6]____________________, was launched by Pepsi Co in 1985 and was the first energy drink introduced by a major US beverage company. It was discontinued in 1999.

Undoubtedly the most popular energy drink today is Red Bull and it is adapted from a Thai energy drink, Krating Daeng, which means Red Bull. The company was founded by [7]____________________ in 1987 along with its famous slogan 'Red Bull gives you wings'. The product is marketed aggressively through advertising, tournament sponsorship and sports team ownership.

Student B

Although Irn-Bru from Scotland has never been marketed as an energy drink, it can claim to be the first. Called Iron Brew at the time, it was first sold in 1901. In Japan, energy drinks have been produced for [1]____________________ years starting with the release of Lipovitan in the 1960s. A lot of Japanese energy drinks do not look like soft drinks at all and are sold in small brown glass medicine bottles. These energy drinks are known as [2]'____________________' and are aimed at the salaryman market.

Lucozade Energy, first sold in 1929, was originally introduced as [3]____________________ for 'aiding the recovery'. However, by the early 1980s it had become an energy drink and was promoted as a 'drink for replenishing lost energy'.

The first drink designed to improve the performance of sports stars was Gatorade. It was invented in the 1960s for [4]____________________, the Gators, hence its name. It was designed to aid hydration and improve performance levels. Gatorade is considered to be [5]____________________ and is known more as a sports drink.

Josta, was launched by Pepsi Co in 1985 and was the first energy drink introduced by a major US beverage company. It was discontinued in 1999.

Undoubtedly the most popular energy drink today is Red Bull and it is adapted from [6]____________________, Krating Daeng, which means Red Bull. The company was founded by a Thai and an Austrian national in 1987 along with its famous slogan 'Red Bull gives you wings'. The product is marketed aggressively through [7]____________________.

Start

Start					Start
	Life was better fifty years ago.	English is destroying other languages.	Football is more important than life or death.	There is nothing wrong with having cosmetic surgery.	Having as many children as you want is not a basic human right.	
	Teachers should be able to use physical punishment.	It's better to be good-looking than intelligent.	Money can buy you happiness.	Terminally ill people have the right to end their life.	We are not alone in the universe.	
	Democracy is the best form of government.	Black is the most elegant colour.	Social networking sites are a waste of time.	Mankind will eventually destroy the planet.	The death penalty is justifiable for some crimes.	
	Citizens carrying guns makes society safer.	Some drugs should be legalised.	Women are more complex than men.	Immigration is generally a positive thing.	You can't be young and wise.	
	Climate change is a myth.	War and terrorism are never justifiable.	The best music has already been written.	Shoplifting is a victimless crime.	A country gets the government it deserves.	

Start

1

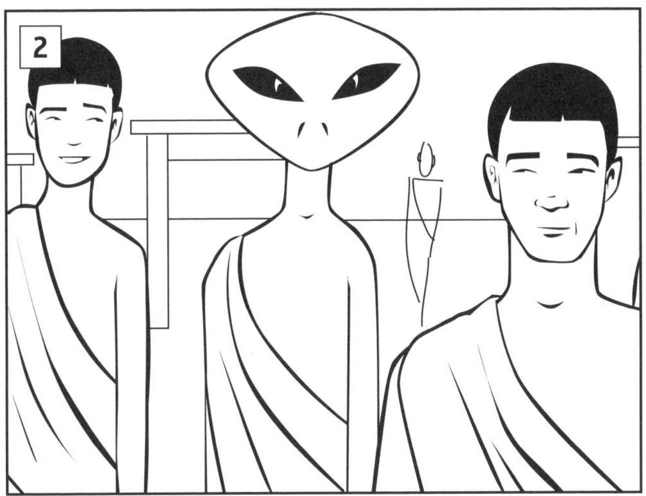
2

3

4
LOTTO

5

Vocabulary *plus*: multi-word verbs

Multi-word verbs
take up
turn down
set up
turn up
run out of
bring up
grow up
pass away
drop out
take up
pick up
look up
stand for
go on
go by
give up

1 They arrived two hours late.	**2** After he left the band, he wrote film soundtracks.	**3** His dog died.	**4** Many years passed before he forgave his brother.
5 He went travelling but used up all his money and had to come home early.	**6** I've recently started doing yoga.	**7** I could never stop eating chocolate, I love it so much.	**8** She started the company with her brother in 2001.
9 She didn't finish university.	**10** Last year she started a new hobby.	**11** Where did you spend your childhood?	**12** He proposed to her but she said no.
13 She has learnt many new skills in her job.	**14** In the story, Tarzan was raised by apes.	**15** Many people admire disabled people.	**16** What does the Olympics represent?

Answers

1 They turned up two hours late.	**2** After he left the band, he went on to write film soundtracks.	**3** His dog passed away.	**4** Many years went by before he forgave his brother.
5 He went travelling but ran out of money and had to come home early.	**6** I've recently taken up (doing) yoga.	**7** I could never give up eating chocolate, I love it so much.	**8** She set up the company with her brother in 2001.
9 She dropped out of university.	**10** Last year she took up a new hobby.	**11** Where did you grow up?	**12** He proposed to her but she turned him down.
13 She has picked up many new skills in her job.	**14** In the story, Tarzan was brought up by apes.	**15** Many people look up to disabled people.	**16** What does the Olympics stand for?

A day to forget, a night to remember

1 It was a cold, dark night. It was ______________ and ______________.	What was the weather like?
2 Jack was tired, he had been ______________ all night and now he was driving home.	What had Jack been doing?
3 It had been the worst twenty-four hours of his life. He had ______________ and ______________.	What two things had he done?
4 As he drove, he ______________. The roads were empty and he felt alone.	What did he do as he drove?
5 He stopped the car at an all-night diner. He had to ______________ and ______________.	What two things did he have to do?
6 It was twenty-four hours since he had ______________ and he was starting to go crazy.	What hadn't he done for twenty-four hours?
7 As he entered the diner, the waitress ______________ and ______________.	What two things did she do?
8 He didn't even notice her but then he suddenly realised ______________.	What did he suddenly realise?
9 In seconds, they were ______________.	What were they doing?
10 '*Could this be real?*' he thought. '*Why had she* ______________*?'*	What had she done?
11 '*And why had she been* ______________*?'*	What had she been doing?
12 But that didn't matter now. All that was important was ______________.	What was important now?
13 She told him that she ______________.	What did she tell him?
14 All he could say was '______________!' **The End**	What did he say?

Grammar: ***I wish, if only***

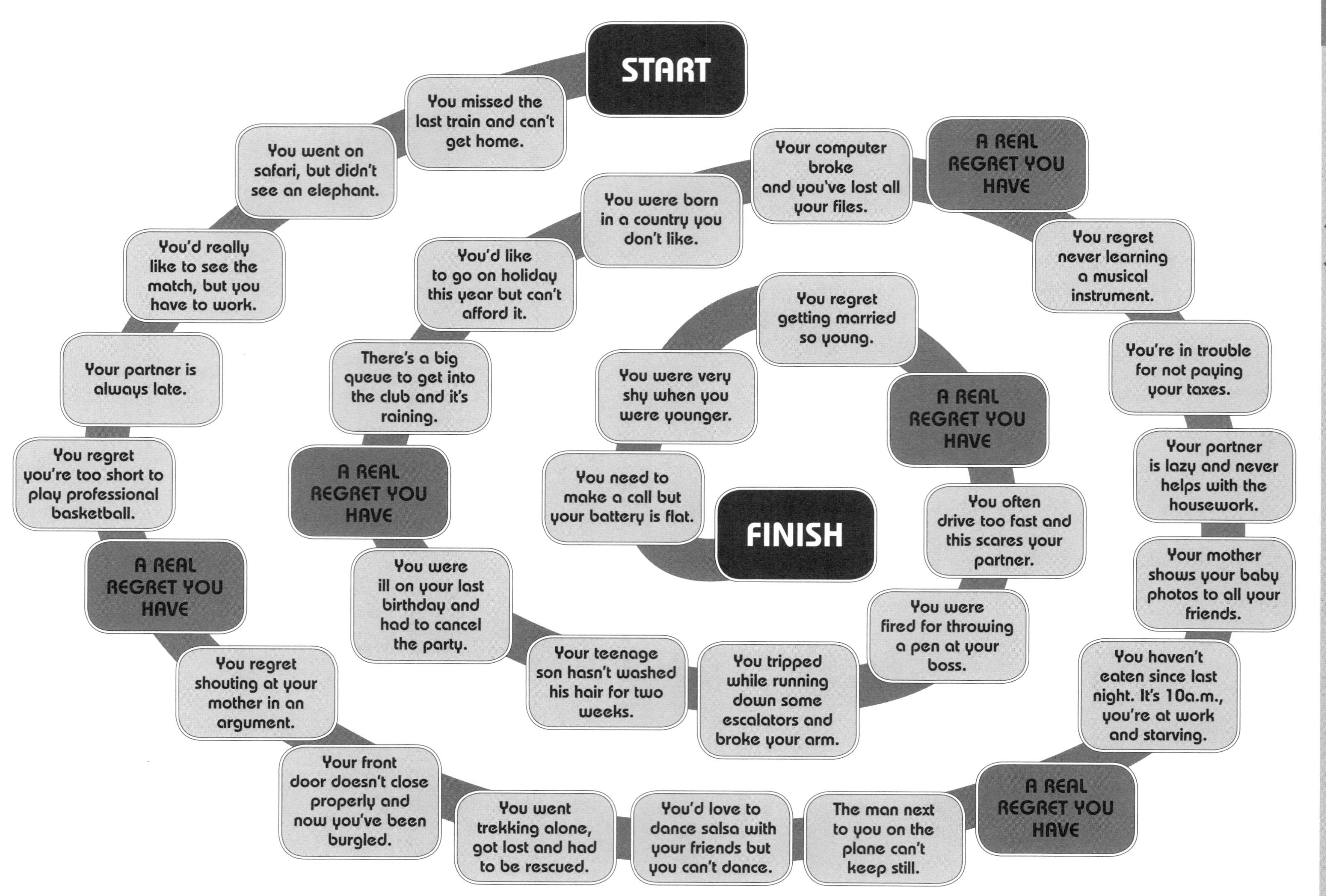

Blurbs

Last Rendition By Jackson Baines Adi is a singer in a band, but through a case of mistaken identity finds himself suspected of terrorism. Transported around the world, questioned and tortured by different intelligence services, to save himself Adi agrees to work undercover for the CIA. Unable to ever go back to his previous life, his world changes forever. Baines is the master of the conspiracy theory and he explores important questions of our time, the way governments deal with the problem of terrorism and the question of human rights. A thrilling, action-packed adventure with an incredible twist at the end.	**Lovosice** By Elzbieta Jabrinska Set in Eastern Europe in the mid 18th century, this is the story of an orphan's battle to survive the horrific experiences of war. Having witnessed the murder of his parents by enemy soldiers, Pavel and his sister escape but his sister later dies. Starving and alone Pavel decides to look for his aunt's family in the city. *Lovosice* describes Pavel's long journey across a war-torn country. Beautifully written with incredible descriptions of the bitter eastern winter and how the cruelty of war is interpreted through the eyes of a child. Moving, heartbreaking but unforgettable.
The Daughters of Altin's By Roma Bazna Set in 1960s Albania, widower Altin is the devoted father of four daughters. Following the death of his wife, Altin is unprepared for raising four girls alone. Despite the financial struggle and the arguments, the strong family bond and his unconditional love for his family shine through. Bazna paints a humorous picture of a rich family life with complex relationships between a grieving father and his children. Share Altin's highs and lows as he watches his daughters grow, find love and eventually experience motherhood. A heart-warming read that is guaranteed to bring a tear to your eye.	**Poison Girl** By Katie G. Elliot Elana Maurice doesn't fit in at school. Her classmates tease her, her busy parents ignore her and she constructs an incredible fantasy world filled with magical creatures and where she has special powers. As she retreats into this world, she loses her sense of what's real and what's imagined. In the end, her visions seem to be of a dark future, a future which ends in terrible catastrophe. This is fantasy writing at its best: imaginative, nightmarish, and at times truly terrifying. Elana may be a child but don't be mistaken, Elliot writes for adults not children.

Role cards

A

A	*Last Rendition*	Really liked characters and the twist at the end.
	Lovosice	Couldn't stand it – far too depressing.
	The Daughters of Altin's	Big fan of Bazna. Liked youngest daughter and the chapter on her wedding.
	Poison Girl	Not fond of this – too far-fetched and a bit childish.

B	*Last Rendition*	Not really into thrillers – too long and too violent.
	Lovosice	Loved it – the intelligence of main character and gentle style of the writer.
	The Daughters of Altin's	Too predictable and sentimental. Altin is a bit of an idiot (but funny).
	Poison Girl	Really scary but great. Loved the creatures and the black ending.

C	*Last Rendition*	Really into this – clever story, lots of action, make a great film?
	Lovosice	Not into it. Pavel was more like an adult than a child. Bad ending.
	The Daughters of Altin's	Not a fan of this kind of book. Slow, boring and clichéd.
	Poison Girl	Wow! Couldn't put it down. Description of Elana's parents' death best bit.

D	*Last Rendition*	Not fond of author or conspiracy theories – plot too complex, too many names.
	Lovosice	Really into historical novels. Child's perspective is original, beautifully written.
	The Daughters of Altin's	Full of humour and can really identify with all the family problems.
	Poison Girl	Put off by the main character being a child. Not a fan of fantasy. Unrealistic.

Vocabulary *plus*: uncountable and plural nouns

Choose the correct alternative in the sentences. If the correct answer is an uncountable noun, follow the black arrow. If the correct answer is a plural noun, follow the white arrow. Which letter do you finish at?

	A	B	C	D	
T	James fell down the *stair/stairs* but he was OK.	The area has such beautiful *scenery/sceneries.*	Before you go hiking, let people know your *whereabout/ whereabouts.*	I like skiing but all the *equipment is/ equipments are* very expensive.	E
S	You need to start wearing *glass/glasses.*	She wore a dress made from beautiful silk *cloth/cloths.*	They used 30 tons of *concrete/concretes* to build that wall.	I love the smell of this *soap/soaps.*	F
R	My mum gave me lots of useful *advice/advices.*	We live on the *outskirt/outskirts* of town.	The subway is a great *mean/means* of transport for getting around the city.	If you ask at reception, they'll be able to give you lots of useful *information/ informations.*	G
Q	The hotel provides free *toiletry/toiletries* for you to use.	**START**		Could you open your bag and show me the *content/contents* please, Sir?	H
P	Do you fancy a game of *card/cards?*	I love going shopping for new *clothe/clothes.*	Can you help me with my *luggage/luggages?*	My university has lots of modern *facility/facilities.*	I
O	The artist has made many sculptures from different types of *wood/woods.*	Hundreds of people visit the *remain/remains* of the ancient temple every summer.	We've just booked some great *accommodation/ accommodations* for our holiday.	It's a lovely place and the *local is/locals are* very friendly.	J
	N	M	L	K	

1 A hobby, sport or interest that takes a lot of **know-how**.

2 A job where it's important to **understand human nature**.

3 An **inventive** person from history.

4 A job where you need to be **cool-headed**.

5 A famous person with **a good sense of humour**.

6 What you need to do in order to be **in great shape**.

7 A job where you need to be **good with your hands**.

8 A game in which you need **a sharp mind** in order to play.

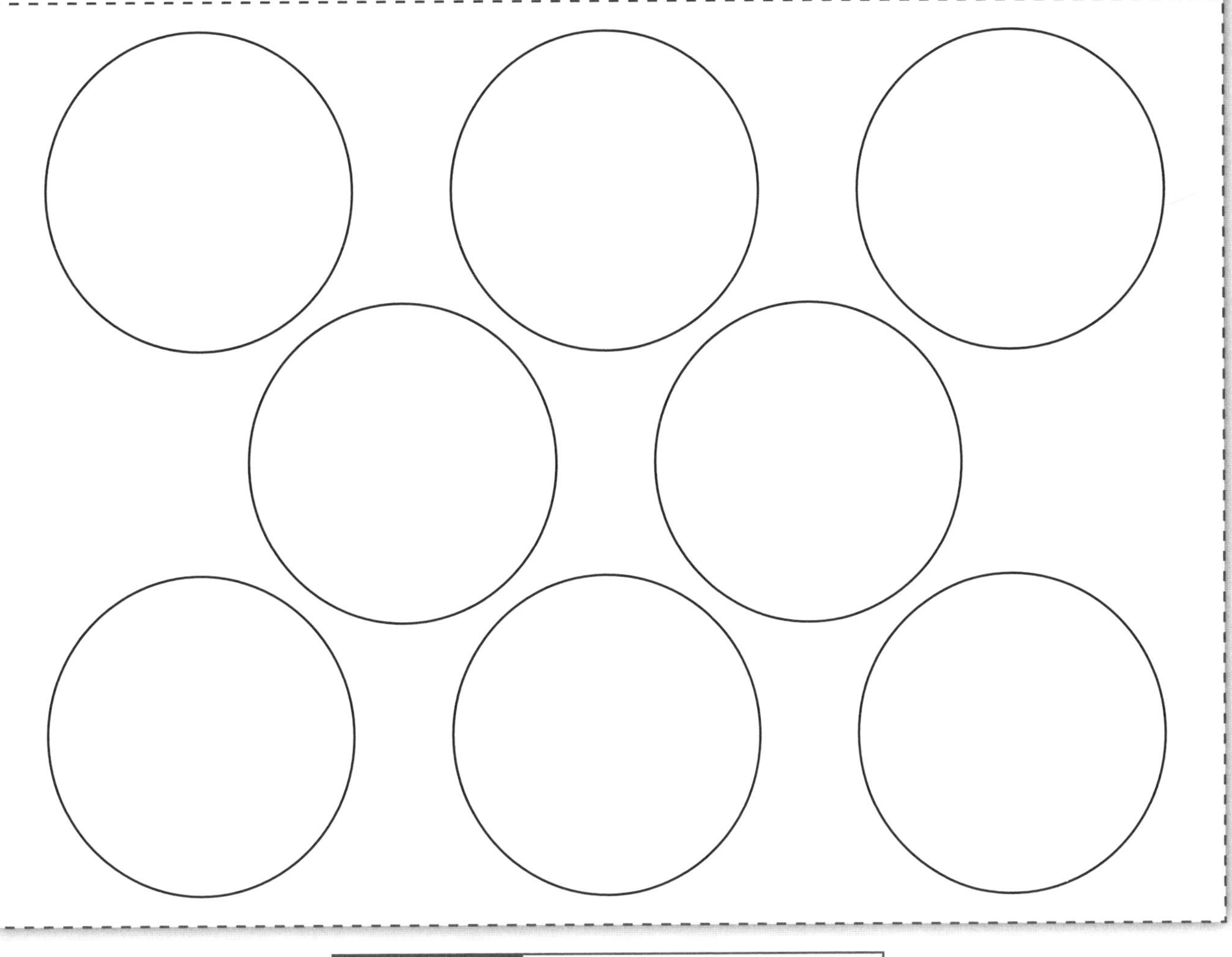

Grammar: present and past habits and future forms

Student A		Answers
1 You're now very old but were a model when you were young.	I ________ appear in fashion magazines. I ________ have grey hair and wrinkles. I ____ never ____ recognised on the street again!	used to/would didn't use to 'll/will, be
2 You moved from Spain to the UK a long time ago.	I ________ eat dinner very late, about 11p.m. I ________ drive on the left. I ____ usually ____ the sun very often.	used to/would didn't use to don't, see
3 You went completely bald when you were young.	I ________ like going to the hairdresser's. I ________ spend a long time doing my hair. I usually ________ a hat.	used to used to/would wear
4 You've recently become a mother/ father for the first time.	I ________ be quite selfish. I ________ buy nappies. I ____ never ____ a full night's sleep again!	used to didn't use to 'll/will, get
Student B		**Answers**
1 You gave up coffee some time ago.	I ________ drink about six cups a day. I ________ sleep well. I ____ always ____ tea instead.	used to/would didn't use to 'm/am, drinking
2 You were a soldier when you were younger.	I ________ wear a uniform all the time. I ________ be very brave. I ____ always ____ letters to my friends and family.	used to/would used to was, writing
3 You've just been banned from driving.	I ________ drive really fast. I ________ have to ask people for lifts. I'm not ________ catching the bus.	used to/would didn't use to used to
4 You've recently got a promotion and are now the boss.	I ________ take orders from people. I ________ have my own office and secretary. I ____ now ____ even harder.	used to/would didn't use to 'm/am, working
Student C		**Answers**
1 You're a famous actress.	I ________ go to lots and lots of auditions. People ________ recognise me. I ________ always surprised by all the attention I get.	used to/would didn't use to 'm/am
2 You've recently got your first job.	I ________ be so lazy and stay in bed until midday. I ________ ask my mum for money all the time. I ____ usually ____ at 6 o'clock.	used to used to/would 'll/will, get/wake up
3 You sold your car and bought a bike.	I ________ drive every day. I ________ spend ages stuck in traffic. I ____ always ____ a shower when I get to work.	used to/would used to/would 'll/will, have/have to have
4 You've recently moved out of the city to a village.	I ________ be woken up by traffic. I ________ hear the birds singing. I ____ generally ____ for country walks at the weekend.	used to/would didn't use to 'll/will, go

1 START
2 Your friend needs a lift to the airport. You're not busy and have a car. What do you say to her?
3 Are you going to go home as soon as the class finishes?
4 Is your country likely to get a new leader in the next twelve months?
5 After you get home, what will you do?
6 What do you think the weather will be like next week?
7 Are you doing anything interesting this weekend?
8 What's the next book you're going to read/film you're going to see?
9 GO BACK 5
10 How many children/grandchildren do you think you'll have?
11 How long are you going to continue to study English?
12 How long is it until the break or the end of the lesson?
13 Are you likely to forget something important soon?
14 Might you live in another country one day?
15 GO BACK 4
16 We're all waiting for your friend. We want you to speak to him and find out where he is. What do you say?
17 When and where are the next Olympic Games?
18 GO FORWARD 3
19 Where's your next holiday going to be?
20 When is the next public holiday?
21 GO BACK 2
22 Are people likely to visit Mars in your lifetime?
23 Your grandma tells you she has lost her glasses. You want to help. What do you say?
24 Are you going to buy anything expensive soon?
25 Do you think you might learn another language?
26 When do you finish your course?
27 GO BACK 3
28 Do you think you'll ever be rich or famous?
29 What are you planning to do this/next summer?
30 The doorbell rings. You offer to answer it. What do you say?
31 Do you think you could become a politician one day?
32 Do you think you'll live for a long time?
33 Are you likely to move home in the next six months?
34 Are you staying in tonight?
35 FINISH

Functional language: describing procedures

You are a group of television executives and you have to invent a new sport or game which will be played on a programme at 7p.m. every Saturday evening. With your group, choose at least four of the items below to be used in the new sport or game. Think about the aim of the game, the way it works and the different stages. What are the key things players need to remember and what's the game called?

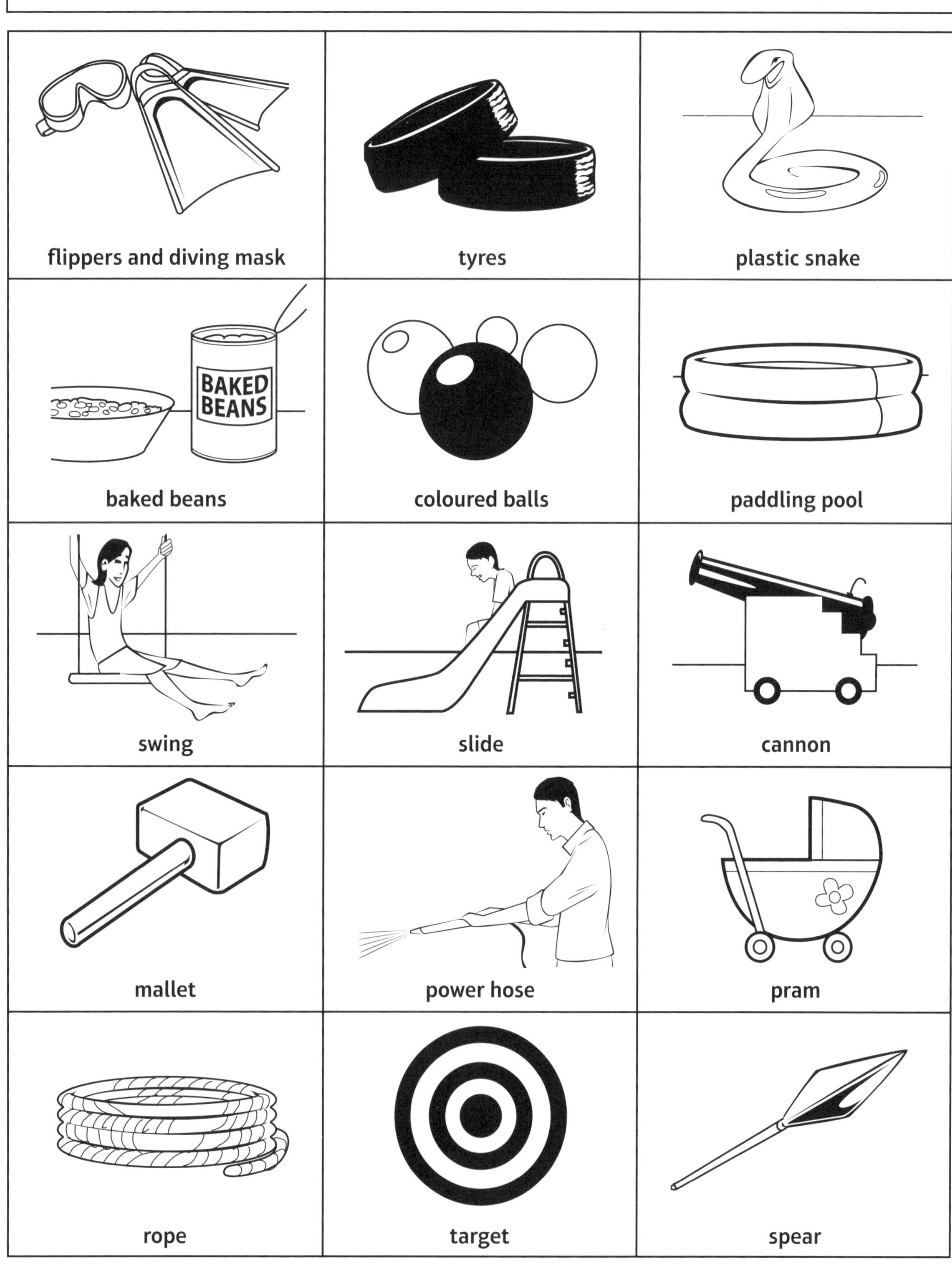

breakthrough	Scientists don't often make ____________s that are this important.	**breakthrough**	The ____________ was made when he was working late in the laboratory one night.
trade-off	There is a ____________ between making the battery bigger and increasing the weight of the product.	**trade-off**	There is a ____________ between the performance of the engine and the need for it to be economical.
breakdown	The engine used in the early model had many ____________s.	**breakdown**	Over 100,000 kilometres, this vehicle had no ____________s.
outcome	The ____________ of the experiment was not possible to guess.	**outcome**	The ____________ of the modifications was an increase in the product's efficiency.
downside	The ____________ of this material is the cost.	**downside**	The biggest ____________ of the product was its reliability.
drawback	The fact it doesn't work underwater is a major ____________.	**drawback**	Even though it had a number of ____________s, the first design was chosen.

Answers

Scientists don't often make **breakthroughs** that are this important.	The **breakthrough** was made when he was working late in the laboratory one night.	The **outcome** of the experiment was not possible to guess.	The **outcome** of the modifications was an increase in the product's efficiency.
There is a **trade-off** between making the battery bigger and increasing the weight of the product.	There is a **trade-off** between the performance of the engine and the need for it to be economical.	The **downside/drawback** of this material is the cost.	The biggest **downside/drawback** of the product was its reliability.
The engine used in the early model had many **breakdowns**.	Over 100,000 kilometres, this vehicle had no **breakdowns**.	The fact it doesn't work underwater is a major **drawback**.	Even though it had a number of **drawbacks**, the first design was chosen.

Vocabulary: advertising collocations

Student A

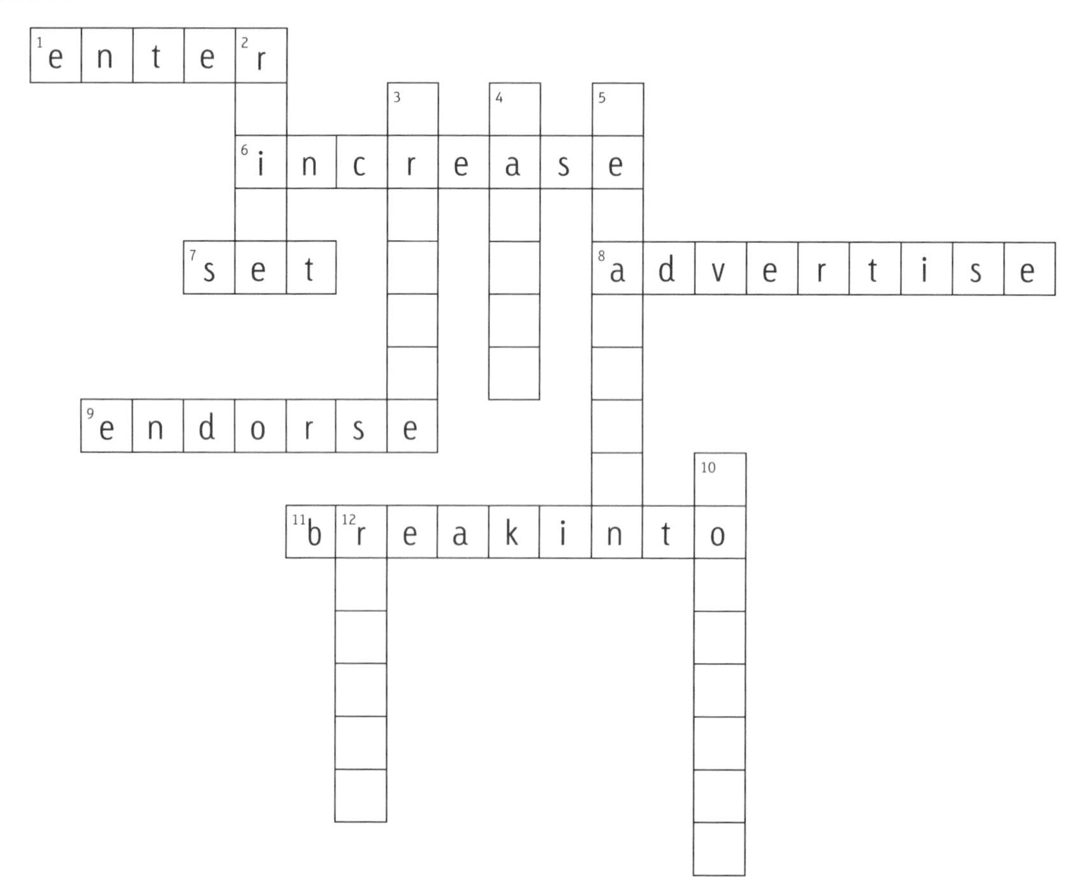

Student B

The Sinclair C5

1	Launched in United Kingdom in 1985, the Sinclair C5 was a battery-assisted tricycle	
2	created by British inventor, Sir Clive Sinclair. The C5 was steered by the handlebar	
3	beneath a driver's knees and powered by a small electric motor making it unnecessary	
4	for the driver to pedal. C5's top speed of twenty-four km/h was the fastest allowed	
5	in the UK without driving licence. The retail price was £399, plus £29 for delivery,	
6	which was expensive for the time. Both media and the public ridiculed the C5 during	
7	1980s and it was a commercial disaster, selling only around 12,000 units. In fact, the	
8	design was an impractical one: from the beginning, there were the serious concerns	
9	about the C5's safety in traffic because it was so low to ground. In addition to this, the	
10	driver was exposed to the wind and the rain and the cold weather tended to shorten	
11	battery life. The lack of gears and seat-to-pedal adjustment and the fact that a motor	
12	overheated on the long hills, were also serious problems. The motor turned out to be	
13	essentially useless for climbing hills, with even the gentle slopes requiring the driver to	
14	pedal. Sinclair spent the millions of pounds on developing the C5 and its failure	
15	bankrupted a company and cost him his reputation. It will long be remembered in the	
16	UK as the spectacular and comic failure, but was Sir Clive's idea just ahead of its time?	

CONDITIONAL DOMINOES

Grammar: real and hypothetical conditionals

I just don't remember it.	If products are endorsed by celebrities,	people are more likely to buy them.	I won't buy sunglasses
unless they are a well-known brand.	If I'm watching something on TV and there is a commercial break,	I change channels.	Provided you take the time to shop around,
you can get good deals these days.	If I see a new product in the shops,	I often try it.	If I go shopping at the weekend,
I might buy something new to wear.	If I buy a new mobile in the next twelve months,	it'll be the same brand of phone as I've got now.	I won't buy another computer for at least a year
as long as my present one doesn't break.	If I need to buy a ticket next week,	I'll do it on the internet.	If luxury goods were cheaper,
people wouldn't want to buy them.	I'd buy a fake watch	if it was a good copy.	If I were to start a business,
I might open a restaurant or sell fast food.	If companies didn't advertise,	we wouldn't buy their products.	If I found out a well-known company used child labour,
I'd stop buying their products.	If there wasn't sponsorship,	a lot of sports couldn't survive.	If an advert isn't funny,

You are a team of advertising executives in the marketing department of a soft drinks company, Swapps. The company is going to expand its portfolio of high-profile brands by launching its first energy drink. The energy drinks sector is very competitive and there is a lot of money at stake, so it is essential that the marketing campaign to launch this new product is dynamic and effective.

Hold a meeting with your colleagues to put together your complete marketing campaign. Discuss the categories below and decide on a strategy for each. Prepare to present your campaign to the board of directors.

1. **Decide on the market.**
   Describe the typical drinker. What are they like? (Think about age, gender, interests, what is important to them.) What do they do for a job and in their free time? Why do they need an energy drink?
2. **Decide on the name.**
   Suggestions for the name include: Tiger Teeth, Sharp, Kick, Hyper, Shark Bite, Black Wolf, Blue Monkey and Craze, but maybe you have better ideas?
3. **Decide on the slogan.**
   It needs to be something short and catchy.
4. **Decide on the packaging.**
   What should the can look like? What are the colours and what's the logo?
5. **Decide on how to spend the budget.**
   You have a budget of €30m. Decide how you're going to spend the money.
6. **Decide on the adverts.**
   What happens in the TV and cinema ads? What are the printed ads going to show?

Type of advert	Cost	
Prime-time TV ads on six major channels (two weeks)	$20m	Which channels?
Whole page ads in ten magazines (three months)	$5m	What kind of magazines?
Ads in all national cinemas (two months)	$10m	
Whole page ads in five national newspapers (one month)	$5m	Which newspapers?
Viral advertising (three months)	$2.5m	Which sites?
Sponsor six major sporting events	$5m	Which events?
Sponsor six other major events	$5m	Which events?
Billboards in the ten largest cities (three months and across the whole city)	$2.5m	
Free samples to public in the ten largest cities (50,000 cans over three months)	$2.5m	Which places – in the street, bars, clubs, etc.?
Celebrity endorsement (two-year contract)	$5m	Who is it?

Tell the group about …

1 a famous person that looks young for ____________.

2 a famous person that is in ____________.

3 a classmate who needs to act ____________.

4 when you came ____________.

5 whether you think teenage boys are more ____________ than teenage girls.

6 at what age you think you had the ____________ to make your own decisions.

7 why it is important to care for the ____________.

8 whether you believe there is age ____________ in the modelling industry.

9 what you see as the dangers of age ____________.

10 what government services are available for the ____________ in your country.

11 a famous person that acts old for ____________.

12 at what age you believe you will be in ____________.

13 a time you haven't acted ____________.

14 when people in your country usually come ____________.

15 whether you think women are more ____________ than men.

16 at what age you believe your father had the ____________ to make his own decisions.

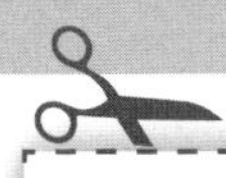

Student A

You work in a large office and you have found out that your boss, Student B, is leaving for another job abroad. You've also heard that your colleague, Marco, has been promoted and is going to replace Student B. You are really unhappy as nobody likes Marco and everyone loved working for Student B. You meet Student B at the coffee machine and have a chat.

Start: Hi. Congratulations on the new job. You must be really excited about it.

a Well, it's hard to **look on the bright** side when your new boss is going to be Marco. Anyway, you never liked him.

b No. Anyway, I guess we'll just have to do the best we can.

c Disappointed!? He told me he was **filled with despair**. The company only made Marco boss to save money. They know nobody likes him and loads of people will quit.

d Wow, that sounds promising! When can I start?

e Yes, we've all had our **ups and downs**. What were the company thinking when they appointed him? I'm really not looking forward to working for him.

f Yes, I'd **look on the bright side** if I were you. You know it's going to be absolutely terrible here without you.

Student B

You are the boss of a large office but you are leaving this job to work for a bigger company in Spain. You have also heard that your colleague, Marco, has been promoted and is going to replace you. Everyone is really unhappy as nobody likes him and everyone loved working for you. You meet your colleague, Student A, at the coffee machine and have a chat.

g Come on, don't be so sad. Try to look at the positives of having a new boss.

Finish: Anyway, must dash. I've got a desk to tidy out! See you later.

h You're not alone. I think all your colleagues **have mixed feelings** about it, too. Jack said he was disappointed about the decision.

i Yes, I'm really **looking forward to** working in Spain and some new challenges. I'm really positive about the future.

j That's better, you're sounding a bit more **upbeat** now. If you're interested, I may be able to get you a job with me.

k I wouldn't say that, I have **mixed feelings** about him but he's good at his job. Sure, we've had a few problems over the years.

l I'm not sure that's true, but it's difficult not to be **filled with despair**. Anyway, whatever the reasons are, a decision like this is not progress or good for the company.

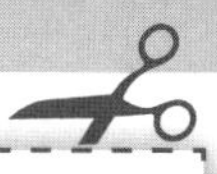

Gyrkyzstan

Beautiful, isolated Himalayan republic. Very difficult to reach but vast unspoilt mountain landscape.

Last year there was a lot of snow. Not possible for planes to take off or leave for one month!

Wealthy Russian holiday-makers have started going there. Visit it before it changes to just another ski resort!

Things to do

Summer: trekking, mountaineering, rafting, bungee-jumping, hunting

Winter: some winter sports like skiing – facilities not great

Things to know

No food or drink allowed into the country.

Alcohol is banned in most places.

No visa needed but $50 exit tax.

Very important to get travel insurance and special insurance for winter sports.

Good idea to take/hire camping equipment.

Travel

Flights are expensive. No direct flights. Change in Moscow or Tashkent.

Public transport poor.

Hire a minibus and driver (quite cheap).

Djamenia

Small newly-independent state in sub-Saharan Africa. It has both desert and rainforest.

Was dangerous and politically unstable but now much better. Government killed thousands of rebels.

Oil has been discovered there, so it's about to change and possibly suffer environmental damage. Visit it now!

Things to do

Desert: camel riding, camel trip across the desert, visit ruined cities

Jungle: gorillas, amazing waterfalls, great wildlife

Things to know

Good idea to take gifts from home to give to people, e.g. pens.

No visa needed. No airport tax.

Get all vaccinations!

Get used to people looking at you and following you – especially kids.

Travel

Fly to Nigeria or Algeria and then get a flight from there.

Local buses OK but be patient! Very slow!

Your guides and drivers will be armed (heavily)!

In the past not safe to travel – still a bit dangerous.

The McKenzie Islands

The smallest nation on earth – a group of about twenty coral islands 1,500 km west of Hawaii.

Rising sea-levels threaten the islands' existence. Last year inhabitants of the fourth largest island were forced to abandon it. Visit this island paradise before it disappears under the waves!

Things to do

Beaches: sunbathing, swimming, relaxing in paradise

Sea: diving, snorkelling, sailing, fishing, incredible surfing

Things to know

Need a tourist visa. Apply through Australian embassy.

Get your diving licence somewhere else. Very expensive!

Learn some of the local language – the locals will love you for it!

Possibly the friendliest people in the world.

Most accommodation is basic beach huts.

Travel

Costs a fortune to get there. Flights from Hawaii, Jakarta and Auckland (not scheduled).

Boats between islands are cheap.

Possible to walk everywhere – taxi if you're feeling lazy!

Kirlian Island

A 1,500 km^2 rock in the Southern Ocean. The windiest place on the planet but with a spectacular volcano.

Once only inhabited by a few scientists and fishermen and hundreds of thousands of penguins.

The island has started servicing cruise ships and is starting to lose its character. Get there before it does!

Things to do

Volcano: crater and lava fields, trekking, spectacular cliffs, rock climbing, bathe in hot springs

Wildlife: penguin and seal colonies

Things to know

Better in summer – long, cold and dark winters.

Bring own food (though can buy some things – very expensive).

Little accommodation and basic. Book in advance.

Electricity only a few hours a day.

Take camping equipment and outdoor gear.

Travel

Ships from Australia take seven days and cheap.

Some flights from Australia and Seychelles (not scheduled and very expensive).

Trips to Antarctica are available by boat and plane.

	Futurologist predictions and questions:	**Your answer/opinion:**
1	All the world's governments will have passed laws to limit the global population by 2030.	
2	You'll be driving an electric car or one that uses an alternative source of fuel by 2025.	
3	There will be tigers and pandas in zoos but they will have become extinct in the wild.	
4	'Space tourists' will be taking trips on special planes out of the earth's atmosphere in the next ten years.	
5	China will have become the world's number one superpower within the next twenty years.	
6	We'll be just as obsessed with money but we'll be living in a completely 'cashless' society within ten years.	
7	The world's fastest athlete will have run 100 metres in under nine seconds by 2025.	
8	In fifty years, the older generation will be playing more computer games than the younger generation.	
9	Space exploration will continue but when will life on other planets have been conclusively proven?	
10	We'll all be watching holographic TV and cinema and reading electronic books before the end of the decade.	
11	Europe will have become completely unified by 2030.	
12	We'll be designing and personalising our own products on our home computers within the next ten years.	
13	Completely different varieties of English will have developed by 2050.	
14	People will commonly be living to 120 by the end of the 2020s.	
15	The sale of unhealthy fast food will have been banned in most countries by the mid 2020s.	
16	More people will be speaking Spanish than English in the USA in thirty years' time.	
17	Climate change will continue but when will the polar ices caps have completed melted?	
18	We'll be choosing the sex and physical characteristics of our babies before they are born by 2080.	
19	Your Prediction 1:	
20	Your Prediction 2:	

Tick two topics you would like to discuss from the list below.

This class believes that …

- a family with two parents is the best environment to bring up children.
- there is a lack of positive role-models for young people these days.
- governments need to censor the internet to protect their citizens.
- protecting culture and traditions from globalisation is not important.
- it's not the government's responsibility to look after sick and poor people.
- celebrity culture is harmless fun.
- money should be spent on protecting people rather than endangered species.
- your school days are the best days of your life.
- cosmetic surgery is only justifiable in extreme cases.
- marriage can't be forever in a modern society.
- art is an expensive waste of money.
- modern technology doesn't make our lives better.
- ______________________________ (your suggestion)

Arguments for

Arguments against

wildlife programme	**reality show**	**costume drama**	**soap opera**
• animals • nature • environment	• ordinary people • famous • competition	• past • clothes • story	• continue • story • week
sketch show	**sitcom**	**documentary**	**docudrama**
• laugh • funny • comedy	• comedy • laugh • Big Bang	• serious • real life • investigate	• real life • people • work
series	**serial**	**thriller**	**detective series**
• every • episode • programme	• episode • story • character	• exciting • action • adventure	• police • crime • investigate
game show	**quiz**	**current affairs programme**	**news**
• prize • money • win	• questions • prize • guests	• events • reports • investigate	• reporter • events • reports

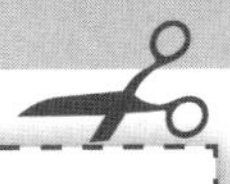

Student A

turn out	take back
bring out	put up
come across	come across
bring out	take back

I can't stand living in this city any longer.
You can't **put up with** living in this city any longer.

I found by chance some delicious English apples in the supermarket yesterday.
You **came across** some delicious English apples in the supermarket yesterday.

I am not a bad-tempered person but she makes me show the worst side of my personality.
You're not a bad-tempered person but she **brings out** the worst in you.

When you meet her, you get the impression that she is a shy person.
When you meet her, she **comes across** as shy.

I am so upset. I really wish I hadn't said that!
You should **take back** what you said.

I was really worried but in the end what happened was OK.
You were really worried but in the end, it/everything **turned out** OK.

The company is launching its new smartphone next year.
The company is **bringing out** its new smartphone next year.

This song reminds me of being a teenager again.
This song **takes you back** to being a teenager (again).

Student B

turn out	take back
bring out	put up with
come across	come across
bring out	take back

When you meet him, you get the impression that he is an outgoing person.
When you meet him, he **comes across** as outgoing.

I found by chance this beautiful antique watch in a market at the weekend.
I **came across** this beautiful antique watch in a market at the weekend.

This pie reminds me of being a student again.
This pie **takes you back** to being a student (again).

My child is not naughty but her friends are a bad influence on her.
Your child is not naughty but her friends **bring out** the worst in her.

I feel regret and didn't mean what I said.
You should **take back** what you said.

The company are introducing their latest computer onto the market tomorrow.
The company are **bringing out** their latest computer tomorrow.

He wants to stay at my house for a couple of days.
He wants you to **put him up** for a couple of days.

Thousands of fans attended in order to welcome their team home from the World Cup.
Thousands of fans **turned out** to welcome their team home from the World Cup.

GAME 1	GAME 2	GAME 3	GAME 4	GAME 5	GAME 6
1 a few	1 every	1 each	1 several	1 a few	1 both
2 hardly any	2 neither	2 a few	2 a great deal of	2 every	2 quite a lot of
3 none	3 a little	3 plenty of	3 hardly any	3 neither	3 lots of
4 a great deal of	4 few	4 quite a lot of	4 a little	4 quite a few	4 few
5 all	5 quite a few	5 little	5 all	5 little	5 both
6 several	6 lots of	6 both	6 none	6 plenty of	6 a little
Topics Advice Friends The media The news Information Population	**Topics** Weather Nature Time Towns/Cities Accommodation Families	**Topics** Government Information People Clothes Food The police	**Topics** Advice Population Money Health Politics Weather	**Topics** The news Equipment Habits Food People Transport	**Topics** Scenery Children Clothes Time Accommodation Nature

Student A
Record company Executive Assistant

You are an assistant for a record company executive at AGM Records. AWOL is your most important band but its lead singer, Vinnie, recently disappeared moments before the start of the first concert of their world tour.

The company has no idea where he is. The tour has been cancelled and your boss is absolutely furious and really anxious to know the situation, especially when the band can resume the tour.

Your boss has sent you to have a meeting with the band manager. You've made notes on the things your boss has said and wants to find out. You are going to report these to the band manager and find out some answers.

Try and sort out the situation so both sides are happy.

Your boss said:

'The cancelled tour will cost $25m and might bankrupt the company.'

'The tour absolutely must go ahead.'

'When is AWOL going to resume the tour?'

'Is it possible for the guitarist to sing instead? He told me yesterday he would.'

'We'll sue the band and terminate its contract at the end of the year if they don't tour.'

'Can I see Vinnie in person or can he phone me immediately?'

'Why didn't he speak to the manager or the band if he had a problem about something?'

'What's Vinnie's mental state? Is he going to kill himself?'

Student B
AWOL's Manager

You are the manager of a famous band called AWOL. The lead singer, Vinnie, recently disappeared moments before the start of the first concert of their world tour. The tour has been cancelled and the record company are absolutely furious. The band is also upset about Vinnie's behaviour and you are worried about his mental state. You also know that if the band split up you lose your job.

You spoke to Vinnie yesterday and made some notes on what he said. You now have a meeting with the assistant of the record company boss to report what Vinnie said.

Try and sort out the situation so both sides are happy.

Vinnie said:

'I don't want to leave the band – I love the guys.'

'I don't want to do the tour now – maybe in the summer.'

'I split up with my girlfriend of two years just before the concert. I couldn't face doing the show.'

'I told the band I wasn't doing the show.'

'I'm addicted to the prescription drugs I was taking for my stage fright and need some time in rehab.'

'I want to be left alone and not see anyone until next week.'

'I'm not suicidal.' (but he does seem very depressed)

'Can I get $10,000? I've spent all my money.'

'Can we remix the album? It could be so much better.'

Sherpa's cleaning up rubbish left by climbers on Mount Everest have found the camera of George Mallory, a British climber who died on the mountain in 1924. Mountaineering's biggest unsolved mystery is whether he and his partner, Andrew Irving, were the first to reach the peak. Both died on the descent. Mallory's body was found in 1999 but not his camera. The perfectly preserved film seems to show the pair at the summit twenty-nine years earlier than the successful 1953 expedition.

Black's news agency

One of Italy's most famous monuments, the Leaning Tower of Pisa, has collapsed. The fifty-five-metre-tall tower had been leaning since its construction in 1173. It was reopened in 2001 after two decades of work and was declared 'stable' for another 300 years. There are reports of the ground shaking before it collapsed and some are blaming a minor earthquake. Some tourists caught the collapse on their mobiles and cameras. A spokesperson for the monument said it would be rebuilt, leaning!

SANA's news agency

A giant anaconda, over twenty metres long, has been shot in the Democratic Republic of Congo. Villagers had reported a giant snake in the river and complained it had been eating their cattle. This was ignored by the local police until they encountered it whilst looking for a missing child. It was shot and opened up but the remains of the child were not found in the stomach. She was found alive and well at a relative's house. The previous largest reliable measurement of an anaconda was about nine metres in length.

Black's news agency

Scientists have grown a baby mammoth using DNA found in a frozen mammoth in Siberia. Finding completely frozen mammoths is not unusual but the DNA is usually unuseable. However, three years ago, scientists found usable mammoth DNA in a well-preserved specimen. It was implanted into unfertilised Asian Elephant eggs, fertilised and implanted into a female. The mammoth, a male, was born two days ago, but died today. The last mammoth to die before this was 4000 years ago.

Glock's news agency

American astronomers have discovered that an asteroid, 5 km in diameter, may collide with the Earth in 2028. Previously, the next big asteroid impact was expected in March 2788. It will be equivalent to ten million megatons of TNT and leave a crater ninety-five kilometres across. For comparison, the largest nuclear weapon was just fifty megatons. Scientists hope that technology will be available to destroy the asteroid before it reaches Earth and we can avoid the greatest catastrophe in modern times.

USN's news agency

Tattoist Jed Michaels has had his whole face tattooed purple, including his ears and eyelids. Jed said he loved his new colour but having his eyelids tattoed was quite painful. Asked why he did it, he just said he liked the colour and thought it suited him. Jed has been getting tattoes done since he was fourteen. Asked if he might regret it, he said he has regretted some, his worse one is Mickey Mouse playing drums on his leg but he thinks the best one is now his face.

USN's news agency

Vocabulary: collocations: decisions

You are a strict vegetarian and have been invited to your partner's parents' home for the first time. You are having dinner and you discover just before you start eating the vegetable soup that it has meat in it. Do you **follow your principles** and explain you can't eat it or say nothing?

You are an unemployed actor and a man selling pirate DVDs comes to your restaurant table and offers you some recent films. You know that your money will help criminal gangs and won't help the film industry but you want to see the films. Do you **betray your principles** and buy them?

You are a police officer and you stop a motorist driving very fast, fast enough for him/her to lose his/her licence for a year. The motorist is a top politician and he/she offers you $2,000 to let him/her drive away without punishment. Do you **stick to your principles** and not take the bribe?

You know your son has been involved in a bank robbery. The police are looking for the robbers. If you tell the police, your son may never speak to you again but if you don't, you could also be in trouble. It's a big dilemma. What **decision** do you **arrive at**?

You've been offered a job in a distant foreign country for three years. You don't like the country, the climate, the people or the food but you will get double your present salary. After **evaluating the situation** what do you decide to do?

Your rich boy/girlfriend wants to marry you. If you do this, you would never worry about money again and would have a very comfortable life. However, you don't really love him/her. Will you **follow your principles**? What's your decision?

You've been trying to sell your house for six months and need to sell it within one week or your dream of emigrating to Australia won't happen. You have a cash offer but for twenty-five percent less than your price. Do you **postpone the decision** to sell to this buyer or accept the offer?

You've just crashed your partner's new car. When you see him/her, he/she is in a really bad mood and you can't tell him/her but if you don't tell him/her soon it could make things worse. You must **reach a decision** about when to tell him/her. What do you do?

You made a big mistake at work which cost your company $10,000. Your boss blames your colleague and he/she will lose his/her job if you don't say something. If you say nothing, there is no way they could ever find out it was your mistake. After **evaluating the situation** carefully, what do you decide?

TRUTH	**TRUTH**	**LIE**
TRUTH	**TRUTH**	**LIE**
TRUTH	**TRUTH**	**LIE**

unhelpful	supportive	diplomatic
tactful	sensitive	sensible
confrontational	collaborative	aggressive
assertive	direct	focused

CONDITIONAL FOX AND HOUNDS

Grammar: past and mixed conditionals

1 Your son has been suspended from school for two weeks for bad behaviour.

You **consider** __________ **(send)** him to a private school. **(5)**

Tell him he **had better** __________ **(improve)** his behaviour. **(9)**

2 Your son says it was the worst experience of his life and **will never** __________ **(forgive)** you. He goes back to his old school unhappier than he was before. **(1)**

3 Choose a hobby:

__________ **(play)** guitar might be a nice idea for him. Buy him an electric guitar and pay for lessons. **(6)**

__________ **(attend)** art classes. He was quite good at drawing when he was younger. **(14)**

4 He goes back to his old school but it's time to try something different.

Arrange for him __________ **(see)** a psychologist. **(17)**

Try and get him **interested in** __________ **(do)** something new, help him find a hobby perhaps? **(3)**

5 **Despite you not** __________ **(be)** able to afford it, he spends the next three months studying at private school. However, he **doesn't enjoy** __________ **(travel)** three hours a day.

You pay for another year of school and hope he gets used to the travelling. **(7)**

You send him to a boarding school instead. **(8)**

6 This is a disaster. He never **wants** __________ **(play)** his guitar and he's rude to his guitar teacher.

You think **it's better** __________ **(sell)** the guitar and use the money for something else. Perhaps buying a set of golf clubs? **(12)**

Send him to art classes. **(14)**

7 Success! He seems to be doing better at school and his teachers see an improvement in his behaviour.

You **intend** __________ **(continue)** sending him to this school. **(11)**

You send him back to his old (local) school now his behaviour is better. You can also save money! **(4)**

8 OK, there isn't any travelling but he really hates boarding school and becomes really quiet and withdrawn.

You **would rather** see him __________ **(behave)** badly than be so depressed. You send him back to his old private school. **(11)**

You **expect him** __________ **(get)** used to it. **(10)**

9 It doesn't improve and he gets expelled from school. No other state school is **prepared** __________ **(take)** him.

You send him to a private day school far away from your home. **(5)**

You send him to a boarding school so he **doesn't have to** __________ **(travel)**. **(8)**

10 He doesn't and runs away. The police find him one week later. This was terrible, you were really worried and **promise not** __________ **(send)** him away again. He goes back to his first school. **(4)**

11 Unfortunately, you lose your job and you really **can't afford** __________ **(spend)** money on private education. Send him back to his old school. **(4)**

12 He's really **good at** __________ **(play)** golf and as you **used** __________ **(play)** too you can spend time with him. You buy him expensive clubs and private lessons.

You don't want to spoil him so you send him to a US camp for problem kids for one month. **(18)**

You send him to a golf camp in the US resort and hope he behaves himself. **(20)**

13 **Try** __________ **(get)** him interested in culture and take him to museums, galleries and the theatre. **(15)**

Do some sport together. Try golf, you play and you never know he **might** __________ **(like)** it. **(12)**

14 He really **likes** __________ **(paint)** and **enjoys** __________ **(be able to)** express himself. He also makes some new friends in the class.

You send him on a two-week painting course in the summer holidays. **(16)**

You don't approve of his new friends and think he should try something else but this time with his family. **(13)**

15 He's not interested and spends most of the time **complaining about** __________ **(be)** bored and talking on his mobile phone.

Either go back to **(13)**

or, try a camp in US for badly behaved children __________ **(make)** him realise how lucky he is and hopefully change him. **(18)**

16 While on the course, he was arrested by the police for graffiting. You **had to** __________ **(pay)** a fine and you think it's time he did things with his family so you can keep an eye on him. **(13)**

17 The psychologist thinks there is not so much wrong with your son. She **suggests** __________ **(do)** a couple of things.

Painting and you send him to art classes. **(14)**

Spending more time __________ **(do)** things together as a family. **(13)**

18 The summer camp **is like** __________ **(be)** in the military and is very strict. Your son phones you every day pleading to come home.

Let him come home. **(2)**

Make him __________ (stay) until the end. **(19)**

19 Bad decision. He gets really angry and is **accused of** __________ **(attack)** one of the organisers. He spends two months in a prison for young offenders in the USA. You send him back to his old school when he gets back. **(1)**

20 Trusting your son was a good move. He didn't get into trouble. He **continues** __________ **(play)** golf and **ends up** __________ **(play)** in tournaments and being quite successful. He has a focus and is more motivated to study. You have a happy son again!

THE END

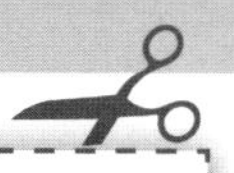

Complaining students

You are studying English for six months at the International Oxford City School of English. You have spent a lot of money to study in an English speaking country and although your English has been improving, there have been some problems with the school. You and a couple of other students are going to see the Director and his/her assistant to discuss these. Even though you are very frustrated, you need to be diplomatic when trying to find a satisfactory solution. You've made a list of your main points.

- Teachers are often late in the morning – this is unprofessional and a bad example for students.
- Some teachers don't seem very motivated (the late ones!). They don't seem to care.
- There are too many students of one nationality in some classes and they naturally speak their first language not English.
- Classes are sometimes cancelled and the lesson is not rescheduled or the fees refunded.
- There are only a few computers for students to use and the internet is very slow.
- The food in the canteen is expensive and not fresh. The sandwiches have hard bread and the coffee is terrible.
- The canteen is always full, so students have to eat in the classrooms, which isn't allowed.
- The library is too small.

Director and Assistant Director

You are in charge of the International Oxford City School of English, a language school in the centre of a busy city. Your school has a good reputation and is very busy but this has caused you problems.
You can't find enough good teachers and the facilities are now inadequate. Some unhappy students have decided to come and see you to discuss the situation but there are some things which the students need to be reminded about, diplomatically! Do your best to keep the students happy and find a solution. You've made a list of your main points.

- Students have been using the computers in the classroom (for teachers), this isn't allowed and teachers have complained.
- Students are often late in the morning, too. The buses are unreliable and both the teachers and the students use them.
- Students are eating food in the classrooms and teachers and students have been complaining about this.
- There is a problem with some of the teachers. Some don't phone to say they are not coming in or just don't turn up. It's a nightmare!
- Good teachers are hard to find but some teachers are fed up with students not switching off their mobile phones, arriving late and speaking in their first language.
- Students leave bags on chairs in the library or use it to go to sleep.
- There are plans to replace all the student computers and add four more.
- You are thinking about getting a new company to provide the food in the canteen.
- There are plans to have no more than fifty percent of students speaking the same first language in a class. This will take time to introduce.

You are guilty of **arson**. You set fire to your neighbour's car. Nobody was injured, but why did you do it?

You are guilty of **kidnapping**. You kidnapped the wife of a wealthy man. You asked for $5m ransom. Why did you do it?

You are guilty of **bribery**. You tried to bribe a planning officer $20,000 to let you build a modern extension to your home in the old part of the city.

You are guilty of **stalking**. You stalked a famous actor for two years. You sent over 500 letters in this time and the police found you in the actor's garden.

You are guilty of **vandalism**. You have sprayed graffiti on over eighty trains. The cost of cleaning them has been $50,000.

You are guilty of **identity theft**. You stole the identity of four people to get bank loans and credit cards. You spent $150,000.

You are a **mugger**. You have been found guilty of mugging fifteen people. You stole their wallets and mobiles at knifepoint but didn't physically hurt anyone.

You are guilty of **counterfeiting**. You have a factory which makes copies of designer handbags. You employ 40 people and made $500,000.

You are guilty of **shoplifting**. You were caught after you stole three pairs of jeans and a T-shirt from a high street clothes store.

You are guilty of **hacking**. You entered military sites, which contained highly confidential and extremely sensitive information. Why did you do it?

Game one

1 I helped her with her bags and she said 'Thank you'.	**2** He said he was sorry he upset her.	**3** It was the driver's fault. He caused the accident. **(P)**
4 The police think I stole the paintings. **(P)**	**5** She said I was wrong to not wear a seatbelt.	**6** I want to be a world famous chef.
7 The court decided he didn't murder his colleague. **(P)**	**8** He was not allowed to drive for a year. **(P)**	**9** The residents stopped the trees from being cut down.

blame clear ban criticise suspect thank dream save apologise

Game two

1 It's your fault we're lost.	**2** He was found not guilty of offering a bribe to a police officer. **(P)**	**3** The court said he can't own a dog for five years. **(P)**
4 I lent him my laptop. He really appreciated this.	**5** She thinks I lied to her.	**6** The charity rescued the building. It was going to be demolished. **(P)**
7 I'm sorry if I offended you.	**8** She told me I was a bad driver and drove too fast. **(P)**	**9** She wishes she lived in France.

thank criticise save apologise suspect dream clear ban blame

Game three

1 Sorry. I was wrong about your mother.	**2** I think you took my phone.	**3** The dogs were going to attack but the farmer saved me.
4 You are the reason we are late.	**5** I raised lots of money for a charity. They were very grateful.	**6** He said it was a big mistake for me to sell the land at this time.
7 What she'd really like to do one day is start her own business.	**8** He's now free. The judge said he didn't start the fire.	**9** He mustn't leave the country or go near a football stadium. **(P)**

clear ban thank blame criticise suspect rescue apologise dream

Answers

Game one

1. She thanked me for helping her with her bags.
2. He apologised for upsetting her.
3. The driver was blamed for causing the accident.
4. I am suspected of stealing the paintings.
5. She criticised me for not wearing a seatbelt.
6. I dream of being a world famous chef.
7. He was cleared of murdering his colleague.
8. He was banned from driving for a year.
9. The residents saved the trees from being cut down.

Game two

1. I blame you for us being lost.
2. He was cleared of offering a bribe to a police officer.
3. He is banned from owning a dog for five years.
4. He thanked me for lending him my laptop.
5. She suspects me of lying to her.
6. The building was saved from being demolished (by a charity).
7. I apologise for offending you.
8. I was criticised for being a bad driver and driving too fast.
9. She dreams of living in France.

Game three

1. I apologise for being wrong about your mother.
2. I suspect you of taking my phone.
3. The farmer rescued me from being attacked by the dogs.
4. I blame you for us being late.
5. The charity thanked me for raising lots of money.
6. He criticised me for selling the land at this time.
7. She often dreams of starting her own business.
8. He's now free. The judge cleared him of starting the fire.
9. He is banned from leaving the country or going near a football stadium.

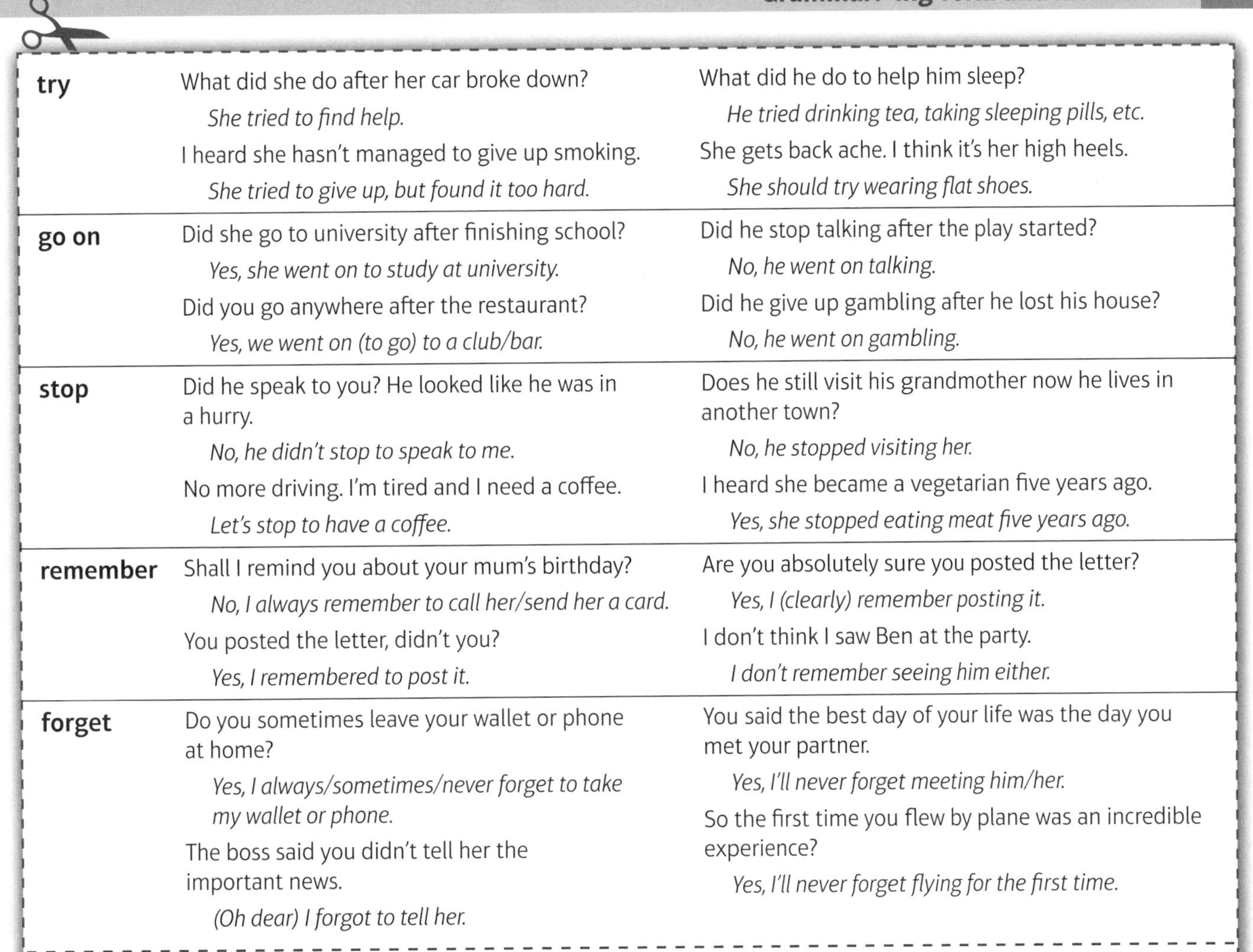

try	What did she do after her car broke down? *She tried to find help.* I heard she hasn't managed to give up smoking. *She tried to give up, but found it too hard.*	What did he do to help him sleep? *He tried drinking tea, taking sleeping pills, etc.* She gets back ache. I think it's her high heels. *She should try wearing flat shoes.*
go on	Did she go to university after finishing school? *Yes, she went on to study at university.* Did you go anywhere after the restaurant? *Yes, we went on (to go) to a club/bar.*	Did he stop talking after the play started? *No, he went on talking.* Did he give up gambling after he lost his house? *No, he went on gambling.*
stop	Did he speak to you? He looked like he was in a hurry. *No, he didn't stop to speak to me.* No more driving. I'm tired and I need a coffee. *Let's stop to have a coffee.*	Does he still visit his grandmother now he lives in another town? *No, he stopped visiting her.* I heard she became a vegetarian five years ago. *Yes, she stopped eating meat five years ago.*
remember	Shall I remind you about your mum's birthday? *No, I always remember to call her/send her a card.* You posted the letter, didn't you? *Yes, I remembered to post it.*	Are you absolutely sure you posted the letter? *Yes, I (clearly) remember posting it.* I don't think I saw Ben at the party. *I don't remember seeing him either.*
forget	Do you sometimes leave your wallet or phone at home? *Yes, I always/sometimes/never forget to take my wallet or phone.* The boss said you didn't tell her the important news. *(Oh dear) I forgot to tell her.*	You said the best day of your life was the day you met your partner. *Yes, I'll never forget meeting him/her.* So the first time you flew by plane was an incredible experience? *Yes, I'll never forget flying for the first time.*

Bingo card one

forget	try
remember	stop
go on	forget
stop	go on
try	remember

Bingo card two

go on	go on
remember	forget
stop	try
try	remember
forget	stop

DEDUCTION BLOCKS

Grammar: modals of deduction

❶	❷	❸	❹	❺	❻
□	□□	□ □□	□ □□□	□□ □□□	□□ □□□□
must + *have* + pp	*could* + *have* + pp	*might* + *have* + pp	*couldn't* + *have* + pp	*can't* + *have* + pp	any modal + *have* + pp
You hear a loud cheer from the local stadium.	Your parents are coming to see your new house but they are late.	You come across a friend you've not seen for two years. He looks really thin.	A motorist pulls out in front of you and you crash into him.	You've eaten some chicken and now two hours later you feel really ill.	You see a man with his leg in plaster.
Your flatmate doesn't seem to be at home.	You see a couple with shopping bags running down the street.	You dog was in your garden this morning but now it isn't there.	A competitor completed a marathon running backwards dressed as a frog.	The match was cancelled but Greg still went to the stadium.	Your teenage son is looking really guilty.
Your neighbour has just bought a really expensive new car. He's usually broke.	You see your neighbour for the first time in a month. She looks tanned and relaxed.	You're a teacher and your worst student has given you some excellent homework.	You are a building inspector and the quality of the work in this building is terrible.	I shouted 'turn right' but he didn't, he went straight on.	You see an old man wearing lots of medals.
You see lots of people leaving the cinema crying.	Your colleague has just arrived for work out of breath.	Your neighbour's curtains are closed all day and you can't hear any noise from her house.	You're a teacher and your best student has just got terrible marks in the exam.	A motorist crashed his car. The road was empty at the time.	You see your teenage daughter looking really sad.
You meet a woman who tells you she got married in a castle.	There was a fire in your house while you were at work.	Your partner usually gets home at 6.30p.m. You hear him/her arrive at 6.00p.m.	There's a guest at the restaurant shouting angrily at the waiter.	The person in front of you at the cash point hits the wall angrily. The machine has just kept his card.	You notice the screen of your mobile is cracked.

Student A

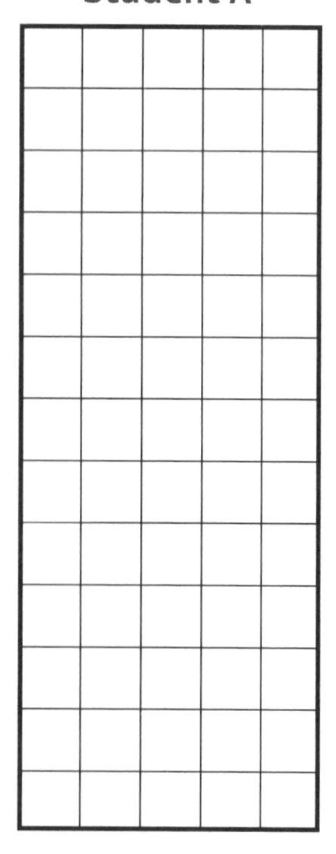

Student B

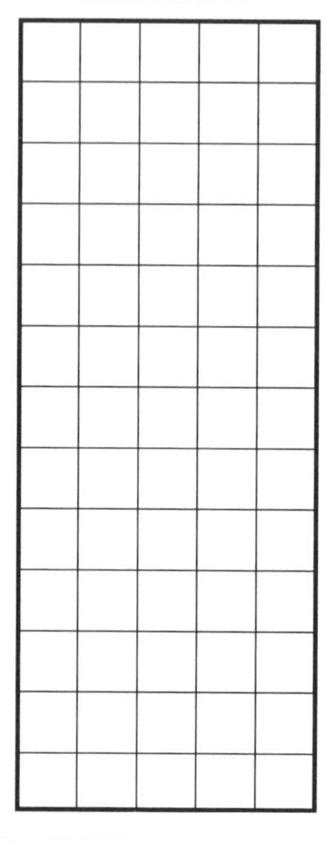

Customers

Employees

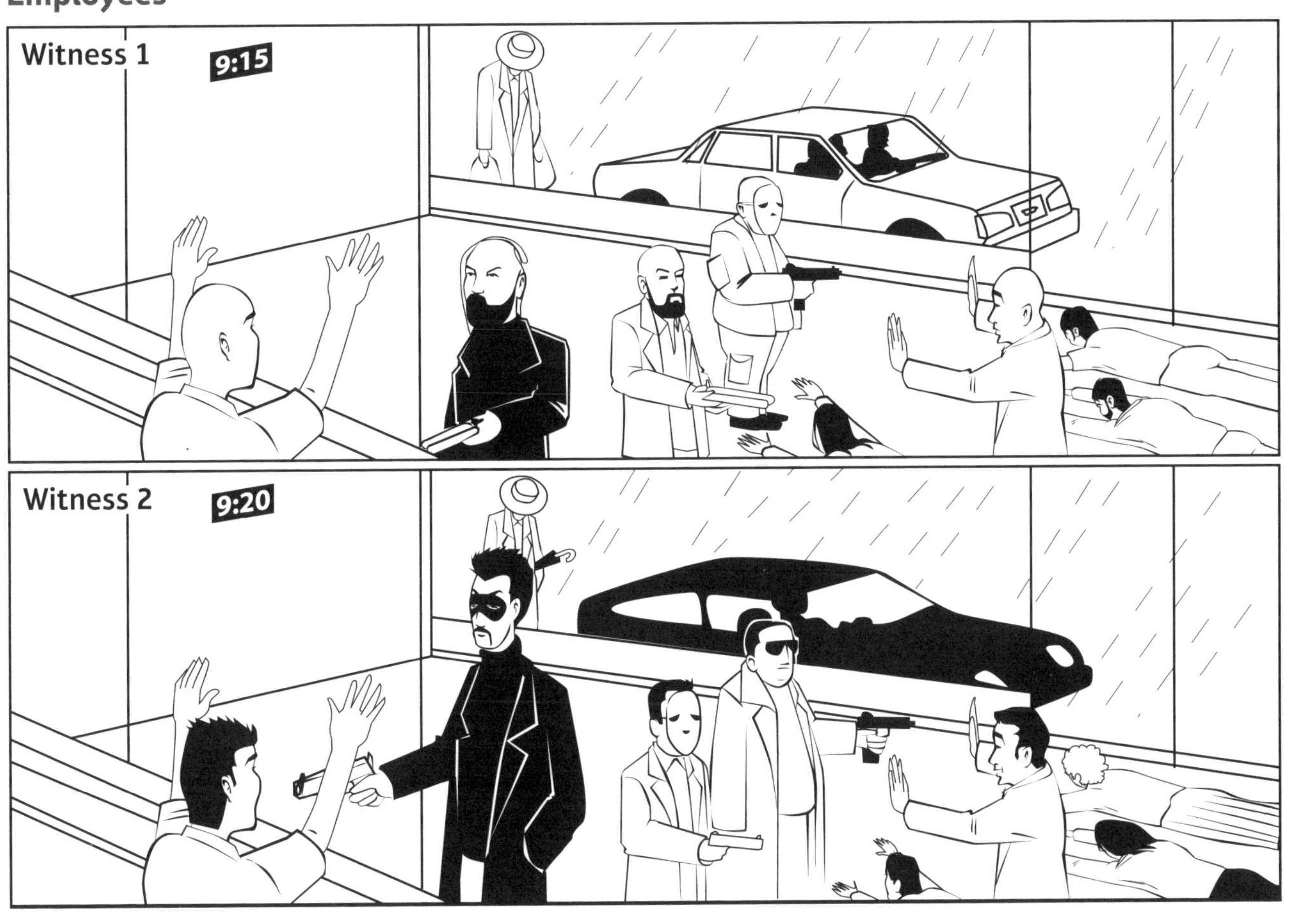

I WOULDN'T RECOMMEND IT!

Vocabulary: adjectives to describe films

1 'I didn't know how the film was going to end. It was so …'	**2** 'It's about the relationship between a dying grandfather and his grandson. It's really …'	**3** 'It was such a sad story. I found it very …'
4 'The way that he helped his wife recover after the accident was really …'	**5** 'At the end, he takes revenge by shooting everyone. It's …'	**6** 'He gave an amazing performance. I thought he was absolutely …'
7 'I was on the edge of my seat all the way through. It was absolutely …'	**8** 'The main character is this strange old man who wears black. He's really …'	**9** 'It really made you think. I'd describe this film as …'
10 'You can't take your eyes off him. His performance was …'	**11** 'The plot is really clever. You could never guess the ending. It's …'	**12** 'The film was really funny. In fact, I'd go so far as to say it was …'
13 'It was non-stop action all the way through. I love films that are …'	**14** 'He was good. I'd describe his performance as a Bond villain as …'	**15** 'It's just about the most shocking film I've ever seen. It's very …'
full of suspense	**poignant**	**moving**
touching	**gory**	**superb**
gripping	**creepy**	**thought-provoking**
stunning	**outstanding**	**hysterical**
fast-paced	**intense**	**controversial**

Answer sheet

1 full of suspense **2** poignant/touching/moving **3** poignant/touching/moving
4 poignant/touching/moving **5** gory **6** superb **7** gripping **8** creepy **9** thought-provoking
10 stunning **11** outstanding **12** hysterical **13** fast-paced **14** intense **15** controversial

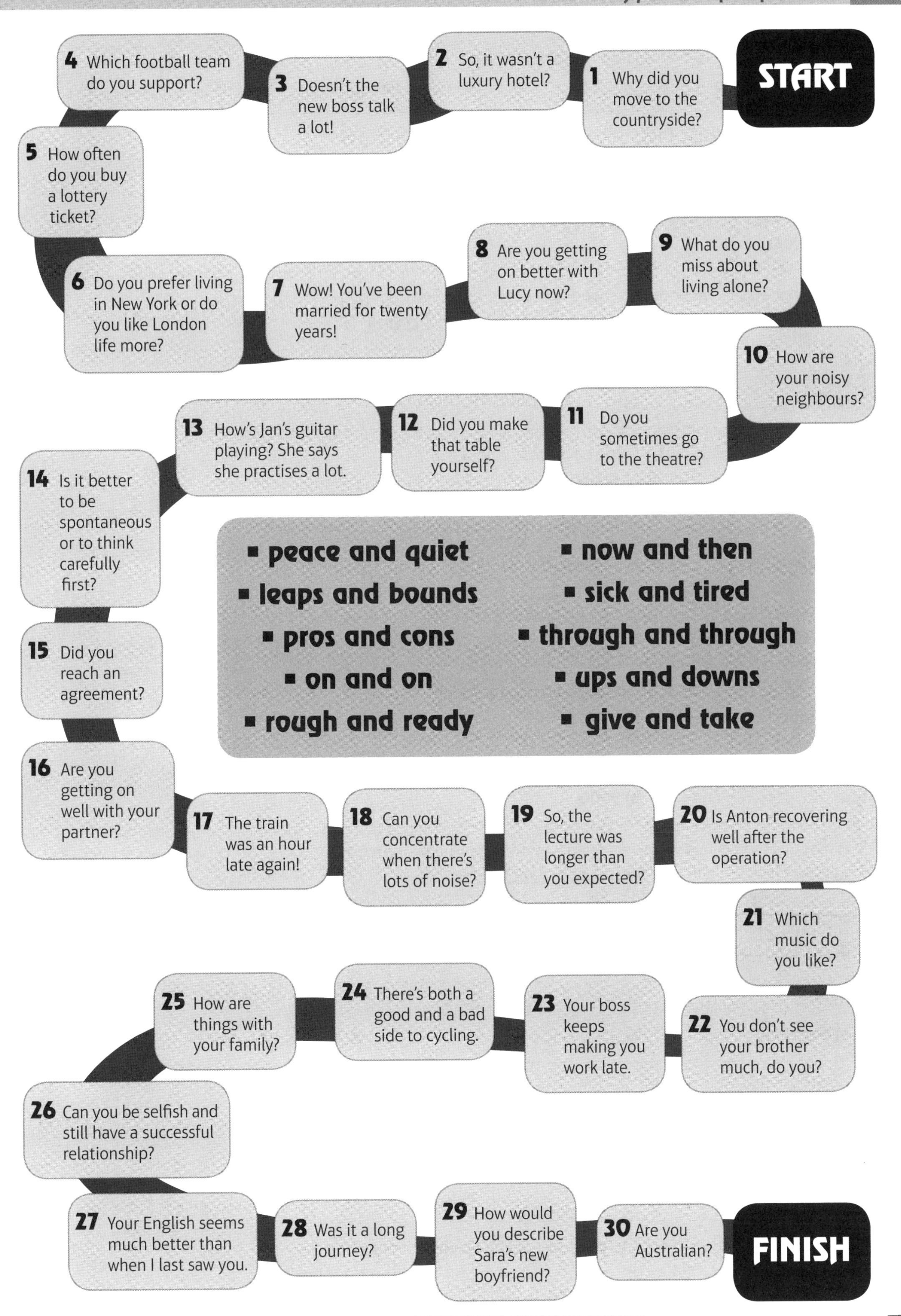
START
1 Why did you move to the countryside?
2 So, it wasn't a luxury hotel?
3 Doesn't the new boss talk a lot!
4 Which football team do you support?
5 How often do you buy a lottery ticket?
6 Do you prefer living in New York or do you like London life more?
7 Wow! You've been married for twenty years!
8 Are you getting on better with Lucy now?
9 What do you miss about living alone?
10 How are your noisy neighbours?
11 Do you sometimes go to the theatre?
12 Did you make that table yourself?
13 How's Jan's guitar playing? She says she practises a lot.
14 Is it better to be spontaneous or to think carefully first?
15 Did you reach an agreement?
16 Are you getting on well with your partner?
17 The train was an hour late again!
18 Can you concentrate when there's lots of noise?
19 So, the lecture was longer than you expected?
20 Is Anton recovering well after the operation?
21 Which music do you like?
22 You don't see your brother much, do you?
23 Your boss keeps making you work late.
24 There's both a good and a bad side to cycling.
25 How are things with your family?
26 Can you be selfish and still have a successful relationship?
27 Your English seems much better than when I last saw you.
28 Was it a long journey?
29 How would you describe Sara's new boyfriend?
30 Are you Australian?
FINISH
peace and quiet
leaps and bounds
pros and cons
on and on
rough and ready
now and then
sick and tired
through and through
ups and downs
give and take

RELATIVE CLAUSE QUIZ

Grammar: relative clauses

Question	Answer			Note
1 Ulan Bator which is in Asia is the capital of which country?	a)	b)	**c) Mongolia**	commas
2 How many people are there who speak English as a first language?	a)	**b) about 380 million**	c)	OK
3 The marriage which lasted the longest was between a Taiwanese couple. How long did it last?	**a) 86 years**	b)	c)	OK
4 What was Napoleon Bonaparte who was emperor of France afraid of?	a)	b)	**c) cats**	commas

Question	Answer			Note
1 Eating eggs which are 100 years old is a delicacy in which country?	**a) China**	b)	c)	OK
2 Polar bears who live in the Arctic have what colour skin?	a)	**b) black**	c)	commas
3 What is the name of the city which had the biggest population 1000 years ago?	**a) Beijing**	b)	c)	OK
4 The Great Wall of China which the Chinese started building in 220 BC is how long?	**a) 6600 km**	b)	c)	commas

Question	Answer			Note
1 A nephophobic is a person who is afraid of what things?	**a) clouds**	b)	c)	OK
2 The man who had the most wives ever was King Mongut of Siam. How many did he have?	a)	**b) 9000**	c)	OK
3 When did the Vikings who were from Scandinavia first visit America?	a)	**b) the 11th century**	c)	commas
4 Until the 1970s people thought that 'kangaroo' which is an aborigine word meant …	a)	**b) I don't know!**	c)	comma

Question	Answer			Note
1 What did Mickey Mouse who was created by Walt Disney use to be called?	**a) Mortimer**	b)	c)	commas
2 What was the city that Bill Gates grew up in?	a)	b)	**c) Seattle**	OK
3 How old was King Tutankhamen when he died?	a)	**b) 18**	c)	OK
4 How fast can the puck which is what ice-hockey players hit travel?	a)	b)	**c) about 220km/h**	commas

Look at the list of statements and questions below. If possible, change them so they contain a participle clause. It is not possible in every case.

1. In your country, is it impolite to make noise while you are eating?
2. People who were born in the last two decades would find it impossible to live without the internet.
3. It is better for companies to employ people who are experienced than employ graduates.
4. Did you always study hard when you took exams at school?
5. It is better to marry someone who you think is funny than someone rich.
6. It's depressing to see so many young people who are endangering their health by eating junk food and smoking.
7. Motorists who are still driving at seventy-five years old should take another driving test.
8. The best nights out are the ones which are unplanned.
9. Do you listen to music while you are travelling?
10. The most beautiful places are the ones which are unchanged by mankind.
11. All the technology which has been created in the last fifteen years has not improved our lives.
12. Company employees who work from home are more productive than the ones in the office.
13. People who have children later in life make better parents.
14. When you read English, do you want to understand every word?
15. A man who holds doors open for women is old-fashioned and sexist.
16. People who have dogs should pick up their dogs' mess.
17. Rail passengers who have to wait more than fifteen minutes should not have to pay.
18. People who have been found guilty of a crime should not be allowed to vote.
19. Cars which are made in Germany are reliable but too expensive.
20. Homes which are located in the centre of cities should be cheaper for nurses, teachers and emergency service workers.

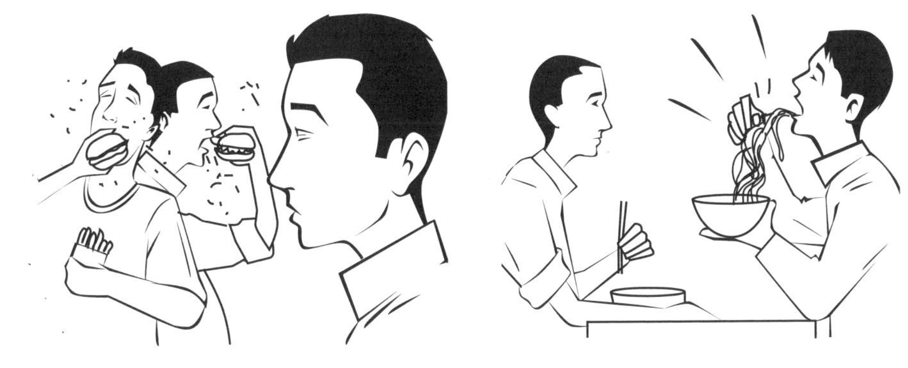

Functional language: giving a tour

UNIT 1

HAPPY FLATMATES

Materials: One copy of the Student A and Student B worksheet per pair of Ss

Ss work in pairs. Give each pair a copy of the Student A and Student B worksheets. They have to share the information on their worksheet to name the housemates in the picture and find the two words or phrases that describe each person's personality. Student A starts by reading the first piece of information labelled 'Start'. Student B listens and looks for any information that links to it. If they have something, they read it to Student A. For example, when Student A says that Sam is a *geek*, the link is Student B's information about a housemate who is *obsessed with computers*. If Student B is unable to find a link with the first piece of information their partner reads, Student A can try reading out others until they do. Ss then continue taking it in turns to read pieces of information. By sharing and matching what they have, they will gradually be able to fill in the gaps below the picture. Check Ss understand that two of the personality words are repeated.

Encourage Ss to read clearly and listen carefully to each other. They must not show each other their worksheets. Explain that they need to listen for words and phrases with similar meanings, e.g. *keeps himself to himself* and *introverted*, and use logic and their powers of deduction to complete the task.

Answers:

1 Lucy – a good laugh, down-to-earth
2 Sam – a computer geek, keeps himself to himself
3 Josh – a people person, witty
4 Gemma – spontaneous, a morning person
5 Sara – a computer geek, keeps herself to herself

HOW DO I FEEL?

Materials: One set of cards per group of Ss

Ss work in groups of three or four. Cut up the cards and distribute one set per group. Ss put them face down on the table. The first student picks up a card and reads the text in **bold** to the others. They listen and have to answer the question on the card, either *How do I feel?* or *What's the feeling?* The first question requires an adjective as the answer and the second a noun. The answers are written in **bold** at the bottom of the card. The first student to give the correct answer wins the card. It is then the next student's turn. This continues until all the cards have been won. Ss need to be quick to win the card and the winner is the student with the most cards.

GOOD COP, BAD COP

Materials: One set of role cards per group of Ss

Ss work in groups of three. Tell them that five valuable paintings have been stolen from a famous gallery and two detectives are going to interview the director of the gallery about the incident. Organise Ss into groups of three – two are detectives and the third is the gallery director. Explain that one of the detectives is the 'good cop' and does not want to upset the important and famous director, but the other is the 'bad cop' and doesn't care. The bad cop will lead the interview and only ask direct questions. However, in order not to upset the director, the good cop will rephrase every direct question the bad cop asks to make an indirect question, e.g. if the bad cop says *Can we see your personal emails?* then good cop will say, *We were wondering if we could see your personal emails?* The gallery director can also ask questions, e.g. *How long are you going to close the gallery?* or *Could you tell me how long you are going to close the gallery?* Distribute the role cards and give Ss a few minutes to read them and prepare. The cops should work together and decide on the questions they are going to ask. When everyone is ready, the two cops interview the director. At the end of the activity, the cops have to say if they think the director is guilty or not.

TALK ABOUT ...

Materials: One copy of the board (A3 size if possible) and a dice per group of Ss and one counter per student

Ss work in groups of four. Give each group a board, enlarged to A3 if possible, a counter each and a dice. Place the counters at the **START**. The first student rolls the dice and moves the number shown. The student then has to talk to their group about the subject in the square for at least 30 seconds (the other Ss should keep time). If the student is successful, they remain on that square. If not, they go back to where they were. Explain that Ss are not restricted to using just the tense form in the question in their answer. On the contrary, they should use as many different tense forms as they can, e.g. for *Talk about something you've just bought* a possible answer could begin *I bought a new phone last week. I was walking past a shop and saw that there was a special offer.* If a student lands on a FREE QUESTION square, they can ask any question to another member of the group using the present perfect, e.g. *What's the funniest thing you have ever seen?* During the activity, monitor for interesting ideas which Ss can share with the class at the end of the activity. Note any errors you hear related to the present perfect. You can either elicit corrections for these at the end or on the spot. The winner is the first student to reach the finish.

HOW CAN I HELP YOU?

Materials: Two role cards per student

Ss work in pairs. Give all Student As and Student Bs their two role cards. Start by discussing Ss' experiences of telephone customer service and call centres. Focus on whether they are generally positive or negative and why. Explain that in the activity Ss will have a chance both to make and to respond to enquiries. Check the vocabulary *to clone a card*, *overdraft* and *overdrawn* and give Ss time to read their role cards and prepare what they are going to say. The role-play begins with Student A phoning Student B about a power cut. Before you start, remind Ss to use the functional language from Lesson 1.3 and to always be polite. Ss continue with the second role-play. At the end, discuss whether the class felt their enquiries were dealt with politely and effectively.

UNIT 2

SCRAMBLED ISSUES

Materials: One copy of the worksheet per pair of Ss

Ss work in pairs. Give each pair a worksheet. They unscramble the social issues vocabulary and write the word or phrase in the second column. Still in pairs, Ss think of three ideas to help with that particular issue and write them in the spaces provided (see example on the worksheet). When they have produced as many ideas as possible, put the pairs into groups of four or six to exchange ideas and discuss which they consider to be the best and most effective for each issue. The groups then report their best ideas to the whole class. Encourage the groups to challenge the ideas presented or to try to build a consensus about the best ways to deal with the issues.

Answers: debt, pollution, unemployment, street crime, homelessness, drought, drug abuse, domestic violence, obesity

YOU'RE ON CAMERA

Materials: One set of role cards per group of Ss

Ss work in groups of four. Tell Ss that they are four councillors (local government politicians) and they are responsible for governing a small town. The town has a number of problems and the possible solutions to these problems could be a range of surveillance measures. Pre-teach/Check *microchip* as a verb (microchipping dogs involves implanting a simple microchip in the dog with information about the dog and its owner). Put Ss into groups of four and distribute the role cards. They are going to have a meeting in their group of four to decide which measures, if any, they will introduce. Give them a few minutes to prepare what they are going to say and make sure they understand that although they should express and defend their views energetically, they should also be prepared to compromise in order to reach an agreement. At the end of the role-play, ask the groups to report back to the class about how they are going to deal with the problems.

IT'S A PERFECT WORLD

Materials: One copy of the Student A, Student B and Student C worksheet per group of three Ss

Ss work in groups of three. Give Students A, B and C their part of the worksheet. The objective of the activity is to guess the situation in **bold** at the bottom of each box from the clues given and to make a similar present perfect simple or continuous sentence. Student A begins with the situation in the first box and reads the first clue about it, i.e. *I feel emotional and I'm crying.* Student B has the first guess. If they guess incorrectly, e.g. *You've split up with your partner*, Student C has a guess. If Student C also gets it wrong, e.g. *You've lost your dog*, then Student A reads the second clue *I love the cinema* and they continue taking it in turns to guess until one of them gets it right. It will then be Student B's turn to start, with Student C making the first guess. This continues until all the sentences in bold have been guessed. Correct guesses win a point and the winner is the student with the most points at the end. Encourage Ss to consider carefully whether to use the present perfect simple or continuous.

A BRIEF HISTORY OF ENERGY DRINKS

Materials: One copy of the Student A and Student B worksheet per pair of Ss

Ask the class if they drink energy drinks, what brands they know and whether they think there are any health risks. Then ask the class when they think energy drinks were first made. Tell them they are going to find out more about the history of energy drinks.

Ss work in pairs. Give them their worksheets. The object is to complete the gaps in their text by asking questions in the passive. For example, Student A asks *What has Irn-Bru never been marketed as?* Student B has the missing information in their text and gives the answer *an energy drink*. Student A writes this in the gap and then Student B asks Student A a question about the next gap. This continues until both Ss have completed all the missing information.

Before Ss start the activity, give them a few minutes to prepare their questions. Make sure they understand that they must not look at each other's worksheet. At the end, discuss as a class whether or not energy drinks are dangerous and whether they should be banned.

NB *A salaryman* is an English-sounding word for a Japanese office worker. *Genki* means healthy and full of energy.

BIG ISSUES

Materials: One copy of the board (A3 size if possible) per group of Ss and one counter per student

Ss work in groups of four. Give each group a board, enlarged to A3 if possible, and four counters. Each student places their counter in one of the four starting positions around the board. The aim of the game is to reach the opposite side of the board. Ss can move one square at a time horizontally, diagonally and vertically, but they can't move to a square which is already occupied. Pre-teach/Check the vocabulary *terminally ill, justifiable, myth, victimless crime* and possibly the phrase *a country gets the government it deserves* (if a government is corrupt and brutal it is because the people are).

The first student begins by moving their counter one space onto any one of the issues in the first row. They then have to give their opinion on the issue and support it with at least two reasons and an example. The other Ss in the group decide if they have completed the task successfully, regardless of whether they agreed with the views stated, and they also have the opportunity to respond to the first student's opinion. If there is a consensus that the first student was successful, the first student remains on that square. If not, they go back to where they were. It is then the second student's turn. Encourage Ss to use the adjectives and expressions from Lesson 2.3. At the end, ask the class which issues they agreed and disagreed on most and why.

UNIT 3

WHAT'S MY SAYING?

Materials: One copy of the worksheet per pair of Ss and two pictures from the worksheet per individual student

Ss work in pairs. Distribute one worksheet per pair of Ss and ask them to look at the pictures and to try to remember the sayings. After you have checked the answers, give Ss two pictures each, which they must not show to anyone, and ask them to prepare short stories or anecdotes based on the sayings in their pictures. Explain that they are going to a party where they will mingle and be able to tell their anecdotes. At the end of each story/anecdote, the student listening has to respond to the storyteller using the correct saying in a natural, conversational way, e.g.

Student A: I went to Spain last year, it's very different from my country – lots of things, like the food and the weather, but especially the time people eat. They eat very late, about 11p.m. This was very difficult for me. I usually eat around 6p.m., but I changed and started eating much later.

Student B: Ah yes that's good. When in Rome do as the Romans do!

Student A shouldn't tell B whether or not they have guessed correctly but should listen, in turn, to B's anecdote and try to respond naturally with the correct saying. Since all Ss have two anecdotes to tell, they should then exchange second anecdotes with a different partner. At the end of the activity, Ss try to guess which sayings they thought the other Ss were given.

Answers:
1 Every cloud has a silver lining.
2 When in Rome do as the Romans do.
3 What goes around comes around.
4 Nothing ventured, nothing gained.
5 Once bitten, twice shy.

CHANGE IT!

Materials: One copy of the board (A3 size if possible) and verb list and one answer sheet per group of Ss

Ss work in groups of three or five. One student has the answer sheet and acts as the referee whilst the other Ss play against each other using an enlarged A3 board. The competing Ss/teams take it in turns to choose a square on the board and try to reformulate the sentences using the phrasal verbs in the column on the left. If they correctly reformulate the phrase, they win that square and should initial it clearly and cross out the phrasal verb. It is then the other student's/team's turn. If Ss don't correctly reformulate the sentence, the referee must not say what the correct answer is so both Ss/teams still have a chance to win it.

The objective of the activity is to make a line of four squares. These can be horizontal, diagonal or vertical. The winning student/team is the first to get four squares. The opposing Ss/teams must try to block each other.

PAST CONSEQUENCES

Materials: One copy of the worksheet per student or pair of Ss

Tell Ss they are going to write a story with the title *A day to forget, a night to remember* using narrative tenses, but they are going to get some help. Ss can work in pairs or alone and are given a worksheet. Ask Ss to read and complete the first stage of the story only, using the question on the right to guide them. They should then fold over what they have written and pass the story to the next student or pair who fill in the next stage. This continues until the story is finished. Monitor closely to make sure Ss are looking at the questions and give ideas where necessary. It is important to ensure that there isn't too much waiting. When Ss have filled in the last section of their story, they can unfold it and read it. Ss must not look at what other Ss have written until then. Ss should decide which story is the funniest, most implausible, etc. Look at any incorrect uses of the narrative tenses or issues about which ones to use.

SPIRALLING REGRET

Materials: One copy of the board (A3 size if possible) and a dice per group of Ss and one counter per student

Ss in work in groups of four. Each group has a board, enlarged to A3 if possible, a dice and a counter for each student. Ss take it turns to throw the dice and move around the board, using the cues in the boxes to express regrets and wishes, e.g. for the first box, *You missed the last train and can't get home*, the student could say *I wish I'd got to the station earlier* (a regret about the past/a past wish) or *I wish I was at home now* (a wish for the present). In most cases, the cue in the box relates clearly to either a past or present situation but in some cases both past and present wishes and regrets can be used (as above). Ss have the opportunity to talk about their own regrets when they land on a 'real regret you have' box. The other Ss should ask follow-up questions, for example, *Why do you regret doing that?* The winner is the first student to reach the end of the spiral.

LITERARY CRITICS

Materials: One copy of the worksheet and one set of role cards per group of Ss

Tell Ss that they are a group of important literary critics who give an annual prize of $50,000 to the best new novel. They have read and made notes on the four shortlisted books and they are now going to meet to decide which book should win the prize. Organise Ss into groups of four and give each group the blurbs to read and each student one of the four role cards. Give Ss about 7 mins to understand the plots and their opinions about the books. Pre-teach/Check *torture, twist at the end, far-fetched* and any other items that you think they might find challenging. Ss then have the discussion and tell each other their opinions about the books. They should generally follow the opinion on their role card, so if it is negative they can't change it to positive. Encourage them to invent further details about the characters and scenes to make their opinions more believable. They should use *What I liked/didn't like was …* or *It was the … that I liked/didn't like* to talk in detail about their ideas and opinions. Each group should decide which book they are going to award the prize to. At the end, the different groups share their ideas and decide on one overall winner.

UNIT 4

NOUN MAZE

Materials: One copy of the worksheet per pair of Ss

Ss work in pairs. Give one copy of the worksheet to each pair. Tell Ss to begin in the START square. Explain that they must choose the correct alternative in the sentence in the first square. If the correct answer is an uncountable noun, they should follow the black arrow. If the correct answer is a plural noun, they should follow the white arrow.

Elicit the first answer as an example (the correct answer is *outskirts*, which is a plural noun, so Ss should follow the white arrow). Ss should continue until they reach the edge of the grid. When they have finished, ask Ss to tell you which letter they finished at. If they chose the correct answers and identified the uncountable/ plural nouns correctly, they should finish at the letter R. If Ss have finished in the wrong place, encourage them to try again.

With ***stronger Ss***, do it as a race. The first pair to tell you the correct letter wins.

Answers: outskirts (plural), cloth (uncountable), glasses (plural), stairs (plural), scenery (uncountable), whereabouts (plural), concrete (uncountable), soap (uncountable), information (uncountable), contents (plural), facilities (plural), luggage (uncountable), accommodation (uncountable), remains (plural), clothes (plural), cards (plural), toiletries (plural), advice (uncountable).
The correct finish point in the grid is R.

I'M GOOD AT SOMETHING

Materials: One copy of the worksheet per student, cut in half so that they have sentences 1–8 on one piece of paper and the empty circles on another piece of paper

Give both halves of the worksheet to every student. Give them 5 mins to think of one example for each sentence 1–8. Ss work alone and write each example in a different circle – they shouldn't fill out the circles in a logical order. Ss need to think about the meaning of the phrases in bold. If necessary, work through a few examples with the whole class before they begin. For example, for *A hobby, sport or interest that takes a lot of know-how*, Ss might write chess, sailing or computer gaming. For *An inventive person from history*, Ss might write Leonardo da Vinci or Isaac Newton.

Once Ss have written an example in every circle, put them into pairs. Ss swap examples and try to match their partner's examples with the correct sentences. They must check their guesses with their partner by making statements, e.g. *I think chess is a hobby that takes a lot of know-how*. If Ss don't guess correctly, their partner should give further information and clues to help them get the correct answer. When Ss have finished, elicit interesting ideas from the whole class.

THEN AND NOW

Materials: One copy of worksheets A, B and C per group of three Ss

Organise Ss into three groups: one group of Student As, one of Student Bs and one of Student Cs. Give each individual student a worksheet, making sure that the answer section is folded over so Ss cannot see the answers. In the first stage of the activity, Ss work together in their groups and read the situations then complete the gaps with the correct form of *used to* or *would* or an appropriate verb form. When Ss have completed the gaps, they unfold the answers and check them in their groups. Answer any questions that arise.

For the second stage of the activity, put Ss into A, B, C groups of three. They take it in turns to read out the three sentences that they completed and the other two Ss have to guess the situation. Correct guesses win a point and the winner is the student with the most points at the end.

QUESTIONS OF THE FUTURE

Materials: One copy of the board (A3 size if possible) and a dice per group of Ss and one counter per student

Ss work in groups of four. Give them a board, enlarged to A3 if possible, a dice and counters. Ss take it in turns to roll the dice and move around the board. They have to answer the questions in the squares they land on. If a student successfully answers a question according to the other Ss, they stay on that square. If they do not, they need to go back to the square they were on before. All the questions use future forms and the answers should usually use the same future form as the questions. However, there are some cases in which a different future form might also be acceptable, e.g. the answer to *Might you live in another country one day?* could be *Definitely! I'm moving to Spain next year.* Encourage Ss to give details with their answers and for the other Ss to ask supplementary questions. The winner is the first student to reach the finish.

THE NEW FOOTBALL

Materials: One copy of the worksheet per group of Ss

Ss work in groups of four. Their task is to invent a new sport or game incorporating at least four of the items on the worksheet. Distribute the worksheets and check the pronunciation of any unfamiliar items in the pictures: *flippers, swing, slide, cannon, mallet, power hose, pram, spear*, etc. Ss brainstorm ideas in their groups and make notes about their decisions. They should make sure they include the name and aim of the new sport, the equipment used, the rules and procedures the players have to follow and any other important points.

When all the groups have finished developing their idea, they take it in turns to present it to the class. At the end of the presentations, Ss vote on which sport or game they like best and which one will be used in the programme. Encourage Ss to use the functional language in Lesson 4.3 when presenting their idea to the other groups, and to use mirror questions if they are unsure about anything they hear when they are listening to a presentation.

UNIT 5

COMPOUND SNAP

Materials: One set of cards and one answer sheet per group of Ss

Ss work in small teams. Two teams compete against each other and one student is the referee. The teams have one set of cut up cards and the referee has the answers. Half the cards are compound nouns and the other half are gapped sentences that can be completed with the nouns. Ss shuffle all the cards together and distribute them equally between the two teams, so that each player has one set of cards face down in front of them. The referee has the answer sheet. A player from each team turns over one of their cards at the same time and places it face up on the table in a pile in front of them. When there is a matching compound noun and sentence card, Ss shout *Snap!* and say the complete sentence. The referee verifies whether the answer is correct. If it is, the student wins the cards. If the student is wrong, Ss carry on turning over their cards until they run out, when they shuffle them and start again. The winner is the student with the most pairs at the end.

PRODUCT, PRICE, MARKET

Materials: One copy of the Student A and Student B worksheet per pair of Ss

Ss work in pairs. Explain that each pair has the same crossword, but that Student A's has words/phrases going across and is missing the words/phrases going down and Student B's has words/phrases going down, but is missing the words/phrases going across. Tell Ss that they must give each other clues for each word/phrase in their crosswords, but must not say the actual word/phrase.

Pre-teach/Check the questions Ss need to ask for clues, e.g. *What's 9 across? What's 4 down?* Tell Ss they should answer their partner's questions by giving the noun the word/phrase collocates with (either *a price*, *a market* or *a product*) and a brief definition, e.g. *What's 12 down? Price. Make it smaller.* (reduce). Ss take it in turns to ask for and give collocations/definitions until their crosswords are complete.

Answers: **1** enter (a market) **2** raise (a price) **3** promote (a product) **4** launch (a product) **5** see a gap in (a market) **6** increase (a price) **7** set (a price) **8** advertise (a product) **9** endorse (a product) **10** dominate (a market) **11** break into (a market) **12** reduce (a price)

AHEAD OF ITS TIME

Materials: One copy of the worksheet per group of Ss

Show Ss a picture of a C5 and tell them it was a real product. Ask them to guess what it is, how it worked (a battery-operated electric tricycle) and whether it was successful or not. Distribute the texts and pre-teach/check *tricycle*, *steer*, *handlebar* and *pedal*. Ask Ss to read the text quickly to check their predictions. Organise Ss into groups of four with two Ss on each team. The teams take it in turns to identify the article mistake on each line. The first team has the first guess on line one. If they are correct, they win that line and can initial the box on the right. If they are wrong, the second team can guess and try to win it. The teams take it in turns until the mistake is identified and the line is won. The second team then has the first guess with the second line. At the end, the winner is the team with the most lines.

Answers: **1** *the* United Kingdom **2** *a* handlebar **3** *the* driver's knees **4** *The* C5's **5** *a* driving licence **6** *the* media **7** *the* 1980s **8** ~~the~~ serious concerns **9** low to *the* ground **10** ~~the~~ cold weather **11** *the* motor **12** ~~the~~ long hills **13** ~~the~~ gentle slopes **14** ~~the~~ millions **15** *the* company **16** *a* spectacular

CONDITIONAL DOMINOES

Materials: One set of cards per group of Ss

Ss work in groups of three or four. Give out one set of cut up cards per group. Pre-teach/Check *endorse*, *shop around* and *sponsor*. Deal out the cards. Each player has the same number of cards which they put face-up on the table in front of them. The cards contain different halves of conditional sentences. To begin, the first player puts one of their cards in the middle of the table. The next student has to add a card to make a correct conditional sentence. They can add to the beginning or the end of the sentence. If a student is unable to put down a correct card, it's the next player's turn. The winner is the first student to get rid of all their cards. When all the cards have been used, check that all the sentences are correct. Then ask Ss to discuss the sentences and say whether or not they are true for them and/or if they agree or disagree with what they say.

CAMPAIGN COMPETITION

Materials: One copy of the worksheet per group of Ss

Explain that Ss are advertising executives and they are going to plan the launch campaign for a new energy drink.

Ss work in groups of three or four and spend a few minutes reading the information on the worksheet. Pre-teach/Check key vocabulary items, such as *sponsorship*, *endorsement*, *billboard*, *slogan*, *logo* and *prime-time*. Ss discuss their ideas and put together their campaign. Remind them to make notes about their decisions to help them with the presentation later. Encourage Ss to use the functional language from Lesson 5.3 when putting forward their ideas and making suggestions and to express reservations about ideas. Monitor and help them with any language they need. When the campaigns are ready, Ss present them to the rest of the class and they vote on which one is the best.

UNIT 6

TELL THE GROUP

Materials: One copy of the worksheet per student

Ss have a worksheet each and work alone to complete the missing words. When they have finished, they check their answers in pairs before checking altogether as a class. Then, put Ss into groups of four and give them a few minutes to collect ideas and prepare what they are going to say about the different things on the list. When Ss are ready, the discussion starts and they share their ideas. Encourage Ss to give plenty of details when speaking and to ask each other questions.

Answers: **1** their age **2** their prime **3** their age **4** of age **5** immature **6** maturity **7** elderly **8** discrimination **9** discrimination **10** elderly **11** their age **12** your prime **13** your age **14** of age **15** mature **16** maturity

COFFEE MACHINE CHAT

Materials: One copy of the Student A and Student B worksheet per pair of Ss

Ss work in pairs. Give them their worksheet. Begin by explaining the scenario outlined at the top: Student A and B work in the same company but Student B, who is a very popular boss, is leaving the office for a better job in Spain and is going to be replaced by an unpopular colleague, Marco. Student A is talking to Student B at the coffee machine about how bad things are going to be after Student B's departure. Ss have to put the conversation in the correct order. Student A starts, Student B finds the correct response, then it's Student A's turn again and so on. Ss take it in turns until the conversation finishes. They are not allowed to look at each other's worksheets at any time. When they have finished, Ss should try to have the conversation again but this time without the prompts. They should try to still use the vocabulary in **bold**, but can invent other details and extend the conversation.

Answers: **1** i **2** f **3** g **4** a **5** k **6** e **7** h **8** c **9** l **10** b **11** j **12** d

OFF THE BEATEN TRACK

Materials: One set of cards per group of Ss

Ss work in groups of four. Give each person a card. The groups are adventurous travellers who are planning a trip together. Each person in the group has to research an interesting destination. Give Ss a few minutes to read and make notes. They have to give their group as much information as possible about the destination on their card using the modal verbs and related phrases they studied on p69. The group then vote on where they want to go. Each student should talk about:

- what they *ought/have/are supposed/need* to do and what they *don't have to* do in order to prepare for visiting this destination or in order to get around, stay safe whilst they are there, etc.
- what they *will/won't be able to* do in this destination.
- specific events in the past when certain things *had to* happen or *couldn't* happen in these destinations.

Write these points up on the board as a reference. When the preparation time is up, collect in the cards. Ss then tell their groups about the different destinations using the notes they have made. The others listen and ask further questions. Ss can invent details if necessary. Monitor and ensure that Ss are using the modals. Remind them they can use the notes on the board as prompts. At the end of the activity, ask each group which destination they want to travel to.

FUTUROLOGIST FORUM

Materials: One copy of the worksheet per student

Tell Ss they are going to be futurologists – people who predict future trends in society. Distribute the worksheet and pre-teach/check any vocabulary you think might be challenging, e.g. *cashless* and *holographic*. Remind Ss that *within* in time phrases means the same as *by*. Tell Ss to look at the predictions and questions on the worksheet. Do they think these things are likely to happen? Ss should evaluate and respond to the predictions in the space provided using the phrases from Ex 5B on p72 to help them. They also make two predictions of their own. When they have finished, put Ss into groups of four and get them to discuss their answers and opinions as well as their own predictions with the group, justifying and supporting their opinions with reasons and examples. The groups should try to agree on which predictions are *likely, possible, impossible*, etc. At the end of the lesson, the groups present their different opinions to the whole class.

IT'S DEBATABLE

Materials: One copy of the worksheet per student

Give Ss a worksheet each and explain the idea of a debate – a formal discussion of a topic. It starts with 'a motion' – something which 'the house' or the class believes. Two Ss support the motion and two oppose it. Each side argues their case for and against, starting with the side that supports the motion and then alternating speakers between the side that supports the motion and the side that opposes it. Finally, having listened to all four speakers and heard both sides of the argument, the group discusses the topic together and takes a vote to decide whether the majority is for or against the motion. Give Ss a few minutes to read the topics on the worksheet and decide which they would most like to have a debate about. Get the class to vote on which of these will be the final topic. Working on their own, Ss then brainstorm ideas to support their views for and against the motion and write notes in the appropriate box. Monitor and help Ss with vocabulary, checking to see who supports and opposes the motion. From these, nominate ***stronger Ss*** to speak for and against it. Hold a debate, as outlined above, with the teacher as the chair. When both sides have had an equal opportunity to present their views, the class can take a vote to determine the majority view.

UNIT 7

WHAT'S MY PROGRAMME?

Materials: One set of cards per group of Ss

Ss work in groups of three or four. Give each group a set of cut up cards. The cards are placed face down in the middle and the first student picks up a card. They have to elicit from the other Ss the word(s) in **bold** at the top of the card by describing it. All the words are types of TV programme.

Ss can say anything to elicit the TV programme, but they are not allowed to use the three bullet-pointed words below it in their descriptions, or any other related forms of these words, e.g. if *investigate* is one of the words on the card, Ss are not allowed to use words like *investigation* or *investigator* in their definitions either. The first student to guess the TV programme being described wins the card. The winner is the student with the most cards at the end.

MULTI-WORD VERB REFORMULATION

Materials: One copy of the Student A and Student B worksheet per pair of Ss

Ss work in pairs. Give them Student A and Student B worksheets. They take it in turns to read each other their sentences which do not contain a phrasal verb. These are the ones written in **bold**. The student who is listening has to reformulate the sentence in a natural conversational way using one of the phrasal verbs in the grid at the top of their worksheet, e.g. if Student A reads the first sentence in **bold** (*I can't stand living in this city any longer.*) Student B looks for a suitable phrasal verb and replies with something like *Oh dear, you can't put up with living in this city any longer*. Student A can check to see if Student B is right by looking at the phrasal verb sentence under the sentence in bold. If Student B is correct, it's Student B's turn to read a sentence to Student A for reformulation and Student B can cross off *put up with* from the grid.

The phrasal verbs are only used once. If a student doesn't reformulate correctly, Ss can go back to the sentence later when there are fewer phrasal verb options.

QUANTIFIER DICE

Materials: One copy of the board and a dice per group of Ss

Ss work in groups of three. Give each group one board and a dice. There are six games on each board, one in each vertical column and the groups should play through all six games to decide the winner, starting with game one. To play, the first student rolls the dice, e.g. four, and looks at the quantifier in square four, game one, which is *a great deal of*. The student then has to make a sentence with this and one of the topics in the box at the bottom of the column for game one, e.g. *Wikipedia contains a great deal of information*. If the other Ss agree that this is correct, the student wins the square and initials it. The topic is crossed off and can't be used again. The game continues with the next student rolling the dice and trying to win another square in game one by making a sentence combining the quantifier in the square with an available topic. If a student rolls a number for a square already won, it's the next student's turn. It will get more difficult to win squares as the game progresses. When all six squares in game one have been won, the next game starts. The overall winner is the student who wins the most games.

AWOL

Materials: One copy of the Student A and Student B worksheet per pair of Ss

Explain to Ss that one of them is the assistant of a record company executive and the other is the manager of one of the label's biggest bands, AWOL. Explain the situation as outlined on the role cards and that Ss are going to have a meeting to resolve the problem. Pre-teach/Check *sue* and *rehab*. Emphasise that the situation is delicate as both parties need each other and therefore both the band manager and the record company executive are going to be polite and diplomatic. Consequently, they are more likely to backshift the tenses of what they say. However, there are situations where they might not do this because the situation is still current. Ss work in pairs and have a role card each. They spend a few minutes deciding what they are going to say and how they are going to report what they have been told. The discussion can then begin. Encourage Ss to reach a compromise. At the end Ss report to the class what they have decided to do.

HOLD THE FRONT PAGE

Materials: One copy of the worksheet per group of Ss

Tell Ss they are journalists for the same paper and they want their story on the front page. Organise Ss into groups of three and give each student two different news stories from the worksheet. Tell them to choose one story to present to their group as the story that should go on the front page. Give them a few minutes to read and prepare before collecting the stories in again. Ss now have to sell their story to the group using as much emphasis as possible to make it sound dramatic and interesting. To do this, they should use ways of adding emphasis from p86, e.g. *The amazing thing is …* . Encourage Ss who are listening to use some of the vocabulary from *Learn to make guesses* on p87 when responding to what is being said. Remind Ss of these phrases by putting them on the board first. When Ss have presented their stories, the group discusses which one will interest their readers the most and use it for the front page. They should also decide what the headline will be.

UNIT 8

COLLOCATION DILEMMAS

Materials: Three situation cards and one lie and two truth cards per group of Ss

Start by asking how you tell when someone is lying and ask Ss if they think they are good at lying. Explain that the activity is about lying convincingly and also being able to identify a liar. Ss work in groups of three and are given three situation cards and one lie and two truth cards per group. Ss with truth cards have to tell the truth, and Ss with lie cards have to lie. Give the groups time to read their situation cards and make sure everyone understands the dilemmas. The first group starts by explaining their first dilemma to the other groups. The individuals in the other groups take it in turns to briefly say what they would do and why, lying or telling the truth according to their cards. Ss should naturally use the collocations from Lesson 8.1 when they do this since they are prompted to by the dilemma cards. When everyone has answered, the first group have to identify the liar in each of the other groups. They get a point for every one correctly identified. It is then the next group's turn to explain a dilemma. At this point everyone should exchange their lie and truth cards so the next group doesn't know who the liars are.

IT'S HOW YOU SAY IT

Materials: One copy of the worksheet per class

Make one copy of the worksheet for your class and cut up the cards. If you have more than twelve Ss, then make a copy for every twelve Ss you have. If you have less than twelve Ss, remove some of the cards. Give one card to each student, and tell them that they have to demonstrate the adjective on the card to their classmates, without saying what the adjective is. Give them a minute or two to decide how they are going to do this. Go round and help where necessary. Make sure they don't show their cards to each other.

When they are ready, bring Ss into the middle of the class to mingle and interact with each other, in the style of the adjective on their cards. Tell them they should speak to all of their classmates at least once.

When they have all spoken to each other, put Ss into pairs and ask them to try and remember what their classmates said and guess the adjective on their cards. Tell them to write a list. In feedback, check answers with the class and give one point for each correct answer. The pair with the most points wins.

CONDITIONAL FOX AND HOUNDS

Materials: One copy of the board (A3 size if possible) per group of Ss and one counter per student

Ss work in groups of three. Give each group a board, enlarged to A3 if possible, and a counter each. Two Ss are hounds and the other student is a fox. The hounds have to catch the fox by landing on the same diamond on the board. The game begins with Ss placing their counters on their starting diamond. Both fox and hounds can only move diagonally, one diamond at a time. The fox starts and moves one space onto any one of the four diamonds next to the start. Subsequently, in order to move from one diamond to the next, both the fox and the hounds have to make conditional sentences using the picture in the diamond they are in. Depending on the shade of the diamond, the sentence has to be either in the past (black), in the present (white) or both past and present (grey). For example, if the fox lands on the picture of the bed in the grey diamond, they could say *If I hadn't come to school this morning, I'd still be in bed now.* (past clause followed by present). If they move to the picture of the police car on the black diamond, they could say *If I'd seen the police car, I would have stopped.* (two past clauses), etc. If the other Ss agree the sentence is correct, the student can stay on the diamond they have moved to. If not, the student has to go back to where they were. The two hounds chase the fox and try to catch it. Ss can then change roles and one of the hounds can become the fox.

BAD BEHAVIOUR

Materials: One set of cards per group of Ss

Ss work in groups of three or four. Give each group a set of cut up cards. Explain to Ss that they are the parents of a fifteen-year-old boy who is having serious behaviour problems at school and they are going to make a series of decisions to help him. Pre-teach/Check *golf clubs, boarding school, private school, expelled from school* and *suspended from school.* Tell Ss to write the numbers of the cards in marker pen on the back and lay the cards out in order, face down in five rows. Do the first card together as a class. Ss turn over card one and one student reads the situation. Ss must first decide what the correct form of the verb is – infinitive, infinitive with *to* or an *-ing* form and complete the options on the card. They can then decide which of the given options to follow. Point out that each option has a number after it. Explain that this is the number of the next card they should turn over as the cards are all linked in some way to create a decision maze. They turn over the number of the card indicated at the end of the option (and put back and turn over the card they have just read). Ss continue doing this, completing verb forms and making group decisions until they reach the end of the maze.

At the end of the activity Ss can discuss which decisions were bad and which were good.

Answers:

1 consider sending, had better improve
2 will never forgive
3 playing, attending
4 Arrange for him to see, interested in doing
5 Despite you not being, doesn't enjoy travelling
6 wants to play, it's better to sell
7 intend to continue
8 would rather (see him) behave, expect him to get
9 prepared to take, doesn't have to travel
10 promise not to send
11 can't afford to spend
12 good at playing, used to play
13 Try to get, might like
14 likes painting, enjoys being able to
15 complaining about being, to make
16 had to pay
17 suggest doing, Spending more time doing
18 is like being, make him stay
19 accused of attacking
20 continues to play/playing, ends up playing

DON'T TAKE THIS THE WRONG WAY

Materials: One role card per student

Tell Ss that they are studying or working at the International Oxford City School of English. The school has recently had some problems and some dissatisfied Ss have made an appointment to see the Directors to discuss the situation. Ss work in groups of four to six. In each group there needs to be a Director and an Assistant Director – they will have the same role card. The rest of the group are complaining Ss and also have the same card. Give Ss a few minutes to read their role and plan what they are going to say. Explain that Ss need to be diplomatic, not confrontational, and remind them to use the functional language from Lesson 8.3 for handling an awkward situation and softening a message.

When Ss are ready, they have the meeting. Both sides have a number of points they want to make, but also need to reach a solution which they are happy with. At the end of the discussion, the class compares what they have agreed in their groups.

UNIT 9

WHAT'S MY PUNISHMENT?

Materials: One set of cards per group of Ss

Tell Ss that the activity involves deciding the appropriate punishments for different types of crime. Revise the different types of punishments and put these up on the board: *a caution (warning), a fine, a ban, community service, imprisonment, a suspended sentence, capital punishment* (though not for these crimes!).

Put Ss into groups of five. Give each student two crime cards and a few minutes to think about why and in what circumstances they committed those two crimes. When they are ready, Ss take it in turns to confess one of their crimes to the group. They should add details and give a justification or reason why they did it. The other Ss listen and ask further questions. They then discuss what the appropriate punishment is. Finally, if everyone can come to an agreement, the group sentences the student. It is then the next student's turn to confess. When everyone has confessed their first crime, they confess their second. At the end, compare the punishments different groups gave for the same crime. Do Ss think any of the punishments are especially harsh/severe or too lenient?

NOUGHTS AND CROSSES

Materials: One copy of the grids (A3 size if possible) and one answer key per group of Ss

Check Ss' knowledge of the rules of noughts and crosses and demonstrate how to play on the board if necessary. Ss work in groups of three and have one set of grids, enlarged to A3 if possible, and a copy of the answers. There are three games and two Ss play each other in a game with the third student acting as referee. Ss should change referee after every game. The players take it in turns to reformulate the sentences in the grid using the appropriate verb from the box at the bottom with the correct dependent preposition. If the sentence in the grid has the letter 'P' in brackets next to it, this indicates that the reformulated sentence has to be passive. All the other sentences are active. The referee checks and confirms the answers (looking at the answers for the game in progress only). If the answer is not correct, the referee must not reveal what the correct answer is so the box can still be won fairly. If the sentence is correct, the student crosses out the verb used and draws either a nought or a cross in the grid. The object of the game is to get either three noughts or crosses in a horizontal, diagonal or vertical line. When the game is finished, Ss can look at any boxes which were not won and guess what the answers are. They then swap roles and start the second game.

VERB FORM BINGO

Materials: One prompt sheet and one set of bingo cards per group of Ss

Ss work in groups of three or five. There is one question master and two teams of either one or two Ss. The question master has the large prompt sheet with the example sentences and the teams have a bingo card each. The first team starts by calling out one of the verbs on their bingo card, e.g. *stop*. The question master then reads one of the prompts for that verb, e.g. *I heard she became a vegetarian five years ago.* The team has to produce a sentence with the same meaning using the verb on the bingo card with the correct form after it (*-ing* or infinitive), e.g. *She stopped eating meat five years ago.* If the answer uses the correct form and is similar in meaning to the prompt (it doesn't have to have exactly the same wording) the team can cross out that word on their bingo card and it is the other team's turn. If the answer is wrong, the team can't cross out the verb and may be given the same prompt or a different one later by the question master. The winner is the first team to cross out all their words. When they do this, they shout 'Bingo!'

DEDUCTION BLOCKS

Materials: One copy of the board and grids (A3 size if possible) and a dice per group of Ss

Ss work in groups of four, with two on each team. Enlarge the board and grids to A3 if possible. The first team begins play by rolling the dice. Each number on the dice corresponds to a modal verb and also to a pattern, as shown at the top of the board, e.g. 1 = *must* + *have* + pp and the pattern is '☐'. The team has to choose a situation from the boxes under the modal (it can be any box in the column) and make a deduction using that modal. For example, for the situation in the first box, *You hear a loud cheer from the local stadium*, the deduction might be *The home team must have scored a goal.* If the other team agree the deduction is correct, the first team has 'won' the pattern and can draw it in their grid. The situation is crossed out on the board and cannot be used again. It is then the other team's turn to play. To win the game, the teams need to use the patterns they win to fill in their grid. The idea is to make horizontal lines without gaps. Each pattern has to 'fall' to the bottom of the grid or until it lands on top of another part of a pattern (the rules are similar to Tetris-type computer games). Each complete line wins a point and the winner is the team with the most complete lines at the end of the game.

TELL ME WHAT YOU SAW

Materials: One set of cards per group of Ss

Tell Ss they have all witnessed a bank robbery and are going to discuss what they saw in order to help the police catch the robbers. They will also decide who the most reliable witness is. Ss work in groups of four: two Ss are bank customers and two are bank employees. Distribute the cards and give Ss a few minutes to look at their card and think about how they are going to describe what they saw. Elicit ideas for the kinds of questions it might be useful to ask the witness of a crime, e.g. the time, what exactly happened in what order, description of people, anything unusual noticed, etc. and put ideas up on the board. The bank employees and the bank customers then take it in turns to interview each other about what they saw. There are two objectives: the first is to build up a picture of events and to see whether Ss reach the conclusion that the robbery was an inside job (the cashier is winking to one of the robbers who appears to be his brother/close relative). The second is for Ss to decide who the most reliable witness was. While Ss are interviewing each other, they need to identify witness descriptions that are the same. If two witnesses describe something identically, it means the witness account is reliable. At the end, Ss look at each other's pictures and can see, if they have not already guessed, that it was an inside job.

UNIT 10

I WOULDN'T RECOMMEND IT!

Materials: One set of cards and one answer sheet per group of Ss

Explain to Ss that they are going to read some comments about films and that they will have to complete them with an appropriate adjective. Ss work in groups of four and have one set of cards and an answer sheet. The cards are divided into two piles – sentences and adjectives – and spread out, face down. Ss take turns to try and turn over matching pairs of a sentence card and an adjective card. If the student turns up a matching pair, they win the cards and have another turn. If the pair doesn't match, they simply turn the cards back over in the same position and it's the next student's turn. The answer sheet should be kept face down on the table and used to check answers. With some sentences there is more than one correct answer, but only the options given on the answer sheet can be accepted since they are the strongest collocations or the most likely answers. The winner is the student with the most pairs of cards at the end.

TWO-PART PHRASE GAME

Materials: One copy of the board (A3 size if possible) and a dice per group of Ss and one counter per student

Ss work in groups of three. Give each group a board, enlarged to A3 size if possible, a dice and a counter each. Ss all place their counters on the 'Start' square. The first student rolls the dice and moves the number of places shown. They have to respond to the prompt in the square they land on using one of the two-part phrases listed on the board, e.g. *Why did you move to the countryside?* could be met with the response *Because I wanted peace and quiet* or *Because I was sick and tired of living in a noisy city.* If the student gives an appropriate response, they can stay on that square. If not, they have to go back to where they were before. The other Ss decide whether the response is possible or not, referring to the teacher if there are disputes. If two Ss land on the same square, they can't give exactly the same response – the second student has to find something different to say with a two-part phrase. The first student to reach the 'Finish' square is the winner.

RELATIVE CLAUSE QUIZ

Materials: One set of cards per class

Ss work in four groups. Give each group a card with four questions, but make sure that the final column is folded over. Ss look at the questions and decide if the relative clause in the question is defining or non-defining. If it is a non-defining clause, then they should add the necessary commas. After completing all four sentences, Ss can unfold the final column to check their answers. They then work with their group to think of two incorrect answers for each of the four questions and write these onto the card. Explain that they should make these as believable as possible as later they are going to use them for a quiz. When all the groups are ready, the quiz starts and the groups take it in turns to read questions to the other groups. The other teams have to guess which of the three given alternatives is the correct answer. A correct guess wins a point. Keep score and the team with the most points at the end is the winner.

CHANGE AND DISCUSS

Materials: One copy of the worksheet per pair of Ss

Ss work in pairs. Give each pair a worksheet. For the first stage of the activity, Ss have to change the statements and questions so that they contain a participle clause, e.g. *In your country, is it impolite to make noise while you are eating?* can become *In your country, is it impolite to make noise while eating?* In some cases, the statement can't be changed and in most cases the change involves removing the relative pronoun. Check the answers with the class. Then put Ss into groups of four or five to discuss the statements and questions. Monitor and listen for the more interesting ideas or controversial opinions. At the end ask Ss to share these with the other groups.

Answers: **1** while eating **2** People born **3** can't be changed **4** when taking exams **5** can't be changed, but 'who' can be omitted **6** people endangering **7** Motorists still driving **8** the ones unplanned **9** while travelling **10** the ones unchanged **11** All the technology created **12** Company employees working **13** People having **14** When reading English **15** A man holding **16** can't be changed **17** Rail passengers having to **18** People found guilty **19** Cars made **20** Homes located

TOP TOURS

Materials: One set of cards per group of Ss

Ss work in groups of four. Give each student in the group a tour. Tell them that they are tour guides who work on an open-top double-decker bus for a company called Top Tours and they are going to prepare a tour in an imaginary city. The tourist bus will visit the places on each tour in the order shown on the tour cards and Ss need to prepare what they are going to say for each place. Tell them to invent names for the places and buildings and facts and stories about them. Make sure you give them plenty of time to prepare this information and make notes. Then, arrange chairs into a row, like the seats on a bus, and Ss take it in turns to be the tour guide and stand at the front to give their tour, showing the 'tourists' the picture of the places as they talk about them.
The tourists have to ask questions about what they are being shown, including at least one question about dimensions, e.g. *What is the height of the tower?* At the end of activity ask Ss which tour they enjoyed the most and what was the most interesting thing they saw.

Pearson Education Limited
Edinburgh Gate
Harlow
Essex CM20 2JE
England
and Associated Companies throughout the world.

www.pearsonelt.com

First published 2016
Second impression 2017
ISBN: 978-1-292-12018-8
Set in Aptifer Sans 10/12 pt
Printed in Slovakia by Neografia
Illustrated by Sean@kja-artist.com

Every effort has been made to trace the copyright holders and we apologise in advance for any unintentional omissions. We would be pleased to insert the appropriate acknowledgement in any subsequent edition of this publication.